# Windows 98 Quick Reference

Though Windows 98 is very much a mouse driven interface, touch-typists will appreciate the keyboard shortcuts for common tasks. Below you'll often find several alternative ways of doing the same task.

## Working in Windows Explorer

The procedures described below for files apply to folders as well.

### Sort Files

Sort the files in a folder in various ways by clicking the column titles in the right-hand pane in the Details view. To sort files by filename, file size, file type, or when modified, click **Name**, **Size**, **Type**, or **Modified**, respectively. Click once to sort in ascending order, and click again to sort in descending order.

### Select Multiple Files

If your Active Desktop is set to single-click mode, hold the mouse cursor momentarily over the file or folder, instead of clicking, in the procedures described below.

Click the first file or folder in the right pane. Then do one of the following:

- To select a range of contiguous files, click the last file while pressing the **Shift** key; or
- To select several non-contiguous files, click each additional file while pressing the **Control** key; or
- To select multiple sets of contiguous files, click the first file of the new range while pressing the **Control** key. Then click the last file of the range while pressing both **Control** and **Shift**. Repeat this procedure for each additional range.

### Delete Files

- Press **Shift + Del** to delete without sending to the Recycle Bin; or
- Drag the selected files to the Recycle Bin; or
- Right-click the file or selected files, then choose **Delete** from the object menu. To delete without sending to the Recycle Bin, press the Shift key while choosing Delete; or
- Select the file(s), then click the **Delete** tool.

### Move Files

- Drag the file or selected files to the destination folder icon in the same drive. If moving to another drive, hold down the **Shift** key while dragging; or
- Right-click the selected files, and choose **Move** from the object menu. Then right-click within or over the destination folder, and choose **Paste**; or
- Right-drag the file(s) from the destination folder, then choose **Move Here** from the object menu that appears.

2. Drag the folder or shortcut with the left or right mouse button to the new location indicated by the moving horizontal bar. To navigate into a subfolder, hold the bar over it until it exposes its contents.

3. Release the button to move the folder or shortcut to the current location of the moving bar. To copy the item instead, press the **Control** key while releasing the button.

## Getting to the Start Menu Program Dialog

■ From the Start Menu, select **Settings**, **Taskbar & Start Menu**, or right-click outside any button on the Taskbar and choose **Properties**. Choose the Start Menu Program tab of the Taskbar Properties dialog box.

## Removing Shortcuts from the Start Menu

■ Click **Remove** on the Start Menu Program tab. Navigate the hierarchy to select the folder or shortcut you want to remove, and click the **Remove** button. Repeat the last procedure for each item you want to remove.

## Adding a Shortcut to a Program or Document

■ Click **Add** on the Start Menu Program tab, then type the path and filename of the program or document in the Command line field. Or, if you don't know the full path, click the **Browse** button instead. If you are adding a shortcut to a document, select **All Files** in the Files of Type field. (If you are adding a shortcut to a program select programs instead.) Navigate your hard-drive or network to the desired program or document file and select it. Click **Open**, so that the filename now appears in the Command line field of the Create Shortcut dialog.

■ Click the **Next** button to get to the Select Program Folder dialog, and select the folder in which you want to place the shortcut. If you want to create a subfolder for the shortcut, click the New Folder button, and type in the name for it.

■ Click the **Next** button to get to the Select a Title for the Program dialog. Type in a readily recognizable name for the program or document.

## Adding a Shortcut to a Folder

■ Click **Add** on the Start Menu Program tab, then click the **Browse** button and navigate your hard-drive or network to the desired folder and select it. Now drag the folder with the left or right mouse button to the Start button so that the Start Menu pops up. Continue dragging the folder to its desired location in the menu hierarchy before you release the button.

## Working Directly with Shortcuts in the Start Menu Folder

This is the most efficient method when you are reorganizing your Start Menu and adding new folders (submenus) to it at the same time.

■ Right-click the **Start** button and choose **Open**, or click the Advanced button on the Start Menu Programs tab of the Taskbar Properties dialog box. This opens an Explorer window with the Start Menu folder hierarchy in the left pane and the files in the right pane. The directory tree you see here corresponds exactly to the Start Menu hierarchy.

■ Create, rename, move, copy, or delete folders. Move or copy shortcuts to other locations in the tree. Create new data files for registered programs by right-clicking an empty spot to open the object menu.

- Place the program icon or its associated data file in the Startup folder in the Start menu. It will run automatically the next time you start Windows; or

- Assign a shortcut key to the program, and then start it by using the keyboard shortcut. (You must create a .LNK file to do this).

## Windows 98 Shortcut Keys

Some of these keys or key combinations can also be used within an application with the same or similar results.

| Key Combination | Purpose |
| --- | --- |
| F1 | Display online help |
| F2 | When an icon is highlighted, lets you rename the object |
| F3 | Access the Find dialog box |
| F5 | Refresh a window (useful after saving files to an already open window) |
| Asterisk (keypad) | Expand all subfolders |
| Plus (keypad) | Expand the selected folder |
| Minus (keypad) | Collapse an expanded folder or, if it's already collapsed, select its parent folder |
| Alt+F4 | Close the active program. You can also use it to exit Windows if you're at the desktop |
| Alt+Tab | Switch to the next window. Keep the Alt key down while tabbing to cycle through open windows until you get to the one you want to activate |
| Alt+Shift+Tab | Switch to the previous window |
| Backspace | Move one level up in the directory structure (same as clicking the Up tool) |
| Ctrl+A | Select all files and folders |
| Alt+Enter or Alt+double-click | View properties of the selected object |
| Ctrl+Esc | Open the Start menu. Use the arrow keys to select program, and press Enter to start it |
| Esc | Cancels the last action in most cases |
| Shift+F1 | Display context-sensitive help when the application supports it |
| Shift+F10 | Display the object menu for the selected object |
| Tab | Use this key while at the desktop to switch between the desktop, Taskbar, (Quick Launch) and Start menu. |

## Adding and (Re-)Arranging Shortcuts on Your Start Menu

Personalize your Start Menu by adding shortcuts to your most frequently used folders, programs, and documents.

### Moving or Copying a Shortcut to a New Location

1. Click the **Start** button, then navigate the Start Menu so as to highlight a folder, or a shortcut to a folder, program, or document.

## Copy Files

- Drag the file or selected files to the destination folder icon in a different drive. If copying to the same drive, drag while holding down the **Shift** key. You'll see a + sign next to the mouse cursor when it's over a destination folder you're copying to; or

- Right-click the selected files, and choose **Copy** from the object menu. Then right-click within or over the destination folder, and choose **Paste**; or

- Right-drag the file(s) from the destination folder, then choose **Copy Here** from the object menu that appears.

## Rename a File

- Right-click the file or folder, and choose **Rename** from the object menu. Type over the existing filename in the rectangular editing box that appears; or

- If you are in double-click mode, you can simply click the filename (and not the file icon) in order to edit the filename; or

- Press **F2** while the file icon is highlighted, then edit the filename.

## Create a New Folder

- Right-click in parent folder, and choose **New**, **Folder** from the object menu. Rename "New Folder" (the default name) as desired.

## Create a Shortcut to a File

- Right-click the destination folder, and choose **New**, **Shortcut** from the object menu. Provide the path to the file in the Create Shortcut wizard; or

- Right-drag the file(s) to the destination folder, then choose **Create Shortcut(s) Here** from the object menu that appears.

# Starting Programs Quickly

Windows 98 provides many ways to start your applications. Here are the easiest ways to do so:

- Double-click a data file associated with the program while in Explorer (for this to work there must already be a file association to the program; otherwise Windows will prompt you to create one for that file extension); or

- Double-click the program icon in Explorer; or

- Right-click the program icon while in Explorer, and then click **Open** in the object menu; or

- Select the program's entry from the **Start** menu; or

- Create a shortcut to the program on the desktop. Start it by right-clicking or double-clicking the shortcut icon; or

- Choose **Start**, **Run** and then type the application's path and filename. Click **OK** to start the program; or

- Choose **Start**, **Run** and then drag-and-drop the program's icon into the Run dialog box. Click **OK** to start the application; or

- Use the **Find** dialog on the **Start** menu (or press **F3**) to find your program, and then right-click or double-click it; or

# Using Windows 98

*Kathy Ivens*

A Division of Macmillan Computer Publishing, USA
201 W. 103rd Street
Indianapolis, Indiana 46290

## Contents at a Glance

# Using Windows 98

Library of Congress Catalog No.: 97-81028

ISBN: 0-7897-1594-5

00 99 98    6 5 4 3 2

Interpretation of the printing code: The rightmost double-digit number is the year of the book's printing; the rightmost single-digit number, the number of the book's printing. For example, a printing code of 98-1 shows that the first printing of the book occurred in 1998.

Screen reproductions in this book were created using Collage Plus from Inner Media, Inc., Hollis, NH.

Composed in *Janson Text* and *Formata* by Que Corporation.

# Credits

**Executive Editor**
Grace Buechlein

**Development Editors**
Sunthar Visuvalingam
Philip Wescott

**Technical Editors**
Craig Arnush
Ron Ellenbecker
Jeff Perkins

**Project Editor**
Tom Lamoureux

**Copy Editor**
Heather Kaufman Urschel

**Indexer**
Tim Tate

**Production Team**
Chris Livengood
Becky Stutzman

**Cover Designers**
Dan Armstrong
Ruth Harvey

**Book Designers**
Nathan Clement
Ruth Harvey

# Contents

## About the Authors

Kathy Ivens has authored and contributed to more than three dozen books on computer subjects. She is a columnist and frequent contributor for national computer magazines.

Before becoming an expert in computing, Ms. Ivens spent many years in television, where she had fun producing sports and was mildly amused producing news and entertainment programs. Preceding that career were several others; as a community organizer for social agencies; providing marketing services for large corporations; and she even spent a few years as a political consultant. She still doesn't know what she wants to be when she grows up.

## Dedication

*For Debby Stead and Mike Shuster, who have asked me to explain stuff, which helped me understand how to explain stuff. And also because it's nice to have a sister and brother-in-law who are nifty people.*

# Acknowledgements

I'm fortunate to have had some superb assistance on this book. Larry Seltzer, one of my favorite bit-heads (a bit-head is somebody even more technically proficient than a weenie), contributed his state of the art equipment and state of the art knowledge. Rob McGregor, one of the best computer book writers I've run across, contributed a vast array of great information. Don Child took on tasks and subjects that I didn't even want to think about, and delivered outstanding material, for which I thank him enormously.

At Que Publishing, Grace Buechlein, as always, provided support, guidance, and general all-around niceness as we struggled to keep up with the forever-emerging beta releases of Windows 98. Philip Wescott, one of the world's great Development Editors, remained calm, professional, and charming throughout the entire process (and I didn't always make it easy). Production Editor Tom Lamoureux kept us all going and actually was able to keep track of the status of chapters and figures as we made change after change to keep up with Microsoft's changes in the product. The technical accuracy of this book is due in large part to the skills of Ron Ellenbecker and Craig Arnush.

# We'd Like to Hear from You!

Que Corporation has a long-standing reputation for high-quality books and products. To ensure your continued satisfaction, we also understand the importance of customer service and support.

## Tech Support

If you need assistance with the information in this book or with a CD/disk accompanying the book, please access Macmillan Computer Publishing's online Knowledge Base at **http://www.superlibrary.com/ general/support**. If you do not find the answer to your questions on our Web site, you may contact Macmillan Technical Support by phone at **317-581-3833** or via email at **support@mcp.com**.

Also be sure to visit Que's Web resource center for all the latest information, enhancements, errata, downloads, and more. It's located at **http://www.quecorp.com/**.

## Orders, Catalogs, and Customer Service

To order other Que or Macmillan Computer Publishing books, catalogs, or products, please contact our Customer Service Department at **800-428-5331** or fax us at **800-882-8583** (International Fax: 317-228-4400). Or visit our online bookstore at **http://www.mcp.com/**.

## Comments and Suggestions

We want you to let us know what you like or dislike most about this book or other Que products. Your comments will help us to continue publishing the best books available on computer topics in today's market.

Que Corporation
201 West 103rd Street, 4B
Indianapolis, Indiana 46290 USA
Fax: 317-581-4663

*Please be sure to include the book's title and author as well as your name and phone or fax number.* We will carefully review your comments and share them with the author. Please note that due to the high volume of mail we receive, we may not be able to reply to every message.

Thank you for choosing Que!

# Introduction

This book is for everyone who wants to learn to use the Windows 98 operating system efficiently without having to pore over long, technical explanations.

It includes the basics, the interesting features, and the tricks I've picked up as I've used Windows 98 in my own office. I've been using Windows 98 since the first beta version was released and I've played with it, tweaked it, and learned about it through each ensuing beta release.

I wrote this book knowing that you don't do your work in Windows 98; you use software. But you have to have a running operating system to use software, and you have to tweak your operating system to get the most out of your software.

If you need to know how to take advantage of the features in the operating system and solve common troublespots, this is the book for you.

This book is a basic primer, not an engineering tome. It's written with the idea of teaching you the things you have to know if you're going to get any real power out of your computer.

You'll find a lot of information about hardware, including configuration options (and problems), and some explanations of why some hardware works the way it does. There's coverage of some of the newer hardware you're probably using (or considering buying) for multimedia.

Personalization and configuration of the look of your system is one of the hallmarks of Windows 98, so you'll find information about making your desktop look exactly the way you want it to. Along the way, you learn how to put more power on that desktop using shortcuts, the taskbar, and a menu system you can configure to make yourself more efficient.

There's plenty of information on using the tools provided in Windows 98 to wander through the Internet.

If you use Windows 98 at work, you'll gain some insights about networking that might help you cope with those pesky network problems that make you feel so frustrated and helpless.

If you use a laptop, you'll find information and tips for using the special features that exist in your system.

I've included a chapter on Windows 98 for home users, because some of the issues that arise in that environment don't seem to be covered much in most computer books.

## Conventions Used in This Book

The *Using* series has some conventions that control the formatting of text, and they are used to help you distinguish between generic information and a discussion about a dialog box or menu you're viewing on your screen.

- *Menu and Dialog Box Choices.* Words that appear in a menu or a dialog box are printed in bold type. For example, you might see text that says "choose **Color**, then select a new background color from the palette that appears."

- *Hotkeys.* We underline references to hotkeys, which are underlined letters in menu commands and dialog boxes that you can use with your Alt key instead of employing the mouse.

- *Combination Keys.* We use a plus sign (+) to indicate that keys should be used together. For example, you may see "press **Ctrl+A** to select everything."

- *Cross References.* If there's information that's connected to the topic you're currently reading, we'll tell you which chapter has it. You can use this information to learn more about the subject, or take the next step in building whatever it is you're building at the moment. For example:

SEE ALSO
➤ *To learn how to turn your 486 computer into a 266MHz Pentium without changing chips, see "I believe in the tooth fairy" in Chapter 21.*

- *Glossary Terms.* Words that have technical or special computer meanings are italicized. This means we know you might not be familiar with them and it's a signal that the definition can be found in the glossary.

- *Tips, tricks, warnings, and sidebars.* Sometimes I'll want to give you a hint to make something work better, or a tip about a clever way to use a particular feature. By giving these valuable notes explicit titles and placing them in the margin, we've made them handy and easy to find, without breaking up the text that explains the procedure you're currently working your way through.

# Getting Started with Windows 98

# Installing and Starting Windows 98

# Installing Windows 98

If you didn't purchase a computer with Windows 98 pre-installed, you must install the operating system over your current operating system (or a clean hard drive, but that's less likely to be the case). Windows 98 is designed to upgrade previous versions of Windows (3.*x* and 95).

The installation has a number of individual processes, which occur in this order:

- The operating system files are copied to your hard drive.
- The setup program detects and analyzes the computer hardware and connected peripherals.
- Hardware and peripheral installation decisions are made.
- The operating system is configured, along with certain peripheral devices such as modems and printers. Depending on the components selected for installation, Dial-Up Networking and the Inbox may be configured.

If Windows 95 is your current operating system, the Windows 98 CD-ROM will launch Setup as soon as you insert the CD. If you use Windows 3.*x*, open File Manager and access the CD-ROM. Double-click **Setup.exe**.

## Decide On an Installation Type

After the temporary files necessary to run the setup program are copied to your hard drive, you must choose the type of installation you want to perform. The choices are as follows:

- **Typical**. This installs the components of the operating system that are commonly used.
- **Portable**. Choose this option for installation onto a laptop; it includes special features for portable computers.
- **Compact**. This option is for computers that don't have great amounts of disk space available. The files necessary to run the operating system are transferred.
- **Custom**. Use this option if you're comfortable with Windows and want to decide which components are installed.

You'll be asked to accept the Microsoft License Agreement for Windows 98; select **I accept the Agreement**, and then choose **Next**.

## Save Your Previous Operating System

Windows checks for installed operating system components and asks if you want to save existing MS-DOS and Windows system files, which gives you the opportunity to uninstall Windows 98 if you want to. It takes about 50MB of disk space to save your previous version of Windows, so it's a good idea to answer **Yes**. Choose the default directory for saving the files (the suggested directory name is c:\XXXMB free, where XXX is the number of free megabytes on your hard drive).

## Create an Emergency Startup Disk

When the setup program asks if you want to create an emergency startup disk, say Yes. If something goes wrong with your system files, the emergency disk can get you into your system so you can repair or reinstall corrupted files. You need a blank formatted disk.

The setup program prepares the emergency files and tells you when to insert the disk. It also tells you when to remove it.

## Find a Diversion While the Files are Copied

Now the operating system files are transferred from the CD-ROM to your hard drive. This can take quite a while, so you might want to find something to do or something to read.

## Setting Up the Drivers

After all the files are copied, the setup program restarts your computer. When the bootup is complete, you'll see a message that says Getting ready to run Windows for the first time.

Yea! You are off and running. Windows 98 initializes the device driver database and gets ready to set up your hardware. This only takes a few seconds. (*Drivers* are software files that control the hardware devices in your computer.)

## Configuring Plug and Play Devices

Windows next searches your system for Plug and Play devices. These are hardware devices that are manufactured with Windows in mind, and Windows knows everything about them. Depending on the number of Plug and Play devices in your system, this can take more than a few moments.

The Plug and Play devices that are located and identified are configured. Then other (non-Plug and Play) hardware is located and identified. The driver database is checked against the hardware so everything in your system will run properly.

Sometimes Setup fails during hardware detection, especially if the computer has older devices that aren't recognized. Windows may ask you to select the devices you want the detection program to look for. If you have a network card or some other peripheral you think may not be supported, deselect it and tell Windows you don't have one of those. After the operating system is up and running, you can install it (it's much easier).

If the setup program freezes or dies, restart the computer, and then start Setup again from the beginning. Don't worry—you'll skid through all the parts you've already been through and Windows will pick up where it left off.

After the hardware is taken care of, a few other details are attended to: The Help files are installed and some technical stuff goes on in the background.

Then Windows restarts your computer once again.

## Welcome to Windows

A large message of welcome greets you. Choose **Continue** to open the Registration Wizard if you want to register your operating system with Microsoft (or choose **Register Later**).

Close the Welcome window by clicking the **X** in the upper-right corner.

## The Last Configuration

There is another set of configuration processes, but don't worry, this is the last. The following devices may be configured, depending on your equipment and the installation options you selected:

- Modem
- Printer
- Internet Explorer
- Inbox
- Dial-Up Networking

You can cancel any or all of these and perform the configuration later. In fact, we cover those topics throughout this book.

# Starting Your Computer

When you turn on your computer, it goes through two different sets of startup tasks: The initial startup procedure starts the computer, and a secondary startup procedure starts the Windows 98 operating system.

## Computer Startup

The first set of steps starts with the *POST* (Power On Self Test). It's a check of the hardware, then the computer moves on to check the commands and information stored in your BIOS chip, and then it loads drivers to control the basic hardware in your computer (hard drive, ports, video, and so on). You can see the beginning of the POST on your screen in the form of a series of numbers in the upper-left corner—that's the RAM check (the final number that's displayed represents the amount of memory in your computer).

At some point, you probably see a message telling you how to enter the computer's own setup program (for example, you may see a message instructing you to press the Del key or F2 to enter setup). You only need to enter the computer setup if you've made a change in the basic hardware (such as memory and hard drives). In that case, you need to configure the setup files to match the new hardware so the computer startup procedure doesn't find a discrepancy between the information it has and the hardware it finds. The documentation that came with your computer explains what to do and how to do it.

## Windows 98 Startup

If your Windows 98 system doesn't load after you see the message that Windows 98 is starting, you probably have some sort of conflict with hardware or configuration settings. This usually occurs after you've added or changed a hardware device. In fact, it's not a good idea to add or change hardware until you've been running Windows 98 for a while and know you have a smooth, functioning operating system.

You can troubleshoot the startup, and sometimes it's a better idea to get someone who has expertise in Windows 98 to advise you as you use the troubleshooting features.

Troubleshooting begins by changing the way the operating system loads. To accomplish this, press F8 when Windows 98 first starts. This produces a menu from which you select the appropriate menu number. A countdown clock runs onscreen, and you have 30 seconds to make a decision before the operating system boots normally.

Here are the menu choices:

1. **Normal**   This is the default, the same as doing nothing. It's the selected option, so just press Enter to start Windows 98 without having to wait for the countdown.

2. **Logged\BOOTLOG.TXT**   This startup option causes everything to run exactly the same as a normal operating system startup, except that behind the scenes, Windows 98 is keeping a log of everything that happens. Each individual step that Windows 98 takes to get you to your desktop is recorded. The filename for the log is BOOTLOG.TXT, and if there are problems, you can examine that file in any text editor or word processor.

**3. Safe mode**     Using this choice is like inventing and loading an operating system named "Windows 98 Lite." Only the bare components necessary to get you to your Windows 98 desktop are loaded during startup. This is useful if you are having problems starting the operating system (especially after making a change in the configuration or adding new hardware). Because there are so few commands executed and files loaded, there's a reduced chance of problems. Use Safe mode to start the operating system so you can undo any configuration changes you made that were probably the cause of your problems. If there are serious problems during startup, Windows 98 will probably recognize that fact and go into Safe mode automatically.

**4. Safe mode with network support**     This is the same as Safe mode, except the drivers that let you join the network are loaded. This is useful if you have to repair a configuration problem and the Windows 98 files are on a network computer instead of a CD-ROM that you could use on your own computer.

**5. Step-by-step confirmation**     This is very much like Normal, except you see each process Windows 98 goes through and you're asked to confirm the decision to move to the next step. If there's a problem, you'll also see the error message that problem causes. This is a useful way to isolate exactly which process is causing problems.

**6. Command prompt only**     This choice is jargon for "don't start Windows, just go to DOS." When the process ends, you see a command prompt (c:\>). You can run DOS software, and examine the DOS startup files for problems (Config.sys and Autoexec.bat).

**7. Safe mode with command prompt**     This is the same as Safe mode, except that Windows 98 doesn't start up and you end up at a command prompt. In addition, the commands in your startup files (Config.sys and Autoexec.bat) are not processed. If your startup problem stems from some change you made to Config.sys or Autoexec.bat, you can undo the damage before trying to restart the operating system.

When your Windows 95 computer doesn't boot (either you see an error message or it just freezes before it has finished the boot-up process and you never get to the desktop), turn off your computer and start again. This time, choose Safe mode by pressing F8 to force a Startup menu. When Windows 98 boots into Safe mode (by the way, your desktop has messages on it that say Safe mode just to remind you), you can fix the problem. Usually, it's just a matter of undoing the last configuration option you messed around with. (If you added hardware, for example, turn off your computer, and take out the hardware before starting again.)

But what if Safe mode doesn't work either? What if your computer still won't boot into Windows 98? There are two common reasons for Safe mode failure:

- You have a virus on your hard drive. Boot the computer with an MS-DOS bootable floppy disk and then run a DOS-based virus checker (always keep one of those around).

- You have a problem in your basic computer settings. Restart the computer and use the appropriate keystrokes to enter the computer's setup program and check the settings (sometimes, your CMOS battery will have died and your computer simply "forgot" its components—check the documentation for your computer to learn how to handle this).

If neither of these solutions works, you probably need to get your computer to a repair expert.

## Windows 98 Welcome

Everything usually runs quite smoothly, however, and when the operating system has completed its startup procedures, a bright and cheerful Welcome to Windows 98 screen greets you. You can use the options on the screen to register your operating system or head for the Internet (both of which require your modem and an Internet service provider). There are also options to tour the Windows 98 features and configure hardware maintenance programs.

# Introducing the Desktop

# Introducing the Windows 98 Desktop

There's been a fundamental change in the look and behavior of Windows with the release of Windows 98. Now you have a choice as to the way your desktop looks and acts. You can use the classic desktop (which looks very much like the Windows 95 desktop) or the Active Desktop, which looks like a Web page. In fact, what's really terrific is that you can move back and forth between the two faces of Windows 98 at will.

Because the primary advantage of the Active Desktop is the ability to open Internet pages as easily as you open files on your local drive, having a permanent connection to the Internet is almost a necessity. In fact, if you don't stay hooked up, whenever you click an object that's on the Internet instead of your local hard drive, you'll hear your modem making a connection.

In addition, you can put live, real-time updates of information from the Internet on your desktop, so the latest stock prices or news stories are always in front of you.

If you're using your Windows 98 computer at work, having access to a permanent Internet connection would be unusual. If your Windows 98 computer is at home, keeping the family phone line tied up with an Internet connection would be equally unusual (to say nothing of dangerous if you have teenagers).

Therefore, it's possible that you'll spend a great deal of your time working in the classic desktop, using your software to write letters, keep your checking account records, and play games.

# Understanding the Active Desktop

The Windows 98 Active Desktop is integrated with Internet Explorer 4, and the word "active" means you can configure your desktop to be dynamic, alive, and all the other synonyms for "active."

You can connect to any Internet site that provides active, changing contents (stock ticker, news headlines) and keep the information flowing onto your desktop so it's always current and always in front of you.

Internet locations and files stored on your hard drive are both treated the same way—click-to-open. If you're not connected to the Internet when you click an Internet site, Windows 98 automatically starts dialing to make a connection.

### Switching to the Active Desktop

1. Right-click on any blank spot on your desktop to see the shortcut menu.

2. Place your mouse pointer on Active Desktop to reveal the submenu (see Figure 2.1).

FIGURE 2.1
Toggle between the classic and Active Desktop modes with a click of the mouse.

3. Choose **View as W̲eb Page** to change to the Active Desktop mode.

A checkmark appears next to the **View as W̲eb Page** selection, indicating that Web mode is active. When you open a desktop icon, the window resembles a Web page (see Figure 2.2). When you want to return to the classic desktop, click again to remove the checkmark.

FIGURE 2.2
The underlined icon titles look and work like Internet links—a single click opens them.

**SEE ALSO**
➤ *Learn all about setting up your Active desktop in Chapter 18.*

# Using the Mouse

If you're new to computing, or you've worked with only text-based computers (PCs running DOS or a terminal), the mouse is a new tool and mousing is a new concept. Working in Windows 98 without being comfortable with a mouse can be tortuous, so you need to spend some time getting used to it.

Here's the best trick I know for getting used to a mouse—play Solitaire. It's true! I've used Solitaire as a training device at every client site that was downsizing from a mainframe (and text terminals) to Windows. It always works. In a short time (okay, a couple of hours), you'll have conquered the mouse. Here's how to get the most out of Solitaire as a training device:

- Single-click the deck to expose cards.
- Drag cards from the deck to the column.
- Drag cards between columns.
- Double-click cards to place them on your pile at the top of the game.

## Getting Used to Pointing

Whenever you move your mouse, your mouse pointer moves in the same direction. In Windows 98, you can simply point at some objects to get information—there's no clicking needed:

- Place your pointer on a listing on the Start menu, and additional menus for that listing automatically display.
- Hover the pointer over a toolbar icon to see information about that icon's function (the little message is called a *ToolTip*).
- If the titles on the software buttons on your taskbar become truncated as you add buttons, linger a second with your pointer to see the whole title appear in a ToolTip.

## Getting Used to Mouse Clicks

The left mouse button is used for selecting, dragging, and opening objects.

- To select an object, move your mouse until the pointer is on the object, and then click once with the left mouse button. The object is highlighted (its text is reversed).

- To select more than one object, select the first object and then hold the Ctrl key while you click on the other objects.

- To drag an object, select it and then hold down the left mouse button and drag the mouse to the target location (the object comes along for the ride).

- If you've selected multiple objects, dragging one of them drags all of them.

- To open an object, double-click on it.

The definition of "opening" an object changes depending on the type of object you double-click:

- A software program file opens the software.

- A document file opens the software that's associated with the document (or you're asked to select a software program to use with the document).

- A container object (a hard drive, floppy drive, or a folder) opens a window to display the objects in the container.

## Configuring a Single-Click Environment

If you're using the Active Desktop, why not go all the way and make it a true Web-like environment—which means you live in a world where a single-click does everything.

### Configuring Web behavior for the Desktop

1. Click the **Start** button and choose **Settings**, **Folder Options** from the **Start** menu.

2. On the General tab, select **Web style** (see Figure 2.3).

3. Click **OK**.

The new single-click configuration applies only to the operating system icons. When you work with your software programs, everything stays the way it was.

**Selecting a contiguous group of objects**

If the multiple objects you want to select are contiguous, select the first object. Then move to the last object in the group and hold the Shift key while you click on it. All the objects between the first and last are selected.

**Double-clicking at the wrong speed renames an object**

Windows 98 expects a double-click to be almost instantaneous, one click immediately after another. If your pointer is on the title instead of the icon, you can have a problem. If there's a slight pause (very slight, almost imperceptible), instead of opening the object, the object's title becomes highlighted. This means the title is in "edit mode" and if you press any key except the Enter key, you will replace the object name with the character you type.

Be careful when double-clicking, and if the title is highlighted, immediately press Enter or Esc to retrieve the title.

You can learn how to adjust the double-click rate for your mouse by reading Chapter 7.

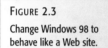

FIGURE 2.3

Change Windows 98 to behave like a Web site.

## Getting Used to Right-Clicking

If you're coming from a Windows 3.*x* environment, you probably wonder why manufacturers bothered to put a right button on the mouse. Well, now you get a chance to use it—in fact, you'll probably use the right mouse button as much as you use the left mouse button.

There's a slew of stuff you can do with the right mouse button, and most of it is quick access to commands you used to have to go to a menu bar to find.

The right mouse button is used for shortcuts to menu commands. Almost every object in Windows 98 will produce a shortcut menu if you right-click on it. (Shortcut menus are sometimes called context menus.) For example, if you right-click on a file while you're working in Explorer or My Computer, you'll see a selection of menu choices that make sense for the type of file you've selected (see Figure 2.4).

You can also drag items with the right button held down instead of the left. This is called right-dragging, and when you use this option to move a file, a menu appears when you release the mouse button (see Figure 2.5).

FIGURE 2.4

Your shortcut menu may differ depending on the file type you select and the software utilities you've installed.

FIGURE 2.5

You won't accidentally move a file you meant to copy if you right-drag it.

# Understanding a Windows Window

When you're actually getting work done on your computer, it means you're working in a software program. Whether you're writing a letter, creating a report, working on a spreadsheet, or putting together a multimedia presentation, there's a software program open.

And where there's a software program, there's a window. In fact, even if you're not working in software, if you open a Windows 98 container (such as a hard drive or a folder), there's a window. You can have a whole bunch of windows open on your screen at the same time (see Figure 2.6).

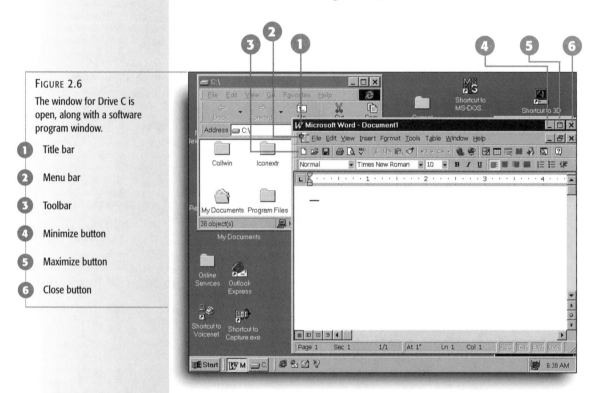

FIGURE 2.6

The window for Drive C is open, along with a software program window.

1  Title bar

2  Menu bar

3  Toolbar

4  Minimize button

5  Maximize button

6  Close button

Most windows in Windows have these common attributes:

- A border
- A title bar
- A menu bar
- Buttons for minimizing, maximizing, restoring, and closing the window

Okay, I listed four things for that last item, and if you look at the upper-right corner of a Windows window you see only three buttons. The Restore button (which looks like two overlapping rectangles) appears only after you maximize a window, and you click it to put the window back to the size it was before you maximized it.

In addition, you can usually configure a window to display a toolbar and a status bar (both of which are on both the windows in Figure 2.6).

## Sizing and Moving Windows

There are three sizes for a Windows window: minimized, maximized, and restored (a window that is neither full screen nor minimized). The jargon for a restored window, which can be any size you want it to be, is "window." That is, if you have a choice about how to open a program, the jargon you encounter is something like "Full Screen or Window?" Full screen means maximized and window means less than maximized (it could be any size, but it doesn't matter because you can always adjust the size to suit yourself).

When you minimize a window by clicking the minimize button (which looks like a minus sign), it disappears. The only evidence that it is still alive is its button on the taskbar.

Minimizing a software program window does not close the software. Before you shut down your computer, you must go through the software's exit routine in one of the following ways:

- Restore the window and click the **Close** button.
- Restore the window and choose **File**, **Exit** from the menu bar.
- Right-click the program's button on the taskbar and choose **Close**.

When a window is "a window" (not maximized), you can change its size. You can stretch any of the four sides individually or move two sides at a time.

### Changing the size of a window

1. To expand or contract one of the sides, place your mouse pointer on that side of the window.
2. When the pointer changes to a double-headed arrow, press and hold the left mouse button while you drag the side in the appropriate direction (see Figure 2.7).

**FIGURE 2.7**

When you widen a window, you see a shadowy line as you drag your mouse. Release the mouse when that line is where you want the new edge of the window to be.

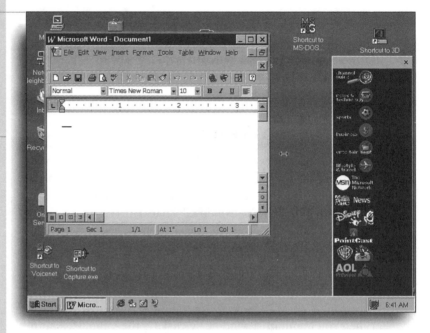

3. To expand or contract two sides proportionately, place your mouse pointer on one of the corners.

4. When the pointer changes to a double-headed arrow, press and hold the left mouse button while you drag the corner in the appropriate direction.

To move a window, place your mouse on the title bar. Then press and hold the left mouse button while you drag the window to its new location.

# Overview of the Default Desktop Icons

The Windows 98 installation program placed some icons on your desktop, and the first time you boot up the operating system, these icons are lined up on the left side of your screen (see Figure 2.8).

Not all Windows 98 desktops have the same icons, although there are some general rules about what to expect:

- My Computer, the Recycle Bin, and My Briefcase are almost always found on Windows 98 desktops. (In fact, I'd say "always" except the few people in the world who don't have all three icons will call me to tell me, so I took the safer route and said "almost always.")

- If you installed the various communications options, you'll have an Inbox and/or an Outlook Express icon, as well as an Online Services folder.

- If you installed support for networks, Network Neighborhood is present.

If you have additional icons on your desktop, as in Figure 2.8, it means you picked a broader range of installation options.

The icons don't have to stay lined up neatly on the left side of your screen; you can move them around, just as you can place the tools on your physical desk anywhere you want.

### Relocate an icon on the desktop

1. Place your mouse pointer anywhere on the icon.

2. Press and hold down the left mouse button while you drag the icon where you want it.

3. Release the mouse button to place the icon in its new spot.

Later, as you use Windows 98 more and more, you'll probably add more icons to your desktop. For instance, you may create icons that are shortcuts for software you use frequently. Double-clicking an icon on the desktop is faster than opening the menu system to find the software's listing. And, some of the software applications you install may place their own shortcut icons on your desktop.

It can get pretty crowded on a busy person's desktop. The more crowded it is, the more you'll need some sort of scheme for placing icons on your desktop in a logical way. Of course, your logic may not match someone else's logic, and as a result most Windows 98 desktops look like a hodge-podge of groups of icons.

In fact, the orderliness of desktops frequently matches the condition of a user's physical desk. My own physical desk is a large trestle table and there are tools, papers, folders, and other paraphernalia scattered all over it. People who see it probably think of the word "messy," but I know where everything is and can find what I need in a split second.

My Windows 98 desktop matches that style. Wanna see it? Look at Figure 2.9. What's important (and the real reason I'm showing it to you) is that the desktop icons are so easy to manipulate that I can make it look neat in one second flat. In fact, I can clean it up and get rid of the messy look by temporarily hiding most of the icons in three seconds flat.

To tell you the truth, the desktop you see in Figure 2.9 is the same desktop you saw in Figure 2.8. It took me only about five seconds to turn it from a crowded mess to the way it looked the day I first started using Windows 98. You'll learn how to perform all these desktop tricks in this book.

**SEE ALSO**

➤ *"Personalizing Your Desktop" to learn more about arranging your desktop, making your desktop neat automatically, and creating desktop shortcuts, page 191.*

## My Computer

My Computer really fits its name—it is your computer. It's a folder that contains all the important parts of your computer. Incidentally, if you don't share your computer with anyone else, you might want to change the name of My Computer to something that's perhaps more personalized, more professional, or more adult (the term "My Computer" always sounds a bit silly to me when I have to refer to it out loud). Try something like Bill's Computer (use your own name, of course).

FIGURE 2.9

The desktop is the place to keep all the tools you need during your working day.

When you open My Computer, you see icons representing your computer's major resources; the contents depend upon the configuration of your computer. You should see at least a floppy drive, a hard drive, the Control Panel folder, and the Printers folder. The My Computer window shown in Figure 2.10 is for a computer that also has a CD-ROM drive and a Dial-Up Networking folder.

Each object in My Computer is a folder. You can open the folders to view their contents or even configure their contents (depending on the object you choose).

In addition, the drive objects in My Computer can be managed right from there. You can diagnose problems, perform maintenance chores, and so on.

FIGURE 2.10

You can view and manipulate the resources in your computer from the My Computer folder.

**SEE ALSO**

➤ *More information about using My Computer is in Chapter 4.*

➤ *Details about setting up and using printers can be found in Chapter 13.*

➤ *For information about Dial-Up Networking, see Chapter 17.*

➤ *To learn about sharing resources with other network users, see Chapter 23.*

## Recycle Bin

Don't let the name fool you—the Recycle Bin doesn't recycle anything. It's a trash bin. When you delete a file from your hard drive in Windows 98, it isn't deleted; it goes into the Recycle Bin. There are two ramifications to this, one good and one not so good:

- If you change your mind, you can get the deleted file back.
- Deleting a file from your hard drive doesn't gain you any disk space.

Of course, once you delete the file from the Recycle Bin, it really is deleted and you get the disk space back (which is, I suppose, a form of recycling).

You also can delete a folder, and all the files in the folder are automatically sent to the Recycle Bin along with it.

You can tell at a glance if the Recycle Bin has any deleted files in it because when it's empty, it looks empty, and when it has even one deleted file, it looks as if it's stuffed and overflowing with paper.

The Recycle Bin is fussy about which files it's willing to accept, so here are the rules:

- The folder or file must be located on a hard drive. Files from removable drives (your floppy drive, a Zip drive, or a Jaz drive) are not sent to the Recycle Bin—they're really deleted.

- The folder or file must have been deleted from Explorer, My Computer, or a dialog box (Open, Save As) in software that is written for Windows 98 (or Windows 95/NT 4). If you delete a file from an MS-DOS command line or from older software that doesn't know about the Recycle Bin, it is not sent to the Recycle Bin. There are, however, third-party utilities that can undelete these files if you work quickly (before the disk space is overwritten). Norton Utilities for Windows 95 comes to mind, and there are probably some shareware utilities on the Internet.

You don't always have to use the Recycle Bin. There are ways to bypass it when you want to delete files and you know there's no chance you're making a mistake and will change your mind later. You can also permanently turn off the Recycle Bin, and you can also change its capacity (it doesn't hold an infinite number of files; it has a limit and starts deleting files itself to make room if you send it more files than the limit).

**SEE ALSO**

➤ *To learn how to restore files you deleted by mistake and how to change the way the Recycle Bin works, see Chapter 4.*

## My Briefcase

Just as a real briefcase, you can use My Briefcase to take work home from the office and then bring it back. The changes you made at home are automatically made to the original file you were working on in the office. If you start a new file while you're working at home, the Briefcase tells your office computer about it when you get back to work. You can take the Briefcase on the road when you're traveling for business, or you can take it to another computer in your office.

**SEE ALSO**

➤ *To learn all the neat tricks for using My Briefcase, turn to Chapter 22.*

# Network Neighborhood

If your computer is on a network with other Windows computers (Windows NT, Windows 98, or Windows 95), you have a Network Neighborhood icon on your desktop.

When you open the Network Neighborhood folder, you can see the other computers that are connected to the same network you're on (see Figure 2.11).

**FIGURE 2.11**

You can see the computers that are connected to your computer in the Network Neighborhood folder.

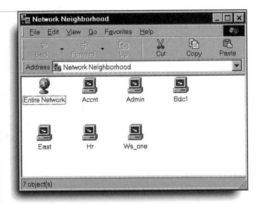

It doesn't necessarily follow that if you can see a computer in Network Neighborhood, you can access it. Each computer on the network (including yours) can be configured independently for the way it shares its resources. Some computers might share all their folders, other computers might share only certain folders, and some may share their folders only with certain users. Some computers might have a printer that's set up for sharing, which means other users can print documents without having to have printers attached to every computer.

To see whether or not a computer has shared resources you can access, double-click its icon in Network Neighborhood. A folder opens to display all the shared resources for that computer. For example, in Figure 2.12, the computer named East is sharing a great many folders, and the computer named Accnt is sharing some folders, some printers, a Jaz drive, and a CD-ROM.

**SEE ALSO**

➤ *Learn about working on a network by reading Chapter 20.*

➤ *All the detailed information about creating shared resources on your computer and accessing shared resources on other computers can be found in Chapter 21.*

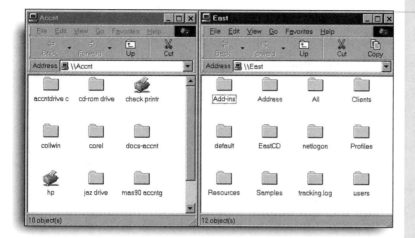

FIGURE 2.12

You can see the shared resources for a connected computer by double-clicking the computer's icon in Network Neighborhood.

## Inbox

The Inbox is your doorway to the world of electronic communication. You'll use the Inbox for email and faxing services, but there are other features (an address book, for example) available that make using those services easy and convenient.

The Inbox is really a program named Windows Messaging, which is the name you see when you double-click on the Inbox icon to open it (see Figure 2.13).

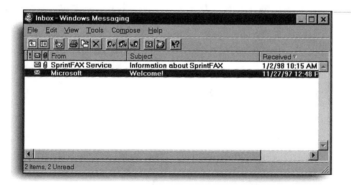

FIGURE 2.13

Open the Inbox to use Windows Messaging for electronic communications.

If you're on a network, your Inbox probably connects to your network mail service (which might be Microsoft Mail or Exchange Server). As mail is received on the network post office, it's delivered to your Inbox. You can configure the software to alert you whenever the network mailbox deposits a message into your Inbox (you can play a sound, have your mouse pointer change its shape, or pop up a message over whatever software window you're using).

If you're not connected to a network, you can use Windows Messaging to connect to your email service. This could be an ISP (Internet service provider), CompuServe, or any other communications service that works with your Inbox.

Windows Messaging requires its own setup program, and usually a wizard appears after you install Windows 98 to walk you through the process of establishing your settings.

After the initial setup, however, you might want to change some of the configuration options, and it's quite easy to do that. Perhaps you changed the way you access email (moving from an ISP to CompuServe or vice versa). Maybe you get mail from other employees through a network mail service, but have to dial out to get your Internet mail.

You can, in fact, have multiple configuration standards for Windows Messaging, and then choose the one you want to use when you open the Inbox. These configuration files are called profiles, and you can have as many different profiles as you need.

Since you have Internet Explorer 4, you may want to use Outlook Express for email, which works similarly to Windows Messaging. More information about Outlook Express is in Chapter 19.

# Quitting Windows 98

You cannot just reach for that Power button on the front of your computer when you're finished working. If you turn off the computer without going through the Windows 98 shutdown routine, you'll damage your system.

While you're working, Windows 98 keeps all kinds of important stuff in memory. Part of the "official" shutdown process is to take that data and put it into files on your hard drive so the information is saved permanently (that's a vast oversimplification, but it describes the general operation accurately).

### Shutting down your computer

1. Click the Start button to open the Start menu.
2. Choose Shut Down to display the Shut Down Windows dialog box (see Figure 2.14).

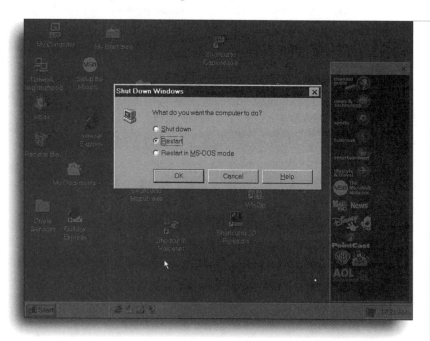

3. Select the appropriate option, and then click OK.

- If you want to turn off your computer, choose **Shut Down**. Windows 98 will notify you when it is safe to turn off your computer. Now you can reach for that power button.

- If you just want to restart the operating system because you've changed settings and those changes don't take effect until you restart, choose **Restart**.

- If you're having a serious problem and a support technician wants you to change or copy files to correct the problem, choose **Restart in MS-DOS mode**.

If you work at the computer in short spurts, don't turn it off between sessions. In fact, there's no particular reason to shut off a computer at all. Many of us believe our computers, CMOS

**Putting the plug in memory leaks**

As you open and close software, something weird happens. The available memory and resources shrink. The software and/or the operating system doesn't always "give back" the memory and resources it uses. This phenomenon is called "leakage," and it just happens. If you don't turn your computer off every night, use the Restart option every once in a while to get everything back to optimum power. Once a week is fine unless you're getting a lot of "out of memory" messages.

batteries, and hard drives last much longer if we never power down the computer.

The exception is when you're expecting a lightning storm, in which case you should power down and then pull the plug out of the outlet (don't tell me about your surge protectors, I don't wanna hear it; trust me, pull that plug).

# Major Desktop Tools

The two desktop tools you'll probably use most often are the taskbar and the Start menu. It makes sense to understand the way these constant companions work so you can get the most out of their features. And, you can configure them to work exactly the way you want them to, making you far more productive.

# Using the Taskbar

Your Windows 98 desktop has a gray area across the bottom of the screen that's called the *taskbar*. The left side of the taskbar has a Start button and the right side has a digital readout of the current time.

Depending on your installation and configuration choices, there may be other objects on the taskbar. For example, the taskbar shown in Figure 3.1 has a Quick Launch toolbar, and the icon for setting Display properties.

## The Start Button

The Start button is the tool you use to get to the Start menu, and a single click is all that's required. When the Start menu appears, it contains nine items by default (see Figure 3.2). There may be additional items at the top of your Start menu, because some software programs place items at the top of the Start menu during their installation program.

For details about using and customizing the Start menu, see the section "Using the Start Menu" later in this chapter.

## Taskbar Buttons

When you open a software program, the taskbar displays a button to indicate that the software is in use. The button contains the name of the software application and an icon (see Figure 3.3).

FIGURE 3.2

The default items on the Start menu provide access to the programs and tools you need to get your work done.

FIGURE 3.3

Opening a software window puts a button on the taskbar.

The same thing happens if you open any type of window; it doesn't have to be a software program window. If you open Explorer, or use a dialog box to set up a Windows 98 feature, you'll see a taskbar button for every window that you've opened. The button doesn't disappear until you close the window.

And therein lies the real power of the taskbar: It's a task switcher. Click a button to bring that window to the foreground so you can work in it. It doesn't matter what the state of the window is when you click its taskbar button (whether it is minimized, maximized, or halfway in between); it's open and active as soon as you click its button on the taskbar.

When you want to work in another window, click its taskbar button. Immediately, that window is in the foreground and the window you just left moves to the background. As you continue to click taskbar buttons to switch among programs, all the programs in the background remain open and running.

As you open more and more windows, the taskbar buttons become smaller to make room for the additional buttons. Eventually, it might become difficult to figure out what window a button represents. The taskbar provides assistance by supplying a tooltip for each button. Just hold your mouse pointer over a button to see any information that's been truncated as the button shrank (see Figure 3.4).

**Taskbar buttons prevent mistakes**

One great advantage of all of this is that with those taskbar buttons staring at you, you'll never forget that an application is open and then accidentally shut down Windows.

Another advantage is that you'll never forget that you opened a software application and then double-click its icon again, resulting in two instances of the software being open. If you've used Windows 3.x, there's a good chance you've done that. I can remember going to client sites and finding a half dozen or more instances of Solitaire running. Users would be playing, then accidentally click outside of the Solitaire window, making the game's window disappear. Instead of bringing up the task list with Ctrl+Esc, they'd go back to the Games Program Group and double-click the Solitaire icon, and they'd do this over and over again.

FIGURE 3.4

Hold your mouse pointer over a button to see details.

Tip

If you hold your mouse pointer over the digital clock on the right side of the taskbar, the current day and date appears.

As you switch among windows, each window's mode is preserved. There are three modes for windows:

- *Maximized*, which means the window fills the screen. Even if you switch to another window that hides it, the maximized window remains maximized in the background.

- *Minimized*, which means the window is not visible and exists only as a taskbar button. The software is still open and running.

- *Restored*, which means the window has a specific size (smaller than maximized) that you can control.

**SEE ALSO**
➤ *Learn all about sizing windows in Chapter 2.*

## The Taskbar Tray

The right side of the taskbar has an indented area that displays the current time, and it may also contain some icons. This indented area is called the *tray*, and it's designed to hold icons representing system functions. In addition to the digital clock display, you may see one or more of these objects in the tray:

- A speaker icon, which appears if you've installed a sound card in your computer.

- A display icon, which you can click to reveal a menu that lets you change the resolution of your screen display.

- A modem icon (complete with blinking lights to indicate connection status), which appears while you're online with a browser or some email software programs.

- A battery meter icon, which monitors the power management features of Windows 98 if they're being used (usually on a laptop).

- A PC card icon, which appears if there is a PCMCIA card installed (also usually on a laptop).

- A printer icon, which indicates that a document is in the process of printing.
- A fax icon, which indicates that faxing is active.

Other programs and utilities you install may place icons in the tray. Tray icons are most common for programs or utilities that are launched during system startup.

## Using the Shortcut Menu for Taskbar Buttons

You can right-click a taskbar button to see a shortcut menu that lets you choose the window's mode as you switch to it (see Figure 3.5).

**FIGURE 3.5**
Change the size of an application window as you switch to it.

This means you can switch to the window and change its size all in one step. For instance, if the window is currently full screen in the background, and you want to reduce its size so you can have two windows open at the same time, you can click Restore on the shortcut menu to see the window in restored mode instead of maximized mode.

The shortcut menu doesn't explicitly tell you which mode the window is currently using, but you can usually figure that out from the choices offered. In fact, it's not very important what the current mode is; all that's important is what you want the window to look like when you switch to it.

You can also exit software or close down a window from the shortcut menu. Choose Close to shut the window—the button disappears from the taskbar. If the button represents a software program and you modified the document you were working on since the last time you saved it, the software will ask if you want to save it before shutting down (see Figure 3.6).

FIGURE 3.6

Closing software without switching to it is a real time saver and poses no risk of abandoning documents without saving them.

**All shortcut menus aren't equal**

The shortcut menus for application buttons sometimes have additional choices that are specific to the application. For example, the button for my email software offers a choice named "Check for Mail" on its shortcut menu.

# Help! A Window's Taskbar Button Doesn't Work

Sometimes you may minimize a program and then later click its taskbar button to return to it and nothing happens. So, you right-click the taskbar button, but the Restore and Maximize choices are grayed out. There seems to be no way to get back to this program. Incidentally, if you choose Close from the shortcut menu and open the program again, there's a good chance that it will open minimized so you have to use the taskbar button to access it. However, the same problem will occur.

What has happened is that the program is minimized in an area off your screen and can no longer be viewed. That's not supposed to happen, but it sometimes does (it's a bug). Here's how to fix it:

### Retrieving a minimized window that seems to have disappeared

1. Minimize all the open windows so you can see the desktop.

2. Click the program button on the taskbar to select the program, and then right-click the button to bring up the shortcut menu. Select **Move** (the Move command is usually grayed out on the button's shortcut menu, but when this situation occurs, it becomes accessible).

3. Move your mouse pointer to the middle of the screen. Don't click. Your pointer has turned into a diamond shape with four squares inside the diamond (see Figure 3.7).

FIGURE 3.7

This pointer shape means control of the movement of the selected window has been passed to the arrow keys on your keyboard.

4. Use the arrow keys on your keyboard to move the program window to an area on the desktop where you can see it in its entirety. You can usually see an edge of this program window so you know which arrow keys to use (for example, if the

window is tucked away past the upper-left corner, use the right and down arrows to bring it onto the desktop).

**5.** When the window is totally available on the desktop, press the Enter key to position the window at its current location.

**6.** Resize the window if you'd like to, and then close it. Don't minimize it before closing it; it will probably do the same thing again.

## Using the Shortcut Menu for the Taskbar

There are a couple of other nifty tricks you can perform from the taskbar. If you are working with multiple applications, and are switching among them with the taskbar buttons, you can use the taskbar shortcut menu functions to perform an action on all the windows at once. To do this, follow these steps:

**Using the taskbar shortcut menu to perform an action on all windows**

**1.** Right-click on a blank spot (where there is no button) on the taskbar to see the taskbar shortcut menu (see Figure 3.8).

**FIGURE 3.8**
Perform actions on all your open windows with one click.

**2.** Choose **Cascade** to arrange all the open windows in a cascade, one over the other from left to right, top to bottom.

**3.** Choose **Tile Horizontally** to arrange the windows without overlapping, from left to right, using multiple rows if necessary.

**4.** Choose **Tile Vertically** to arrange the windows without overlapping, from top to bottom, using multiple columns if necessary.

**5.** Choose **Minimize All Windows** to minimize every open window. This is a quick way to get to your desktop.

After you use one of the above commands, you'll see an additional command on the shortcut menu—an "Undo" command for the last process you used.

(The Toolbars item on the shortcut menu is discussed later in this chapter in the section "Using the Toolbars.")

# Customizing the Taskbar

You can make all sorts of changes to the taskbar and the way it works. Customizing the taskbar can make it more useful, because your customization efforts let you match the taskbar's behavior and appearance to the way you want to work.

## Moving the Taskbar

You don't have to keep the taskbar at the bottom of your screen; you can place it on any of the four sides. To move the taskbar, follow these easy steps:

### Moving the taskbar

1. Put your mouse pointer on the taskbar, choosing a place where there are no buttons (on a crowded taskbar, you can usually find a space to the left of the taskbar tray).

2. Hold down the left mouse button while you drag the taskbar to either side of the screen, or to the top of the screen.

3. When you see the shaded gray area on the new edge (along with any buttons that are on the taskbar), release the mouse pointer to let the taskbar drop into its new space (see Figure 3.9).

When the taskbar is positioned on the left or right edge of the screen, it takes up more space. That's because taskbar buttons are always horizontal (if they weren't, you'd have to keep tilting your head to read them when you place the taskbar on the left or right side of your screen).

## Sizing the Taskbar

You can make the taskbar larger, which is an advantage if you generally have a lot of buttons on it because it gives each button more room. This, of course, makes the buttons easier to read.

When you don't have a lot of buttons on the taskbar, making the taskbar smaller is an advantage because it gives your application windows more room.

FIGURE 3.9
To move the taskbar, drag it to a different edge of your desktop.

### Changing the size of the taskbar

1. Place your mouse pointer on the edge of the taskbar that's closest to your desktop. When the pointer is on the right spot, it changes into a double-headed arrow.

2. Press the left mouse button and hold it down while you drag in the appropriate direction (toward the desktop to make the taskbar larger, toward the outside edge of your monitor to make it narrower).

3. Release the mouse button when the taskbar is the size you want it to be.

Resizing the taskbar works differently for different edges of the screen:

- If you are resizing a taskbar that is on the top or bottom of your screen, you cannot fine-tune the size. The taskbar jumps up or down in increments the size of the height of the buttons.

- If you are resizing a taskbar that is on the left or right edge of your screen, you can release the mouse at any point and the taskbar will maintain that width.

When you enlarge the taskbar, all the icons on your desktop scrunch over so that the taskbar doesn't hide any of them. When you make the taskbar smaller again, the desktop icons move away from each other to take advantage of the additional space on the desktop.

Programs written for Windows 98 (or Windows NT 4 or Windows 95) do the same thing: They adjust to the size of the taskbar. Actually, they do a quick mathematical computation that notes the space the taskbar is using and then they reduce or enlarge their own screen metrics as you reduce and enlarge the taskbar.

If you are running multiple Windows programs and have the windows all open at the same time (tiling or cascading them), they will all avoid overlapping the taskbar.

MS-DOS programs and programs that were written for earlier versions of Windows don't know about the taskbar and therefore don't adjust for it. If you want to see your taskbar, don't run those applications in full-screen mode.

## Setting Taskbar Properties

**Bringing back a hidden taskbar**

You can still access the taskbar quickly even if you are running software programs that hide the taskbar when they run in full-screen mode. Just press Alt+Esc to see the taskbar. Use the taskbar buttons to switch to other windows. When you want to return to the original program (the one that hides the taskbar), click its taskbar button.

You can set the properties of the taskbar in order to control its behavior, including whether or not it's always visible. This is accomplished in the Properties dialog box for the taskbar. You can get to the Taskbar Properties dialog box in either of two ways:

- Right-click on a blank spot on the taskbar and choose Properties from the shortcut menu.
- Click **Start** to display the Start menu, and then choose **Settings**, **Taskbar & Start Menu**.

The Taskbar Properties dialog box, shown in Figure 3.10, offers several options that you select or deselect by clicking the appropriate check box.

The "Show Clock" option is self-explanatory.

The "Show small icons in Start menu" option is for the Start menu, and we'll discuss that later in this chapter.

**FIGURE 3.10**
Use the Taskbar Properties dialog box to configure the taskbar's behavior.

The other two options are directly related to the way the taskbar operates and behaves.

### Keep the Taskbar Always On Top

Select **Always on top** if you always want to keep the taskbar on top of any open windows.

If you deselect this option, programs will stop adjusting their windows in order to make room for the taskbar. That means that any software you use in full-screen mode, including software written for Windows 98, will overlap the taskbar so you can't see it. To get to the taskbar, you will have to either resize the software window or press Alt+Esc.

However, if the taskbar isn't always on top, your maximized software window has more screen space, which sometimes makes it easier to work in the software. For instance, your word processor is able to display several more lines of text if it doesn't have to adjust its size for the taskbar. And, some people find the taskbar disconcerting when they're using graphics software or playing games.

## Auto Hide the Taskbar

Select **Auto hide** if you want to have the taskbar disappear when you're working in a window and then reappear automatically when you need it.

When Auto hide is enabled, the taskbar disappears as soon as you click anywhere on your desktop or in a window, or as soon as you move your pointer about 10 pixels away from the taskbar.

While the taskbar is hidden, you can see a very thin black line at the bottom of your screen, which represents the edge of the taskbar. As soon as your mouse pointer gets within two pixels of that line, the taskbar reappears.

When the taskbar is visible and you click on the taskbar, you temporarily stop the Auto hide function. You can move your mouse anywhere on your screen and the taskbar remains visible. As soon as you click anywhere else on your screen, however, Auto hide is re-enabled.

## Manually Hide the Taskbar

There may be times when you don't need to have the taskbar in front of you and you'd prefer to have the desktop space it consumes available for the software window you're working in. You don't have to change the configuration of the taskbar to hide it; you can do it yourself. Just follow these steps:

### Manually hiding the taskbar

1. Move your mouse pointer on the edge of the taskbar until it turns into a double-headed arrow.

2. Press the left mouse button while you drag the taskbar edge away from the desktop toward the edge of your monitor. The taskbar disappears, but if you look carefully, you can see the same thin black line that exists when the taskbar is configured for Auto hide.

3. To bring the taskbar back, move your mouse pointer to the thin black line until the pointer turns into a double-headed arrow.

4. Press the left mouse button and drag the line toward the desktop until the taskbar returns.

What you're actually doing is resizing the taskbar to make it smaller; in fact, you're making it so small that it isn't visible.

---

**Make the taskbar float or hop**

As the taskbar hides and reappears, it may seem to either float gracefully on and off your window, or just jump off and jump back on. The graceful animation is called smooth scrolling and if you care about it (or don't like it), you can enable or disable it by following these steps:

1. Open the Display Properties dialog box in Control Panel and move to the Effect tab. (You can also get to the Display Properties dialog box by right-clicking on a blank spot on your desktop and choosing Properties from the shortcut menu, or by double-clicking the Display icon on your taskbar tray).

2. Select the "Show Window Contents While Dragging" check box (if it already has a checkmark, the feature is enabled).

3. Click OK.

# What To Do If You Can't Get the Taskbar Back After Manually Hiding It

Sometimes after you hide the taskbar (or get too energetic when you're resizing it to make it smaller), you cannot get it back. The thin black line disappears, or you cannot get your mouse pointer to turn into a double-headed arrow. Here's how to fix the problem:

**Rescuing the taskbar after manually hiding it**

1. Press **Ctrl+Esc**. This selects the taskbar (you can't see it, but trust me, it's selected) and also displays the Start menu.

2. Press **Esc**. The Start menu disappears, but the taskbar is still selected (you still can't see it).

3. Press **Alt+Spacebar**, which brings up a shortcut menu.

4. Choose Size from the shortcut menu.

5. Your mouse pointer turns into a diamond shape with four squares inside the diamond. Do not click the mouse button.

6. Use the arrow keys to resize the taskbar (if the taskbar is on the bottom, use the Up arrow, if it's on the right edge of the screen, use the Left arrow, and so on).

7. Your pointer turns into a double-headed arrow and each time you press the arrow key, the pointer moves farther away from the edge of your screen. You can also see a red line moving with the pointer. The red line indicates the new position for the inside edge of the taskbar.

8. Press **Enter** as soon as the red line (and your mouse pointer, which is moving along with the red line) is a good distance away from the edge of your screen.

9. Now you can resize the taskbar—carefully.

If this doesn't work, you'll have to press **Ctrl+Esc** to bring back the Start menu so you can select **Shut down**. Then restart the computer in Safe mode. This restores the taskbar to its default location.

To start Windows 98 in Safe mode, when you see the "Starting Windows 98" message, press the **F5** key. Or, press the **F8** key and then choose **Safe Mode** from the Startup menu that appears.

However, a Safe mode start restores all the default options for the taskbar and Start menu, so if you changed the options, those changes will be lost and you'll have to reconfigure the taskbar.

**SEE ALSO**

➤ *Information about all the ways to start your computer, including Safe mode, can be found in Chapter 1.*

## Customizing the Objects in the Taskbar Tray

Every icon that appears in the tray can be used to configure or customize the object it represents. All you have to do is double-click the icon, and you see its window. The configuration options vary, depending on what the icon's object is. Here are a few examples:

- While printing is active, a printer icon appears in the tray. Double-click it to open the printer's window, where you can perform a variety of actions including deleting or pausing a document that's being printed.

- If you have a sound card in your computer, there's a speaker icon on the tray. When you double-click the icon, the Volume Control dialog box appears so you can change the volume or balance of the sounds coming from your speakers (or mute everything if you wish).

- Single-click the Display icon to change your video settings (see Figure 3.11). Double-click the icon to open the Display Properties dialog box.

**FIGURE 3.11**

Make a quick change to your video settings from the taskbar tray.

- Double-clicking the power management icon that appears in the tray of a laptop computer brings up a dialog box in which you can configure the way you want power management options to work.

The icon that appears by default in the taskbar tray of every Windows 98 computer is the digital clock. When you double-click the clock, the Date/Time Properties dialog box appears (see Figure 3.12). This is the same Date/Time dialog box you can access in the Control Panel.

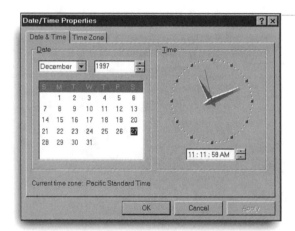

FIGURE 3.12

Set the date and time with the Date/Time Properties dialog box.

If the date or time (or both) are incorrect, you can reset them by following these steps:

**Resetting the date and time**

1. Click the arrow next to the Month box to choose a different month.

2. Click the appropriate date in the calendar.

3. Use the up or down arrow next to the Year box to change the year.

4. To change the time, place your mouse pointer to the left of the element you want to change (hour, minute, second, or AM/PM). Then use the up or down arrow to make your changes. (You can also drag the mouse across the element to highlight it, and type in the new numbers directly instead of using the arrows.)

5. Choose Apply to apply your changes without closing the dialog box, or choose OK to apply the changes and close the dialog box.

You can also adjust the time zone (necessary only if you move to another time zone or if you made a mistake when you first set up Windows 98). Move to the Time Zone tab (see Figure 3.13) and click the arrow next to the time zone display. Scroll through the choices to find your time zone.

**FIGURE 3.13**

Keep track of your time zone and Windows 98 will keep track of daylight saving changes.

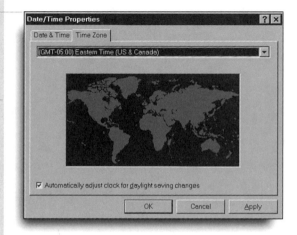

By default, Windows 98 selects the option to adjust the clock for daylight saving changes, and you can leave that selection alone even if your home town doesn't participate. Windows 98 knows that if you live in certain parts of Indiana, you don't have to reset your clocks (there's even a specific choice for Indiana in the drop-down list of time zones).

If you're using your computer in a company that regards the correct time as a sacred item (such as a broadcasting company), you probably shouldn't pay a lot of attention to the clock on your taskbar. Very few computers keep accurate time, and in fact when I glance at the five computers on my network, I can see that no two of them are displaying the same time, and the range of discrepancy is nine minutes. They all started out with the correct time, but over a period of months that has changed.

**FYI**

The "GMT" reference in the time zones refers to Greenwich Mean Time, and all the time zones display an amount of time ahead of or behind GMT.

**SEE ALSO**

➤ *Information about using a printer window to configure printing is in Chapter 13.*

➤ *Detailed information on setting display properties is in Chapter 8.*

# Using the Taskbar Toolbars

New in Windows 98 are toolbars on the taskbar. You can choose the toolbar(s) you want to display, configure their display, and invent your own toolbars.

## The Built-In Toolbars

There are four toolbars built into Windows 98: Quick Launch; Address; Links; and Desktop.

### Putting a toolbar on the taskbar

**1.** Right-click a blank spot on the taskbar to display the taskbar shortcut menu.

**2.** Place your mouse pointer on the Toolbars command to see the submenu of available toolbars (see Figure 3.14).

**FIGURE 3.14**
A checkmark indicates the toolbar is on the taskbar.

**3.** Click a toolbar to add it to your taskbar. A checkmark appears next to the toolbar name.

**4.** Remove a toolbar from the taskbar by clicking its name.

You can also create your own toolbars, and the steps to accomplish that are covered later in this chapter.

## Quick Launch Toolbar

The Quick Launch toolbar is on your taskbar by default. It contains icons for those features that Microsoft assumes you'll use the most (see Figure 3.15):

**FIGURE 3.15**
Use the Quick Launch toolbar for one-click access to programs and features.

■ Internet Explorer, the browser included with Windows 98.

■ Outlook Express, the Windows 98 built-in email program.

**Synchronizing time across an NT network**

The issue of correct time can carry more importance than whether or not you're a fanatic about time being correct to the second. For some multi-user software programs that run from network servers, the time assigned to a transaction that affects a data file can be very important. If more than one user is writing to a file and the software is watching to see which new data is the latest (and therefore the data that is kept), the time is very important.

If your Windows 98 computer is attached to a Windows NT network, there's a way to synchronize the time on your computer's clock with the time on the clock of another computer. You need to ask your network administrator which computer has the correct time, of course.

This is accomplished by going to an MS-DOS command prompt and entering **net time \\computername /set**. Substitute the name of the computer with the good clock for computername. The /set parameter forces your clock to synchronize with that target computer's clock. If you omit the /set parameter, you'll see a message telling you what the date and time is on the target computer.

Many network administrators include a **net time** command in the logon script for workstations, ensuring that all the computers on the network are operating on the same time. (In fact, one of these days I'm going to get around to doing that.) Of course, that means the administrator must keep a careful eye on the accuracy of the clock in the computer that's being used as the standard.

- Show Desktop, a one-click way to minimize all the windows on your screen and make your desktop accessible.

- View Channels, to make a quick trip to the Internet and visit (or change) your favorite channels.

**SEE ALSO**

➤ *Information about Internet Explorer and channels is found in Chapter 18.*

## Address Toolbar

The Address toolbar is a replica of the URL box on your Internet browser. Enter a URL and press Enter to launch your browser and head for that location. The Address toolbar saves your URL entries so you can get to your favorite places quickly (see Figure 3.16).

The Internet addresses that appear in the Address toolbar are the URLs you entered from that toolbar. Once you're working in the browser, any additional Web sites you visit are not memorized in the Address toolbar.

## Links Toolbar

The Links toolbar is a replica of your Links toolbar on Internet Explorer (see Figure 3.17). Just click the link you want to use and IE4 automatically launches and takes you there.

If you're not sure of the location, hold your mouse pointer over a link to see its URL.

## Desktop Toolbar

The Desktop toolbar is a miniature version of your desktop, which is incredibly handy when your screen is filled with software windows. Every icon on your desktop is on the toolbar (see Figure 3.18).

# Customizing the Toolbars

You can change the appearance, position, and contents of a toolbar with ease. What's nifty is that you can configure each toolbar independently.

FIGURE 3.16

A quick click takes me to the Internet site I want to visit.

FIGURE 3.17

Click a link and your trip to the Internet is on automatic pilot.

FIGURE 3.18

Any shortcut or other icon you need to access is right in front of you with the Desktop toolbar.

## Adding Titles and Text to Toolbars

You may want to see more information than an icon-filled toolbar displays. You can add the toolbar's name (title) and also add text for each icon.

- To display the toolbar's title, right-click on a blank spot on the toolbar and choose Show Title from the shortcut menu.
- To display the text for each icon on the toolbar, right-click on a blank spot on the toolbar and choose Show Text from the shortcut menu.

There is no option to show icon text for the Address toolbar (it has no icons, so that makes sense). Figure 3.19 shows the Quick Launch toolbar with both the title and text displayed.

FIGURE 3.19

There's no confusion about the toolbar when everything is spelled out.

Of course, when you add either a title or text, the toolbar takes up more room. When the toolbar doesn't fit in the available space, an arrow appears at the right end of the toolbar (refer to Figure 3.19). The arrow acts as a scroll bar; use it to expose the hidden icons to the right. When you reach the end of the toolbar, the arrow jumps to the left so you can scroll back.

## Resizing Toolbars

Both the icons on the toolbars and the toolbars themselves can be resized, so you have all sorts of options for designing the way your taskbar looks.

You have two choices of icon size for your toolbars: Large and Small. To change the size of the icons on an individual toolbar, follow these steps:

### Changing the size of the icons on the toolbar

1. Right-click on a blank spot on the toolbar
2. Place your mouse pointer on the View command.
3. Choose Large or Small.

Figure 3.20 shows the Quick Launch toolbar with large icons next to the Desktop toolbar with small icons.

**FIGURE 3.20**

The larger icons are easier to recognize, but you can see and access more icons if they're small.

### Expanding and shrinking a toolbar

1. Place your mouse pointer on the ridged edge on the left end of the toolbar. The pointer changes to a double-headed arrow.
2. Press and hold the left mouse button and drag to the left to expand the toolbar.
3. Drag to the right to shorten the toolbar.

If you have multiple toolbars on the taskbar, expanding one toolbar shrinks the toolbar to its left. Shrinking the toolbar expands the toolbar to its left.

## Moving Toolbars

You can drag a toolbar from the taskbar and park it anywhere on your screen by following these steps:

### Dragging a toolbar to park it anywhere on the desktop

1. Place your mouse pointer on the ridge on the left edge of the toolbar so that the pointer becomes a double-headed arrow.

2. Press and hold the left mouse button while you drag the toolbar to any spot on the desktop.

3. Resize the toolbar to make it perfect (see Figure 3.21).

FIGURE 3.21
When the toolbar is on the desktop, resize it to fit your taste.

You can also drag the toolbar to any edge of your screen and it becomes a second taskbar. All the right-click functions of the taskbar are available.

If you place a toolbar on the desktop, you can drag another toolbar from the taskbar into its window. Now you have two toolbars in the same window. In fact, you can continue to drag toolbars to that window and have one window for all your toolbars. The toolbars are separated by a ridged edge and can be configured independently (see Figure 3.22).

FIGURE 3.22
You can configure each toolbar in the window separately.

## Creating Toolbars

You can create your own toolbars so that all your frequently used items are together in one handy place. Here's how to accomplish this:

### Creating your own toolbars

1. Right-click a blank spot on the taskbar and choose **Toolbars**, **New Toolbar** from the shortcut menu.

**2.** When the New Toolbar dialog box appears (see Figure 3.23), select a folder (or enter a URL if the toolbar is a shortcut to an Internet address).

**3.** Choose **OK**.

Any item you place into this folder while you're working in software applications (or dragging items to folders) is reflected on the toolbar.

You'll probably have to create the folder first (unless you already have folders you created to hold shortcuts to oft-used items).

My first new toolbar was created from a folder named Current Projects. This is the ideal use of a toolbar because instead of having to open the folder and select the document I want to work on (or open software and find the document in its folder), I can click its icon on the toolbar. The icon works exactly the way it does in Explorer, and clicking on it opens the software associated with it. What's better is that a toolbar icon requires only a single-click, instead of the double-click Explorer needs.

# Using the Start Menu

Almost everything you'll ever need to do when you're working with your computer can be accessed from the Start menu. You can start software, install software, configure hardware, get help, find files...the list goes on forever.

As if that weren't enough, you can even customize the Start menu to match your own needs.

The Start menu appears when you click the **Start** button (or if you press **Ctrl+Esc**). All Windows 98 Start menus have at least the items you see in Figure 3.24.

**FIGURE 3.24**
Your Start menu is the launch pad for anything you need to access on your system.

The Start menu items that have an arrow to the right of the menu item have additional menu items available. In fact, some of those additional items have arrows pointing to more items. All of this depends on the software and utilities you install in your Windows 98 system (which means that your menu items won't look the same as mine).

As you move your mouse over the items on the Start menu that have arrows, the additional items display automatically (you don't have to click on the arrow to see them). The additional menu you see is called a *cascading menu*.

Many software applications install cascading menus when they place their programs on your Start menu. If you've installed a lot of software and a lot of Windows 98 accessories, your cascading menus can fill your desktop (see Figure 3.25).

In this section, we'll go over the Start menu items briefly, starting from the bottom and working our way to the top of the default menu system. Then we'll discuss ways to customize the Start menu to make it easier to navigate.

**Some software programs add items to the basic start menu**

If you've installed Microsoft Office or Corel Suite or any of several other software suites, you probably have additional menu items at the top of your Start menu. For instance, if you install Microsoft Office, your Start menu probably has two additional choices at the top: New Office Document and Open Office Document.

FIGURE 3.25

Meandering through a large
menu system can take some
time.

## Shut Down

Starting from the bottom of your Start menu, your mouse first
encounters the Shut Down menu item. Use this menu choice
every time you want to turn off your computer; do not just hit
the power button. When you click Shut Down, you see the Shut
Down Windows dialog box shown in Figure 3.26. Your selection
depends on what you need to do next on your computer, and all
of the choices are explained in Chapter 2.

FIGURE 3.26

Choose a shut down option
that matches what you want to
do next.

## Log Off

New to Windows 98, this command closes all open software and
presents a new logon dialog box so you can log on again with a

different user name. If you used Windows 95, this command replaces the choice on the Shut Down dialog box that was named Close all programs and log on as a different user.

## Run

Using Run is a bit like going to an MS-DOS command prompt and entering a command to start an application. You can also use Run for functions other than entering a command; we'll cover those later in this section.

When the Run dialog box opens, the name of the last command you entered is displayed in the entry box, in case you want to run the same command again (see Figure 3.27). If you do, just click **OK**. Of course, the first time you use Run, the entry box is empty.

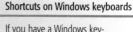

**Shortcuts on Windows keyboards**

If you have a Windows keyboard, hold down the Windows key and press R to open the Run dialog box without having to go to the Start button.

**FIGURE 3.27**

The last Run command you entered is displayed automatically.

Click the arrow to the right of the entry box to see a list of commands you've previously entered (see Figure 3.28). If the command you need is listed, select it and then click **OK**.

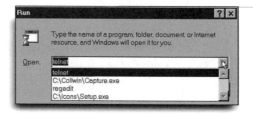

**FIGURE 3.28**

After you've used Run several times, you'll probably find the command you need in the list of commands you previously used.

If the command you want to use isn't listed, just enter it and click **OK**. Some commands require you to enter the *path* along with the command. The path is the location of the command, and it's entered by specifying the folder (and subfolder if applicable) in which the command file resides. Each level of the path is separated by a backslash (\).

For example, if you want to open a program named MyProgram that is located in a folder named MyStuff, enter **\mystuff\ myprogram** and click **OK**. If your program were located in a subfolder under MyStuff named YourStuff, you would enter **\mystuff\yourstuff\myprogram**. (Notice that you don't have to go to the trouble of using capital letters in a command.)

If you don't remember the name of the folder or subfolder that contains the command file you need, click **Browse**. The Browse dialog box appears, displaying the components of your desktop (see Figure 3.29).

Select **My Computer**, and then select the hard drive that has the folder you need. (If you're on a network and you want to use a file from another computer, you can choose Network Neighborhood.) Continue to select folders and subfolders until you find the file you're looking for. Double-click the filename (or single click it and choose Open on the Browse dialog box). The filename is placed in the Run dialog box, and you can click **OK** to execute the command.

You can use Run for more than executing commands. Here are some of the shortcuts Run provides for you:

- Enter the path to a folder or subfolder to open a window that displays the contents of that folder. This is faster than opening My Computer and then opening the folder and subfolder you want to look at.

- Enter the name of a document, and Windows 98 will open the software program associated with that document and put the document in the software window. (If the document is one you've worked with recently, you can also open it from the Documents item on the Start menu, which we'll discuss later in this section.)

- You can open a shared folder on another computer on your network by entering its name with a *UNC* (Universal Naming Convention). The UNC is a format for accessing shared resources on a remote computer. It is very much like a path, except the first entry is a double backslash (\\). The double backslash indicates the next item in the path entry is a computer instead of a folder. For example, to open a shared folder named Budgets on a remote computer named Accntg, enter **\\accntg\budgets**.

- Enter a *URL* (Universal Resource Locator, which is the name of a site on the Internet) in the Run dialog box to open your Internet browser and head to the site.

**SEE ALSO**

➤ *More information about Network Neighborhood is found in Chapter 20.*

➤ *For information about associating documents with software programs, turn to Chapter 4.*

➤ *To learn more about using Windows 98 on a network, see Chapter 20.*

## Help

The Help menu item opens the Windows 98 Help system. If you previously used Windows 95, you'll notice a whole new look and functionality for Help.

**SEE ALSO**

➤ *Complete explanations about using Help can be found in Chapter 5.*

## Find

You can use Find to search for practically anything that's in your computer or accessible from your computer.

The cascading menu for Find offers four choices: Files or Folders; Computer; On the Internet; and People. Each choice displays a specific Find dialog box.

## Finding Folders and Files

The dialog box for finding folders and files has a wealth of options you can use to make your search productive (see Figure 3.30). Those options are covered in detail in Chapter 4.

**FIGURE 3.30**

Use a name, a partial name, file specifications, or any other specific information to find the files you need.

The dialog box for finding a computer doesn't offer very much in the way of assistance, not even a Browse button (see Figure 3.31). You have to know what you're looking for. Enter the name of the computer you want to find in the Named box and click Find Now.

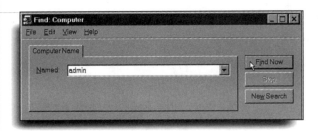

**FIGURE 3.31**

Use Find to locate a computer you need to access.

The only assistance for this function is available if you've successfully searched for a computer before and you want to find the same computer this time. You can click the arrow to the right of the entry box and see the name of computers you've searched for previously.

When the computer is located, its icon appears in the Found section of the dialog box (see Figure 3.32). Double-click the icon to open a window that displays all the shared folders and resources for that computer.

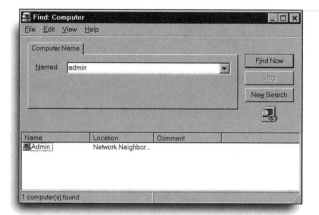

FIGURE 3.32

When Find locates the computer you're seeking, its icon is displayed.

The truth is, it's far more productive to use Network Neighborhood to find a computer because you can browse your network (which I find much easier because my memory isn't what it used to be and I can't remember the names of all the computers on the network).

## Finding Stuff on the Internet

When you choose On the Internet from the cascading menu, your browser opens and you can use any Internet search engine to find the information you need.

## Finding People

When you're using Find to search for information about a person, Windows 98 assumes you want to search your address book first (see Figure 3.33).

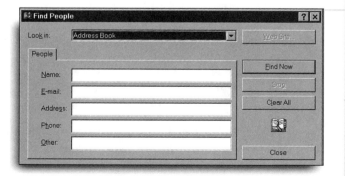

FIGURE 3.33

Fill in whatever information you know in order to search your Windows 98 address book.

If the person you want to locate isn't in your address book, but instead can be found on the Internet, follow these steps to play detective:

### Locating people on the Internet with Find

1. Click the arrow to the right of the Look in box and select an Internet search engine from the drop-down list.

2. When you're connected to the Internet, use the functions available for the search engine you chose (see Figure 3.34).

**FIGURE 3.34**

Try all the Internet people-searchers to see which one you like the best.

## Settings

The Settings menu item has a cascading menu that lists the items you use for setting up your system (see Figure 3.35).

These configuration settings are discussed throughout this book (of course, the taskbar settings are discussed in this chapter).

The Windows update listing connects you to the Microsoft Web site so you can get updates for your Windows 98 system.

FIGURE 3.35

Use the Settings menu item to reach your system configuration functions.

**SEE ALSO**
- ➤ *Control Panel information is found in Chapter 7.*
- ➤ *Information about setting up printers is in Chapter 13.*

## Documents

The Documents menu item has an arrow, which might make you think it has a cascading menu. It doesn't. The arrow points to a list (which isn't the same thing as a menu). This list is the last 15 documents you worked on, as long as you accessed those documents with a software program that is written for Windows 98 (or Windows 95 or Windows NT 4). Programs written for Windows 3.*x* or MS-DOS do not send the document name information to this list.

When you select one of the documents, Windows 98 opens the software program that created the document and then loads the document in the software window.

You can clear the list using the Properties dialog box for the Start menu (which we'll discuss later in this chapter).

## Favorites

This Start menu item stores all your favorite Web sites. When you first install Windows 98, you have an entire collection of favorite sites (Microsoft has made the decisions for you). The sites are divided by category, so this menu item has an abundant set of cascading menus (see Figure 3.36).

**What's the point?**

Now you know how the Documents menu works, and I'll bet you never use it. In many years of visiting client sites and training users, I've never found anyone who used this menu item. It's pointless. It's easier to open the software application and click the File menu to see a list of recently used documents. In fact, even software programs written for earlier versions of Windows maintain a recently used list in the File menu option, so it's more productive to go to the software.

I have a theory that there was a Committee for the Design of the Start Menu at Microsoft and they did what most corporate committees do—they got carried away with their mission and didn't notice when they'd crossed that line we refer to as "logical reasons for doing something."

FIGURE 3.36

You're bound to find something that interests you in some of these sites.

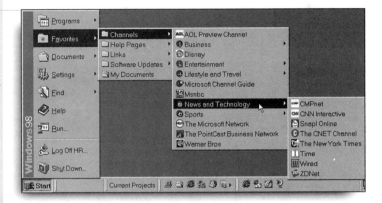

This folder is a mirror of the Favorites menu item in Internet Explorer 4. As you make changes there, your Start menu Favorites folder reflects them. See Chapter 18 for information about setting up your Favorite sites in IE4.

## Programs

The Programs item on the Start menu is where you'll spend a lot of time, because running software is what you do most when you're at your computer. It would be pretty sad if the only use you got from your computer was configuring and tweaking your operating system.

When you install a software program, it should place either a program item or a program group on the Programs menu item. The reason I say "should" is that some software fails to do this (MS-DOS software almost always fails to do this). However, you can add a program item to the menu, and we'll discuss how to do that later in this chapter.

A *program item* is a listing for that software, and you click it to launch the software.

A *program group* is really a folder because the listing is a container for multiple items. Program group listings have an arrow to indicate a cascading menu, and the individual programs you can launch for the program group are on that cascading menu.

# Customizing the Start Menu

Are you tired of moving your mouse through cascading menu items to find the program you want to use? Wouldn't it be easier to have the programs you use all the time listed right on the Start menu instead of in the Programs menu?

Have you uninstalled software programs, but still see the listings on your Programs menu?

Is your Program menu so large that it threatens to outgrow the size of your monitor?

I hear a resounding chorus of "yes" from the peanut gallery.

You're not alone; it happens to everyone. The larger the size of your hard drive, the longer your Programs menu grows—it's a law of nature.

There are a number of options for customizing the Start menu so that everything you need to get your work accomplished is handy, convenient, and easy to get to.

The easiest way to begin is to use the Taskbar Properties dialog box (don't be fooled by the name; it's also the Properties dialog box for the Start menu). To reach that dialog box, use one of these methods:

- Right-click a blank spot on the taskbar and choose Properties from the shortcut menu.
- Choose **Settings**, **Taskbar & Start Menu** from the **Start** menu.

Either method opens the dialog box with the Taskbar tab in the foreground.

Okay, let's get to the important stuff. To access the options for customizing the Programs menu, you must click on the Start Menu Programs tab (see Figure 3.37).

## Removing Items from the Programs Menu

One of the things that I find very annoying is that most of the time, an Uninstall program fails to remove the program's listing in the Programs menu when it uninstalls the software. As a

**One Start menu option is on the taskbar tab**

There is one Start menu customization item on the Taskbar tab, "Show small icons in Start menu." If you select that option, the icons (and the text) of the Start menu are reduced in size. This makes the Start menu smaller when you use it (which means it doesn't cover up quite as much of your desktop or the software window that is on your desktop).

The cascading menus that appear as you use the Start menu are already configured for small icons, so it is only the Start menu itself that is changed when you select this option.

Try it yourself and see if it makes a difference to you. Personally, I find it's no big deal either way.

result, you can have a very long Programs menu list, and some of the entries don't work because you've eliminated the software program. When that happens, you should delete the Programs menu item manually.

FIGURE 3.37

You can add and remove items from the Start menu with its Properties dialog box.

**Clear that document list!**

Notice that the bottom half of this dialog box has a button to clear the contents of the Document menu item. Just click the button to get rid of the list of documents.

Also, if you use desktop shortcuts to launch your favorite programs and don't have to open the Programs menu for them, you might as well remove those items from the Programs menu. This should make the Programs menu shorter and less confusing to wade through.

To clean up your Programs menu, follow these steps to remove items:

### Removing items from your Programs menu

1. Choose **Remove** from the Start Menu Programs dialog box, which brings up the Remove Shortcuts/Folders dialog box shown in Figure 3.38.

2. Scroll through the list to find the item you want to remove. Click the plus sign next to a folder to see the individual items it contains and select the target item.

3. Click on the item you want to remove, which selects and highlights it.

FIGURE 3.38
You can remove a folder or an individual program listing from the Programs menu.

4. Click **Remove** to delete the selected item. The item disappears immediately; you are not asked to confirm the removal. However, the item is sent to the Recycle Bin so you can retrieve it if you make a mistake.

5. Choose **Close** when you have finished your housekeeping. You are returned to the Start Menu Programs dialog box.

Here are some things you should know about removing items from the Programs menu:

- You are not removing the program; you are removing a shortcut to the program. A shortcut is a pointer to a file and removing a shortcut does not remove the file. That's why it's okay to remove menu listings for programs you still use, which you can do if you have a desktop shortcut or you're going to place a shortcut on the main Start menu.

- If you remove a folder, you automatically remove all the items contained in that folder. Don't remove a folder unless you expand it with the plus sign and look at all the individual items to make sure you realize what you're removing.

- Don't remove the Startup folder even if it's empty.

SEE ALSO
➤ *Learn how to create desktop shortcuts for your favorite software programs in Chapter 12.*

## Folders equal cascading menus

Folders represent those Programs menu items that have arrows indicating there is an additional menu available. The individual items you see when you expand the folder by clicking the plus sign are the program items that display on the cascading menu.

**About the Startup folder**

The Startup folder has a special function: It holds shortcuts to programs or utilities that start up when you first start the operating system. Some software programs place items in the Startup folder (and most of the time I head for the Startup folder and remove them because I don't always want to have that software function running automatically). If there's a program or utility you'd like to launch while you're starting Windows 98, you can place a listing in the Startup folder. One of the common utilities found in Startup folders are virus checkers.

# Adding Items to the Programs Menu

You can add menu items to the Programs menu or directly onto the Start menu. You can even create new folders for the Programs menu and put new items into them (or move existing items into them in order to reduce the length of your Programs menu). We'll start this discussion by adding a program item, and then we'll create a new folder for the Programs menu and place items in it.

## Adding a Single Item to the Programs Menu

If you've installed software that didn't place a listing on the Programs menu, you can add it manually by following these steps:

### Adding a single item to the Programs menu

1. From the Start Menu Programs dialog box, choose **Add**, which brings up the Create Shortcut dialog box shown in Figure 3.39.

**FIGURE 3.39**

The Create Shortcut function works like a Windows wizard, guiding you through all the steps.

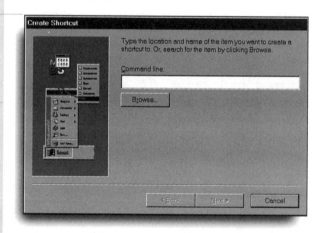

2. If you know it, enter the path and/or filename of the program you want to place on the menu.

3. If you don't remember the path and/or filename, choose **Browse** to open a Browse dialog box, which opens to display all the folders and program files on Drive C. (If you have two hard drives and the folder you need is on Drive D, find the icon for Drive D and choose it.)

4. Move through the folders to locate the program file you need. When you find it, double-click it to place its path and name in the Create Shortcut dialog box.

5. Choose **Next** to move on to the Select Program Folder dialog box (see Figure 3.40), where you get to choose a location on the Programs menu for your new item.

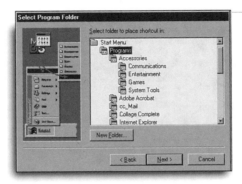

FIGURE 3.40

By default, the system assumes you want to put your item directly on the Programs menu instead of one of the sub-menus.

6. Unless the item is a program that's connected to one of the existing subfolders, you should select the Programs menu. Then click **Next**.

7. Now you must choose a name for the item. By default, the system enters the filename including the extension, which isn't very elegant, but it does provide an accurate description. You can change the name entirely or just get rid of the extension.

8. Choose **Finish** to complete the process. You are returned to the Start Menu Program dialog box and the new item is now on your Programs menu.

## Adding a Folder to the Programs Menu

You can add a folder to your Programs menu and place program items in it. This is a good way to reduce the size of a very long Programs menu, because you can put similar types of programs together in one folder instead of having a separate listing for each program.

To add a folder to the Programs menu and then move program listings into it, follow these steps:

**You can create a new folder for this program**

If you're adding a group of programs that are related to each other, you can add a folder for them instead of adding each listing to the Programs menu.

In the Select Program Folder dialog box, choose New Folder. Give the folder a name and select it as the target folder for your program listing(s).

### Adding customized folders for programs to the Programs menu

**1.** In the Start Programs Menu dialog box, choose **Advanced** to launch an Explorer window that displays the section of your hard drive that contains the Start menu information.

**2.** Click the **Programs** folder to select it. The right pane of the window displays all the subfolders and individual items on your Programs menu (see Figure 3.41).

**FIGURE 3.41**

All the items on your Start menu exist as objects on your hard drive.

**3.** Choose **File, New, Folder** from the menu bar to create a new folder under the selected Programs folder (or right-click on a blank spot in the right pane and choose New, Folder from the shortcut menu).

**4.** The new folder appears in the right pane, and it is named New Folder by default. The name is selected and highlighted (which means it is in Edit mode), so as soon as you begin typing characters for the folder's real name, the default name disappears. Enter a name that describes the type of programs you're planning to put into this folder (perhaps all your word processors, or accounting programs). When you have entered the name, press **Enter**.

**5.** In the left pane, click the **Programs** folder to select it again, and then click the plus sign to the left of the Programs folder. This expands the folder so that all of the subfolders appear in the left pane. Your new folder is there. Don't click on it to select it; you want to leave the Programs folder as the selected folder. The items on the right pane are always the contents of the selected folder, and you want to work with the items in the Programs folder.

**6.** In the right pane, select the Program items you want to move into the new folder. To select multiple items, hold down the Ctrl key as you click each item you want to move.

**7.** Use one of the following methods to move all the select items into the new folder (when you select multiple items in the right pane of an Explorer window, whatever you do to one item you do to all the selected items):

- Right-click any one of the selected items and choose **Cut** from the shortcut menu. Then right-click on your new folder in the left pane and choose Paste from the Shortcut menu.

- Press and hold the right mouse button to drag one of the selected items to the new folder (the others all come along for the ride) and release the mouse when the pointer is on the new folder. Then select **Move Here** from the menu that appears when you release the right mouse button.

- Press and hold the left mouse button to drag one of the selected items to the new folder (all the selected items move along with it). Release the mouse button when the pointer is directly on the new folder.

- Choose **Edit, Cut** from the menu bar. Then click on the new folder in the left pane to select it and choose **Edit, Paste** from the menu bar.

**8.** Close the Explorer window to return to the Start Menu Programs dialog box. Choose **OK** to close the dialog box.

Now open your Start menu and look at the Programs menu. Your new folder is listed with an arrow to the right of its name. Place your mouse pointer over the listing to see that the cascading menu contains the items you placed in the new folder.

You can continue to use this process to combine individual listings on your Programs menu. Perhaps you'd like to put all the kids' games in one folder. If your children have their own preferences, create a folder named Judy's Games and another one named Mike's Games.

## Drag and Drop New Start Menu Items

You can place items on the Start menu itself, the menu you see when you click the Start button, instead of placing them on the Programs menu. This is useful for creating easy access to the item because you don't have to move your mouse to the Programs menu and then work your way through cascading menus to get to the item you need.

Windows 98 creates a special area above the regular, default Start menu to hold those items that are placed directly on the Start menu. It's separated from the main Start menu with a thin line. The items in this section are arranged alphabetically.

To put a software program listing on the Start menu, open Explorer or My Computer and find the program file you want. Drag the file to the Start button. That's "Start button," not "Start menu." Of course, you have to make sure Auto hide isn't on so you can get to the Start Button.

Making your Start menu easy to use makes it so much easier to open software, use the Windows 98 tools, and access all the utilities in your system. Customizing these important parts of your operating system is so easy to do that it doesn't make sense not to.

# Managing Files and Folders

# Understanding Icons, Folders, and Files

Getting around in Windows 98 is pretty easy thanks to the wealth of navigational tools at your disposal. These tools also make it quite easy to manipulate the elements you find in your system, moving and deleting items as you need to.

Before you can use these tools efficiently, it helps to have a basic understanding of the system elements involved, such as icons, folders, and files.

## Icons

Every element in your Windows 98 system is an object, and *icons* are pictures that represent these objects. Objects include hardware objects (such as drives and printers), system objects (such as folders, Properties dialog boxes, and fonts), and a variety of software objects (program files and document files).

One interesting result of using Windows 98 for any period of time is that after a while you learn to recognize the objects in your system by their icons. Your interaction with icons always involves your mouse:

- Double-click an icon to open it (or single-click a Windows 98 icon if you've configured your Active Desktop for single-clicking).
- Click an icon and hold down the mouse button while you drag the mouse to move the icon's object.
- Right-click an icon to see its shortcut menu, which lists all the options for manipulating the icon's object.

Most of the icons you see are stored inside Windows 98 system files or the program files for software; there's usually no file for the icon that you could locate on your drive. Windows 98 knows which icon to display for each type of object by checking the information in the Registry.

### How Objects Are Guaranteed Uniqueness

If you find behind-the-scenes technical stuff absorbing, you may be interested in this (otherwise, you can safely skip this information).

Every object type has a unique class identifier (CLSID) and all the information about the object type is kept in the Registry. If you look in the Registry, you'll see all sorts of information about the object type, including its default icon. The default icon is displayed in two parts: the file it's in, and the icon number within that file. For example, a default icon notation may be Syncui.dll,0. This means the icon is contained in the Windows system file named Syncui.dll and it is the first icon in that file (computers start counting with 0).

The actual CLSID key isn't English, it is a 16-byte number that is formatted as 32 hexadecimal digits, which is a technical way of saying it uses special characters that can be translated to English if you know how (not many people know how; I certainly can't glance at a hex character string and interpret it). The CLSID is a group of characters arranged in a format of 8-4-4-4-12. For example, the CLSID for My Briefcase is 85BBD920-42A0-1069-A2E4-08002B30309D. Each object type has a totally unique CLSID in your Registry.

Object types are identified the same way on every PC in the world (like a Social Security Number). The term for this identification is a Globally Unique Identifier (GUID). The GUID is the same as the CLSID, but we only use the term CLSID when we're referring to a specific computer.

When programmers invent a new object type for Windows (usually for software that runs in Windows), they have to create a GUID for it. Microsoft has a program that does this work for them. The way GUID creation works is to generate the first 8 digits as random numbers, then the next 4 digits use the current date and time on the computer being used to generate the GUID, and the last 20 digits are generated using information from that computer's hardware setup. It would be an enormous coincidence if two GUIDs ended up the same; the odds are so far against it that it's not considered something to worry about.

# Folders

I have a large box on the floor of my office labeled "to be filed." It's overflowing, because I can't seem to find time to file paperwork (and I hate doing it so I use every possible excuse to avoid it). It's almost impossible to find anything in that box when I need it, so eventually I do take the time to transfer every object in it to a filing cabinet.

When I open the filing cabinet I have two different devices for holding all my information: hanging file folders and manila folders. The manila folders are inserted inside the hanging folders and some hanging folders contain multiple manila folders.

Your computer works very much like my file cabinet (and your file cabinets are probably similar to mine). Instead of dumping every file in your system onto a drive, your computer is neatly arranged into folders. Most folders contain files. Some folders contain folders (which we call subfolders). If it weren't for folders, your computer system would be like the box on my floor and you'd go crazy looking for the files you need.

Most of the time you don't have to worry about creating all the folders you need. Windows 98 creates folders to hold all the operating system files in a logical manner, and the software you install creates the folders needed to operate the software in a manageable way.

*Folders* (which have icons that look like manila folders) represent directories on your drive and subfolders represent subdirectories. Back in the days of MS-DOS computing, we used to type out the name of directories and subdirectories to move around a hard drive (clicking a folder icon is far easier). The format for a directory statement is `Drive:\DirectoryName\SubdirectoryName`.

The directory statement is known as a *path*. A path is a map to a location on your hard drive. When you open Explorer and select a folder or subfolder, the title bar on the Explorer window displays the path for that folder (see Figure 4.1).

Paths start with a drive letter and then describe a hierarchical location, much like a corporate organization chart. The drive letter itself represents the root (or root directory) and the hierarchical format is called a *tree*.

**Some folders are empty**

Some software programs install extra folders during the setup process. Sometimes these folders are used to hold temporary files that are needed by the software while it's running and when you exit the software, those folders are emptied. Sometimes these folders are set up to prepare for special files that are created when you use special features in the software. If you never access those special features, the folders remain empty.

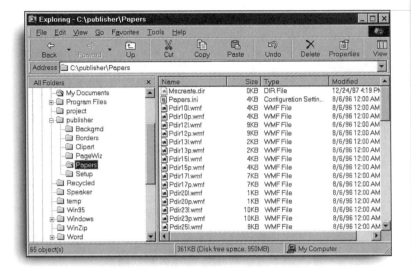

FIGURE 4.1

Check the title bar to see the path for the folder you've selected.

## Files

A *file* is a piece of information. If it's a document file, the information is whatever you or a software company created. If it's a program file, it's the information a programmer created (which includes instructions and codes).

Files, too, are represented by a path and the format is `drive:\Directory\Subdirectory\filename`. There may not be a subdirectory in a specific file's path (or there may be multiple subdirectories if the file is tucked way down on the tree).

## Naming Rules for Folders and Files

The rules for naming a folder or file in Windows 98 aren't very complicated, because there aren't really a lot of rules. You can use up to 255 characters in your filename and you can use any character on your keyboard except \, /, *, ?, :, <, >, |, ".

Folder names and file names must be unique within the level of the tree. That means you cannot have two folders named `Letters` that are on the root directory of your drive, but you could have a folder named `c:\letters` as well as a folder named `c:\My Documents\letters`.

**Even the desktop is a folder**

Your desktop is a folder and the only difference between it and all the other folders in your system is that you cannot close the desktop folder.

**Windows 98 uses long filenames**

The capability to use up to 255 characters in a filename is called *long filenames*. The other file naming convention is DOS filenames, which are limited to eight characters (no spaces allowed) and an extension of up to three characters. The jargon nickname for DOS filenames is "8.3" (pronounced eight point three).

Likewise, you cannot have two files named Report in the same folder, but you could have multiple files named Report scattered throughout your drive as long as each is in a different folder or subfolder.

# Browsing with My Computer

When you open My Computer (which is a folder), you see the major components in your Windows 98 system. All the drives attached to your computer are displayed, and Windows 98 places folders for the Control Panel, Printers, and Dial-Up Networking into the My Computer folder (see Figure 4.2).

FIGURE 4.2

This computer has a floppy drive, a hard drive, and a CD-ROM. The hand icon indicates the drive is shared with other network users.

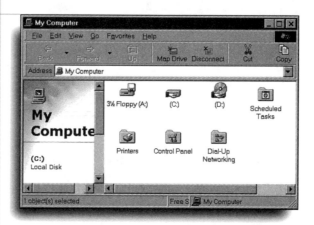

Each object in My Computer is also a folder, and if you double-click an object it opens a folder window. (Don't double-click a floppy drive if there isn't a floppy disk inserted because there are no contents to show you. In fact, you'll see an error message telling you the drive isn't ready.)

Double-click the hard drive object to see all its folders and files (see Figure 4.3).

To see the contents of any folder, double-click it, and if there are additional folders, you can double-click them to see their contents (there's a path statement on the window's title bar).

After you open a few folders, your screen can get crowded. Just click the close button (the X in the upper-right corner) of any window you're not interested in anymore.

The ability to see the contents of several folders at once is an advantage if you want to move files from one folder to another.

FIGURE 4.3

All the folders and files on the hard drive are displayed in the window.

# Browsing with Explorer

Open Explorer and you'll notice that the view from here is different than the view from My Computer (see Figure 4.4). You're looking at the same objects, but this vista is a view of your computer's hierarchical tree.

Explorer splits the view between two panes: the left pane (named All Folders) shows only containers; the right pane (named Contents) shows the contents of the containers. You have to select a container in the left pane to see its contents in the right pane.

By default, Explorer opens with Drive C selected in the left pane and the contents of Drive C in the right pane. Drive C has been expanded, which means its folders are displayed in the left pane.

- You can expand any folder that has a plus sign next to its icon (the plus sign indicates there are additional subfolders).

**Container really means folder**

All the objects I'm calling containers in the left pane, including drives, are folders (like all folders they can be opened to reveal their contents). However, calling a drive a folder (Folder C:???) seems silly, even though technically it is a folder, because all of us think of a drive as a physical entity.

FIGURE 4.4

Explorer offers a treetop view of your computer's hierarchy.

- When a folder is expanded, its icon changes to an open folder and there's a minus sign to the left of the icon. Click the minus sign to collapse the folder.

- You can keep expanding folders until there are no more subfolders to display, but the left pane never displays anything but folders (you cannot expand down to the files in the left pane; instead you must select a folder to see its files in the right pane).

You can adjust the size of the panes by placing your mouse pointer on the bar between the panes. When your pointer turns into a double arrow, drag the bar in the appropriate direction.

Incidentally, if you can't read the name of a folder because the left pane is too narrow, position your mouse pointer on the folder for a second or two to have a ToolTip appear with the folder's full name.

You can also adjust the width of the columns in the right pane. Place your pointer on the bar between any columns and when your pointer turns into a double arrow, drag the column in the direction you need. If you double-click the bar to the right of the column, the column widens to display the widest item in that column.

# Setting the View

Both My Computer and Explorer have a default way of showing information, which is called the *view*. You can change the view to accommodate your own preferences and work habits.

There are a host of options for viewing the contents of your system on the View menu (see Figure 4.5) for both My Computer and Explorer. You can change the information that's displayed, the graphics used, and the order in which information is sorted.

**FIGURE 4.5**

Use the View menu to change the way My Computer displays information.

The format in which the objects are presented varies depending on the graphics option you choose from the View menu. There are four format options for the display of objects:

- *Large Icons*, which displays each object as an icon with the object name below the icon.

- *Small Icons*, which displays each object as a smaller icon with the object name to the right of the icon. The objects are arranged in the window in rows from left to right.

- *List*, which also displays each object as a smaller icon with the object name to the right of the icon. However, the objects are arranged in columns.

- *Details*, which presents several columns of information about the objects (see Figure 4.6).

FIGURE 4.6

Explicit information about each folder and file is available in the Details view.

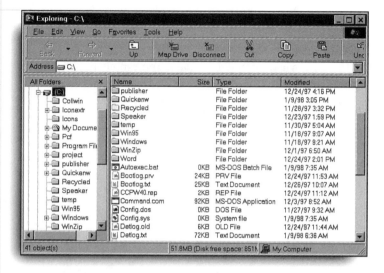

If you choose **Details** view, you can sort the objects in the window by any of the column categories. Just click the column heading to sort by that category. Click again to change the sort to descending order.

You can also use the options on the View menu to arrange the objects in a specific manner. Choose **View**, **Arrange Icons** and then order the icons by Name, Type, Size, or Date.

When you view a folder with large or small icons, you're free to move the icons all around the window. For instance, you can bunch similar object types together. If, however, you want to "tidy up" your window, choose **Auto Arrange** from the Arrange Icons submenu. Windows 98 will place each icon neatly in the window, following a grid pattern. The grid starts at the upper-left corner and moves across the window from left to right, filling in each space of the grid with an icon (see Figure 4.7). As long as there's a checkmark next to the Auto Arrange selection, trying to move icons out of these grids is impossible.

The Line Up Icons command on the View menu works in a similar fashion to the Arrange Icons. The difference is that scattered icons are placed in a grid, but placed in a grid area that is closest to the column and row in which they started (see Figure 4.8).

FIGURE 4.7
Use Auto Arrange to keep all
the objects neat and tidy.

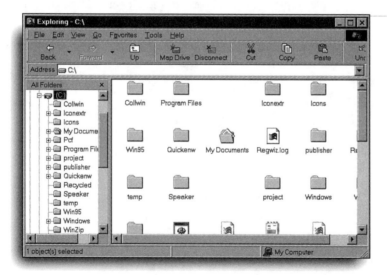

FIGURE 4.8
The result of the Line Up Icons
command probably qualifies as
organized chaos.

In addition to choosing the display mode and arranging icons,
Windows 98 offers a view choice called "View as Web Page." In
Explorer, this causes almost no change in the view (although in
My Computer or other folders that offer the traditional folder
window, the Web Page choice creates a two-pane view).

# Configuring View Options

Both My Computer and Explorer offer additional options in the
View menu that let you configure views for the entire system. (In
fact, all the folders you open from these two folders offer options
for configuring the global view.)

You can configure system-wide options for the following:

- The way the desktop looks
- The way files are viewed in folders
- The associations between data files and software programs

## Setting Desktop View Options

Choose **View, Folder Options** from the menu bar to open the
Folder Options dialog box with the General tab in the foreground (see Figure 4.9).

FIGURE 4.9

Configure the way the folder
and your desktop look.

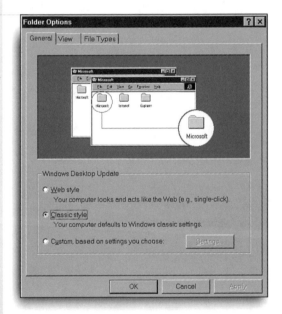

- Choose **Web style** to make the folder and your desktop
  look (and behave) like a page on the World Wide Web. In

addition to changing the overall look and feel, objects are treated like Web links, with one-click access.

- Choose **C**lassic style to use the familiar Windows look and feel.

- Choose C**u**stom and then choose **Settings** to design the view yourself (see Figure 4.10). For even more control, choose **Customize**.

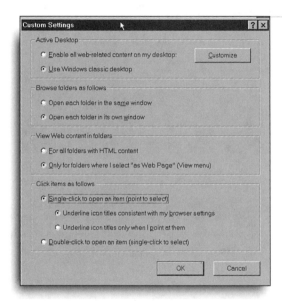

**FIGURE 4.10**
Select the behavior modification options you want to impose on your system.

## Setting Folder View Options

Move to the View tab to set options for viewing files and folders (see Figure 4.11).

In the top section of the dialog box you can configure the look of the folders you open:

- Choose **L**ike Current Folder to make all your folders resemble the configuration you're creating here.

- Choose **R**eset All Folders to undo any configuration options you regret and put everything back the way it was immediately after you finished installing Windows 98.

FIGURE 4.11
Choose what you want to see
and how you want to see it.

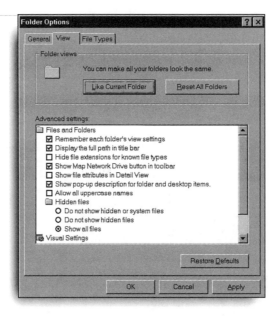

In the Advanced settings section, scroll through the list and select or deselect options to match the way you want to work. If you regret any of these choices later, you can return to this dialog box to make different selections, or choose **Restore Defaults** to put everything back the way it was.

## File Types and Associations

The information on the File Types tab of the Options dialog box represents one of the most powerful features in Windows 98: the automatic association between a data file and a program. This means you can double-click a file in Explorer and the correct software opens.

The registered file types are displayed on the File Types tab of the Options dialog box (see Figure 4.12).

When you install software that is written for Windows 98 (or Windows 95 or Windows NT), part of the installation process notifies the operating system about the program's file types. This means that any files created in that program by a user are automatically associated with the program.

---

**HTML customization is available for folders**

All folders have a Customize This Folder command on the View menu. Choosing that command launches a customization wizard that walks you through the process of turning the folder into an HTML document so it can be viewed and manipulated as if it were a Web page. If you're comfortable with HTML commands, you might want to experiment with this option.

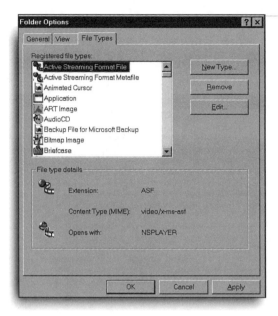

The association is made between a software program and the extension to a filename. For example, files with an extension of .doc are associated with Microsoft Word, while files with an association of .wpd are linked to WordPerfect. If an association between an extension and a program exists, that means there is a registered extension.

Older software, such as software you used in Windows 3.*x* that you continue to use in Windows 98, may not have an automatic file type registration process. And DOS software never registers file types. Additionally, if your company has rules about filenaming conventions and requires all customer reports from the company database to be saved with an extension of .cus, there's no association between the files and the software that can read them.

## Creating an Association

If you save files with a specific extension that isn't registered, you can create the association yourself. Then, when you double-click any data file of the same type (with the same extension), the right software program will open.

**Registered extensions shouldn't be changed**

The default for Windows 98 is not to display the extensions of registered file types. The reason for that default selection is to protect those extensions against modification. If you change the extension of a registered file type, you break the association.

### Notifying Windows about file types

**1.** Find the file with the unregistered extension in Explorer or My Computer.

**2.** Double-click it, which brings up the **Open With** dialog box seen in Figure 4.13. (If you right-click instead, the shortcut menu offers Open With instead of the Open command you'd see on a registered file type. Choose **Open With** to get to the same dialog box.)

FIGURE 4.13

Windows 98 needs some help from you to open this file.

**3.** Enter a description of this data file type.

**4.** Scroll through the list of programs to find the software that you want to use when you work with this file type.

**5.** If the program you need isn't on the list, choose **Other**. In the Open dialog box that appears, move through the folders to find the software program file you want to use. Choose **OK** to return to the **Open With** dialog box.

**6.** If you're absolutely sure that this data file type can be handled by this software, select **Always use this program to open this file**.

**7.** If you're not sure and just want to experiment, deselect the **Always use** option. (If it works, return to the **Open With** dialog box and make the association permanent.)

There are some hints for using this feature:

- If the data file is a report from a database that was saved to disk, it's probably a text file. Think about associating it with your favorite word processor so you can dress it up with all the formatting options available.

- If the data file is text and is used to move information through a network or over the Internet, associate it with WordPad or any other text editor you're sure is available to recipients.

- If the data file is not text and can only be manipulated with the software that created it (and the software is not registered and listed), use the Other option to place the software program in the programs list at the same time you register the data file type.

## Changing an Association on a One-Time Basis

Want to use a different program to open a data file that already has an association?

### Configuring associations

1. Select the file in Explorer or My Computer (single-click to select).

2. Hold the Shift key while you right-click the file.

3. An Open With command appears on the shortcut menu in addition to the Open command.

4. Choose **Open With** and then select the appropriate program from the **Open With** dialog box.

I've found this to be extremely useful when I need to use certain software with data files but the installation process of another software program has "grabbed" the file type. For example, I like to use Collage Image Manager to open .pcx files when I have to print them (there are features in the printing functions I use). However, Windows 98 grabs the .pcx extension for Kodak Imaging Preview. If I'm going to edit the .pcx file, I double-click to open Imaging Preview. If I don't need to manipulate it in any way, I can load it in Collage by using the Shift key.

I learned another handy use for this function from a number of people who discovered the same great idea independently. They all used Microsoft Word and frequently had to send documents to users who did not have Microsoft Word. Now, it's not difficult to load a document into Word and then save it as a text file. But all of these people had discovered that WordPad launched faster than Word (in fact, WordPad does everything faster) and when there was a request for a document they all used the same procedure to convert it. It's a handy trick.

### Using WordPad instead of Word

1. Open Explorer or My Computer and find the file you need.
2. Select it, and then right-click it while holding down the Shift key.
3. Choose **Open With** from the shortcut menu.
4. When the **Open With** dialog box appears, choose **WordPad**.
5. Make sure the **Always use this program to open this type of file** option is not selected, and then click **OK**.
6. When WordPad opens the document, choose **File**, **Save As** from the menu bar.
7. Select **Text Document** in the Save as type box and change the file extension to .txt.

I actually timed this myself with a file that was about 60,000 bytes. The WordPad technique was much faster than Microsoft Word 97.

## Registering File Types and Associations

You can configure new file types and associate them with any software program, or change existing file type associations.

### Permanent registration of a file type

1. Open Explorer or My Computer and choose **View**, **Folder Options**.
2. When the **Options** dialog box opens, move to the File Types tab.
3. Choose **New Type** to bring up the **Add New File Type** dialog box (see Figure 4.14).

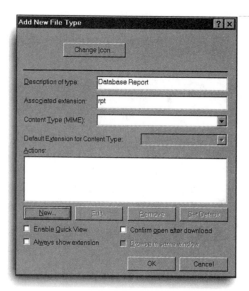

**4.** Fill out the options in the dialog box using these guidelines:

- *Description of type:* Enter a description that will appear in Explorer and My Computer when you use the Details View.

- *Associated extension:* Enter the three letter filename extension this file type uses (you don't need to enter the period before the extension).

- *Content Type (MIME):* (This is an optional choice, and if you don't want to configure this file type for MIME, you can skip all the related options.) Specify the MIME type you want to associate with this file. When you open a file of this file type on the Internet, your browser will use the association. Click the down arrow to the right of this field to see the available options.

- *Default Extension for Content Type:* Choose a filename extension for the MIME association. This becomes the default extension for this particular file type (MIME types usually have multiple choices for extensions).

- *Actions:* Specify the action that occurs when you double-click this file listing (see the next section on attaching associated programs to file types).

- *Confirm Open After Download:* Select this option if you want a dialog box to ask you whether you want to open this file type instead of opening it automatically after you download it.

- *Enable Quick View:* Select this option if this file type is supported by Quick View.

- *Always show extension:* Select this option if you want the file type's extension to be displayed in Explorer or My Computer (even if you have configured View not to show extensions for registered file types).

## Attaching Associated Programs to File Types

The Action box on the Add New File Type dialog box is where you specify what happens when you double-click on a file in Explorer or My Computer. The action must be an executable file (program file), and that executable file becomes the software association for this file type.

### Associating an action with a file type

1. Choose **New** on the **Add New File Type** dialog box, which opens the **New Action** dialog box (see Figure 4.15).

FIGURE 4.15

The program you add will be associated with all files of this type.

2. In the **Action** box, specify the wording for the command that will appear on the shortcut menu. Most of the time this would be Open.

3. In the **Application used to perform action** box, enter the path and filename of the executable file you want to associate with the file type (use the Browse button to search your computer for the file).

**4.** If the application can use DDE, select the **Use DDE** check box. DDE is the capability of different Windows programs to share elements in data files.

**5.** Choose **OK** when you are finished, then choose **Close** to exit the **Add New File Type** dialog box.

If you don't add an action to the file type, when you double-click any file of this type, the **Open With** dialog box displays so you can pick the software you want to use.

# Copying, Moving, Renaming, and Deleting Folders and Files

You can manipulate the files and folders in your system in a variety of ways using either My Computer or Explorer. When you have to work with files, you can work with multiple files and whatever you do to one, you do to all.

## Selecting Multiple Files

You can manipulate files in bunches using the following procedures:

- Choose all the files in a folder by pressing Ctrl+A.
- Choose a group of contiguous files by clicking the first file in the group and holding down the Shift key while you click the last file in the group. All the files between the first and last are selected.
- Choose multiple files that are not contiguous by selecting the first file and holding down the Ctrl key as you click each additional file.

After you select a group of files, any action you take on one (dragging, using menu commands) is also performed on the others.

## Dragging Objects

You can drag objects in Explorer or My Computer to move or copy them. This is also referred to as drag and drop. Dragging

**Tip**

I've found that when I want to select multiple items, it's easier to do so in Explorer with the Details view. Every object is in a straight column and easy to find and select.

objects isn't a clear-cut, easy proposition. First, you have to decide whether you want to drag with the left mouse button or the right mouse button. And there's a big difference in the procedures.

If you use the left mouse button, here's what happens:

- Dragging an object from one folder to another folder on the same drive moves the object. It no longer exists in its original location. Dragging the object with the Ctrl key held down copies it so it exists in both places.

- Dragging an object from one drive to another drive copies the object. It exists in both places. Holding the Shift key when dragging between drives moves the object (it no longer exists in the original location).

- If the object is a program file, the new location accepts only a shortcut to the program file. The original program file itself stays where it was.

However, if you use the right mouse button to drag, when you drop the file at its new location you see the menu shown in Figure 4.16.

**FIGURE 4.16**

Right-dragging is much safer because you get to choose the results instead of trying to remember what does what.

You can cancel a drag while you're in the middle of it by pressing the Esc key.

## Using the Shortcut Menu

After you select the object (or objects) you want to work with, right-click to see the shortcut menu. The available commands give you plenty of choices for manipulating the object.

- Choose **Cut** to remove the object from its current location. Then select the new location and right-click. Choose **Paste** to put the object in the new location. You've moved the object.

- Choose **Copy** followed by **Paste** to copy the object to a new location (leaving the original object where it was).

- Choose **Delete** to send the object(s) to the Recycle Bin (hold down the Shift key to skip the Recycle Bin and delete the object permanently).

- Choose **Rename** to change the name of the object. You cannot use the Rename command if you've selected multiple objects. (You can also left-click an object to select it, then press F2 to rename it).

You may have additional commands on the shortcut menu depending on your installation selections and the file type.

# Using the Recycle Bin

The Recycle Bin is your desktop trash can, and you can indulge in some trash picking when you throw something away you didn't mean to.

There are three ways to put deleted files in the Recycle Bin:

- Delete objects from your hard drive when you're working in My Computer or Explorer.

- Delete objects from your hard drive when you're using a software program that's written for Windows 95, Windows 98, or Windows NT 4.

- Drag objects from your hard drive to the Recycle Bin icon.

Deleting the following objects does not involve the Recycle Bin and you cannot recover the objects:

- Objects deleted using DOS commands.

- Objects deleted from removable drives (floppy, Jaz, or Zip drives, for example).

- Objects deleted from connected computers on a network.

- Objects deleted while working in software written for Windows 3.*x* or DOS.

**Tip**

If you're working in a software window (instead of full screen) and you can see the Recycle Bin on your desktop, you can delete files by dragging them to it. Keep the Recycle Bin in an easy-to-reach corner of your desktop if you use this method.

## Emptying the Recycle Bin

As soon as you place any item in the Recycle Bin, its icon changes so it looks as if it's absolutely overflowing with paper. The files and folders you place in the Recycle Bin are the same size as they were before you deleted them; they're just hidden from you so you can't see them (unless you open the Recycle Bin). That means deleting files doesn't gain you any disk space until you empty the Recycle Bin.

- To empty the Recycle Bin, right-click its icon and choose **Empty Recycle Bin** from the shortcut menu. Poof! Everything is gone. For good and forever. And your disk space is back.

- To delete only certain files from the Recycle Bin (while you wait to make up your mind about the other files), open the Recycle Bin and select the files you're sure you can delete. Right-click any selected file and choose **Delete** from the shortcut menu (or choose **File**, **Delete** from the menu bar).

## Recovering Files from the Recycle Bin

If you realize there's a file you shouldn't have deleted, double-click the Recycle Bin to open it and see its contents (see Figure 4.17). I find it best to choose **View**, **Details** from the menu bar so I can see all the information about the files (the default view is icons). Right-click the file you need and choose **Restore** from the shortcut menu. (You could also select the file and choose **File**, **Restore** from the menu bar.)

- Files are restored to their original folders.

- You can drag a file from the Recycle Bin to a different folder to restore it in that location instead of its original location.

- If the folder has been deleted, it's re-created to hold the restored files.

## Customizing the Recycle Bin

You can customize the Recycle Bin to make it as efficient as possible, matching the way you want to work. To configure the

Tip

After you delete a file or folder, you can restore it immediately if the very next thing you do is right-click a blank spot on the desktop and choose Undo Delete from the shortcut menu.

Recycle Bin, right-click its desktop icon and choose **Properties**.
The **Recycle Bin Properties** dialog box appears (see Figure
4.18).

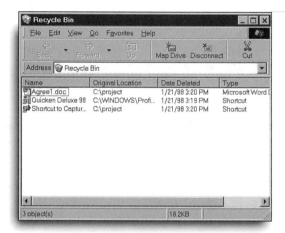

FIGURE 4.17

All the items in the Recycle Bin
are displayed when you open
its window.

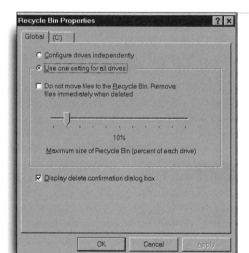

FIGURE 4.18

Customize the way the Recycle
Bin works to make sure your
productivity is enhanced by its
features.

## Configure the Size

The Recycle Bin is like your trash cans—there's a point at which
they get stuffed to the gills, all filled up. However, unlike your
trash cans, the Recycle Bin has two behavior characteristics that
make it more manageable:

- You can change the size of the Recycle Bin.

- When the Recycle Bin is full, old trash is removed to make room for the new trash. This means you can keep adding deleted items but the items that are removed to make room won't be recoverable.

The size of the Recycle Bin is based on a percentage of the size of your hard drive. If you have more than one hard drive, you can use different percentages for each drive or set a percentage figure to be used for all drives.

Most of the time it's easier to keep all drives set at the same percentage figure. By default, Windows 98 sets 10 percent of your hard drive aside for the Recycle Bin:

- Raising the percentage gives you more opportunity to restore files because they'll remain there longer. This is more noticeable if you routinely clean up your hard drive by deleting large groups of files at one time.

- Keeping the percentage low means you'll run less risk of running out of the necessary free space you need to maintain a swap file, create new document files, and install more software.

It's a delicate balance and you should observe the results of any changes you make carefully, and reconsider them if necessary.

## Skip the Recycle Bin

You don't have to use the Recycle Bin. You can delete files permanently instead of having to go through the steps of re-deleting them in order to get rid of them for good. To accomplish this, select the check box with the label Do Not move files to the Recycle Bin. Remember, that means no more picking through the trash for files you didn't really mean to delete.

There's a compromise position you can adopt: Keep the Recycle Bin active, and when you're really, really sure that it's safe to delete objects, hold down the Shift key while you press the Del key (or when you choose **Delete** from the shortcut menu). The Shift key causes Windows 98 to bypass the Recycle Bin.

---

**The Recycle Bin uses first in first out**

When the Recycle Bin is full, the oldest files are removed to make room for your new deletions. The determination of what is the oldest file is the date and time the item was sent to the Recycle Bin. The original date and time of the file has no impact on the decision.

**Different settings for different drives**

While it's true that most of the time it's easier to keep multiple drives set for the same percentage for the Recycle Bin, there are situations when it is advisable to configure drives separately.

**Recycle Bin on the data drive**

If you use one drive for software and the other drive to store data, it's probably a good idea to set the size of the Recycle Bin on which you keep the data for a larger percentage of the drive. That's because data is more volatile, it gets deleted more frequently, and it gets recovered more frequently (that's just the way it seems to work).

Incidentally, if you have multiple drives and have opted to configure each drive separately, you can also configure this option separately. You may have one drive on which you want to use the Recycle Bin, while feeling perfectly safe to perform permanent deletions on the other drive.

### Skip the Warning When Deleting

By default, Windows 98 warns you when you delete any object. It's actually a confirmation request, asking if you're sure you want to send the object to the Recycle Bin. You must answer Yes before the file is deleted.

Some people feel this is unnecessary, compulsive behavior that creates extra work. After all, the files aren't really being deleted. If you agree, deselect the option named Display delete confirmation dialog box. However, if you get rid of the confirmation step, you really should get into the habit of opening the Recycle Bin and examining its contents before emptying it.

# Using Find to Locate Files

The computer I'm using to write this chapter has more than 20,000 files on Drive C. I use several different word processors, each of which saves files to any of a group of specific folders. Frequently I can't even remember which word processor I used to write that letter to the electric company or send a report from my accounting system to my accountant. So, of course, I have no idea which folder to look in.

People who create folders for specific types of documents (letters, reports, poetry, whatever) frequently forget to change folders as they save various documents during the day, so it's possible to put a poem in the reports folder.

Finding a file by moving in and out of all the possible folders is a frustrating experience, and a total waste of time. Windows 98 to the rescue!

# Setting Up the Search

Click the **Start** button and then choose **Find**, **Files** or **Folders** from the Start menu. The **Find** dialog box has everything you need to locate that missing file (see Figure 4.19).

FIGURE 4.19

When you can't remember where you put a file, Find is like sending a bloodhound out to search.

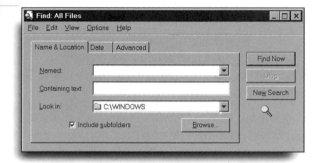

Here's how to use all the power of Find:

- Use the Named box to enter a word or partial word you used in the filename. The characters you enter can appear anywhere in the filename. For instance, if you enter **port**, Find will locate files named Report To Bob, Important Please Read, Reapportionment Memo, and so on.

- The Containing text box is the place to enter text that's in the file if you remember any of it. Find will search the files to find the phrase you enter here. This works well only if you remember the phrase exactly, and if it's unique enough to have appeared in only a few letters.

- The Look in box lets you select the folder you want Find to search. To search subfolders, select Include subfolders.

- Move to the Date tab if you remember approximately when you last worked on the file (see Figure 4.20).

- On the Advanced tab you can choose a specific file type or a size range to narrow down the search. Use these options in addition to the options on the other tabs to make the search more efficient.

When you have filled in the information you think will suffice, choose Find Now.

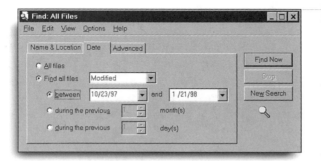

FIGURE 4.20
Most people can usually find a way to search successfully by using date criteria.

## Other Methods of Launching Find

You don't have to use the Start menu to open Find; you have two other choices.

### Start Find from the Desktop

Click a blank spot on the desktop to make the desktop the foreground program, and then press F3. The same Find dialog box opens.

However, the Look in box uses your profile folder as a starting point from the search. To change the starting point, click the arrow to the right of the box and choose your hard drive or another folder. Then enter the criteria.

### Start Find from Explorer

One of the most efficient ways to use Find is to start it from Explorer. The reason it's more efficient is that you can select the folder you want to start the search in before you invoke Find.

Choose a folder, and then press F3. The Find dialog box opens with the Look in box displaying the name of the folder you selected in Explorer.

This saves Find the trouble of searching every single folder on your hard drive if you know the files you need are found in subfolders under the selected folder. For instance, if you keep all your data documents in subfolders under My Documents, start the search in My Documents.

## Working with the Results

All the files that match the specifications you enter are displayed in the bottom of the Find dialog box (see Figure 4.21).

FIGURE 4.21

All the files that meet the specs are here.

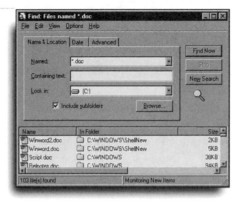

You can use the search results listing as if you were working in Explorer or My Computer. Right-click any file and use the shortcut menu to open it, copy it, and so on.

## Saving the Search and the Results

You can save the search criteria in order to use it again later (useful if you're working on a Project and you use several different programs to create information).

To save the criteria, choose **File**, **Save Search**. Nothing special happens, there's no dialog box to fill out, you don't have to enter a name for the saved search. Windows 98 takes care of everything.

Look on your desktop and you'll find a new icon. It looks like a stack of papers and it's named to reflect the search criteria you used. The extension .fnd on the icon title reminds you that it's a saved search. Double-click the icon to open the Find dialog box with your criteria intact. You can search again, or make any modifications you want to the criteria.

If Find yields a rich mine of information and there are multiple files you need in the search results, you can save the results. This is really helpful if you don't have time to work on each file you found and you don't feel like finding pen and paper to write down the path and filename of all the files you need.

**To save the results as well as the search criteria:**

**1.** Open the **Options** menu and make sure the **Save Results** command is checked.

**2.** Choose **File**, **Save Search**.

The same icon appears and when you double-click it, both the Find dialog box and the search results at the bottom are available.

# Using Find for Housekeeping

You don't have to restrict your use of Find to locating files you can't find on your own. I use it to clean up my hard drive.

My word-processing documents are kept in numerous folders. Two of the word processors I use make a backup copy of a file each time I save the file. Word names those backups "Backup of xxxx" where xxxx is the filename. WordPerfect uses the filename with an extension .bk!

These files aren't lost, I know exactly where they are. But to clean up my drive manually I'd have to open each individual folder, select the backup files, and delete them.

- I opened Find and enter **\*.bk!** in the Named box. The search results list every backup WordPerfect file in all my WordPerfect data folders. I select all of them and press the Del key.

- I repeated the exercise with **Backup of** in the Named box.

- I saved the search criteria for each Find procedure.

Now I double-click on each desktop icon to repeat the search. Performing this task every few days or once a week is amazingly efficient; sometimes I empty my drive of 100 or more unneeded files.

# CHAPTER 5

# Using Windows 98 Help

Even after you've been using Windows 98 for a long time, you're probably going to get stuck trying to make the operating system do something or install something. In fact, even if you've performed a task in the past, you'll probably need a reminder about the actual steps needed to accomplish your mission.

Online help is always available, just a couple of mouse clicks away, and it's robust and easy to use.

Get started by clicking the Start button, and then choose Help (or, if you're at your desktop, press F1).

# The New Look of Help

If you've used earlier versions of Windows, you'll notice that the Help window doesn't look the way it used to. When Windows 98 Help opens, it's a two-pane window like Explorer (see Figure 5.1).

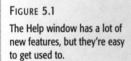

**FIGURE 5.1**

The Help window has a lot of new features, but they're easy to get used to.

Not only does this Help window look different from previous versions, it behaves differently, too. The way you move through the Help system is similar to the way you move around the Internet with your browser.

## Getting to Help Topics

You'll find the Help system is very easy to understand and use. Navigating through the books and topics is quite simple and intuitive.

- When you point to an element, your mouse pointer turns into a pointing hand.

- To open a book (expand it to show its contents), just single-click. No more double-clicking anywhere in Help!

- When you expand a book, you may see additional books. Pick the book of interest and continue to expand books until you reach a list of topics (see Figure 5.2).

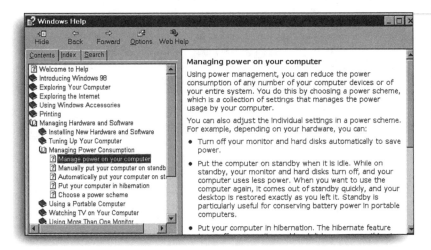

**FIGURE 5.2**

The icon for a topic is a page with a question mark.

- When you select a topic in the left pane, the contents display in the right pane.

- You can change the width of the panes by putting your mouse pointer on the bar between them. When your pointer becomes a double-arrow, press and hold the left mouse button and drag the bar in either direction.

## Using the Help Toolbar

The toolbar on the Help window is like a browser toolbar, and in fact, has some of the same buttons your browser has.

**Use Hide to make room for dialog boxes**

One helpful reason to hide the left pane is to make screen room for a dialog box. Many help pages are easier to understand if you open the dialog box that's under discussion and follow along.

The Hide button makes the left pane disappear so you can concentrate on (and enlarge) the Help topic window (see Figure 5.3). When you want to pick a different topic, click the Show button to bring back the left pane.

The Back button takes you to the previous Help window and the Forward button moves you ahead again after you've gone back.

**FIGURE 5.3**

Hide the left pane at will, and then use the Show button to bring it back.

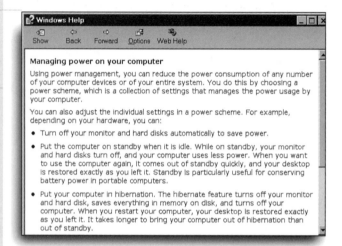

The Options button displays a menu that includes the toolbar button commands in addition to printing the current topic.

The Web Help button opens Internet Explorer, which sends you to Microsoft Windows 98 technical support on the Web.

# Using the Contents Tab

The Contents tab displays a group of books that cover all the important subjects about Windows 98. The titles in this online library provide a complete encyclopedia of information about the operating system.

- Clicking a book expands its topic (you'll likely find more books).

- Clicking an expanded book collapses it.

- Clicking a secondary level book expands its topics.

- Clicking another book closes the first book and expands the new one.

The right pane doesn't change its contents while you're opening books. When you find your way to a topic listing, that topic's Help page appears in the right pane.

Many Help pages have underlined words or phrases, and if you place your mouse pointer on them, the pointer changes to a hand with a pointing finger. This, of course, means there's a link to more information:

- When you click **click here**, a dialog box, wizard, or program launches so you can walk through the steps discussed in the Help page.

- Click **Related Topics** to see a list of additional help topics related to the current help page (see Figure 5.4).

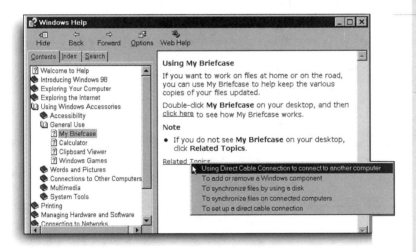

FIGURE 5.4

Move quickly to a new help page by selecting a related topic.

- Click an underlined word or phrase to see its definition.

Right-click any object in the Contents list and choose **Print** to see a Print dialog box that lets you choose what you want to print (see Figure 5.5).

FIGURE 5.5

Don't choose to print everything; you'll print for hours, they'll have to cut down more forests to replace the paper you use, and it's available on the screen when you need it anyway.

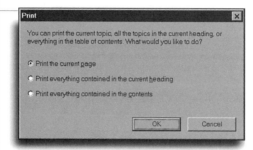

# Using the Index

The Index tab lists all the topics and phrases that have been indexed by Microsoft. The major, important topics (such as printing, audio, backup, and so on) are in the index, and this is often the place you'll begin your search for help.

There are two sections: an entry box on the top where you can enter the topic you're looking for, and a list of the entire index below that (see Figure 5.6). The list is in alphabetical order, of course, the way an index is supposed to be arranged.

FIGURE 5.6

Enter a word you think may be in the index, or just scroll through the index to find the topic you need.

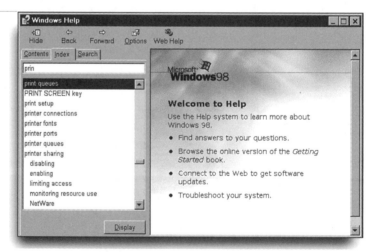

As you enter characters in the top box, the index listing jumps to the index listing that matches your characters. For example, as soon as you type the letter "p," the index listing for the first instance of "p" is highlighted. If the next character you type is an "r," the first instance of an index listing that starts with "pr" is highlighted. It keeps going that way and eventually you get to the entry you need and you can stop typing. It's rare to have to enter an entire word; there's always a point at which you're either on the entry you need or you're close enough to it to select it with an arrow key or the mouse.

When you find the entry you want, select it and choose Display. Depending on the topic, you'll either see a list of Help topics (see Figure 5.7) or a Help page.

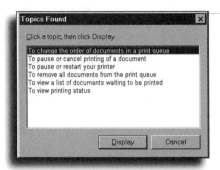

## Using Search

Sometimes you can't find exactly the help you're looking for in the Contents books or the Index. Just move to the Search tab to search all the help pages for a specific word (see Figure 5.8). This works because not all the important words are indexed, and also because sometimes topics are indexed under one word, but other similar words are in the text of the Help page.

### The Search feature works in a three-step fashion:

1. In the entry box at the top, enter the word you want to search for.
2. Choose **List Topics** (or press **Enter**) to see a display of all the help pages that contain your word.
3. Select the topic you want to read, and then choose **Display**.

**FIGURE 5.8**

The Search tab is used to find specific words in the help topics that you need information about.

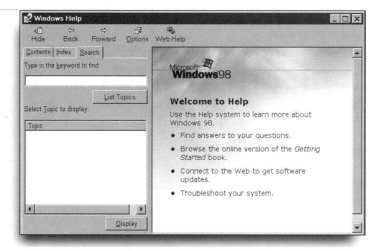

The resulting Help window contains your word, the topics that include your word, and the Help page for the topic you selected (see Figure 5.9).

**FIGURE 5.9**

Your word and the list of topics remain in the Help window so you can make another choice quickly.

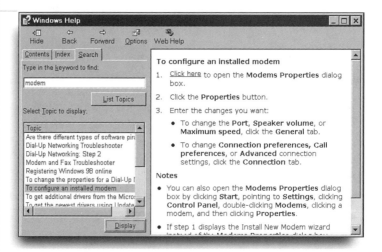

# Using the Help Pages

When you select a topic, the type of Help page you see may take any of several forms. There are text pages that offer descriptions and instructions and Help pages that have hot links to dialog boxes so you can perform tasks under the watchful eye and advice of the Help page (which remains on the screen as a reference). Troubleshoots are available for a number of topics, and they provide interactive help as you try to solve a problem.

## Standard Help Pages

Figure 5.10 shows a fairly typical Help page. There are instructions about performing a task, some tips about the task, and a link to Help pages on related topics.

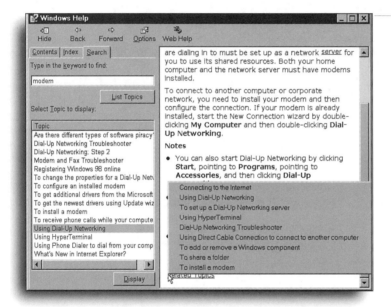

**FIGURE 5.10**

Read the instructions, take advantage of the tips, and check out any other related subjects.

## Demonstration Help Pages

Some Help pages do more than instruct; they provide an opportunity to perform a task while the Help page stays on the screen (see Figure 5.11).

## Troubleshooters

Troubleshooter Help pages are designed to walk you through a series of processes after you encounter a problem with a Windows 98 feature.

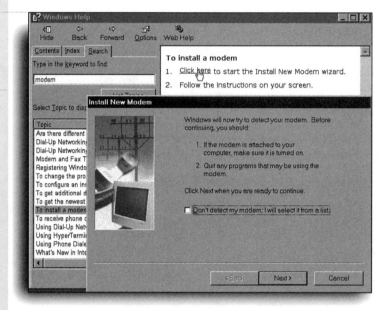

Some troubleshooters appear automatically when you complete a
task. For example, when you install a printer and print a test
page, Windows 98 asks you if the test page printed correctly. If
you answer No, the print troubleshooter opens automatically.

However, you can open troubleshooters yourself because they're
all listed in the Contents tab (see Figure 5.12).

### The opening page of a troubleshooter asks you what's wrong

 **1.** On the **Contents** tab, open the **Troubleshooting** book.

 **2.** Select **Windows 98 Troubleshooters**.

 **3.** Select the specific troubleshooter you want.

After you select the appropriate problem, you move through a
series of pages. The troubleshooter asks additional questions to
narrow the problem and then offers suggestions. As each suggestion is made, you're asked whether or not the problem was
solved. If it wasn't, the troubleshooter continues to offer
suggestions (see Figure 5.13).

**FIGURE 5.12**
All the built-in troubleshooters can be accessed directly as a Help topic.

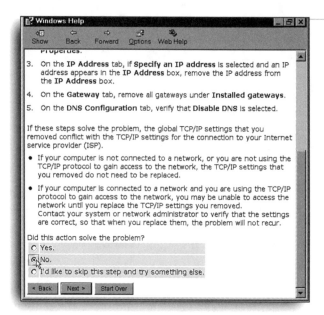

**FIGURE 5.13**
The troubleshooter moves deeper and deeper into the problem and possible resolution.

Eventually, if none of the suggestions work, you're advised to call technical support at Microsoft (or the manufacturer of a device, if that's where the problem is).

## Help Page Options

There are a slew of options available for Help pages, and all the commands are available by right-clicking anywhere on the right pane (see Figure 5.14).

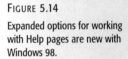

FIGURE 5.14

Expanded options for working with Help pages are new with Windows 98.

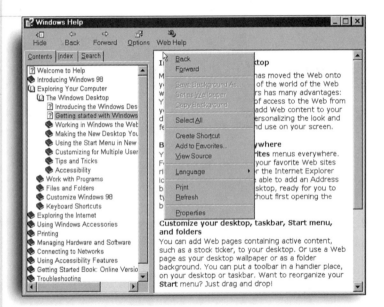

Some of the options are self-explanatory (or familiar if you've used previous versions of Windows). But there are a few that present some interesting possibilities for keeping yourself well-informed as you work in Windows 98.

- **Create Shortcut** puts a shortcut to the current Help page on your desktop. You can open it whenever you need to read it by double-clicking (Internet Explorer opens to load the document).

- **Add to <u>F</u>avorites** puts the page in one of the folders on your Favorites menu item. You can choose an existing Favorites folder or add a new one on the spot (see Figure 5.15).

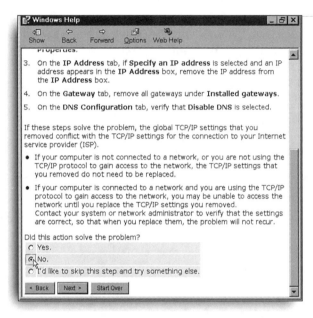

FIGURE 5.15
Adding a folder for help topics is a good idea.

- **<u>V</u>iew Source** opens Notepad with the HTML source document for the current page. You can use the Notepad features (Save, Print, and so on) if you want to keep this page as a discrete document.

There's also an interesting set of options if you choose to print the Help page. When the Print dialog box opens, there are two options available because the document you're printing has links:

- **Print all linked documents**, which prints every document that has a link displayed on the current help page.
- **Print table of links**, which places a list of all linked documents on the printed copy of the help page.

You can use these options to ensure that you have a complete set of printed files about the current topic.

# Getting Help in Dialog Boxes

When you open a dialog box in Windows 98 (or in your Windows 98 software programs), look in the upper-right corner to see if there is a question mark next to the Close button. If there is (and there almost always is), you can ask the Help system "What's This?" about any item in that dialog box. In fact, you have three different methods for asking that question, so you can use the one you find easiest:

- Click the question mark in the corner, which turns your mouse pointer into a question mark. Then click the label of the field or check box you're investigating.
- Right-click the field label.
- Click the field or check box itself and press F1.

No matter how you do it, a small pop-up that says What's This? appears. Click the pop-up to see the answer in the form of a pop-up box (see Figure 5.16). You can right-click in the pop-up box to see a shortcut menu that offers choices to copy the contents to the Clipboard, or print the contents.

FIGURE **5.16**

The answer to What's This? can be viewed, copied, or printed.

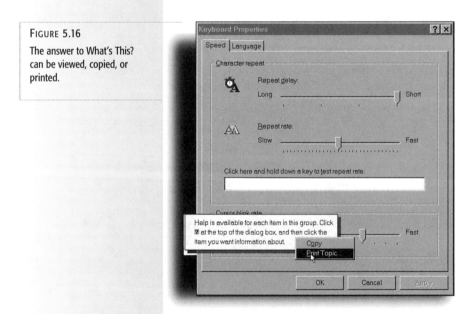

# Getting Command Line Help

I still spend a lot of time at the command line. It's part of my computer heritage, I guess, because by the time graphical user interfaces were available, I'd already been playing around with computers for many years. Also, I type fast. And, I never really learned to love the fact that I have to take my hand off the home keys of a keyboard to reach for a pointing device.

Also, there are still some tasks that are easier to do at the command line, such as renaming groups of files that share a common characteristic in their filenames. By the time I'd work out a way to display only those files in Explorer (and sometimes that can't be accomplished), I could have performed the task at the command line three times over. For example, suppose you have the following files in a folder:

1230101.ext

1230102.ext

1230103.ext

1230201.ext

1230202.ext

1230203.ext

1230301.ext

1230302.ext

1230303.ext

All the filenames that end in 01 have to be changed so they end in AA.

Try using Explorer. While you do that, I'll open an MS-DOS command prompt and enter **ren 123??01.ext 123??aa.ext**. Okay, I'm finished—and you're still clicking away in Explorer.

There are many commands that offer a number of choices about the way they work. When you use those commands, it's important to know the *syntax* the command expects. Syntax means the proper format for the command and any additional parameters available for the command.

To get help for a command, open an MS-DOS command window and enter **command /?**, substituting the name of the command for "command."

The syntax and all available parameters are displayed as shown in Figure 5.17.

```
MS-DOS Prompt                                                    _ 8 X

Auto     ▼    □ 🖺 🖺  🔁  🖽 🖶  A

C:\WINDOWS>copy /?
Copies one or more files to another location.

COPY [/A | /B] source [/A | /B] [+ source [/A | /B] [+ ...]] [destination
  [/A | /B]] [/U] [/Y | /-Y]

  source       Specifies the file or files to be copied.
  /A           Indicates an ASCII text file.
  /B           Indicates a binary file.
  destination  Specifies the directory and/or filename for the new file(s).
  /U           Verifies that new files are written correctly.
  /Y           Suppresses prompting to confirm you want to overwrite an
               existing destination file.
  /-Y          Causes prompting to confirm you want to overwrite an
               existing destination file.

The switch /Y may be preset in the COPYCMD environment variable.
This may be overridden with /-Y on the command line

To append files, specify a single file for destination, but multiple files
for source (using wildcards or file1+file2+file3 format).

C:\WINDOWS>
C:\WINDOWS>
```

If the information is too long to fit in a single window, and it scrolls so that you can't see the beginning of the help information, use **command /? | more**. This causes the information to pause when the screen is full, and the word "more" appears on the last line to indicate that there is more information available. Press any key to display the rest of the information.

If you want to save the information in a file so you can save it to examine it later, or print it, enter **command /?>filename**. Substitute a filename for the word "filename." The resulting file is a plain text file.

I usually use the name of the file and an extension .txt for the filename, so if I enter **xcopy /?>xcopy.txt**, I have a file on my hard drive named xcopy.txt that I can use in the following ways:

- I can print the file by entering **copy xcopy.txt prn** at the command line.

- I can enter **notepad xcopy.txt** at the command line to open Notepad with the xcopy.txt file loaded in the window.

- I can open Explorer and double-click on the file to open it in Notepad (the file extension .txt automatically causes Notepad to open because Notepad is the associated program for .txt files).

- I can open a word processor and load the file so I can read it or print it from the word processor.

# Help on the Web

If you can't find the information you need in the Help files, or you just want to find out what's new with Windows 98, talk to Microsoft.

There are Windows 98 Help sites on the Web and you can get there right from your Help window.

Click the Web Help icon on the Help window toolbar to see the Web Help topic page and then click the underlined hot link (which says click here).

Windows 98 does everything automatically, dialing out to your Internet connection (if you're not already connected) and connecting you to the Microsoft Help.

The Microsoft technical support site has links to more information you can access as you search for assistance.

All the help you can find in Windows 98 is available in your software applications. The help system looks the same and acts the same (of course, the topics are different; they're specific to the software). Don't forget that F1 is the universal help key for Windows and Windows software, so when in doubt, reach for F1.

# System Maintenance

**Installing the system tools**

If any of the system tools you want
to use are missing from the System
Tools submenu, you can install
them now by following these steps:

1. Open the Add/Remove
   Programs icon in Control
   Panel and move to the
   Windows Setup tab.

2. Select the System Tools listing
   and choose Details.

3. Click the check box next to
   each of the system tools you
   want to install.

4. Choose OK and follow any
   instructions.

Housekeeping isn't a lot of creative fun, and that applies to
housekeeping chores for computers. There are those tasks that
should be performed every day and then there are those larger
jobs that are performed less frequently (like spring cleaning).

This chapter goes over the maintenance routines that you
should know about and use to keep your computer running at
peak efficiency.

# Backing Up

This is the most important task you perform and it should be a
daily routine. But for most people, I'll bet it isn't. After you lose
data (important data that you can't replace and is incredibly difficult to reconstruct), you'll back up. For a while. Then, when the
memory fades, you'll become less conscientious. Until the next
disaster.

Disasters occur. There's no avoiding them. Without backups,
they're far more devastating than they need to be. It's not *if* your
hard drive will die, it's *when*.

You have lots of choices as to the way you want to back up the
data on your computer:

- You can use Microsoft Backup software.
- You can use the proprietary backup software that came with
  a tape backup device.
- You can devise a scheme for copying files from your hard
  drive to another drive.

The important rule to keep in mind when you're planning a
backup strategy is that backup strategies should not be designed
to make backing up easy, but instead to make restoring easy.

## Creating a Backup Strategy

Your decision about how to approach backing up should be made
based on the hardware available to you.

## Back Up Everything Every Day

If you have a tape drive or a Jaz drive that is as large (or larger) than your hard drive, there's no thinking required: Back up the entire drive every day.

There's no work, no user action, none of your time required for such a backup. Just start the backup software and leave the computer.

If your tape drive is not as large as your hard drive, or if you are using a Zip drive (which holds 100MB of data), you have a couple of choices:

- Do a complete backup every day, knowing that at some point, the backup software will prompt you to insert the next media.

- Select only those folders for backup that contain your data. If disaster strikes, you can always reinstall the software programs.

A full backup is the best backup strategy there is, because even if you have to replace one file (because you inadvertently deleted it), you know it's on yesterday's backup. There's no need to search through a whole mess of backup media. And, if you lose your hard drive or motherboard, here's how easy it is to get back to work:

### Installing from a full backup

1. Install the operating system on the new drive/computer.

2. Open the backup software (if you use proprietary software, you'll have to install it first).

3. Put your backup in the drive.

4. Choose **Restore**.

5. Go away, have coffee, chat with neighbors.

When you return, you can go right back to work knowing everything is there.

---

**Most backup software compresses files**

Because most backup software does enable compression, you can often get 1.5 to 2 times the amount of data on your backup compared to your hard drive. 1.5 gig of data will probably fit on a 1 gig Jaz drive.

### Back Up the Files That Changed Every Day

If you have to back up to floppy disk or to another removable drive that is much smaller than your hard drive (for instance, a 100MB Zip drive, if your hard drive is much larger than 100MB), you cannot back up the whole system every day.

You start by backing up all your data, and then each day do a backup of the data that's new or changed. If you use floppy disks, each of these daily backups must be on a different floppy disk. Eventually, rather than having hundreds of disks, you begin the procedure all over again.

Here are the caveats to consider about this backup strategy:

- If you need to restore an individual file, you need to know which day you last changed it so you know which backup set it is on.

- If you need to restore the entire system, you must start with the last full backup, and then restore each daily backup in the order in which it was backed up.

The first time you have to restore, I'll bet your next action is to rush to the computer store to buy a tape drive or a Jaz drive.

## Planning Media Usage

Never back up on the media that holds the last good backup; it's an invitation to the computer devils who notice when you do that and create major computer problems that are transferred to the media. It's never a good idea to overwrite good files with files that may not be good. You not only don't get a good backup, you lose the last good backup.

The ideal solution is to have a different tape or removable drive for each day of the week. If you can't manage the expense, buy one for even days and one for odd days.

## Other Backup Issues

There is important information in your computer and about your computer that cannot be backed up by copying files. There

**What's your data worth?**

Don't judge the value of your data by trying to determine what you paid for the software that's installed. Try and figure out what the data you've put into that software is worth to you. The calculation involves much more than money. Important letters and legal documents, your bookkeeping information, all the notes and knowledge you've poured into your hard drive have a value. It may be that the value is measured in time, energy, sweat equity, or another computation that has nothing to do with the coin of the realm.

Match that value against the cost of a tape drive or a Jaz drive (there are 1GB and 2GB Jaz drives, so it's probable that you can use a Jaz drive to back up your entire hard drive). Match that value against the cost of extra tapes or removable disks.

are some chores to perform that you'll be grateful you did when your hard drive dies.

## Track Your Hardware Settings

If you have to reconfigure your system, it will be much easier if you have a complete list of all the settings for your hardware. The IRQ, I/O addresses, and all that other techy stuff is terribly important. It's also extremely difficult to reconstruct. To print the information about hardware configuration, follow these steps:

### Printing out your hardware configuration

1. Right-click My Computer and choose **Properties** from the shortcut menu to open the System Properties dialog box (or choose Settings, Control Panel from the Start menu and double-click the System icon).

2. Move to the **Device Manager** tab.

3. Choose **Print**.

4. In the Print dialog box, choose System Summary to get a printout of all the devices in your system and their settings.

Put the printout away in a safe place. If you make changes to any settings or add any new devices, repeat this procedure.

## Keep Software Disks Safe

Your original software disks are important and precious, and should be stored in a safe place. A fireproof box is the best place.

If you use software that you've downloaded, copy or back up the files. Most of the time the original downloaded file won't fit on a floppy disk, but the individual files that were extracted will fit across several floppy disks.

Although you could use the backup command to transfer a very large file to multiple floppy disks, there's a better choice: Get yourself a copy of WinZip (**http://www.winzip.com/**) and use it to back up large files across multiple floppy disks. There are far fewer restore problems with WinZip than with the MS-DOS Backup command. And don't forget to put a copy of WinZip away with your other software.

### More information is available

While the information in the System Summary is really all you need if you have to reconfigure hardware, there's another choice in the Print dialog box when you're printing device information. You can choose All Devices and System Summary, which provides information about drivers and other technical specifications for the hardware in your computer. This report is longer and can be confusing, but it probably isn't a bad idea to print it once and file it. I've seen situations where the information in this report was handy when a technical support representative needed information to solve a complex problem.

### Software floppy disks should be copied

If you have software that arrived on floppy disks, it's also a good idea to make a backup copy of each disk. The best way to perform that task is to use the `Diskcopy` command, which copies any hidden files and disk labels. Put each floppy disk into the floppy drive, and then enter **Diskcopy A: A:** and follow the instructions for inserting the original (source) and target disks. If you have two floppy drives on your computer, enter **Diskcopy A: B:** and the system will make the copies automatically.

**Don't count on fireproof containers**

Here's a true story to illustrate the need for offsite storage of backup tapes: I had three clients in one high-rise office building. All the clients had been on the receiving end of my notes and speeches about the need for safe storage of software disks and tapes and offsite storage. One client had created a Friday night protocol of waiting for the backup to finish and taking the tape home (and bringing it back the next Friday morning). The other clients did not use offsite storage for backup tapes, although they were careful to store backups in fireproof containers.

One Sunday afternoon there was an enormous, disastrous fire. When people were finally permitted back into the building, two of the clients rescued their fireproof containers in which they'd stored the tapes. Sure enough, the container provided a bulwark against flame, nothing in the box had gone up in flames. But the tapes had melted.

The client with the offsite tape storage protocol lost absolutely no data. Within two days the company was back at work in a new office with new computers and the files looked exactly as they'd looked the Friday night before the Sunday fire. The other two clients have never fully recovered from the disaster, having lost all kinds of important customer and accounting information that could not be reconstructed.

### Keep Backup Tapes Safe

On a regular basis (once a week is good), get your backup media to a remote site. If you do full backups every night, pick one day for this exercise. For instance, if you pick Monday, then every Monday you either wait for the backup to finish and take the backup to the remote location, or take it during the day on Tuesday.

If you do full backups once a week and incremental backups thereafter, take the full backup offsite that night or the next day.

If you have a fire, the worst that can happen is that you lose a week's worth of data.

If your computer is at home, find a neighbor or friend to swap backups with.

# Backing Up with Microsoft Backup

You can use Microsoft Backup, the backup program that comes with Windows 98, to back up to any type of media.

If you have a tape drive, you can either use the software that came with it, or use Microsoft Backup if it supports your tape drive. Contact Microsoft for details because the list of supported drives changes constantly (or contact the manufacturer). To launch Microsoft Backup, follow these steps:

### Launching Microsoft Backup

1. From the Start menu choose **Programs**, **Accessories**, **System Tools**, **Backup**.

2. The opening window asks what you want to do (see Figure 6.1). Until you've created a backup set (a list of folders and files to back up), select **Create a new backup job** and choose **OK**.

3. The Backup Wizard asks whether you want to do a full backup or choose a specific array of files and folders to back up. Make a choice and choose **Next**.

Each choice initiates a different set of procedures, and we'll go over the different operations in the following sections.

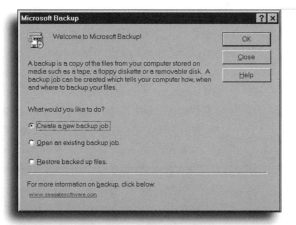

FIGURE 6.1
Select a procedure to start the appropriate Backup Wizard.

## Performing a Full Backup

If you choose to do a full backup, the Wizard asks if you want to back up all the selected files (it's assumed that the list of selected files includes everything in your computer) or just those that have changed. Here's how to proceed:

### Performing a full backup

1. Choose **All selected files** and then choose **Next**.
2. Specify where to back up the files. If you have a tape drive, it is listed and you should select it.
3. If you don't have a tape drive, choose **File**. Then click the folder icon to the right of the text box for choosing files to open the Where to back up dialog box (see Figure 6.2).

**Don't save backup files on the same drive**

The default choice is a file that is placed on the root directory of your hard drive. Don't choose this option; it's ridiculous. If your hard drive dies, you'll also lose your backup files.

FIGURE 6.2
Choose a drive to use as the target for your backup file.

**4.** Give the backup file a name: The day or date is a good choice. (Backup files have an extension of .qic.) Then choose Open to return to the Wizard and click **Next**.

**5.** The next window asks you to decide whether or not you want to take advantage of two features available in the back-up software (both of which are good ideas):

  • If you opt to compare the backup files to the original disk files, it means you'll be verifying that the files were copied correctly. It does, however, mean that the back-up takes more time.

  • You can opt to compress the backup data, which enables you to fit more data on the target media.

**6.** Click **Next** to move to the summary window in which you name the backup job (see Figure 6.3). Naming the backup job means you are saving the configuration options (in this case, a full backup), not the specific files or the name of the backup file itself.

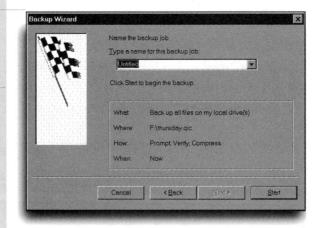

**7.** Choose **Start**.

If you've used the target media before, you're asked if you want to overwrite the existing backup file. Choose **Overwrite** (remember, you have multiple disks or tapes, so it's safe to over-write this one).

The backup begins, and unless you're needed to change tapes or disks, you can leave the computer. When the backup procedure is complete, a message appears on the screen to announce it. Choose OK to clear the message and return to the Microsoft Backup window and close the software.

The next time you back up, you can choose Open an existing backup job from the opening window and select the name you gave the backup job (not the name of the backup file).

## Performing an Incremental Backup

The term "incremental" is jargon for "files that have been added or changed since the last backup." This is a way to keep accurate backup sets of your data files without doing a full backup. Another term for incremental backup is differential backup.

The time and aggravation involved in restoring incremental backups are considerable. Remember, your goal is *not* to make backing up easy; it's to make restoring the backup easy.

The only reason to perform an incremental backup is that you have no choice but to back up to floppy disks. If you have media that can hold a substantial amount of data (even if it can't hold all the data on your drive), there's no reason to use an incremental backup scheme. Instead, back up selected folders, an action which is covered in the next section.

Here's how to tell Microsoft Backup to perform an incremental backup:

### Performing an incremental backup

1. Launch Microsoft Backup.
2. Open an existing backup job (assuming you've created a full backup job as described above) and choose **OK**.
3. The Open Backup Job window opens, from which you should choose a backup job you already created.
4. In the Microsoft Backup window, choose **New and changed files** (see Figure 6.4).

**Backing up to drives instead of tape**

You can choose any drive as the target for your backup file, including a floppy disk drive. If you're on a network and backing up to a network drive, that drive will not appear in the list of drives presented by Microsoft Backup unless you've mapped it. See Chapter 22 for more information on networks and mapping drives.

**An incremental backup is a subset of an existing backup job**

If you create a backup job of selected files and folders (described later in this chapter) instead of a full backup, you can select that job for the incremental backup.

FIGURE 6.4

There's an option for a quick
backup of new and changed
files.

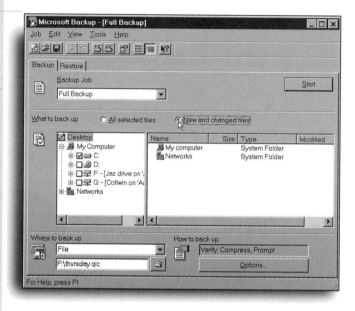

**5.** The other settings on the window remain the same as you
configured them when you created the backup job. There's
usually no reason to make changes, but if you want to
change any options you can.

**6.** You have to save this backup job configuration (or you'll be
asked to save it under the original job configuration name).
Choose Job, Save As from the menu bar. You're saving settings for an incremental backup job so name the job something appropriate (such as partial or incremental).

**7.** Choose **Start**.

Follow the remaining procedures as described above.

## Backing Up Selected Folders

You can decide to back up a specific array of files and folders and
make that group your normal backup. If you don't have a tape
drive or a Jaz drive (or the drives you have aren't large enough to
do a full system backup), this is the next best thing.

Here's the pecking order for choosing the files and folders to back up (keep picking objects until you reach the limit of bytes your destination drive can handle):

- The files in the root directory of Drive C
- Folders that contain utilities for booting (such as a folder that holds the files that are loaded by config.sys and autoexec.bat for your CD-ROM or a folder that holds the configuration program for your Network Card or SCSI controller)
- All your data folders, which are the folders you use to hold the documents you create while using your software
- The folder that holds your email
- Software folders for those software programs that you have customized
- Software folders for software programs that you haven't customized
- Any other folders you've created to hold data that would be difficult to reproduce

### Creating a backup set of selected folders

1. Launch Microsoft Backup.
2. Choose **Create a new backup job** (only necessary the first time you do this), and then choose **OK**.
3. In the next window, expand the hard drive by clicking the plus sign. Place a checkmark in the check box next to each folder you want to include in your backup set (see Figure 6.5).
4. To select files instead of folders, click the icon for the drive or folder instead of the check box. You may have to scroll through subfolders to see the filenames. Then put a checkmark next to each file you want to include in the backup set.
5. Choose **Next**, and then choose whether you want to back up all the selected files or only changed files (the first time you do this, choose all the selected files).
6. Choose a destination and backup filename as explained earlier, and then choose **Next**.

FIGURE 6.5

FIGURE 6.5

Select each folder you want to back up by placing a check-mark next to it.

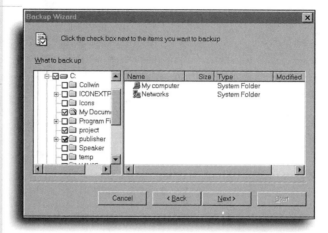

7. Choose options for verify and compression as explained earlier, and then choose **Next**.

8. Name the backup job (you're naming the configuration, not the actual backup file).

9. Choose **Start**.

Everything happens automatically again.

The next time you want to back up these particular files and folders, select this backup job.

# Restoring a Backup

When you need to restore the contents of a backup, you must start with the last full backup. Put the backup tape or disk in its drive (for floppy disk backups, put the first disk in the drive) and follow these steps:

### Restoring a backup from a backup file

1. Launch Microsoft Backup.

2. Choose Restore backed up files from the opening window and choose **OK**.

3. Select the backup file you want to restore from (see Figure 6.6). Then choose **Next**.

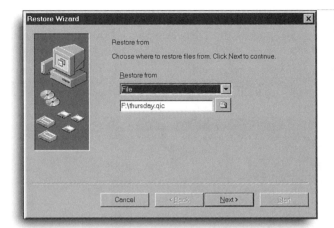

FIGURE 6.6
Choose the backup file to restore.

**4.** Choose the appropriate backup set (you can store multiple backup sets on a tape or drive so there may be more than one).

**5.** Backup reads the contents of the backup set (it takes a few seconds to accomplish this) and displays them (see Figure 6.7). Select the folders and/or files you want to restore. Then choose **Next**.

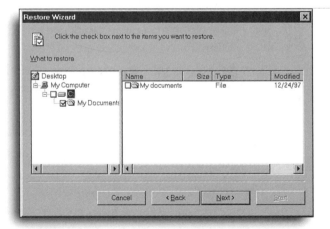

FIGURE 6.7
Anything I backed up can be restored.

**6.** Select a restore location. By default, files are restored to their original location, but you can restore them to different folders if you want. To choose a different location, click the arrow and select **Alternate Location** from the drop-down list. Then click the folder icon to see a Browse dialog box, from which you can select an alternate folder (see Figure 6.8).

FIGURE 6.8

Choose a target location for the restored files.

7. Choose **Next** after you've selected the target location. Then specify how to restore the files:

   • Do not replace the file on my computer means any file that exists on your drive won't be overwritten by the restored version.

   • Replace the file on my computer only if the file is older means that a file on the backup set that is newer than an existing file will be restored.

   • Always replace the file on my computer means that the files on the backup set will be written to your hard drive no matter what.

8. Choose **Start** to begin restoring files.

You may see instructions on the screen and if so, just follow them. There may also be messages on the screen, and the last message tells you that the restore is complete.

# Using System Recovery

Sometimes, you can have a catastrophic crash. Instead of just having to restore some files, you may have to restore the entire operating system from scratch. This is where the System Recovery feature comes in.

Essentially, the System Recovery feature is just a combination of the Windows 98 setup program and the program for restoring your system files. When you have a catastrophic crash, you should perform the following steps:

### Recovering your system after a crash

1. Boot your system with the Windows 98 Emergency Boot Disk.

2. Go to the CD-ROM drive by typing its drive letter followed by a colon (for example, D:) and then the **Enter** key.

3. Change to the System Recovery directory by typing cd \tools\sysrec followed by the **Enter** key.

4. Run the batch file pcrestor by typing it on the command-line followed by the **Enter** key.

This will start Windows 98's setup program, which will install a minimal version of Windows 98, including the Microsoft Backup program. When the minimal installation is complete—it'll take between a half-hour to an hour, depending upon the speed of your system—the restoration process will begin, and you will be asked to provide the media with the full backup on it.

# Copying Files for Backup

You don't have to use backup software to copy your data; you can use the copy or xcopy command. There's an upside and a downside to this technique:

- The upside is that restoring, especially restoring a single file, is a breeze. You don't have to search a backup set; you just find the file and copy it back.

- The downside is that there's no automatic "clean off the target drive and start over" (backup software performs this step), which means that eventually the target disk contains copies of files you've deleted from your hard drive and you have to perform a manual cleanup.

## Copying Files to Floppy Disk

If you don't have a removable device for backing up, you must at least copy your data files to floppy disks. That way, in the event of a disaster (or a semi-disaster, such as an inadvertent deletion of an important file), you can recover.

The easiest way to do this is to use the Send To option that's available when you right-click on a file. Select all the files in a folder (Ctrl+A) and then select the floppy drive as the target. Here are some guidelines for making it easier and more efficient:

- Keep all your data in specific data folders; don't mix data with software files.
- Earmark two floppy disks for each data folder (one for odd days and one for even days) so you never back up onto a good backup.
- When you delete a file from your hard drive, delete it from the floppy drive to make room.

If you have too many files to fit on a single floppy disk, use WinZip on all the files in the folder and save the compressed file on the floppy disk (Winzip will automatically span over multiple disks if necessary).

## Copying Files to Large Removable Media

If you have a Jaz or Zip drive, you can copy all your data folders (and probably some software folders, depending on what fits on the target drive).

The best way to do this is to create a batch file that uses the MS-DOS Xcopy command. A *batch file* is a program you can write to execute MS-DOS commands. You can create the file in any text editor (Notepad works well), and there are only two rules to remember:

- There can be only one command to a line.
- The filename must have an extension of .bat.

While it's beyond the scope of this book to delve into lengthy explanations of MS-DOS commands, here's an example (with some elucidation) of a batch file used to move the contents of a variety of folders to a Jaz drive. Some of the folders have sub-folders, and Xcopy is capable of handling them automatically.

```
xcopy c:\*.* d:\ /h/r/c
xcopy "c:\my documents\*.*" "d:\my documents" /s/e/h/i/r/c
xcopy c:\outlook\*.* d:\outlook /s/e/h/i/r/c
xcopy c:\regback\*.* d:\regback /s/e/h/i/r/c
xcopy c:\windows\*.* d:\windows /s/e/h/i/r/c
```

This batch file copies the files in the root directory of Drive C, and then copies the contents of the important folders. The folder named Outlook holds email, and the folder named regback holds backups of the Registry (because there's no backup software, there's no automatic backup of the Registry, so the backup is performed manually and then copied).

The exit command closes the MS-DOS window.

Table 6.1 explains the Xcopy parameters used in this batch file.

**TABLE 6.1 *Xcopy* parameters**

| Parameter | What It Does |
| --- | --- |
| /s | Copies subdirectories |
| /e | Copies subdirectories even if they are empty |
| /h | Copies hidden and system files |
| /i | Assumes the target name is a directory (and creates it if it doesn't exist) if the source is more than one file |
| /r | Overwrites read-only files |
| /c | Continues to copy if an error occurs |

If you're on a network and you save your data to your local computer, make arrangements with the system administrator to create a shared folder on the server and make that folder the target drive for a batch file such as this one.

After you copy all your important files to the server, the nightly backup of the server will include your stuff. That's like getting double protection.

**Copying to a server requires mapping**

You will have to map the shared folder to a drive letter and include a command to use that mapped drive. That means the first line of the batch file must be **net use x: \\ComputerName\ ShareName** (substitute the appropriate drive letter and names).

Your network administrator can help you design this batch file.

# Using the System Tools

Part of the installation of Windows 98 includes tools to help you keep your system running smoothly. The range of system tools available to you depends on your installation decisions. All the system tools you install are found on your Start menu at Programs, Accessories, System Tools (see Figure 6.9).

**FIGURE 6.9**

Your list of tools may differ from these, depending on what you chose to install.

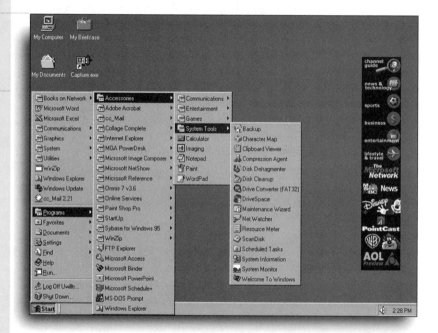

Three very useful (and most commonly used) tools in this list are the following:

- ScanDisk, which repairs damaged drives.
- Disk Defragmenter, which corrects fragmentation of files.
- System Monitor, which tracks the way resources are used in your computer.

We'll discuss those three tools in this section.

# Preventing Damage to Drives

There are two common causes of damaged drives (including having pieces of files floating around your drive):

- An unexpected power down (including a failure to exit Windows 98 properly).
- Low-voltage conditions. Well before you see your lights flicker when voltage is low, your hard drive can feel the effects and suffer damaged sections.

The cure for unexpected power loss is to have your computer plugged into a Uninterruptible Power Supply (UPS), which is the techie term for a computer battery backup unit. And, of course, always make sure you use the Shut Down menu item before turning off your computer.

The cure for low voltage may not be as easy to resolve, because it may not be anything you're causing.

If you plugged a laser printer or a copy machine into the same circuit as your computer, it's your problem. Move something to another circuit (and read the instructions for the copy machine or laser printer, which almost certainly warn you about the amps the machine pulls).

The problem could, however, rest with your local power company. Most power companies have difficulty maintaining 110 volts, especially during the summer when air conditioners are draining the power grid. Also, most power companies report serious drops in voltage every weekday morning between 8:30 and 9:30, when copy machines are being turned on all over the place (copy machines and laser printers, which have the same engines as copy machines, use a lot of amps during startup and warm-up).

If it's the power company's fault, an inexpensive line conditioner will resolve the problem. Check with your local computer store; you should find adequate line conditioning for around $50.

Of course, you should also ask the power company to check your voltage (have them install a voltage-checking machine that monitors continuously for several days; don't accept a brief check). If

**Real protection is line conditioning and a UPS**

You can buy a UPS that includes line conditioning, but it's much more expensive than a plain UPS. In fact, it's usually cheaper to buy a plain UPS and a separate line conditioner.

If your computer and its data are mission critical, get both devices. Plug the line conditioner into the wall, and then plug the UPS into the line conditioner.

the voltage drops frequently (these machines produce a print-out), tell them to do something about it. I complained to my electric company and they moved the transformer so I'm "first off the pole," which I guess gives me first dibs before my neighbors can suck out any voltage. It seems to have made a difference: my line conditioners don't click nearly as much (they make clicking noises when they make voltage adjustments). However, they also installed new lines, so that may be the major difference.

## Using ScanDisk

ScanDisk is a program that checks the general health of your hard drive, specifically looking for two problems:

- Damaged sections of the drive
- Pieces of files that don't seem to belong anywhere (or the computer can't figure out where they belong)

If a damaged section is identified, ScanDisk will attempt to repair it (usually ScanDisk just takes any files out of the damaged section and moves them, and then marks the section as damaged so it isn't ever used again to store files).

If floating pieces of files are found, ScanDisk will put them into files that you can look at to see if you can identify them. However, there's usually nothing you can do with them except delete them.

### Using ScanDisk

1. Select it from the System Tools submenu.
2. In the ScanDisk dialog box (see Figure 6.10), make sure your hard drive is selected (if you have multiple hard drives, you must scan them one at a time).
3. Select **Standard** as the type of test.
4. Be sure **Automatically fix errors** is selected.
5. Choose **Start**.

ScanDisk checks the components of your file system and then reports back (see Figure 6.11). After you read the report, you can close ScanDisk.

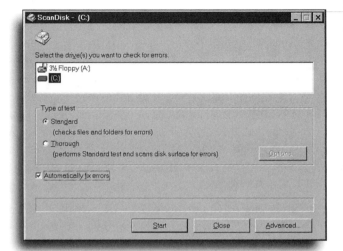

FIGURE 6.10

Select the options you want to use in ScanDisk.

FIGURE 6.11

ScanDisk tells you if it found any errors and displays all sorts of statistics about the state of the drive.

If there were errors reported, and the statistics show no bad spots on the drive, the errors were probably floating pieces of files. That means there are some files on the root directory of the drive with filenames of FILE0000.CHK, FILE0001.CHK, and so on. You could try to read them if you want, but even if they're readable (frequently they're not), there isn't anything you can do with them. Delete them.

ScanDisk also offers a type of test called Thorough. There's really no reason to perform this test (or change any of the Advanced options) unless you're asked to do so by a technical support person.

# Using Disk Defragmenter

Disk Defragmenter is a program that takes fragments of files and puts them together so that every file on your drive has its entire contents in the same place. Fragmentation is not the same as floating pieces of files because the operating system knows where each part of a fragmented file is and can fetch all the parts when you need the file. A floating piece of a file is a file fragment that the operating system has lost track of and has no idea where it belongs.

Files get fragmented as a matter of course; it isn't caused by anything you do or any problem with your computer. The more a drive fills up with files, the more it's likely to become fragmented.

The reason is basically that you cannot put 10 pounds of potatoes into a sack designed to hold 5 pounds of potatoes. Let's look at that in terms of files instead of potatoes.

Here's the scenario: Your hard drive is getting filled up. You open your word processor and load a document from the disk. That document is 60,000 bytes in size. You add another chapter to this great novel and when you save the document, it's 75,000 bytes. The section of the drive it was stored on holds 60,000 bytes, so the operating system puts 60,000 bytes of your new version back where it was and finds another spot on the drive to lay down the remaining 75,000 bytes. Then, the operating system makes a note to itself about that file, and the note says "I stuck the first 60K here and put the next 15K there." The note isn't a note, though; it's an entry in an index-like component of the operating system that's called the File Allocation Table. (It's from that component that we get the acronym FAT for the file system used in Windows 98.)

Two days later, you open that file again and the operating system fetches it, in the right order, after checking the FAT to see where the pieces of the file are.

You add another chapter. The operating system puts the first two sections back where they were, and then finds another spot for the additional bytes you appended to the file. The next day, you add more and there are more sections of the disk being used to hold the pieces of the file. Each time you load the file, it has to be fetched from more and more separate locations.

And, the same thing is happening to the other files you're creating and saving in software programs.

After a while, your system seems slower: It takes a long time to load a document and save a document. That's because there's all this running around your drive to fetch and lay down the file pieces.

It's time to pick up all the pieces and lay them down so that all the parts of every file are contiguous. This is what the Disk Defragmenter does. To do this, it juggles file segments, holding some in memory while it finds room, moving some stuff on the drive out of the way to make room for the stuff in memory. There are short bursts of time when file segments are neither here nor there—they're waiting to be laid down. Don't turn off your computer while the Disk Defragmenter is working, or anything in memory will become a floating piece of a file.

Now, before we discuss using the Disk Defragmenter, it's important to learn a piece of jargon. Nobody who is "with it" ever uses the term Disk Defragmenter. In fact, nobody uses the terms fragmented or defragmented.

When your disk is "fragged," you "defrag" it. That's the terminology used. In fact, computer users will tell you it's time to run the defragger. You won't find an entry on the tools menu for the defragger, but when you see the listing Disk Defragmenter, mentally translate that to defragger.

To defrag your disk, launch the defragger from the tools menu and select the drive you want to defrag when the Select Drive dialog box appears. Then choose OK.

There's a progress report as the process proceeds (see Figure 6.12).

Technically, you could continue to work while the defragging goes on, but it's slow going. And, I've found that every time I save a file, the percentage of completed work backs up a bit (and I don't think it's a good idea to work unless I save constantly). So, this is probably a good time to take a break.

**No FAT check means floating pieces**

When your computer unexpectedly shuts down while files are open, the operating system has no opportunity to tell the FAT where the file segments are. As a result, those pieces of files are on the drive, but Windows 98 has no reference in the FAT for them. That's how those floating pieces of files that ScanDisk takes care of come into existence.

**You may want to check the settings**

There's a Settings button on the Select Drive dialog box that opens a list of default settings for defragging your drive. They're the right settings for performing the operation, so there's no need to change them.

**FIGURE 6.12**

You can track the progress as defragging goes on.

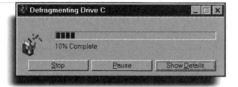

Incidentally, if you want to see a visual representation of the file segments being lifted from the fragged portion of the drive and laid down contiguously, choose Show Details (see Figure 6.13).

**FIGURE 6.13**

Take a closer look at the process with a detailed view.

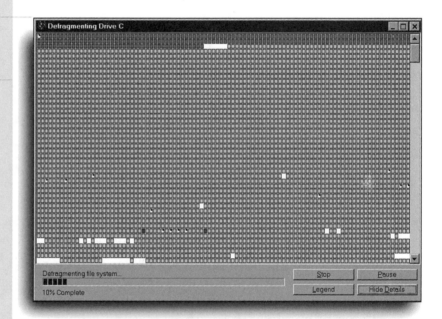

**You can pause or stop the defragging process**

If you absolutely have to do something at the computer during this procedure, you can click the Pause button. After you finish your work, choose Resume. You can also choose Stop to end the process.

If you pause or stop defragging, the response isn't immediate. The program finishes the file it's currently working on and makes sure everything is written to the drive properly and the FAT is updated. Then it responds to your selection.

You can choose Legend to see an informational chart of what each little square means (everything is color-coded, so it wouldn't make much sense if we printed the legend here).

When everything is neat and tidy on your drive, you should notice a much peppier response when you load or save a file. Of course, as you work, you're beginning the process all over again, and eventually your system will slow down and you'll have to repeat this.

# Using System Monitor

System Monitor is a tool you can use to locate the source of a problem. Most of the time it's used to locate bottlenecks when the response time of your computer seems to have suffered a setback. When things just don't seem to be operating correctly, you can monitor the computer resources to see what's not behaving properly.

Open System Monitor from the System Tools submenu to begin setting up your monitors.

The first time you use System Monitor, the software window is unremarkable, and the only thing of interest is the toolbar (see Figure 6.14).

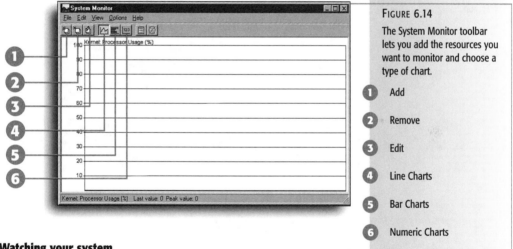

**FIGURE 6.14**

The System Monitor toolbar lets you add the resources you want to monitor and choose a type of chart.

**①** Add

**②** Remove

**③** Edit

**④** Line Charts

**⑤** Bar Charts

**⑥** Numeric Charts

## Watching your system

1. Choose **Add** to open the Add Item dialog box, which displays a list of categories available for monitoring (see Figure 6.15).

2. Choose a category, and the items available for that category are displayed in the Item list.

3. If you aren't sure what the item is or does, choose **Explain** (see Figure 6.16).

4. If you think you should monitor this item, choose **OK**. Otherwise, pick a different item.

FIGURE 6.15

The list of categories available for your computer may differ.

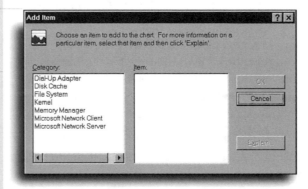

FIGURE 6.16

You can learn about any item by asking System Monitor for an explanation.

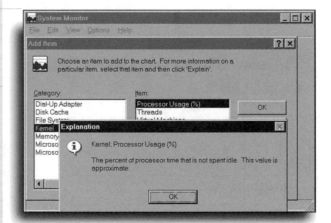

**5.** System Monitor begins keeping an eye on the item and charting its behavior (see Figure 6.17).

**6.** You can add additional items and change the type of chart by using the toolbar buttons (see Figure 6.18).

There are some assumptions you can make about your system when you view the charts:

- If you see a lot of swap disk activity, you probably should think about adding more memory to your system.

- If you see constant high use of the processor, you should probably close a program or two to maintain a productive level of performance.

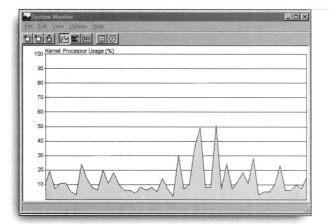

FIGURE 6.17

Watch the chart to see this item's activity level.

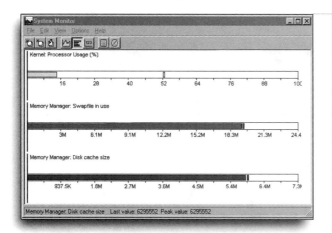

FIGURE 6.18

Two more items were added to this chart, and the chart type was changed to a bar chart.

For the most part, however, this tool is handy for computer professionals who are investigating problems. You may occasionally be asked to chart specific items to assist a support-desk person who is trying to find solutions.

## Using Windows Maintenance Wizard

This system tool is like having a mechanic check out everything under the hood. This mechanic, however, is a wizard, and it performs its job automatically and regularly. There are a number of maintenance tasks you can assign to the wizard for these tune-ups:

- Run the defragging tool (weekly).

- Run ScanDisk (weekly).

- Do general housekeeping on your file system to clean out files that aren't needed, such as temporary files and the files left behind when ScanDisk writes those FILE0000.CHK files (monthly).

Each tune-up task is scheduled for a specific time, and you can choose the time period that's best (the middle of the night is usually a good choice).

Start Windows Maintenance Wizard by selecting it from the System Tools submenu. The first wizard window appears so you can choose the way you want your tune-up to run (see Figure 6.19).

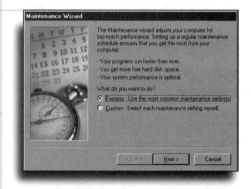

## Using the Express Maintenance Settings

If you opt to use the Express setup for the maintenance, choose Next to decide when the maintenace takes place (see Figure 6.20).

The next wizard window lets you select the option to run all the maintenance tasks right now for the first time. If you don't have anything important to do at the computer, you might want to select it. Otherwise, just choose Finish to let the wizard store your settings.

FIGURE 6.20

Pick a time when it's least likely you'll be working at your computer.

You can see the settings in the Windows 98 Task Scheduler, which is covered in the next section of this chapter. Don't forget to leave your computer on so the maintenance tasks can run.

### Customizing the Maintenance Settings

You can select the tasks and the schedule yourself by choosing Custom from the first wizard window.

After you choose the time period for performing tasks, the wizard walks you through each of the three maintenance tasks and asks you whether or not you want to run the scheduled program.

For those tasks you opt to include in your maintenance, you can customize the program's schedule by choosing Reschedule from the wizard window. Then use the Reschedule dialog box to determine the schedule you want to use (see Figure 6.21).

Repeat this for each task you want to schedule. Then choose Finish.

## Using Scheduled Tasks

Windows 98 has a program called Scheduled Tasks that keeps track of any automated chores scheduled for your computer. Anything you schedule through the Maintenance Wizard is placed in the task scheduler automatically, and you can add additional tasks whenever you choose.

---

**Maintenance also looks at your Startup folder**

Software programs sometimes add objects to your Startup folder without telling you, and as a result you can have a Startup folder with lots of stuff in it you don't care about, but all the programs start every time you start Windows 98. In fact, there may be a program you don't ever want to run, much less run it all the time.

If you do have objects in your Startup folder, the wizard will show you a list during the process of setting up the maintenance. You can deselect any programs you don't want to run at startup. Just by presenting that option, the maintenance has helped speed up the operating system's startup.

FIGURE 6.21

Design the schedule to meet
the intervals you think are necessary and convenient.

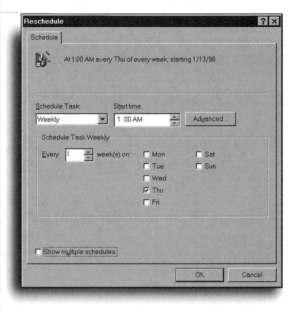

When you install Scheduled Tasks, it's available on the System
Tools submenu and in your My Computer folder, and it also
places an icon on your Taskbar tray. This makes it easy to keep
an eye on what's happening and when it's happening.

To open Scheduled Tasks, double-click on its taskbar icon. The
Scheduled Tasks window displays a listing of every automated
procedure you've scheduled (see Figure 6.22).

FIGURE 6.22

The results of an Express setup
for the Maintenance Wizard
are displayed in the Scheduled
Tasks window.

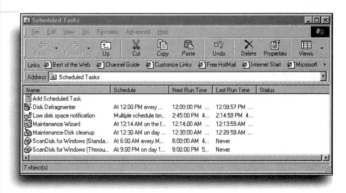

**Adding another task**

1. Double-click the Add Scheduled Task listing (which is always at the top of the list). The Scheduled Task wizard opens to walk you through this procedure. The first wizard window is an introduction and there's nothing you have to do, so after you've read about the wizard, choose Next to move on.

2. A list of Windows programs and utilities is displayed so you can choose the application you want to schedule (see Figure 6.23). Use the Browse button to find programs that aren't listed (you may have some DOS software and utilities that could be scheduled at automatic intervals).

**FIGURE 6.23**

The most common choice is backup, but first I'll schedule a daily playback of my favorite audio CD.

3. On the next window, give the task a name and choose the schedule interval (see Figure 6.24).

4. The next window asks you for more specifications, which depend on the interval you selected. For example, a daily task needs a time, while a monthly task needs a day and time. You also need to give a starting date.

5. The last window has an option that lets you see advanced settings for the task after you conclude your scheduling configuration. If you select it, a dialog box similar to the one shown in Figure 6.25 appears.

FIGURE **6.24**

There's a wide range of choices for scheduling a task.

FIGURE **6.25**

The Settings tab of the dialog box for advanced settings offers additional options.

After you've completed your configuration, the task appears in the Scheduled Tasks window.

■ To remove a task from the schedule, select it and press the Del key or drag it to the Recycle Bin. You'll be asked to confirm the deletion.

- If you don't want tasks to run (perhaps you're planning to work very late), right-click the Scheduled Tasks icon on the taskbar and choose Pause Task Schedule from the pop-up menu.

- To resume scheduled operations after you've paused them, right-click on the icon and choose Continue Task Scheduler.

# Using the System File Checker

One of the tools included in your Windows 98 operating system is System File Checker. This is a utility that can stop panic attacks, because it can check all the Windows 98 system files and ascertain trouble or potential trouble. Of course, most people don't use it until they've had some sort of fatal error, or near fatal error, but the more prepared users utilize the tool as a preventive measure.

The System File Checker is part of Microsoft System Information tool, which you can find on the System Tools menu (which is under the Accessories menu).

## Checking and Replacing System Files

When the System Information window opens, choose **System File Checker** from the Tools menu to open the System File Checker window (see Figure 6.26). Click **Start** to check all your Windows 98 system files.

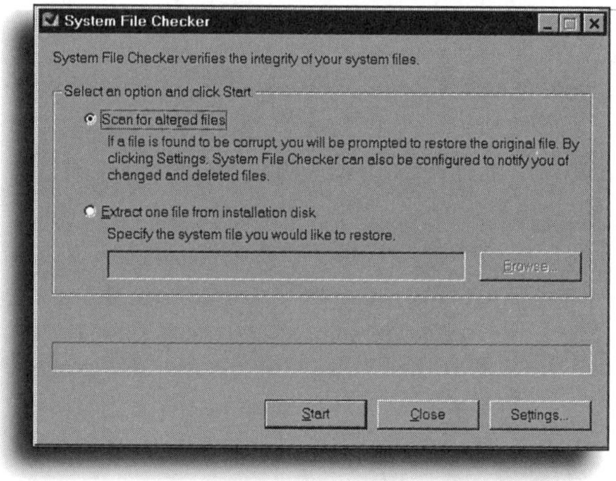

**FIGURE 6.26**
The System File Checker can look for bad files, and then replace them.

If a file is found to be corrupted, the original file (on the Windows 98 CD-ROM) is copied to your hard drive to replace the damaged file.

You can also use System File Checker to extract a file from the installation CD and place it on your hard drive. Because most of the files on the CD-ROM are packed, the System File Checker needs to use the Microsoft extract feature in order to copy a packed file to your hard drive.

## Configuring Settings

To configure the way System File Checker works, choose **Settings** to open the System File Checker Settings dialog box seen in Figure 6.27.

**FIGURE 6.27**

Configure the way System File Checker will work for you.

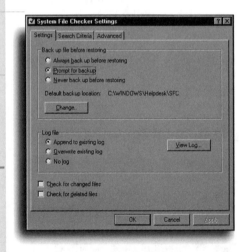

**System file checker uses a file for comparison**

When you install Windows 98 (or install additional features after the original installation), the details of the installation are kept in a file named Default.sfc. This file, which is stored in your Windows folder, has detailed information about the files that were installed, along with their original location. Note that not all Windows 98 systems are installed from a CD-ROM. Some systems are installed from Network servers, and some systems have the original Windows 98 installation files installed right on the hard drive. Don't open or edit Default.sfc unless you are extremely comfortable with operating system technologies.

Here are some guidelines for setting the options:

- You can force an automatic backup of the corrupted file instead of asking you if you want one, or you can eliminate that step. If you want to, you can change the folder in which those backups are stored.

- You can add information about the software's execution to an existing log, create a new log every time you run it, or skip the log altogether. Choose **View Log** to see the current log (it's a text file that opens in Notepad).

- You can add more functions to the System File Checker's job. Choose **Check for changed files** or **Check for deleted files** to add those tasks.

# Managing Drives

There are a few housekeeping chores that you can perform on drives without opening a program from the Start menu. First, open My Computer and right-click the icon for your hard drive, and then choose Properties from the shortcut menu.

## Using the General Tab of the Drive Properties

When the Properties dialog box opens, the General tab is in the foreground (see Figure 6.28).

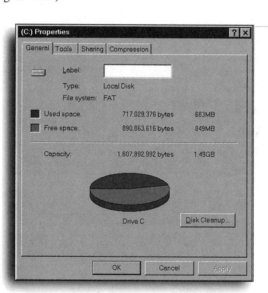

**Floppy drives have similar properties**

If you're looking at the properties of a floppy drive, the General tab is the same except there's no button for Disk Cleanup.

**FIGURE 6.28**

The General tab of the drive Properties dialog box displays information about the drive, along with some utilities you can use.

You can do a couple things with the General tab (your first job is to panic if the amount of free space is down to double digits):

- You can create a Label for the drive. Some people like to do this, but the fact is there's no particular advantage or reason.

- You can run Disk Cleanup, which finds temporary files that aren't needed by running programs. Sometimes there are a large number of unnecessary temporary files on hard drives, and you can recover quite a bit of disk space by cleaning them out.

Disk Cleanup is polite enough to check with you before it removes files (see Figure 6.29). You can give permission to remove files by category.

**FIGURE 6.29**

Some of the categories are preselected for you because there's no need to keep those files.

If you upgraded to Windows 98 from Windows 95 or Windows 3.*x*, during the installation process you were asked whether you wanted to make provisions for returning to your previous operating system. If you responded affirmatively, your hard drive has a great many bytes filled with the files needed to uninstall Windows 98 and go back to your old Windows version. Those files are included in the list of files that can be safely cleaned off your drive. If you're happy with Windows 98 and you don't plan to go back to a previous version of Windows, select those files as targets of the cleanup.

After you make your selection, you have to confirm that you want the selected files deleted. Then they're gone!

# Using the Tools Tab of the Drive Properties

The Tools tab is identical for both hard and floppy drives. As you can see in Figure 6.30, there are three utilities you can run to perform maintenance on the drive.

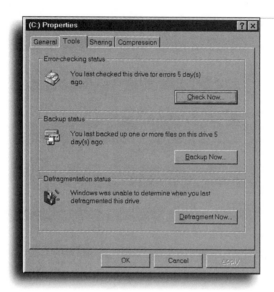

FIGURE 6.30

The tools available on the Properties dialog box are ScanDisk, Backup, and the Defragmenter.

There are two other tabs on the Properties dialog box for drives—Sharing and Compression:

- Use the Sharing tab to enable other users on a network to access all or some of this drive. More information about sharing drives is found in Chapter 23.

- If you're not using FAT32, you can use the Compression tab to install Microsoft compression. This is a feature that compresses files when they are stored on the drive and uncompresses them when you run the associated software. Running compressed drives is more complicated than it seems, and you shouldn't install the feature without a lot of research. Talk to experts, read magazine articles, and make up your mind carefully.

Computer safety, which includes keeping your data safe and your computer running efficiently, is an important part of your responsibilities as a computer user. If you don't take the responsibility seriously, you won't be able to count on your computer to continue to serve you well.

# Customizing Windows

# Configuring Windows 98

# Introducing the Control Panel

Whether you need to make a major change to the way your system operates, or fine-tune its behavior, you'll end up working in the Control Panel. In this chapter, we'll take a look at the Control Panel and go inside some of the specific controls for basic computer functions (the mouse, keyboard, and so on).

The Control Panel is like the master control room of your Windows 98 system. You can liken it to Mission Control at NASA or the deck of the Enterprise on "Star Trek;" it's the place you go to push the buttons that make sweeping changes or minor adjustments to your system.

In this chapter, we'll discuss a few of the Control Panel options—many of them are covered in other chapters. Table 7.1 shows you where to find more information on Control Panel configuration.

**TABLE 7.1  Control panel icons and where to find information**

| Icon | Chapter |
| --- | --- |
| Display | Chapter 8 |
| Passwords | Chapter 9 |
| Add/Remove Programs | Chapter 11 |
| Printers | Chapter 13 |
| Add New Hardware | Chapter 14 |
| System | Chapter 14 |
| Multimedia | Chapter 15 |
| Modems | Chapter 16 |
| Network | Chapter 21 |

To use the Control Panel features, the first thing you have to do is get there:

### Accessing the Control Panel

1. Click the **Start** button to open the **Start** menu.
2. Place your mouse pointer on **Settings** to see the submenu.
3. Choose **Control Panel**.

The Control Panel opens to reveal all of its icons (Figure 7.1).

Most of the icons in the Control Panel open to Properties dialog boxes in which you can set options to control the way your system operates.

## Understanding Properties

Properties are essentially the personality traits of an object in your Windows 98 system. An object's properties can determine how the object behaves, what it can do (and what it can't do), how it looks, and so on. To see an object's properties, right-click any object in Explorer or My Computer and choose **Properties** from the shortcut menu.

Almost every object in your Windows 98 system has properties attached to it that you can view by right-clicking. The only exceptions are the objects in the Control Panel. If you right-click any of the icons in the Control Panel, you won't see Properties on the shortcut menu.

That's because the objects in the Control Panel are containers for system properties. These system properties are accessible by topic instead of one big "system properties" dialog box. This makes it much easier to configure exactly the system feature you want to tweak.

## Shortcuts to Control Panel Applets

The Control Panel icons are also called *applets*, meaning "mini-applications." That's because there's an executable file for each icon. If you look in Explorer in the folder \Windows\System (assuming Windows is the name of the folder in which you installed Windows 98), you'll see a number of files with the extension .cpl. Double-click one of them to open the same dialog box you see if you double-click the icon in the Control Panel Window.

If there's a Control Panel applet you find you use frequently, you can create a desktop shortcut for it by following these steps:

### Creating a desktop shortcut for a Control Panel applet

**1.** Right-drag the .cpl file to the desktop.

**2.** Choose **Create Shortcut(s) Here** from the menu that appears when you release the mouse button.

Control Panel shortcuts are handy if you travel a great deal and are constantly changing dialing properties (use the Modem applet), or if you change display settings for certain games the kids like to play (the Display applet, although this is available already by right-clicking the desktop and selecting properties from the resulting pop-up menu).

Table 7.2 lists most of the applets/icons in the Control Panel, along with their .cpl files. Note that your list will be slightly different depending upon what sort of hardware and installation you have.

TABLE 7.2  **Control Panel applets and their files**

| Applet | File |
| --- | --- |
| Accessibility | access.cpl |
| Add/Remove Programs | appwiz.cpl |
| Date/Time | timedate.cpl |
| Display | desk.cpl |

| Applet | File |
| --- | --- |
| Fonts | main.cpl |
| Joystick | joy.cpl |
| Keyboard | main.cpl |
| Modems | modem.cpl |
| Mouse | main.cpl |
| Multimedia | mmsys.cpl |
| Network | netcpl.cpl |
| Passwords | password.cpl |
| Printers | main.cpl |
| Regional Settings | intl.cpl |
| System | sysdm.cpl |

There are a few things to take note of about the information in Table 7.2:

- There is no executable file for Add/Remove Hardware.
- Several applets use the file named Main.cpl.

If you double-click Main.cpl, you'll see the Mouse Properties dialog box. But there is a way to configure a shortcut for any of the applets that run from Main.cpl:

### Configuring shortcuts for Control Panel applets that run from Main.cpl

1. Create a desktop shortcut to Main.cpl as described previously.
2. Right-click the shortcut and choose **Properties** from the shortcut menu.
3. Move to the **Shortcut** tab (see Figure 7.2).
4. The path and filename of the shortcut's target file is highlighted (ready to edit). Press the right arrow key to go to the end of the path.
5. Add a space after the path followed by the name of the applet you want to use for this shortcut. Use the name on the title of the applet's icon in **Control Panel** (printers, keyboard, mouse, and so on).
6. Choose **OK**.

Of course, you'll probably want to change the name of the shortcut to reflect the applet it's linked to:

**Changing the name of a shortcut**

1. Click the shortcut to select it.

2. Press **F2** to put the title in Edit mode.

3. Press the right arrow to go to the end of the title, and then backspace to delete Main.cpl and replace it with the correct title.

4. Press **Enter** (or click a blank spot on the desktop) to save the new title.

# Tweaking the Mouse

Most people are amazed the first time they take a careful look at the mouse settings that are available in Windows 98. There's a whole lot you can do to enhance the features your mouse is capable of providing.

## Setting Buttons and Speed

If you're on the tennis court or a pitcher's mound, being a southpaw can be a real advantage. However, when graphical computer environments and mice were introduced, there apparently weren't a lot of left-handed people involved in the design process. Today's mice are curved and shaped for right-handed people, and finding one that's curved for a lefty is no easy trick. You can, however, make some adjustments that make your mouse southpaw-sympathetic.

Double-click the Mouse icon in Control Panel and when the Mouse Properties dialog box opens, the Buttons tab is in the foreground (see Figure 7.3).

## Make the Mouse a Lefty

Select Left-handed to reverse the actions of the left and right mouse buttons. This means that when you place your mouse to the left of the keyboard, your index finger rests on the primary button (the one that selects and drags).

## Set the Double-Click Speed

One of the trickiest maneuvers for new mouse users is the double-click. There's a difference between a double-click and two clicks one after another:

- A double-click opens an object.
- Two clicks one after another tells Windows 98 to edit an icon name.

If you double-click too slowly on an object, you suddenly find its title is reversed (it's in edit mode). Then, if you press a key, that key replaces the title even if the key you touched was the space-bar. This is nerve-wracking at best and dangerous at worst.

What's the difference in elapsed time between two clicks and a double-click? It's less than a second. This is a very tight window, so it behooves you to let Windows 98 know what your own interpretation of a double-click is.

The bottom of the Buttons tab has a place where you can demonstrate your idea of a double-click to Windows 98. What you have to do is set the timing to match the speed with which you're able to click the left mouse button twice in a row.

- If you think you need more time between clicks, move the slider to the left.
- If your reflexes are incredibly good (or you drink a lot of coffee while you're working at your computer), try moving the slider to the right.

After you've positioned the slider, test your double-click in the Test area. If the elapsed time between clicks matches the slider setting, the jack-in-the-box pops out of the box. If the little guy doesn't jump up, adjust the slider and try again.

After you've set your double-click time, you can fine-tune it by moving the slider in very small increments and double-clicking in the test area. Each time you match your action to the slider's setting, the jack-in-the-box goes into his box or comes out of it (he alternates between the two with each successful double-click).

## Changing Mouse Pointers

You don't have to stick to those mundane mouse pointers that everybody else uses; you can assert your individuality with a new shape.

To investigate all the possibilities, move to the Pointers tab on the Mouse Properties dialog box (see Figure 7.4).

### Selecting a Whole New Set of Pointers

Windows 98 has some collections of pointers put together in what's called a *scheme*. Each scheme has a complete array of

**Counting the milliseconds**

The left (slow) end of the slider bar is 900 milliseconds, which is nine-tenths of a second. The right (fast) end of the slider bar is 100 milliseconds, which is one-tenth of a second.

If you can't manage to click twice within the space of 900 milliseconds, you need to find an exercise for your index finger, because that's as slow as you can get Windows 98 to work.

pointers and you can see the choices by clicking the arrow to the right of the Scheme box (see Figure 7.5).

FIGURE **7.4**

The current pointers are displayed in the dialog box.

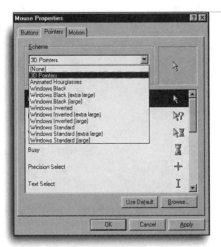

FIGURE **7.5**

You can see that the 3D Pointers scheme lives up to its name.

Some of the schemes don't change the design of the pointers; they merely change the size. If you occasionally find it difficult to find your pointer on your screen, try one of the schemes designed for large pointers.

**The selected pointer is in the preview box**

Notice that when you select a pointer, it is shown in the preview box on the upper-right portion of the dialog box. If the cursor is animated, you can observe its movements.

## Selecting New Individual Pointers

You don't have to change schemes to change pointers; you can elect to change individual pointers and keep the others. Here's how to make specific changes:

### Changing individual mouse pointers

1. Choose a scheme that has a number of pointers you like (which may be the default scheme).

2. Select (highlight) the pointer you want to change.

3. Choose **Browse** to open the **Browse** dialog box with the contents of the Cursors folder displayed (see Figure 7.6).

**FIGURE 7.6**

There's a number of pointers to choose from.

4. Choose a new pointer to replace the pointer you previously selected. (Pointers that are animated have filename extensions of .ani.) Then choose Open. Alternatively, you can just double-click the new pointer.

5. The new pointer is displayed on the Pointers tab.

It's not a great idea to use animated pointers for normal select or text select pointers because it will drive you crazy. However, a little animation on a "busy" pointer (I always refer to that hourglass as a "wait" pointer) isn't terribly distracting.

## Creating Your Own Pointer Schemes

You can replace several (or all) of the existing pointers for a scheme and then make that arrangement of pointers permanent by making it a scheme in itself. Here's how:

**Creating your own pointer schemes**

1. Follow the steps to replace a pointer for all the pointers you want to change.

2. When you're happy with your new set of pointers, choose **Save As**.

3. When the **Save Scheme** dialog box appears, enter a name for your new scheme.

4. Choose **OK** to return to the Pointers tab; then choose **OK** again to save your configuration and close the dialog box.

You can create as many schemes as you want, then use them according to your mood. If you're in a 3D mood, use your scheme of 3D pointers, and if you're down in the dumps, use your scheme of animated pointers to raise your spirits.

## Installing Pointers

If you can't find additional pointers in your Cursor folder or you don't have a Cursor folder, it means you didn't install the additional pointers.

You can add the pointers to your Windows 98 installation in the same way you can add any component after you've installed the operating system. Put your Windows 98 CD-ROM in its drive and follow these steps:

**Installing mouse pointers in Windows 98**

1. In the Control Panel, double-click the **Add/Remove Programs** icon.

2. When the dialog box opens, move to the **Windows Setup** tab (see Figure 7.7).

3. Click **Accessories** to select that component group.

4. Choose **Details** to display the list of Accessories that can be installed.

5. Scroll through the list to find **Mouse Pointers** and select it (put a check mark in the box next to its listing).

6. Choose **OK** to return to the **Windows Setup** tab.

7. Choose **OK** to begin the process of transferring the mouse pointer files.

<br>

FIGURE 7.7

Add the mouse pointers to your installation if you didn't install them previously.

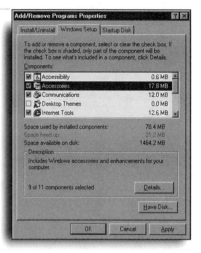

You can also find additional pointers on the Internet. To use them, when the Browse dialog box opens select the folder in which you stored them.

## Configuring Mouse Pointer Motion

The Motion tab of the Mouse Properties dialog box (see Figure 7.8) has two configuration settings: Pointer speed and Pointer trail.

FIGURE 7.8

Configure the pointer's screen characteristics on the Motion tab.

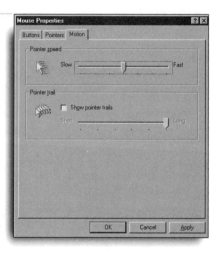

## Setting Pointer Speed

The dialog box has a slider where you can adjust the speed of the pointer. What this really means is the speed of mouse motion to pointer motion. As the mouse moves, Windows 98 applies a speed factor. If the mouse is moving slowly, the pointer is slowed down. When the mouse is moving quickly, the pointer is speeded up. All of the reduction and acceleration is within the limits set by you when you adjust the slider.

Think of it as the operating system applying the brakes or gas pedal as you move your mouse around the screen. However, there's a governor on the engine and the brakes cannot slow the engine down lower than the point you establish, nor rev the engine faster than the limit you set.

Having said all of that, I'll have to admit that no matter where I move this slider, I don't see very much difference in the interaction between my mouse movements and the pointer's movements.

## Configuring Pointer Trails

Pointer trails are repetitious clones of your mouse pointer that trail behind the pointer. A short trail looks like a pointer with a drop shadow effect (you really don't see any additional pointers) and a long trail adds about ten pointers. Those additional pointers chase behind your pointer as you move your mouse around the screen. (Did you ever watch a family of geese or ducks following the mother? or watch lemmings?)

On a regular desktop computer, pointer trails are annoying. But if you're sitting in front of a computer and the output of the computer is being sent to an LCD device that's projected on a screen, you'll love pointer trails. Unless the room is pitch dark and the contrast of the picture on the projection screen is very high (neither of which ever seems to be the case), it's very difficult to figure out where your pointer is.

I've run seminars in which my most frequent question to my audience was "where's my pointer?" Then I had to listen to people yell things like "upper-right corner," or "near the toolbar." As I moved my mouse, squinting at the screen, people yelled

---

**Animated pointers may not work**

There are three situations in which you'll be unable to use animated pointers:

- Your hard drive is not using 32-bit drivers.

- Your display settings are set to display fewer than 256 colors.

- Your video card has a problem with animated pointers.

To learn whether Windows 98 is using 32-bit drivers for your hard disk, open the System icon in Control Panel and move to the Performance tab. Check the File system and Virtual Memory settings to see if they indicate they're running 32-bit drivers. If they're not, you're loading drivers for your disk in your Config.sys file during bootup because your hard disk requires this step.

Some video cards can't seem to handle animated pointers and it's not because they're not powerful cards. For example, I have one Windows 98 computer in which animated pointers won't work. The computer has a Diamond Viper video card with plenty of power and memory on it; it just doesn't like animated pointers (I have no explanation for this, which is when I start using the word "bug").

"getting warmer" or "no, no, the other way." It certainly inter-fered with the smoothness of my presentation (to say nothing of the lack of professionalism involved in having an audience play hide-and-seek with you). After I discovered pointer trails, I stopped losing my pointer during presentations and training ses-sions.

# Tweaking the Keyboard

You can gain more control over the way your keyboard behaves by tweaking its settings. In addition, there are a number of key-board shortcuts you probably should know about but don't (or have forgotten), so we'll cover them here.

## Setting Character Repeat Speed

Double-click the keyboard icon in Control Panel to see the Keyboard Properties dialog box (see Figure 7.9). The Speed tab is in the foreground, which is where the settings are.

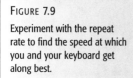

FIGURE 7.9

Experiment with the repeat rate to find the speed at which you and your keyboard get along best.

There are two slider bars to manipulate, one for Repeat delay and one for the Repeat rate.

## Setting Repeat Delay

The repeat delay is the time you can hold down a key without having it repeat. If you make the delay time very long, you can lean on a key for a bit and it won't repeat. This is very useful for any typist who has a heavy hand and types slowly.

If you make the delay time very short, any keypress longer than a light touch will repeat the character. Only rapid typists who touch the keys lightly and then move immediately to the next key can use this setting.

## Setting the Repeat Rate

The repeat rate is the speed at which characters are repeated when you hold down a key. If you move the repeat rate slider to the left (slow) and lean on a key for two seconds, you'll probably see about five repeated characters. Move the slider all the way to the right and in the same two seconds you'll probably see about 15 characters.

You can find a comfortable rate of repeat by moving the slider and then using the test area to see how fast a pressed key repeats its character. Don't forget to click the test area before holding down a key.

I can hear your question; you're asking, "what's the difference; how often, if ever, do I need to repeat the letter r?" Or any other letter for that matter?

Good question, and most of us have never had a need to worry about how many character repetitions there are when we lean on a key—because we never deliberately lean on a key.

However, these settings affect the arrow keys and we've all used arrow keys to move up and down, or horizontally, through a document. Remember that even if you're holding down the Ctrl key along with the arrow key, the repeat rate you set determines the speed with which you move through your document.

Do you always overshoot your mark when you do this? Slow down the repeat rate.

**Key resistance plays a role here, too**

I happen to be a very fast typist and I touch the keys rather than press them. I'm quite fussy about the resistance the keys offer my fingers because if there's a need to press hard, it slows my typing. I've found there's a great deal of difference between keyboards in resistance. Once I settle on a keyboard with little resistance, I set my repeat delay to the shortest interval (that's my keyboard setting you see in Figure 7.9).

People who are not touch typists tend to have heavier hands (I think it's because they use their index fingers for most of their typing and the index finger is stronger than the pinky). If they buy a keyboard with more resistance from the keys and then set the repeat delay for a longer interval, they'll avoid inadvertent repeated characters.

Do you usually lift your finger from the arrow key and then have to press the arrow again to get to your target location? Speed up the repeat rate.

The test area on the dialog box is only marginally useful for testing the movement of arrow keys. The best way to really test the settings is to set the slider, then work for a while. If necessary, reset the slider. Eventually, you'll find the right speed.

(Incidentally, all the keys on your keyboard are affected, such as Page Up, Page Down, Backspace, and Delete.)

## Setting the Cursor Blink Rate

The Cursor Blink Rate setting is also manipulated in the Keyboard dialog box. This setting is exactly what it seems to be—how fast the cursor blinks at you.

If you sometimes have trouble finding your cursor, set a faster blink rate. It works! The trick is to set it fast enough to get your attention, but not so fast that it drives you nuts to see it.

## Making the Keyboard Multilingual

If you have the need to prepare documents in another language, you can configure the keyboard so it supports that language. Don't panic; you're not replacing English with Portugese— you're adding a second language. In fact, you can add many additional languages.

Use the Language tab of the Keyboard Properties dialog box to add languages and specify the keystrokes that will switch between languages.

### Adding a new language to your keyboard

1. Choose **Add** to open the **Add Language** dialog box.
2. Click the arrow to the right of the Language box to see the list of languages supported by Windows 98 (see Figure 7.10). Select the language you need.
3. Choose **OK** to return to the Language tab, where the new language is listed (see Figure 7.11).

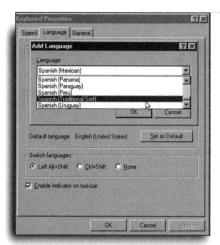

**FIGURE 7.10**
Choose an additional language for your keyboard.

**FIGURE 7.11**
All the languages you install are displayed on the Language tab.

**4.** By default, Windows 98 assumes the default language is United States English. If you want to make another language the default, select it and choose **Set as Default**.

**5.** Specify the keystrokes you want to use to switch languages (if there are more than two languages installed, the keystrokes take you through all of them).

**6.** Select **Enable indicator taskbar** to put a language menu on the taskbar tray (see Figure 7.12).

**You can omit keystroke language switches**

You can choose None and have no keystroke combinations established for switching languages, but if you do, you must select the taskbar indicator. Otherwise, the only way to switch languages is to open this dialog box and change the default language.

FIGURE 7.12

Switch languages by making a menu choice—the current language is indicated on the taskbar.

**7.** Choose **OK** when you have finished installing a new language. Windows 98 transfers the appropriate files to your drive and closes the Keyboard Properties dialog box.

To remove a language from the keyboard, select it and choose Remove.

## Using a Windows Keyboard

Many people have purchased a Windows keyboard (or purchased a computer that came with one). This is a keyboard that has three extra keys, all on the bottom row:

- On the left, between the Ctrl and Alt keys, a key with the Windows logo. Press it to see the Start menu.

- On the right, to the right of the Alt key, a key with the Windows logo. Press it to see the Start menu.

- On the right, to the right of the Windows logo key, a key with an icon representing a menu with an arrow pointing to a menu item. Press it to right-click at the current location of your mouse pointer or cursor.

When used with other keys, the Windows key does more than bring up the Start menu. Table 7.3 is a quick reference for using it.

TABLE 7.3  **Use these keys with the Windows key**

| Additional Key | Shortcut |
| --- | --- |
| D | Toggles the view of the desktop |
| E | Opens Explorer |
| F | Opens Find Files |
| Ctrl+F | Opens Find Computers |
| M | Minimizes all windows |
| Shift+M | Undoes Minimize all windows |

| Additional Key | Shortcut |
|---|---|
| R | Opens Run |
| V | Mutes/Unmutes sound |
| Tab | Switches through taskbar application buttons |
| Break | Opens System Properties dialog box |

It takes a while to get used to these key combinations, but after you force yourself to use them a few times, they become second nature. Many of us who are touch typists believe that any keyboard combination is better and quicker than reaching for a mouse.

# Assigning Sounds

It's not an accident that you hear music when Windows 98 starts up, or that you hear a noise when you make a mistake and click something you shouldn't. Those sounds have been assigned to those events.

You can impose your own taste or sense of whimsy by assigning sounds to events that are currently soundless, or by changing the sounds that are assigned to events.

This all takes place in the Sounds applet in the Control Panel (see Figure 7.13).

**FIGURE 7.13**

All the sound-enabled events that could occur in your system are displayed in the Sounds Properties dialog box.

As you scroll through the list of events, notice that there's a two-level hierarchical display, with the secondary level indented. The first level of the hierarchy is the program, the second level is the list of events.

It starts with Windows (which isn't really a program, of course) and then each sound-enabled software program you've installed is displayed along with its events. For example, you may see a listing for Microsoft Office, Quicken, CompuServe, or any other program that's installed in your system.

There are some anomalies, however:

- Windows Explorer, the Sound Recorder, the Media Player, and several other system utilities are listed as programs (instead of falling under the listings for Windows).

- Sometimes America Online puts its sound files directly into the Windows listing instead of installing a separate listing for itself (that obnoxious, ungrammatical "you've got mail" is not really a Windows 98 sound even though it's listed under Windows).

## Installing Sounds

If you didn't install all the sounds when you installed Windows 98, you can install them now. Or you can collect sound files from friends, the Internet, or shareware CD-ROMS. There are gazillions of sound files available.

To install all the sounds that come with Windows 98, put your Windows 98 CD-ROM in its drive and take these steps:

**Installing the sound schemes supplied with Windows 98**

1. Open the **Add/Remove Programs** icon in Control Panel.
2. Move to the **Windows Setup** tab.
3. Select **Multimedia** and choose **Details**.
4. Mark all the sound schemes you want to install.
5. Choose **OK** to return to the **Windows Setup** tab.
6. Choose **OK** again to save your choices and have the necessary files transferred to your hard drive.

The files are transferred and your Sounds applet lists all the schemes you've installed.

To install sounds that you downloaded or have on disk, copy the sounds to the default folder for sounds, which is \Windows\Media (assuming the folder in which you installed Windows 98 is named Windows).

You can, of course, copy those sound files to any folder in your system, and you can even create a new folder for them.

## Assigning Sounds to Windows Events

Windows 98 has numerous events for which sounds can be applied, and also provides plenty of sound files so you have lots of choices. You can apply an entire scheme to all the events, or apply individual sounds to individual events.

### Assigning Entire Schemes

Instead of making a decision about sounds for each event, you can start by assigning a sound scheme. Then you can change any individual sound assignment that doesn't please you.

Click the arrow to the right of the Schemes box to see the list of sound schemes installed in your system (see Figure 7.14).

**FIGURE 7.14**

Perhaps one of the sound scheme names seems intriguing, or you could just make a random selection.

After you've selected a sound scheme, sounds from that scheme are assigned to a number of Windows events (events associated with programs aren't affected).

If you want to hear a sound, select it and click the play arrow next to the preview box.

## Assigning Individual Sounds to Events

Either starting from the sounds assigned by a scheme, or starting from scratch, you can assign a sound to any Windows event by following these steps:

### Assigning a sound to any Windows event

1. Select the event for which you want to assign or change the sound.

2. Click the arrow to the right of the Name box to see a list of available sounds (see Figure 7.15).

**FIGURE 7.15**

Choose any sound that seems suitable (or unsuitable if you think it would be more fun).

3. Choose a sound. If you want to hear it, click the play arrow in the Preview section of the dialog box.

4. If you don't see anything interesting in the list and you've installed additional sounds, choose **Browse** to open the Browse dialog box.

5. Move to the appropriate folder and choose a sound file by double-clicking it. Then choose **OK** to return to the Sounds Properties dialog box.

6. To remove an existing sound, choose **None** from the list of sounds.

7. Continue to select events and assign sounds until you're satisfied with your sound configuration.

It's easy to continue to tweak and change your system sounds and some of us never finish playing around with this feature.

## Assigning Sounds to Software Events

If you have software programs that established sound assignments, you can change the sound.

Scroll through the Events list to find the software program's listings. Then select an event and add a sound or change the sound that's assigned.

Most of the time, you'll find that the software application put its sound files into its own specific folder (for example, Microsoft Office creates a subfolder named Office that is one level below the Media folder that holds the system sounds). The easiest way to find that folder is to select a sound and then choose Browse. The Browse dialog box opens to the folder in which the selected sound file is stored.

You can Browse the software application's sound files or move to the Media subfolder and assign a Windows 98 sound to a software event.

You can also do it the other way around—if there's a really nifty sound that's been provided for a software event, you can use that sound for any Windows 98 event.

Don't go crazy with sounds. If you choose a sound for every possible event in Windows, you'll quickly reach the state where you want to rip your sound card out of your computer (or your neighbor in the next cubicle will do it for you).

# Setting Accessibility Options

The accessibility options were installed in Windows 98 to make computing easier for people with disabilities. However, some of the options are extremely useful for everyone and this Control Panel applet is certainly worth investigating.

Double-click the **Accessibility Options** icon to configure any adjustments you want to make to your system.

Each set of options has a keyboard shortcut to turn the option on and off. To use the keyboard shortcut, choose Settings and select it.

## Keyboard Options

The Keyboard Options tab presents a number of helpful adjustments you can opt to use (see Figure 7.16).

**FIGURE 7.16**

You can adjust the way the keyboard works to make it easier to type.

### StickyKeys

StickyKeys provide a way to press two keys, one at a time, with the same result that occurs if you press both of them at the same time. This is useful for all those Ctrl, Alt, and Shift key combinations if you cannot manage to press two keys at a time.

Just select StickyKeys to turn the feature on. Press the first key (Ctrl, Alt, or Shift) twice. This makes the keystroke "stick." Then press the second key. The effect is the same as if you had held down the first key while pressing the second key.

You can choose Settings if you want to make changes to the way the option works (see Figure 7.17).

**FIGURE 7.17**
You can change any of the options for using StickyKeys in the Settings dialog box.

### FilterKeys

If you are seeing repeated characters because your keypress action is too long, you can use this option to change the sensitivity of the keyboard. Choose **Settings** to test the new sensitivity.

### ToggleKeys

Activate the ToggleKeys option if you want to hear a sound whenever you press the Caps Lock, Num Lock, or Scroll Lock key. You don't have to be physically handicapped to find this option attractive.

## Sound Options

If you're hearing impaired, it may be useful to see a visual clue when your system produces a sound. For example, if a beep sounds on an error, it's a way to know there's a problem.

The Sound Options tab provides some assistance if you can't hear system sounds (see Figure 7.18).

**FIGURE 7.18**

You can receive visual reminders that a sound is being played.

The ShowSounds option is for software programs, and it instructs programs to display text or icons whenever an event occurs that normally produces a sound. Most programs written for Windows 98 can accommodate this request.

## Display Options

If you need to make your screen easier to read, turn to the Display Options tab (see Figure 7.19).

**FIGURE 7.19**

You can choose high contrast colors to make it easier to see individual elements on your screen.

If high contrast colors don't provide the right amount of assistance, choose **Settings** to see other display settings or to design
your own (see Figure 7.20).

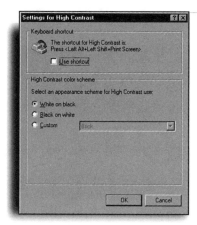

**FIGURE 7.20**

More easy-to-see choices are
offered or you can design your
own color scheme to match
your needs.

## Mouse Options

If using the mouse is difficult, you can use the numeric keypad
to control the mouse pointer. (Take a look at that keypad and
notice that there are arrows on the 4, 8, 6, and 2 keys).

Move to the Mouse tab and select the option to use MouseKeys.
Once MouseKeys are turned on, here's how they work:

- Move the pointer (point) by using the arrow keys on the
  numeric keypad.

  Hold down the **Ctrl** key to move in larger increments.

  Hold down the **Shift** key to move more slowly and precisely.
- Left-click with the 5 key.
- Right-click with minus sign (-).
- Double-click with the plus (+) key.
- Left-drag by following these steps:
  **1.** Point to the object.
  **2.** Press **Ins** (Insert).
  **3.** Use the keypad arrow keys to drag the object.
  **4.** Press **Del** (Delete) to drop the object in the new
     location.

- Right-drag by following these steps:

    **1.** Point to the object.

    **2.** Press the minus sign, and then press Insert (which locks the minus sign key as if you were continuing to hold it down).

    **3.** Use the keypad arrow keys to drag the object.

    **4.** Press **Del** to drop the object.

Personally, I don't think you have to be physically handicapped to find these handy. If you're comfortable with the numeric keypad (which anyone who spends time in accounting software is), you may find that this is better than the mouse.

You can choose Settings on the Mouse tab to customize and configure the way you use MouseKeys (see Figure 7.21).

**FIGURE 7.21**

Configure the way you want MouseKeys to operate.

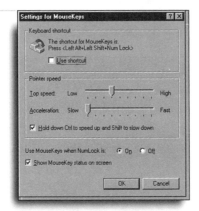

## General Accessibility Settings

If you use any of the accessibility options, you should consider carefully the configuration preferences displayed on the General tab (see Figure 7.22).

The SerialKey device option is used if you are unable to use the standard keyboard and have purchased a special input device. Use the Settings dialog box to install the device onto the appropriate port.

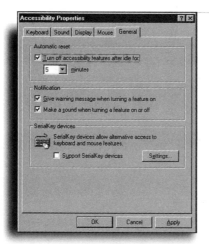

FIGURE 7.22

Complete your accessibility setup by choosing the system options that work best for you.

The Control Panel applets we discussed in this chapter are those that most of us tend to revisit over and over. That's how we continue to tweak our Windows 98 system to make it easier, faster, or more fun to use.

# Personalizing Your Desktop

Configuring desktop specifications

Decorating your desktop

Using a screen saver

Your Windows 98 desktop is your personal workspace, just like your physical desk. The things you keep on it are arranged just so, and "just so" doesn't necessarily mean neat and attractive, it means "just so I can find everything I need."

There's a remarkable mélange of decorative and practical touches you can add to your desktop, and they fall into two categories: the technical settings you establish and the aesthetic taste you exhibit.

New to Windows 98 is a fundamental change in the way the desktop looks and acts. It's called the Active Desktop, and it makes your Windows 98 desktop very much like a Web page. What's terrific about this is that you have a choice; you can use the classic desktop (if you used Windows 95, that's the desktop we call classic) or the Active Desktop.

After you set up the Active Desktop, you can switch between the two desktop styles with a click of the mouse.

In this chapter, we'll discuss the classic Windows desktop.

**SEE ALSO**

➤ *For information about setting up the Active Desktop, see Chapter 19.*

# Configuring Desktop Specifications

Your desktop is displayed as icons on a background and it's all really a bunch of pixels. Pixels are little dots that are placed on your monitor to create the image you see. There are a specific number of pixels arranged in a specific mathematical order. That arrangement is called your video resolution. If you're working at 640×480 (which is pronounced six forty by four eighty), there are 640 pixels if you count from left to right and 480 pixels when you count from the top to the bottom.

## Understanding Screen Resolution

If you increase your resolution to 800×600, it means a lot more pixels are placed on your screen to create the same picture. To fit more pixels on the same size monitor, each pixel has to be a little smaller and a little closer together. That makes each image a bit smaller and a bit sharper (sharper as in "focus"). For example, Figure 8.1 is a desktop at 800×600, and Figure 8.2 is a desktop with a resolution of 1024×768.

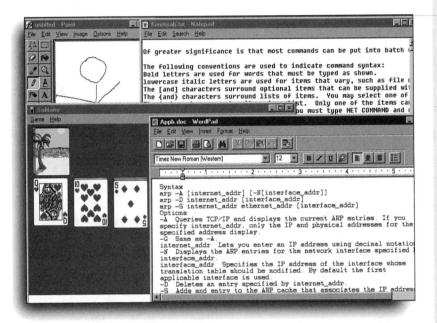

**FIGURE 8.1**

At 800×600, working in multiple windows means a crowded screen with a lot of overlapping.

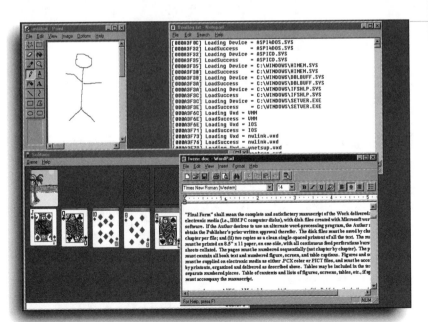

**FIGURE 8.2**

At 1024×768, multiple windows fit on the screen more easily, but the smaller characters might be a problem for your eyesight.

## Changing the Screen Resolution

The level of resolution you can have depends on two things: the capability of your video controller and the sharpness of your own eyesight (as everything gets smaller you may have some problems).

### Quick Change via the Taskbar

The quick way to change the resolution is to click the **Display** icon on the taskbar (if there's one there, if not, stand by and I'll tell you how to put one there). When you click the icon, a pop-up menu appears (see Figure 8.3):

**FIGURE 8.3**

The video controller for this computer doesn't support high resolution above 800×600.

- The resolution and color combinations supported by your video controller are displayed.
- The current selection has a checkmark.

Click a different resolution and your screen goes black for a second, and then reappears with the new settings.

### Using the Display Properties Dialog Box

You can also change the settings in the Display properties dialog box:

#### Changing the settings in the Display Properties box

1. Open the **Display Properties** dialog box using one of these methods:
    - Right-click a blank space on the desktop and choose **Properties** from the shortcut menu.
    - Choose **Settings**, **Control Panel** from the Start menu, and then double-click the **Display** icon.
2. When the Display Properties dialog box opens, move to the Settings tab, which looks like Figure 8.4.

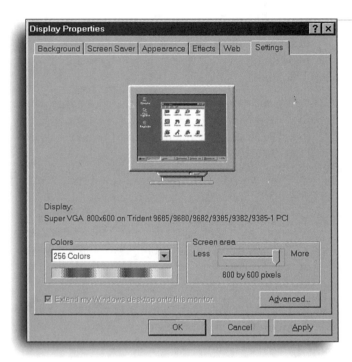

FIGURE 8.4

Technical settings for your video controller are manipulated here.

If you don't know what the possible resolutions are for your video controller, you can open the documentation that came with your computer, or you can do it the easy way—move the slider in the Desktop area portion of the dialog box and see what numbers pop up. Table 8.1 is a brief overview of the four common resolution choices.

**TABLE 8.1   The commonly available screen resolution settings**

| Resolution | Result |
|---|---|
| 640×480 | Normal; works fine if you usually have only one program window open at a time. |
| 800×600 | Smaller images; works well for fitting multiple program windows on your screen. |
| 1024×768 | Like a wide angle lens without the distortion; you can fit much more on your screen (but you need good eyesight). |
| 1280×1024 | The view from the Empire State Building; everything is quite small but you can fit tons of program windows on your screen. You should have an enormous monitor if you are considering this resolution. |

**Don't change laptop resolution**

If you're using Windows 98 on a laptop, you'll probably find that if you increase the resolution you'll lose the edges of your screen. Most laptop displays have no capability to zoom out to see everything when you make things smaller (which is what higher resolution does). That means you'll have to scroll to see anything that's displayed on any of the edges of your screen. This will drive you nuts.

Move the slider slowly, because it's possible that there are several different resolutions available for your video. When you see the resolution you want to try, choose **Apply** (at the bottom of the dialog box).

Apply means you want to make the change but you're not ready to close the dialog box because there are other settings you want to adjust. If the only thing you want to do is change the resolution, choose **OK** instead of **Apply**.

Whether you choose **Apply** or **OK**, a message appears to tell you that Windows is going to resize your desktop. You're warned that you might see some screen flickering for a few seconds and you're reassured that if Windows has a problem doing any of this, it will put everything back the way it was. Press **OK** on the message dialog box to indicate that you're ready for Windows to proceed.

In a few seconds, your desktop is resized and Windows asks if you want to keep the new settings. Answer **Yes** if everything looks good to you.

## Setting the Color Palette

This is another setting that has a range of choices, and the range for some video controllers is narrower than others. It's the number of colors you want to use to display images on your screen. If you do a lot of text-based work, you probably won't see very much difference among the choices. However, if you work in graphics software and do high-end, complicated work such as retouching digital photographs, you need a larger palette.

**You may have fewer choices**

If you have a modern video controller, you may not see the 16-color choice (with all the power on today's video cards, the manufacturers seem to have decided "feh, 16 colors is for wimps"). You may also see two True Color modes, one for 24 bit and another for 32 bit.

There are usually four choices in the color palette list box (click the arrow to the right of the color palette box). The choices are:

- *16 Colors*, which is a bit bland, but fine for text work.
- *256 Colors*, which is more effective if you're doing minor graphics work.
- *High Color*, which is 65,536 colors, which makes all graphics images look real.
- *True Color*, which is 16.7 million colors, probably more than you would ever need.

Now, wait—before you rush to set your system for True Color just to have a nice, jazzy display, there's something else you have to know. It takes a great deal of memory and work for your computer to deliver a lot of colors. You could slow down your system.

To try to protect you, Windows 98 watches what you do when you change any video settings and balances things out for you in an effort to keep your system from crawling along just because you wanted high resolution and lots of colors. You may find that if you choose High Color or True Color, Windows will automatically lower your resolution (if you'd set it for 1024×768 Windows may reset the resolution to 800×600). Or, if you already chose True Color and then reset your resolution to a higher level, Windows may lower your color palette selection.

After you choose **Apply** or **OK** to change your color palette, you may see a message from Windows 98 telling you that the new settings won't take effect until you restart your computer. Here's how to respond to that message:

### Applying a new color palette without restarting Windows 98

   **1.** Choose **Advanced** to open the Advanced Display Properties dialog box (see Figure 8.5).

   **2.** Select **Apply** the changes without restarting.

   **3.** Choose **OK**. Your new color palette is applied to your system.

## Setting Fonts

Also on this General tab is a Font Size selection box. You can change the size and appearance of the fonts in your system and the change affects the titles of icons and menu items.

Click the arrow to the right of the selection box to see the list of font options. You should see Small (which is the default setting) and Large. You may see an additional choice named "Other" depending on your video controller.

Unless you substantially increase the resolution of your Windows 98 system, the default Small font size probably works best. If you make the fonts larger, the titles under your desktop

---

**Restart versus apply now**

Some software programs don't adapt well to a change in the color palette without a restart. That's because they get their settings information from the Registry during startup and are really confused when the settings change after startup.

There are a couple of ways to deal with this problem:

- Make sure there are no software programs open when you make changes.

- If you make changes and then open software that behaves erratically, close the software and restart the computer.

- If you seem to have a number of software programs that really hate it when you change the color palette, select the option to restart the computer before applying your changes.

icons might be too large. This isn't an aesthetic judgment; large fonts make it more difficult to arrange your desktop if you've placed a lot of objects on it because the titles take up a lot more space. (In fact, you may find that if you change your fonts to Large, Windows 98 will resize your desktop to a lower resolution.)

**FIGURE 8.5**
You can decide for yourself how you want Windows 98 to apply color changes.

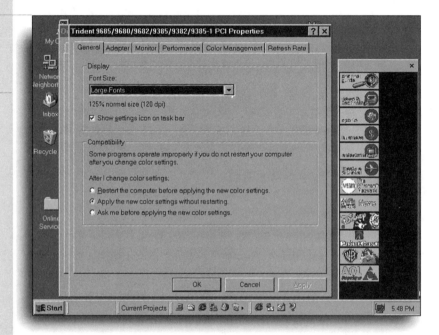

You can experiment with the font choices available in your system to see if you want to change fonts. However, each time you make a change, you'll have to restart your system to see the effect.

## Put a Settings Icon on the Taskbar

Select Show settings icon on taskbar to put the Display settings icon on your taskbar tray, as discussed earlier in this chapter.

# Decorating the Desktop

You can decorate the look of your Windows 98 work area just the way you decorate your office or home. Hang wallpaper, use decorative pictures, place tiles on the desktop, or go in the other direction and create a monochrome minimalist look.

## Using Patterns and Wallpaper

Before you begin decorating, let's understand the terminology:

- A *pattern* is a repeating design element—actually black pixels that sit on top of your desktop, letting the desktop color show through. Use a pattern to add texture to your desktop.

- *Wallpaper* is a graphic image, usually a picture.

### Choosing Wallpaper

We'll start the decorating process by going over the steps for selecting wallpaper:

#### Selecting a wallpaper and modifying it to suit your taste

1. Open the **Display Properties** dialog box, and make sure you're on the **Background** tab (see Figure 8.6).

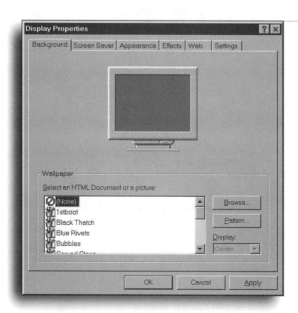

FIGURE 8.6
Keep an eye on the monitor in the dialog box—it previews your design decisions.

2. Scroll through the Wallpaper list and find one you like and select it.

3. Choose the way you want the wallpaper to be displayed on your desktop:

    • **Center** puts the wallpaper graphic in the center of your desktop.

    • **Tile** repeats the wallpaper graphic multiple times, covering the desktop.

    • **Stretch** expands the wallpaper graphic to fill the desktop.

4. If the graphic pattern wallpapers on the list hold no thrill for your sense of decor, try a picture. Choose **Browse** to open a **Browse** dialog box for your Windows folder (the folder where Windows 98 is installed).

5. Scroll through the listings—filenames that have extensions of .gif are pictures (filenames that have extensions of .bmp are the patterns that are on the list).

6. Double-click any picture file of interest and check it out in the preview monitor on the dialog box. If you don't like it, choose **Browse** and try again.

7. When you find the one that's just perfect, select **Center**, **Tile**, or **Stretch** for the display mode.

8. Choose **OK** to place the wallpaper on your desktop and close the dialog box.

9. Choose **Apply** to place the wallpaper on your desktop and keep the dialog box open so you can continue to decorate your desktop.

## Choosing a Pattern

If you decide you'd like to consider a pattern, follow these steps:

### Decorating your wallpaper with patterns

1. Choose **Pattern** to bring up the Pattern dialog box (see Figure 8.7).

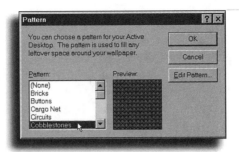

FIGURE 8.7

Select a pattern for an overall desktop decoration.

**2.** Scroll through the Pattern list to find a design that suits your fancy. As you select each pattern, the preview monitor shows you what it will look like on your desktop. When you find the one you like, choose **OK** to return to the Background page.

**3.** Choose **OK** to close the Display Properties dialog box.

## Designing Your Own Patterns and Wallpaper

If you're not wild about anything you see, you can embark on a do-it-yourself decorating project for your desktop.

### Designing a Pattern

The choice of patterns is quite large and there's probably one pattern you saw that contained an element you think you can live with. You can use that pattern as the basis for designing your own pattern. To accomplish this, follow these steps:

**Designing your own pattern for the desktop**

**1.** Select the pattern you sort-of-liked.

**2.** Choose **Edit** to bring up the Pattern Editor (see Figure 8.8). A close-up view of the element that makes up the pattern is displayed, and the overall pattern appears in a Sample box.

**3.** Click any black part of the pattern element to eliminate that pixel. Click any blank part of the pattern element to insert a black pixel.

**4.** If you change your mind, click again to return the pixel to its original state.

**The pecking order of desktop decor**

- Patterns cover desktops (except that the desktop color shows between the dots on the pattern).

- Wallpaper covers patterns. This means if you select wallpaper and either tile it or stretch it, you won't be able to select a pattern (a small wallpaper graphic will be surrounded by a pattern).

FIGURE 8.8

A single element of the all-over pattern can be edited to alter the entire pattern.

**5.** Continue to add and eliminate black pixels until the pattern shape is to your liking.

**6.** To give this pattern a new name, enter the name at the top of the dialog box (in the Name box). Then choose **Add** to add this name to the list of available patterns. Then choose **Done**.

**7.** To keep the changes under the old pattern name, choose **Change**. Then choose **Done**.

If you fail to either rename the pattern or indicate you want to save the changes under the current pattern name, when you choose **Done**, Windows will ask if you want to save the changes to this pattern. Here's how to respond:

- Click **Yes** if you do want to save the changes and keep the pattern name.
- Click **No** if you want to abandon your changes and close the dialog box.
- Click **Cancel** if you want to return to the dialog box and create a new name for your new pattern.

## Creating Your Own Wallpaper

If you don't like any of the pictures in the list of wallpaper, you can't edit them, but you can substitute a picture of your own. That picture has to exist as a file and the file has to be in a format that has an extension of .bmp or .gif.

Perhaps you have a picture of your cat or your sports car, and you'd like to have it in front of you as your work in Windows 98. This is like putting framed pictures on your physical desk.

You can scan a photograph and have your scanner software save it so you can use it for wallpaper. Or, you can download a graphic image from the Internet.

If you're artistic (or even if you're not), you can draw your own picture in a graphics program and use it.

### Creating your own wallpaper from a graphic file

1. In the Wallpaper section of the dialog box, choose **Browse**, which brings up the Browsing for Wallpaper dialog box.

2. By default, the Windows directory is the folder in which the system searches for picture files. If you stored your file in a different folder, change to that folder.

3. Select the file you want to use for wallpaper and choose **OK** (or double-click the filename).

4. Your wallpaper graphic appears in the preview monitor on the dialog box.

5. Choose **Center**, **Tile**, or **Stretch** as the display mode.

6. Choose **OK** to place the graphic on your desktop and close the dialog box (see Figure 8.9). Or choose **Apply** to place the graphic on your desktop and continue to work in the dialog box.

Here are some guidelines for using your own pictures for wallpaper:

- It rarely works well if you try to use your own wallpaper graphic as a tiled image; the pictures aren't usually neat patterns that lend themselves to duplication.

- Most of the scanned pictures I've produced end up as full screen graphics and they fill the desktop. The desktop icons sit on top of the picture and sometimes that's not very attractive. You can use Microsoft Paint to reduce the size of the picture so it fits neatly and attractively on your desktop.

FIGURE 8.9

Here's Pam on a camel; the picture she sent was scanned so I could use it on my desktop.

**SEE ALSO**

➤ *For information on using Microsoft Paint, see Chapter 10.*

## Customizing the Appearance Schemes

You can customize the way all the software windows and dialog boxes look in your Windows 98 system with the Appearance tab (see Figure 8.10).

### Check Out the Existing Schemes

Windows 98 has a bunch of predefined combinations of colors and fonts for the windows and dialog boxes in your system. These combinations are called *schemes*, and you can find all of them in a list that appears when you click the arrow to the right of the Scheme box. As you select a scheme, the preview window on the dialog box changes to show you what that combination will look like.

If the ready-made schemes don't quite do it for you, you can tailor any element in any scheme for yourself. Suppose you just love the lilac hues in the window borders but you think the white font on the title bar is just too, too dull. You can change the title bar—it's easy.

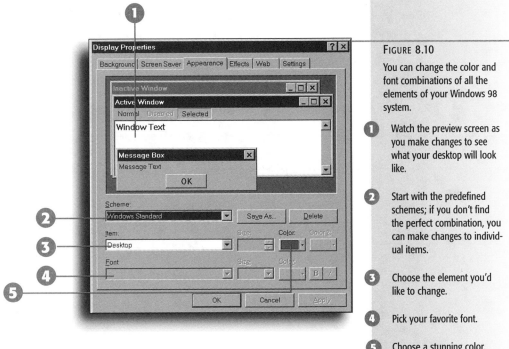

**FIGURE 8.10**

You can change the color and font combinations of all the elements of your Windows 98 system.

1   Watch the preview screen as you make changes to see what your desktop will look like.

2   Start with the predefined schemes; if you don't find the perfect combination, you can make changes to individual items.

3   Choose the element you'd like to change.

4   Pick your favorite font.

5   Choose a stunning color.

## Customize Individual Items in a Scheme

In the Item list, select the element you want to change. Depending on the item you pick, the changes differ. Some items need color, some need fonts, and some need size specifications.

## Make Your Own Scheme

After you select a scheme and change a couple of items to match your own taste, you can save the new combination as a new scheme. Just choose **Save As** and give the scheme a name (a small Save Scheme dialog box opens to accept the name).

## Change the Desktop Color

One of the entries in the Items list is Desktop, and that item is the background for your desktop. The only thing you can change is the color. Even if you're not changing schemes, you may want to get rid of the default desktop color and select something else. Follow these steps to create a new desktop hue:

### Creating a new desktop color

1. Click the arrow to the right of the Color box to see a palette of colors. Click the color you want to use.

2. If there's nothing there that strikes your fancy, choose **Other** to display the Color dialog box (see Figure 8.11).

**FIGURE 8.11**

Drag your mouse through all the color variations to find exactly the shade you want.

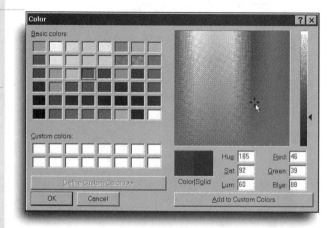

3. In the Color dialog box, press the left mouse button and drag your mouse through the color variations and watch the preview box below the color swatch.

4. When you find a color you like, choose **Add to Custom Colors**. Your color appears in the Custom Colors section of the dialog box.

5. Choose **OK** when you have added one or more new colors to your choices. You're returned to the Display Properties dialog box.

6. Choose **OK** to change the desktop color.

# Using a Screen Saver

Years ago, when computer monitors used phosphorus to create the display, any text that was on the monitor for a long time burned itself into the screen. It was annoying to try to work in a software program when a faint image of the computer's startup menu stayed on the screen like a ghost. The animation in screen savers prevented any image from sitting on the screen long enough to burn in.

Today's monitors don't need screen savers to avoid burn-in, but many people continue to use them. According to my own non-scientific poll, there are three major reasons for using a screen saver:

- Some screen savers are status symbols. The screen savers in this category include scanned pictures (because it proves you can) and techie-looking animated images (for a while, every computer consultant I knew was using "3D Pipes").

- Some screen savers are amusing and they're used as a distraction. Frequently, there are sound effects or musical backgrounds for these screen savers. People who use screen savers for this reason tend to change screen savers often.

- Screen savers can be used for security. Adding password protection to your screen saver means that nobody can get to your computer after the screen saver is displayed.

Screen savers work by timing your time away from the keyboard or mouse. Every time you press a key or click a mouse button, the screen saver starts a countdown. If there are no other key or mouse movements (including moving the mouse without clicking a mouse button) when the countdown ends, the screen saver springs into action, planting itself on your screen. You're the one who decides the length of the countdown.

## Installing a Screen Saver

We'll start by installing a screen saver so your screen is hidden if you stop working for a while (perhaps you walked away from the computer, or you got involved in a lengthy conversation on the telephone or with a visitor).

### Installing a screen saver

1. Open the **Display Properties** dialog box.

2. Move to the **Screen Saver** tab, which looks like Figure 8.12.

**Uh oh, these colors are really messed up**

Sometimes, without realizing it, you may pick text and background colors that are the same, or very close. Then you can't read the text.

Or, you may design a scheme that looked wonderful in the preview box but as you open software windows and dialog boxes, you're learning to hate it, it's making you ill to look at it, and perhaps people who pass your desk make rude noises when they see your screen (or maybe they huddle in the corner, laughing at your screen).

Open the Display Properties dialog box, return to the Appearance tab, and choose **Windows Standard** as the scheme. Everything is back to square one.

FIGURE 8.12

Pick a screen saver name that
sounds as if it has an interesting graphic.

3. Choose a screen saver by clicking the arrow to the right of
   the Screen Saver box and scrolling through the list. As you
   select a screen saver, you can see a miniature preview of its
   graphics (and animation if it's animated) in the preview
   monitor on the dialog box.

4. To see a real preview of the screen saver, choose **Preview**.
   The screen saver fills your screen and remains there until
   you move your mouse, click a mouse button, or press any
   key on the keyboard.

5. Specify the number of minutes you want to pass before the
   screen saver kicks in by entering a number in the **Wait** box.
   You can use the up and down arrows to change the existing
   number or enter a number directly.

6. Choose **OK** to close the dialog box.

The next time there's no mouse or keyboard activity for the period of time you specified, the screen saver will kick in.

# Customizing the Screen Saver

After you've lived with your screen saver for a while, you may decide you'd like to improve its appearance or animation. You can tweak the screen saver by changing the options that control it.

### Configuring your screen saver

1. Open the **Display Properties** dialog box and move to the **Screen Saver** tab.

2. Choose **Settings** to open the screen saver Setup dialog box.

3. Make the changes you desire and choose **OK** to return to the **Display Properties** dialog box.

4. Choose **OK** to close the **Display Properties** dialog box and save your new settings.

The options for screen saver settings are specific to the screen saver. For some screen savers, you can change the colors and texture; others let you change the shape of the elements in the graphic. You can even change the way some screen savers perform their animation effects.

# Adding Password Protection to a Screen Saver

When you password protect a screen saver, using the mouse or keyboard to remove the screen saver no longer returns you to your Windows 98 screen. Instead, a password dialog box appears, and if the correct password isn't entered, the screen saver doesn't leave.

### Adding password protection to a screen saver

1. Open the **Display Properties** dialog box and move to the **Screen Saver** tab.

2. Select the **Password** protected option.

3. Choose **Change** to bring up the **Password** dialog box (see Figure 8.13).

4. Enter your password (you can use up to 14 characters) in the New password box, and then press the Tab key to move to the Confirm new password box and enter it again. You see

an "x" for each character you type; you don't see your password (in case someone is looking over your shoulder). Choose **OK**.

FIGURE **8.13**

Enter a password, then enter it again to confirm it.

**5.** Windows displays a message informing you that your password has been changed successfully and you return to the **Display Properties** dialog box.

**6.** Choose **OK** on the **Display Properties** dialog box to save all your new settings.

After the screen saver has kicked in, mouse or keyboard actions activate the Windows Screen Saver dialog box for passwords instead of returning you to your Windows 98 screen. You have to enter the password to go back to work.

If the password that's entered is incorrect, a message appears to inform you of that fact, and to suggest you try again.

If you ever want to change your password, use steps 3 to 6 to make the changes.

## Using Energy-Saving Techniques Instead of Screen Savers

Instead of having a screen saver kick in after the elapsed time, you can power down your monitor to save electricity. If your monitor is energy compliant, you can use the Screen Saver tab to enable the energy-saving features:

### Using energy-saving features instead of a screen saver

**1.** Choose **Settings** to open the **Power Management Properties** dialog box, which has the **Power Schemes** tab in the foreground (see Figure 8.14).

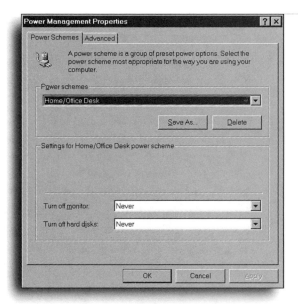

**2.** Click the arrow to the right of the Power schemes box to see the available schemes:

- Home/Office Desk, which has no power saving functions in effect.
- Portable/Laptop, which turns off the monitor after 15 minutes, and turns off the hard drive after 30 minutes.
- Always On, which turns off the monitor after 15 minutes and turns off the hard drive after 1 hour.

**3.** To create your own power scheme, click the arrow to the right of each device to display a list of choices and select the elapsed time for turning off the device.

**4.** Choose **Save As** and give your power scheme a name.

**5.** Choose **OK** to return to the **Display Properties** dialog box.

## Screen Saver on Demand

The elapsed time you specify for having the screen saver kick in shouldn't be too short because it's annoying to have to clear it

> **Always On sounds like a misnomer**
>
> The Always On power scheme doesn't refer to the monitor and hard drive always being on; it's a power saving scheme for computers that are always on. Some of us never turn our computers off, and this scheme is a way to save on energy costs.

when you just stop working for a couple of minutes to think about the work you're engaged in.

On the other hand, if you specify a long interval, leaving your desk means your Windows 98 screen is exposed to all passersby for a long time.

Wouldn't it be great if you could make the screen saver kick in at the exact second you wanted to leave your desk? You can. The way to do it is to create a shortcut key. That key is any letter you select that you press while holding down the Ctrl and Alt keys at the same time. For example, if you choose the letter "s" (for screen saver), when you want to leave your desk and hide your screen while you're gone, you just press Ctrl+Alt+S.

### Creating an on-demand screen saver

1. Open Explorer and select the \Windows\System folder (if the folder where your Windows 98 software is installed is named something other than Windows, substitute that folder name).

2. Find the file for your screen saver. The filename matches the name of the screen saver, and all screen saver files have an extension of .scr.

3. Right-drag the screen saver file to your desktop.

4. When you release the right mouse button, a menu appears. Choose **Create Shortcut(s) Here**.

5. Right-click the new shortcut icon and choose **Properties** from the shortcut menu.

6. When the Properties dialog box opens, move to the Shortcut tab (see Figure 8.15).

7. Place your mouse pointer in the text box labeled Shortcut key.

8. Enter the letter you want to use for your shortcut key. Just enter the letter, you don't have to press Ctrl and Alt. (You can't delete the word "none" that appears in the text box, but as soon as you enter a character, it disappears.)

9. The shortcut key text box displays Ctrl+Alt+your letter.

10. Choose **OK**.

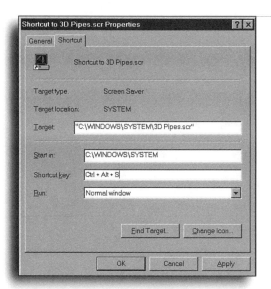

FIGURE **8.15**
Configuring a shortcut is the
same as configuring the file it's
linked to.

Hereafter, when you leave your computer, press the shortcut key
combination and your screen saver will appear instantly. This is
an especially effective security measure if you've password protected your screen saver.

# Tricks and Tips for Using Windows 98 at Home

Creating individual user profiles

Tricks and tips for home computing

# Creating Individual Users

Last year, consumers purchased more computers for home use than television sets. That's rather incredible, considering that just a few years ago a home computer was something only a computer geek would buy.

Home computers are usually shared by all members of the family, and in some households this causes problems. There's nothing worse than getting your desktop set up just the way you like it, only to find it turned upside down the next time you boot up. If you're tired of trying to find your checkbook or word processing program amid the clutter of Junior's game icons, it may be time to set up individual user profiles for each member of the family.

Windows 98 provides a feature called a *user profile* that lets each user have a personalized version of the same computer. Each family member can create his or her own "perfect" desktop. Think of the tension and friction this eliminates!

Before you turn on user profiles, the software that has been installed and the icons that have been placed on the desktop create the default environment. After you enable user profiles, the changes that each user makes (including the software installation) are seen only by that user.

So, if there is a software program that every user in the household will need to access, install it before you begin setting up user profiles. Details about the way all of this works are found in this chapter.

## Turning On the Profiles Feature

The first step is to tell Windows 98 that you want to have individual profiles for each person who uses the computer.

### Turning on Profiles

1. Click the **Start** button and choose **Settings**, **Control Panel** from the **Start** menu.

2. Double-click the **Passwords** icon to open the Passwords Properties dialog box.

3. Move to the User Profiles tab (see Figure 9.1).

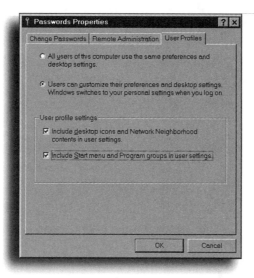

**FIGURE 9.1**
Start by configuring Windows 98 for user profiles.

**4.** Select the second option (Users can customize their preferences), which activates the Settings options.

**5.** If you want desktop icons to be exclusive to each user's settings (and Network Neighborhood if you've networked your home computers together), choose that option.

**6.** If you want the Start menu programs to be specific to each user, select that option.

**7.** Choose **OK**. You see a message telling you that you have to restart your computer to put the new settings into effect. Choose **Yes** to restart.

## Creating Users

When Windows starts again, you're presented with a dialog box that asks you to fill in your username and a password. This is what's called logging on, and the first time each user enters a name and password, that user is created.

### Creating a username and password

**1.** Enter a username. The name you use becomes your official username. You can use a first name, a nickname, your full name, your cat's name, whatever you want.

---

**How exclusive desktops work**

When you opt to have separate desktops, it means that Windows 98 will remember the icons (and their locations) that each user places on the desktop.

**How Program menu items work**

Separate Program menu items means that the software programs that appear on the menu are those installed by the current user. However, if every user needs access to the same software, you don't have to make each user install it—there are some tricks and shortcuts to making anything available to anyone. See the section "Advanced Home Computing" later in this chapter.

2. Enter a password or press the Enter key to have no password. The password you enter becomes your official password. When you enter the password, you won't see what you're typing; the dialog box shows asterisks instead of the characters you enter. After you enter the password, you'll be asked to enter it again to confirm it. If you choose no password, just press **Enter** again.

3. A dialog box tells you that this is the first time you've logged on and asks if you want to retain individual settings for yourself. Answer **Yes**.

Now you're logged on to Windows 98 and any configuration changes you make to the desktop are saved for you. They'll be waiting the next time you log on.

The next time you shut down and restart your computer, the logon dialog box appears again. The name of the last user who logged on is already filled in. Now let another family member create a logon name.

**Creating additional users**

1. Click the User Name box and replace the existing username with this person's username.

2. Follow the previous steps to enter a password and answer the question about retaining individual settings.

The quick way to let everyone in the family establish a username and password is to let each person log on quickly just for the purpose of entering the next person's credentials.

**Logging off without shutting down**

1. Click Start, and then choose Log Off from the Start menu.

2. Choose **Yes** in the log off confirmation dialog box to have Windows 98 display the logon user dialog box without going through a complete shutdown process (see Figure 9.2).

FIGURE 9.2

There's a Log Off option designed especially for changing the current user.

The Log Off menu item is also the way to get to your own desktop if you want to work on the computer and someone else's desktop is on the screen.

## Working with Passwords

You may find it faster to set up each family member quickly by ignoring passwords (use the Log Off option to permit the next user to log on just to install his or her profile). Press the **Enter** key to omit a password as you log on each member of the family. You can establish the passwords later.

If you opt to enter passwords as each person logs on for the first time, changing passwords is quite simple and uses the same procedure as entering a first password for a user who used the **Enter** key to skip a password.

After you've established user profiles, the password settings can be manipulated only for the current logged on user. Each user sets or changes his or her own password.

### Setting the password for the current user

1. Click **Start** and choose **Settings**, **Control Panel** from the **Start** menu.

2. Double-click the Passwords icon in the Control Panel to open the Password Properties dialog box with the Change Passwords tab in the foreground (see Figure 9.3).

3. Choose **Change Windows Password** to see the Change Windows Password dialog box shown in Figure 9.4.

4. Enter your old password (to prove you are who you say you are). If you didn't have a password, use the Tab key to move to the next field.

5. Enter the new password and press the Tab key.

6. Re-enter the new password to confirm it.

7. Choose **OK**.

The next time you log on, this is the password you must enter in the logon dialog box.

**You may be asked about other passwords**

Depending on your computer's configuration, you may see an intermediate dialog box before you see the Change Windows Password dialog box. If so, it means you're being asked if you want to use this new password for other password-protected services such as a network logon.

If you are logging on to a network, you should say **Yes**. It's confusing to try to maintain two separate passwords.

**Understanding security**

Windows 98 has absolutely no security, so using passwords is really unnecessary. Once anyone understands how the file system is set up, he or she can make changes to your desktop. The only thing another user cannot do if you use a password is log on in your name and change the password.

If you need real security, you'll have to use Windows NT 4.

**FIGURE 9.3**

You can enter a new password, either as a first password or to change an existing password.

**FIGURE 9.4**

Just follow the instructions to effect your password changes.

## Forget Your Password?

Another advantage of the lack of security is the ability to use the computer even if you forget the password.

To skip the password entry, when the logon dialog box appears, choose **Cancel** (or press **Esc**). The default desktop configuration greets you.

Of course, you don't want to leave it that way; you need your password so you can find your own personalized desktop. There's no way to get Windows 98 to show you your password, but you can eliminate any record of it. Then, the next time you log on, you'll be asked to provide a new password (as if you were logging on for the first time).

## Removing your password

**1.** Open Explorer and move to the folder that holds your Windows 98 software (usually called Windows).

**2.** Scroll through the file listings looking for a file that contains all or part of your username. The file you're looking for has an extension of .pwl (see Figure 9.5). You may not find a file that matches the name you use when you log on because Windows truncates that name to eight letters (it ignores spaces).

**FIGURE 9.5**
This user logs on as Bruce Hallberg, but the password filename is truncated.

**3.** Select the file and delete it (press the Del key, or right-click on the filename and choose **Delete**). Confirm the fact that you want to delete this file.

**4.** Close Explorer and choose **Log Off** from the **Start** menu.

**5.** The logon dialog box returns; your name is in the username field as the last logged-on user.

**6.** Enter a new password in the password text box.

**7.** Confirm the new password in the confirmation box that appears.

Your desktop is back! Everything is exactly the way it was except you have a new password.

## Understanding the Default Desktop

After you enable user profiles, the first time each user logs on to the computer, here's what is waiting:

- All the configuration of the desktop that was performed by any users before you enabled user profiles was saved by Windows 98 as the default desktop.
- All the programs that were installed prior to enabling user profiles are on the Programs menu.
- Each user can change the desktop configuration at will, and the configuration is saved in that person's profile.

Change colors, move icons, delete shortcuts, add shortcuts—mess around with the desktop to your heart's content. It doesn't matter how awful everyone else thinks your decorative efforts are; they'll never see it. The desktop you design appears only when you log on.

**SEE ALSO**
➤ *Learn all about customizing the desktop in Chapter 8.*

## Working with Software

As I mentioned, all the software programs that were listed on the Programs menu before user profiles were enabled are available to all users.

After user profiles are enabled, the user who installs a software program finds that program listed on the Programs menu. No other user sees that listing; the installation belongs to the user who installed it. This has some advantages and disadvantages.

On the upside:

- A parent can install a bookkeeping program for the household bills and the kids won't have that program on their Programs menu.
- The young folks can install their games and parents won't have to wade through all those listings on the Programs menu.

On the downside:

- If a user wants to use the software installed by another user, there are some procedures involved to make the software available. Don't worry—you don't have to install the same software over and over again for each user.

Remember that even though a user may not have a software program listed on his or her Start menu doesn't mean it's inaccessible. Because of the lack of security features in Windows 98, you can't prevent any user from launching software from Explorer or My Computer.

And therein lies the solution for giving access to software to other users. Any user who needs software that isn't on his or her Programs menu can create a desktop shortcut to the program.

### Creating a desktop shortcut

1. Open Explorer and find the program file for the software.
2. Right-drag the file to the desktop.
3. Choose **Create Shortcut(s) Here** from the menu that appears after you release the mouse button.

(There's also a way to put the software on the Start menu and we'll go over that in "Tips and Tricks for Home Computing," the next section of this chapter.)

# Tips and Tricks for Home Computing

There are some potential problems faced by many families when a computer is installed in the home.

The most common headache is the one caused by access demands: Who gets use of the computer when, and for how long. Good luck; there's nothing I can tell you. Depending on the dynamics of your family, you'll either work it out or live with constant complaints.

However, when it comes to the issues of productivity and privacy, I can offer some assistance.

## Keeping Documents Private

**Microsoft software works differently**

If you're using any of the Microsoft Office applications (Word, Excel, and so on), there's no password protection check box on the Save As dialog box. Choose Options on the Save As dialog box to see the choices for protecting document privacy.

Even though Windows 98 has no real security, almost all of the software written for Windows has a security feature that you can use to keep other people from viewing the data documents you create. Usually the feature is called Password Protection, but some software uses the term File Locking.

Most of the time the option to password protect is on the Save As dialog box. The first time you save a file, you see the Save As dialog box. If the file has been saved without password protection, choose Save As from the File menu and look for the password protection option (see Figure 9.6).

**FIGURE 9.6**

When you save a file in your Windows software, look for the Password Protection selection box.

**Don't create chaos with passwords**

If you are password protecting documents, use the same password for every document. Otherwise, you'll find you can't open your own data. I've never met anyone who worked out a scheme for using different passwords on each document who made it work. In fact, it's not a bad idea to use your logon password for document passwords.

After you opt for password protection, you'll be asked to enter a password (in fact, you'll probably be asked to enter a password, and then re-enter it to confirm it).

Then, when you (or anyone else) tries to open the file, a password text box is presented (see Figure 9.7). Without entering the correct password, there's no access.

FIGURE 9.7
You can't open this document
without knowing the password.

## Keeping Documents from Being Changed

If you have a document you use as a boilerplate or a template
that's been configured to a state of perfection, you may want to
let other family members use it. However, you probably won't
want to permit anyone to change it. You can prevent alterations
by making the file read-only. (Read Only is one of the attributes
available for all files.)

Some Windows software lets you perform this action right in the
software. It offers a Properties choice and you can select Read
Only (for example, WordPerfect provides this capability).

Other Windows software programs (those from Microsoft, for
example) do not provide the capability to change attributes in
the software. Instead, you must change attributes in Explorer.

### Setting a file's attributes to read-only in Explorer

1. Open Explorer and find the file you want to protect from
   changes.

2. Right-click on the file listing and choose **Properties** from
   the shortcut menu.

3. Select Read Only as an attribute (see Figure 9.8). Then
   click **OK**.

Hereafter, if anyone tries to save this file, an error message
appears. Most software will also automatically offer the Save As
dialog box and tell the user that the only way to save this document is under a different filename.

Don't forget that even you can't save your read-only documents
if you want to make changes to them.

**Warning!**

You can't change the attributes
of a file that's in use. If it occurs
to you to make a document
read-only, be sure to save the
document and close it. If it's
loaded in the software window,
you can't make changes to its
properties.

FIGURE 9.8

Make a file non-changeable by changing its attributes to include read-only.

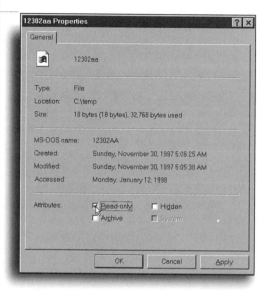

### Making changes to read-only documents

1. Remove the read-only attribute.

2. Open the file in its associated software.

3. Make changes.

4. Save the document and reinstate the read-only attribute if the software permits it. Otherwise, clear the document from the software window and use Explorer to make it read-only.

You're not restricted to documents; you can make templates or other types of files unchangeable by applying the read-only attribute.

## Controlling All the Desktops

**Use My Computer instead of Explorer**

For this example, I'm using My Computer instead of the Windows Explorer. That's because the default view of My Computer is folders and I can open multiple folders and move objects between folders. The default hierarchical view of Explorer makes this more complicated.

Again, the lack of security in Windows 98 makes it possible to manipulate all the desktops in the system, not just your own. I guess that's both good and bad (depending on whether you're the manipulator or the "manipulatee").

When you enabled user profiles, some new folders were created in your system to handle the individual user configurations. You can change the objects in these folders in order to change the desktops. Let's look at what's going on in your system.

### Viewing all profiles

1. Open My Computer and double-click on your hard drive to open it.

2. Open the folder that holds your Windows 98 files (usually it's named Windows).

3. Open the folder named **Profiles**. The folder was created when you enabled user profiles and it contains a folder for each user who has ever logged on to the computer (see Figure 9.9).

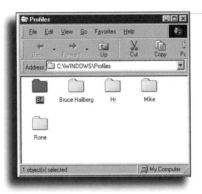

**FIGURE 9.9**
The subfolders in the Profiles folder act like a user list for this computer.

You can open each profile and change the settings that were established by the user who owns the profile. Now, this is not necessarily a nefarious act; it can be an efficient way to make sure that each user has a desktop shortcut to specific software programs.

Each user profile folder contains several subfolders and a file named User.dat, which is the Registry information for that user and should never be touched (see Figure 9.10).

There may be other objects, but these should appear consistently in all profile folders.

FIGURE 9.10

User profiles have subfolders that hold information about the user's activities and preferences.

### Adding shortcuts to multiple desktops

1. Open the Desktop folder for the user who has that program shortcut on the desktop. If no user has one, open Explorer and create a program shortcut on the current desktop (you'll use it to make the copies you need).

2. Right-click the program shortcut and choose **Copy** from the shortcut menu.

3. Right-click the **Desktop** folder of the user who needs this shortcut on his/her desktop. Choose **Paste** from the shortcut menu. You don't have to open the Desktop folder to paste an object in it.

4. Right-click the Desktop folder of the next user who should have this shortcut. Choose **Paste** from the shortcut menu.

5. Continue to add the desktop shortcut to any additional users who need it.

The next time each of these users logs on to the computer, the desktop shortcut will be available.

You can, of course, remove any desktop shortcuts from a user's Desktop folder. Usually you'll do this only if the default desktop that each user started with had shortcuts that shouldn't have been there. If you remove a desktop shortcut that the user created, that user will probably put it back (he or she obviously knows how to).

**Paste can be repeated multiple times**

Once you've placed something on the Clipboard, you can paste it as many times as you want. The Paste command works with the same object until you either change the contents of the Clipboard (by selecting another object or text and choosing Cut or Copy) or shut down Windows.

# Controlling All the Start Menus

You can accomplish the same thing (add and remove items) with any user's Start menu. The Start menu folder inside a user's profile folder really doesn't represent the entire Start menu the user sees after clicking the Start button. It contains only the Programs Menu folder and also contains any items that have been added to the top of the Start menu (see Figure 9.11).

**FIGURE 9.11**

A user's Start menu folder contains a subfolder for the Programs menu and objects representing menu items that have been added to the top of the Start menu.

The first thing to understand is that the items on the Programs menu are nothing but shortcuts. Open the Programs folder to see what's on this user's Programs menu (see Figure 9.12).

**FIGURE 9.12**

The Programs subfolder contains objects that represent the listings on the user's Programs menu. Subfolders indicate listings that have additional cascading menus.

You can place program shortcuts in any user's Programs folder and that user will see a new listing on the Programs menu.

**Placing shortcuts in other users' programs menus**

1. Find or create a shortcut to the program (you can use a desktop shortcut from another user, an existing program listing from another user's Programs menu folder, or create the shortcut yourself).

2. Right-click on the shortcut and choose **Copy** from the shortcut menu.

3. Right-click on the **Programs** folder in the target user's Start Menu folder and choose **Paste** to place the listing on the Programs menu. You don't have to open the Programs folder to paste an object in it.

That's all there is to it. The item will appear on the user's Programs menu the next time the user logs on.

Notice that some of the objects in the Programs folder are subfolders. These represent the program groups on the menu—those items with arrows that lead to cascading menus.

If you want to place a shortcut on one of those cascading menus, paste the shortcut on that subfolder. You could also create a new folder in the Programs folder and place shortcuts in it. The Programs menu would reflect that new group and the shortcut would be on its cascading menu.

## Controlling Internet Access

The issues of email and Web crawling can become major points of contention with a home computer. The amount of time spent on the Internet, the privacy of email, and the megabytes added to the hard drive from downloads and browser caches are all of concern.

### Email on Home Computers

A family email address is the most convenient approach to electronic communications. Unfortunately, when the children reach a certain age, it can also become a source of unending grief. The issue, of course, is privacy. The solution is separate mailboxes.

If you use an Internet service provider (ISP) for email, you'll probably have to pay an additional fee for each additional mailbox. However, there are two well-known Internet services that provide multiple mailboxes as part of the basic service:

- America Online (AOL), which has free software you can download from **http://www.aol.com**. You can have five email accounts on AOL.

- IBM Net, which also provides free software you can download. They're at **http://www.ibm.com**. You can have six email accounts on IBM Net.

Both AOL and IBM also provide parental control features, which lets you set up Internet accounts for children that limit the places they can visit on the Internet.

## Downloading Files from the Internet

Downloading files from Internet sites presents two potential dangers to your home computer:

- Virus programs that are sometimes attached to files available from download sites can infect your computer.

  Make sure you download files from sources you can trust. And get a good virus checker (search the Internet for anti-virus software or purchase a program).

- Your hard drive can fill up rapidly as you continue to download files without deleting those that were previously downloaded.

  Only use downloaded software that you really have a need for. After you've examined other downloads, remove them if you're not going to use them.

  Limit the number of multimedia files you download; these tend to be real disk space hogs.

If you use the Net for gathering information, almost every page on every site can be printed (you may not get all the graphics, but you'll get the information). This is better than downloading everything you see.

**Do some ISP homework**

There may be other services that permit multiple accounts, and you should do some research. You can buy computer magazines or search the Internet for information and comparison studies. One popular magazine, *PC World*, reviewed national ISPs recently and rated them in groups of Best, Good, Fair, Poor, and Worst. Incidentally, IBM was Best and AOL was Worst. However, the reasons for that may not match your reasons for joining, so you should check the criteria.

# Sharing a Printer with Two Computers

If you have a two-computer household and the computers are in the same room, you can share a printer between the computers. The device for sharing is known as a switch box, and you can buy an intelligent switch box or a dumb (manual) switch box.

## Intelligent Switch Boxes

Intelligent switch boxes are expensive (a couple of hundred dollars, and usually that includes cable) and they work by connecting to both computers on one side of the box, and connecting to the printer on the other side of the box. When the box senses data coming from one of the computers, it connects that computer to the printer. If the other computer sends data, it has to wait until the first print job is finished.

The advantage to an intelligent switch box is that the computers can be separated by a greater distance and you can put the switch box anywhere because you never need to touch it.

## Dumb Switch Boxes

Dumb switch boxes usually cost less than $30.00. You also have to buy special cable for the two connections between the computer and the box, which will probably double the price (the cable between the box and the printer is standard printer cable). They are hooked up in the same manner, but switching between computers is performed manually. There's a button that moves from A to B. When computer A needs to print, switch the button to A.

The disadvantage of the dumb switch box is that you have to keep the computers close together (with the box in the middle) so that either user can reach the box. You also have to remember to switch the setting before you begin printing.

The money you spend for either device is less than buying a second printer and maintaining it (toner, print heads, ink cartridges, and so on can add up to real money).

There are similar devices for serial peripherals, which means you can share an external modem between two computers.

# Networking Multiple Computers

If you connect two or more computers together in a Windows 98 network, all the computers can share all the peripherals, including printers, CD-ROM drives, and large removable drives such as Jaz or Zip drives. In addition, you can share files or move files between computers without transferring them to floppy disk and walking them to the other computer.

The computers don't have to be in the same room, or even on the same floor.

Network kits are available at most computer stores, and all you need is a Network Interface Card (NIC) for each computer and sufficient lengths of cable to connect everything.

The instructions for the physical installation usually come with the kit (or ask an expert for a bit of help). The cost should be less than $300 for a basic two-computer kit. The NICs are under $100.00, and cable is about $.25/foot for both 10BaseT (which looks like telephone wire) or 10Base2 (which is thin coaxial cable). It's easier to run 10BaseT through the house (although I have three floors of my house wired with coax and I found plenty of clear chases to get to all the rooms I wanted to).

The Windows 98 setup for Networking is performed through the Control Panel by using the Network icon. There's more information about networking with Windows 98 in Chapter 21.

Having a computer at home is fun, and it's becoming a necessity. In fact, if you have an older computer and are considering moving up, a second computer is probably a better investment than that super-large-screen television you were thinking about (I mean, after all, do you really need to see each sweat globule on that right guard's face)?

# Working with Software

# Using Pre-Installed Accessories

Games for fun and relaxation

Notepad and WordPad

Paint for graphics designing

HyperTerminal and Telnet for special modem connections

Multimedia for more fun

# Introducing the Fun and Utilities– Accessories

Windows 98 is chock-full of programs in addition to the files that are necessary to run your computer. These programs provide entertainment, utilities, and tools, some of which you'll learn to love and rely on.

### Starting the accessories

1. Click the **Start** button.

2. On the **Start** menu, move your mouse pointer to **Programs**.

3. On the **Programs** menu, move your mouse pointer to **Accessories** (see Figure 10.1).

FIGURE 10.1

Your Accessories menu may have different programs depending on your installation decisions.

Some of the menu items on the Accessories menu have arrows; those items are folders. Placing your mouse pointer on a folder displays a submenu that lists the programs in that folder.

# Windows 98 Games

Let's begin with the most important accessories, the games. Think of these programs as therapy, because after all, sitting in front of a computer for long periods of time is mentally and physically exhausting. These games are absolutely necessary for keeping your equilibrium and mental health (are you buying this? will your boss?).

All the Windows 98 games are contained in the Games folder on the Accessories menu (see Figure 10.2).

**FIGURE 10.2**

The games you installed are listed on the Games folder menu.

We won't go over all the rules and the how-to-play, but I'll give you an overview of the important stuff for each game in this section.

## FreeCell

When you first open FreeCell, there's nothing much in the game window. To get a game started, choose **Game**, **New Game** from the menu bar. This puts the FreeCell deck on the game window (see Figure 10.3).

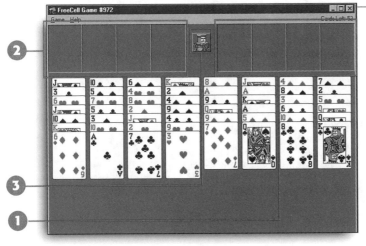

**FIGURE 10.3**

All 52 cards are waiting for you to move them into the home cells.

**1** Home cells only accept cards in ascending order, so you have to start with an Ace.

**2** Free cells hold any card you need to dump, but one card to a cell please.

**3** The King follows your mouse as you move along the cells— it's eerie.

The first time I started a FreeCell game I thought the programmers at Microsoft had all lived through distorted childhoods and didn't really understand how Solitaire was supposed to work. It looked like I'd come in on the middle of a Solitaire game that was being played by an illiterate lunatic.

The game isn't difficult to play, it's just a matter of learning to think several steps ahead: If I do this, can I still do that? Here are some guidelines I've found to be helpful:

- Try not to use up a free cell unless removing that card reveals a card you can move to another column (or to a home cell).

- Piling up one suit in a home cell in an unbalanced fashion will probably impair your ability to move cards between columns.

- Unless all the Kings are near the tops of columns, try to use strategies that empty columns.

## Hearts

The classic game of Hearts is always fun to play, and if you're on a network, you can play against other users across the network (see Figure 10.4).

**FIGURE 10.4**

If you can't find four players on the network, Hearts will fill in the missing seats.

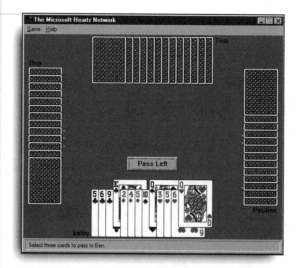

The opening window asks how you want to play, and here are the guidelines for answering:

- If you're not playing on a network (or nobody else on the network wants to play with you), tell the opening Hearts window that you want to be the dealer. Then press F2 to start playing.

- If you're initiating a network game, tell the opening Hearts window that you want to be the dealer, then sit back and wait for the other players to join in.

- If you're on a network and want to play (assuming somebody has started the game), tell the opening Hearts window that you want to join an existing game. You'll be taken to the game that was opened by the network dealer.

There's really only one hint for strategy in Hearts: If you start getting hearts or the Queen of Spades, make an aggressive effort to take all the hearts.

## Minesweeper

This game is more luck than strategy (although I know people who argue with that point of view.) You just try to expose as many squares as you can without blowing yourself up (see Figure 10.5).

**FIGURE 10.5**
When I get this close I get the feeling that my luck can't hold, and I'm waiting for a major explosion.

The only tip I can offer is that when you uncover a square that has a 3 or a 4 in it, and there are hardly any squares left except those near that square, close your eyes and click randomly—it's probably all over for you.

## Solitaire

This is a Windows classic, of course (see Figure 10.6). The game is easy and fun (and addictive to a great many people).

FIGURE 10.6
On my way to another victory!

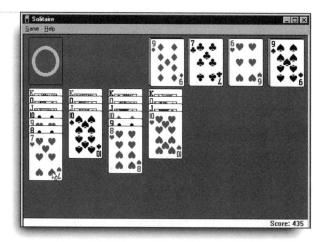

There are a couple of things you might want to consider about Solitaire. First, this is the best way to get a new user comfortable with a mouse. The game involves clicking, dragging, and double-clicking (don't drag cards to the pile, double-click to place them there). Trainers use Solitaire for mouse training all the time.

To add more excitement to the game, play it for points. Here are the games rules that the folks in my office invented:

- You give up 50 points (that's minus 50) points when the cards are first dealt.
- Each card that lands on the pile is worth 5 points.
- Each time you start from the top of the deck again, you lose a point.

## Notepad

Notepad is a *text editor*. A text editor is like a word processor, but it works with files that are composed of plain text.

This is a quick and easy tool for creating small text files. You'll find it very useful if you have to send a quick note to somebody, either via a printed copy, a floppy disk, or e-mail. Because all word processors can handle a text file (and because almost everybody you know will probably also have Notepad or another text editor), this is the universal editor.

If you see a small file with a .txt extension (such as a file named Readme.txt that is part of a software program), double-click the file in Explorer and Notepad will open automatically with that file in the window (see Figure 10.7).

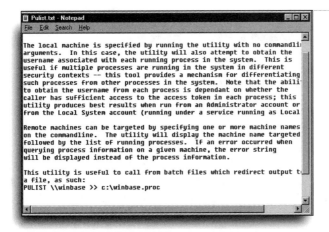

FIGURE 10.7

Text files are on your screen in a couple of seconds with quick-loading Notepad.

However, Notepad can't handle large files (anything over 50KB), and if the file you try to open is too large for Notepad, Windows 98 displays the following error message:

```
This file is too large for Notepad to open.
```

```
Would you like to use WordPad to read this file?
```

Say Yes to open WordPad or No to open Notepad without a document (you can close Notepad and use a word processor instead). WordPad is discussed in the next section.

Incidentally, I've also seen a different error message when users try to load a large text file into Notepad:

```
Not enough memory available to complete this operation.
```

```
Quit one or more applications to increase available memory,
and then try again.
```

If you receive this error message, don't bother closing applications or worrying about the amount of memory you have; the error message is specious and really means "This file is too large for Notepad to open. Would you like to use WordPad to read this file?"

I'm not really sure why that error message occurs occasionally, and the only clue I have is that it seems to occur only in computers that upgraded to Windows 98 from Windows 3.*x*. But, it certainly doesn't occur in all Windows 3.*x* to Windows 98 conversions. It's one of those little mysteries that computer users have to live with.

## Notepad Editing Tools

Even though this isn't a full-fledged word processor, some of the tools that you expect to find in a word processor (and couldn't work without) are available in Notepad. For example, on the Edit menu you'll find the following:

- Cut and Copy, which places any text you've selected onto the Windows 98 Clipboard.

- Paste, which places any text on the Clipboard at the Insertion Point in your document.

- Automatic insertion of time/date in the format HH:MM AM/PM MM/DD/YY (use F5 for a shortcut key).

- Undo, which only tracks your last edit.

## Notepad Word Wrap

There's another command on the Edit menu that is unique to Notepad: Word wrap. It exists because Notepad doesn't automatically wrap the text you load (or type) so you can see it in your window. Until you choose Word wrap, text just keeps going past the right edge of the window.

However, this doesn't change the printed output of your document. When you print, the word wrap matches the margins established in the Page Setup dialog box (choose **File**, **Page Setup** from the menu bar to see it). This is NOT What You See Is What You Get.

# Printing in Notepad

Another unique thing is the way Notepad prints. It just prints. There's no Print dialog box, you cannot choose a printer (the Windows 98 default printer is chosen automatically), you just choose Print from the File menu and there's nothing else you can do.

# One File at a Time in Notepad

Because it's not a full-fledged word processor, Notepad doesn't know about multiple windows. Instead, it swaps one file for another:

- To open a new file, choose **File**, **Open**. If the current file has not been saved, you'll be given an opportunity to save it. When you select the new file from the Open dialog box, it replaces the current file.
- To start a new document, choose **File**, **New**. If the current file has not been saved you'll be given an opportunity to save it.
- There is no File, Close command.

# Notepad Log Files

There is a very clever feature in Notepad that makes it ideal for keeping a log or diary. Once you've established your log document, every time you open it Notepad inserts the current time and date. Just type your notes and save the file.

### Creating a log file

1. Open Notepad. If Notepad is already open, choose **File**, **New**.
2. Enter **.LOG** as the first characters in the document. Don't forget the period, and don't enter anything (not even a space) before this entry.
3. Save the document using any filename you want. Notepad automatically adds the extension .txt to the filename.

Whenever you open this document, the current time and date appears on the next available line. Your insertion point is waiting on the line below the time/date entry.

# WordPad

WordPad is what Notepad would be after a couple of months at the gym and intensive vitamin therapy. You can use WordPad for text files and text file functions, but there are far more features and options to play with (see Figure 10.8):

- Toolbars and a ruler are available.
- You can load and save documents that are formatted for text, Rich Text Format (RTF), Microsoft Write, or Microsoft Word.
- You can format text for Bold, Italic, Bold/Italic, and color.
- You have a full selection of fonts.
- You can use bullets (and customize the bullets).
- You can insert objects such as pictures.
- The Print dialog box controls printing so you can change printers or options.
- Automatic time/date insertion is available.

There are two important similarities between WordPad and Notepad:

- You can only load one document at a time.
- There is no automatic word wrap in the WordPad window.

**WordPad Word wrap is a permanent option setting**

Unlike Notepad, which requires you to reset the word wrap option with each session, you can establish permanent word wrap settings in WordPad. Use the Options command on the View menu to get to the settings. You can set specific word wrap options for each type of document format. The word wrap options are a choice among none, wrap to window, and wrap to ruler settings.

**FIGURE 10.8**
The WordPad window looks very much like a word processor.

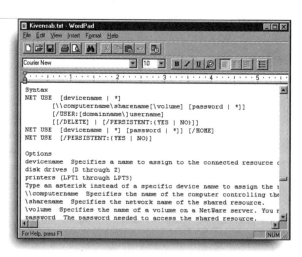

# Paint

If you have more artistic talent than I do (okay, your cat has more artistic talent than I do), you'll love Paint even more than I do. It's fun and it's extremely easy to use (see Figure 10.9).

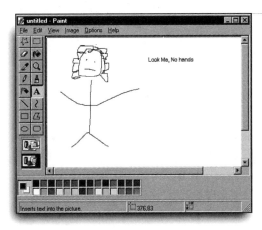

FIGURE 10.9

Paint is an artist in a box, providing plenty of tools for aspiring (and perspiring) artists.

The drawing tools on the left side of the Paint window are like specialized paint brushes. In fact, your mouse pointer changes to reflect the type of tool you selected. There's even a spray can for airbrushing.

The color swatches on the bottom of the window are for selecting foreground and background colors for your masterpiece. Click a color with the left mouse button to select that color for the foreground. Click with the right mouse button to indicate you want to use that color for the background.

One of the neat things you can do with paint is design your own wallpaper and then use your magnum opus on your desktop. After you save the file choose **File, Set as Wallpaper** (you can choose Tiled or Centered). Your wallpaper is placed on your desktop immediately.

SEE ALSO

➤ *Information about creating and using wallpaper is in Chapter 8.*

Warning

If you have to edit a document that absolutely, positively will not have any characters that aren't pure ASCII text (such as your autoexec.bat or config.sys files), use a text editor for absolute safety. Open a command prompt and enter **edit** **filename** to launch the editor. Or, try Notepad, which is less likely to insert any control characters. It's not a good idea to trust important text files to WordPad.

# Using HyperTerminal

HyperTerminal is a communications program that lets your computer connect directly to another computer. That other computer can be a Bulletin Board Service (BBS), an Internet service such as CompuServe or MCI Mail, or another individual computer.

Because, like most people, I use Windows 98 Dial-Up Networking for my Internet connections, I use HyperTerminal to exchange messages and text files with other users. The two computers connect and we exchange the files.

## Configuring HyperTerminal to Dial Another Computer

To use HyperTerminal for this handy function, you have to configure a connection, which is a simple matter. A wizard walks you through all the processes.

### Dialing another computer

1. Double-click the Hypertrm.exe icon in the HyperTerminal window.

2. Enter a name for the connection you're creating and choose an icon for it.

3. Enter the phone number you dial to reach the host computer.

4. In the next wizard window, choose **Modify** to open the **Properties** dialog box for this connection.

5. Move to the **Settings** tab and choose **ASCII setup** to establish the settings for entering text (see Figure 10.10).

6. Select **Send line ends with line feeds** to make sure new lines include a return.

7. Select **Echo typed characters locally** so you can see what you're typing (otherwise, the user on the receiving computer is the only one to see your characters).

8. Click **OK** twice to return to the HyperTerminal window, which displays your new connection.

FIGURE 10.10
ASCII settings determine how
the text looks when you're
sending text with
HyperTerminal.

**9.** Choose Dial to make the connection immediately, or choose
Cancel if you're not ready to dial out.

**10.** When you exit HyperTerminal you'll be asked if you want to
save this connection. Answer Yes.

The new connection now has its own icon in the HyperTerminal
window. Double-click it whenever you want to dial that computer.

## Configuring HyperTerminal to Receive a Connection

Just as you can call another person's computer, you'll probably
want other people to be able to dial you. In order to answer the
call, you have to establish settings.

### Establishing settings for HyperTerminal

**1.** Double-click the Hypertrm.exe icon in the HyperTerminal
window.

**2.** Name the new connection. Use a name that indicates that
this configuration is for answering calls (Answering Calls
strikes me as an appropriate name).

**3.** In the next window enter your own phone number. Actually,
you can enter any series of numbers you want to; the only
reason you're entering anything is that HyperTerminal will
not permit you to leave this field blank.

**4.** In the next wizard screen, choose **Modify** and move to the
**Settings** tab of the dialog box that appears.

**5.** Choose **ASCII Setup** and make the same selections as noted
for dialing out.

**6.** Click **OK** twice to return to the HyperTerminal window, which displays your new connection.

**7.** If you choose **Dial**, you'll get a busy signal (and you'll know the connection works). Choose **Cancel**.

**8.** Save the connection when you exit HyperTerminal.

## Making a HyperTerminal Connection

If you're dialing out to another computer, double-click the connection for that computer and choose **Dial** from the **Connect** dialog box.

If you're receiving a call from another computer, double-click the connection you configured for answering calls. When the **Connect** dialog box appears, choose **Cancel**.

### Starting communication

**1.** If you're dialing out, there will be some squawking noises from your modem. Then you should see a message from HyperTerminal indicating that a connection has been made.

**2.** If you're receiving a call, you'll hear the phone ring. You may see the words RING RING on your HyperTerminal window, or you see your modem's Answer light go on (or both). Enter **ata** in the HyperTerminal window. The modem will squawk, then you'll see a message indicating a connection has been made.

**3.** Type a note to the other person (Hi, hello).

**4.** Hopefully the other person is polite enough to answer (Hello to you too).

**5.** Type back and forth until your fingers are tired. To end the call, click the **Disconnect** icon on the toolbar or choose **Call**, **Disconnect** from the menu bar.

As you continue to type back and forth you'll both realize it would be far more productive to have conversations via voice. Almost everyone can speak faster than they type. Chatting is not a great reason to establish a HyperTerminal connection.

What is a good reason is the exchange of files, although you can "chat" to inform each other that a file is about to be exchanged.

# Exchanging Files with HyperTerminal

### Exchanging files with another user

1.  To send a file to the other computer, choose **Transfer**, **Send File** from the menu bar.

2.  To receive a file from the other computer, choose **Transfer**, **Receive File** from the menu bar.

3.  If you are sending a file, the **Send File** dialog box opens (see Figure 10.11). Enter the name of the file (and its path) or choose Browse to move through the folders on your computer to find the file you want to send.

**FIGURE 10.11**

Usually you'll need to use the Browse button, because most of us don't remember the full path and file name of every file in the system.

4.  Select a file transfer protocol. Click the arrow to the right of the Protocol box to see the choices. Usually choosing Zmodem works best. You and the receiver must select the same protocol.

5.  Choose **Send** to send the file.

6.  If you're receiving a file, choose **Transfer**, **Receive File** from the menu bar to bring up the **Receive File** dialog box (see Figure 10.12).

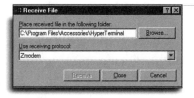

**FIGURE 10.12**

You probably don't want to save this file in your HyperTerminal folder.

7.  Choose **Browse** to move to the folder in which you want to receive this file.

8.  Pick a protocol to match the sender's protocol.

9.  Choose **Receive**.

Whether you are sending or receiving, a dialog box opens so you can watch the progress of the file transfer. When the transfer is complete, you can send or receive additional files. Disconnect when you're finished (don't forget to type a good-bye to be polite).

# Telnet

Telnet is usually used to connect to a UNIX host system and it lets you use the UNIX operating system while you're connected.

If you don't have to dial in to UNIX systems (and very few PC users do), don't stop reading. I've found another great use for Telnet. You can use Telnet to peek into the mail server of your Internet service provider (ISP), and from there you can manipulate the contents of your mailbox.

It's not often that this is a necessary task, but when it is, you'll be grateful for Telnet. The necessity arises when a message has blocked your mailbox. Many ISPs have a maximum size for message storage for each user. If a very large file arrives in your mailbox, it's quite possible your mailbox will shut down, locked tight. You won't get any messages, even those messages that are not enormous. Eventually, your messages may bounce back to the sender with a message stating that the mail could not be delivered to you. This can cause all sorts of confusion with the people who send you messages.

If you have a mysterious dearth of mail and then you hear from someone that he or she has sent you a message with a 7MB file attached, the odds are your mailbox is locked up. You can call your ISP and ask a technician to go into your mailbox and delete the enormous message. However, most of the time you sit on hold for a very long time. Then, after all that time, the technician may be reluctant to delete a message, especially if there are several large messages (for fear of deleting the wrong one).

With Telnet you can do it yourself. Before you begin you must connect with your ISP (usually through a Dial-Up Networking connection. Do NOT open any email software such as a browser, Outlook, or any other email program. Once you're connected, Telnet can get into your ISP mail server.

### Accessing a mail server with Telnet

**1.** Click **Start**, and then choose **Run** from the **Start** menu.

**2.** Enter **telnet** in the **Open** box of the **Run** window.

**3.** When the **Telnet** window opens, choose **Terminal**, **Preferences** from the menu bar to open the **Terminal Preferences** dialog box (see Figure 10.13).

**4.** Select **Local Echo** and **VT100/ANSI** and click **OK**.

**5.** Choose **Connect**, **Remote System** from the menu bar to bring up the **Connect** dialog box (see Figure 10.14).

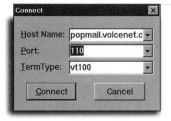

FIGURE 10.14

Configure the Connection for this Telnet session.

**6.** In the **Host Name** box, enter the name of your ISP mail server. This information is available in the setup information you received from your ISP. It's usually something like postoffice.yourisp, popmail.yourisp, or mail.yourisp.

**7.** In the **Port** box, enter **110**. Then choose **Connect**. Your Telnet window displays +OK followed by the name of the mail server you've just connected with. Now you have to move to your mailbox on that server.

**8.** Enter **user** and then enter a space followed by your user name, and then press **Enter**. Use just the name, not your

full email address. For instance, if your email address is
bettyboop@someisp.com, enter bettyboop.

**9.** Enter **pass** and then enter your password, followed by the
**Enter** key.

You are now on your ISP mail server and you are in your mailbox. You have several commands available:

- list displays all the messages in your mailbox. The format
  of the list is a message number (starting with 1) followed by
  the size of the message in bytes.

- uidl # displays information about the message number you
  enter in place of #. This is header information (identification
  of the Internet source). Most of the time you'll see a series
  of numbers with periods (that's called dotted notation) representing the Internet address for the source. Sometimes the
  source actually names an ISP along with those numbers.
  Usually it's difficult to figure out what the sending source is.

- Uidl (with no number) lists all the messages along with the
  header information, but does not display the size of the messages.

- Dele # deletes the specific numbered message (substitute the
  number for #).

Most of the time you can tell which message should be deleted
because the size is so enormous.

Figure 10.15 shows part of a typical Telnet session when using
Telnet to peek into your mailbox without downloading messages.

# Multimedia

There are several programs on your Windows 98 system that
work with your multimedia devices (see Figure 10.16). Just click
the program you want to use.

## CD Player

This is a great program, because my computer isn't anywhere
near my stereo equipment. However, when I'm not loading or

configuring software, my CD-ROM drive is free to hold my music CDs, preventing withdrawal.

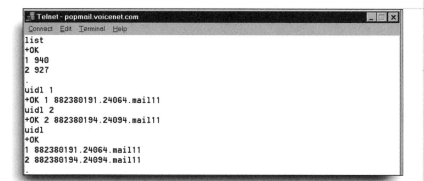

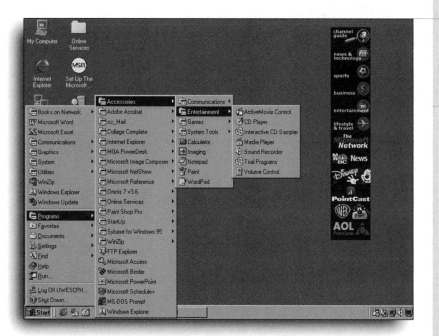

## Configuring the Play List

CD Player doesn't just play the CD, it gives you all sorts of controls over the tracks. You can store information about a single track and play that track over and over (when my kids used to do that I ran out to buy headsets for them).

The first time you play a specific CD in CD Player, you can store the information about the disc and the tracks.

### Storing disc information

1.  Choose **Disc, Edit Play List** from the menu bar to display the **Disk Settings** dialog box (see Figure 10.17).

2.  Enter the name of the artist and the title in the top of the dialog box.

3.  In the Available Tracks box, click the track you want to store a name for and enter the name in the Track box at the bottom of the dialog box. Choose **Set Name**.

4.  Repeat Step 3 for each track you want to store.

5.  Remove a track from the Play list by selecting it and choosing **Remove**.

6.  To change the order in which tracks are played, choose **Clear All**. Then select each track in the Available Tracks list in the order in which you want them played. Use the Add button to move that track to the Play List (you can also drag the track to the Play List).

You can, of course, opt to play only a few of your favorite tracks, and you can repeat the same track as often as you want (see Figure 10.18).

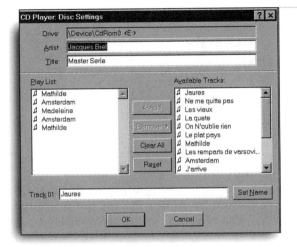

FIGURE 10.18
There are always a handful of
favorites on any CD.

## Sharing CD Play Lists

If you have more than one CD-ROM equipped computer in
your home, or your network at the office includes other computers with CD-ROMs, probably other people are entering their
music CDs in CD Player.

You don't have to reinvent the wheel if you want to share the
music—you can copy and merge the Play Lists from a variety of
CD Players.

The settings for Artist, Track, and Title for each disc are in a file
named Cdplayer.ini, which is in your Windows folder. For example, the contents of Cdplayer.ini for the computer used in Figure
10.18 and preceding figures looks like this:

```
[1A30470]
EntryType=1
artist=Jacques Brel
title=Master Serie
numtracks=16
0=Jaures
1=Ne me quitte pas
2=Les vieux
3=La quete
4=On N'oublie rien
5=Le plat pays
```

```
6=Mathilde
7=Les remparts de varsovie
8=Amsterdam
9=J'arrive
10=Ces gens-la
11=Jef
12=Vesoul
13=Au suivant
14=Madeleine
15=Track 16
order=6 8 14 8 6
numplay=5
```

If you haven't yet set up any play lists, you can copy the Cdplayer.ini file from a user who has. If you've already set up some play lists, you can merge multiple lists into one Cdplayer.ini file.

### Merging play lists

1. Rename your Cdplayer.ini file Cdplayer.xx, where *xx* stands for your initials.

2. Copy the Cdplayer.ini file from another user to your Windows folder.

3. Launch Notepad (or another text editor) and open Cdplayer.xx.

4. Select the entire file (**Edit, Select All** from the menu bar) to place the contents on the Clipboard.

5. Open the Cdplayer.ini file you received from another user.

6. Move to the bottom of the file and choose **Edit, Paste** from the menu bar.

You can continue to do this to merge play lists from multiple sources. Just make sure that when you save the merged file you use the name Cdplayer.ini and save it to your Windows folder.

## Media Player

The Windows 98 Media Player is an entertainment center. It's a small control panel you can use for audio files, video files, or audio CDs (see Figure 10.19).

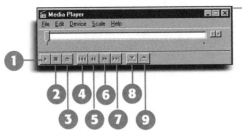

FIGURE 10.19

This little control panel can run almost any type of multimedia file.

1. Play (Pause when media is playing)
2. Stop
3. Eject
4. Previous Mark
5. Rewind
6. Fast Forward
7. Next Mark
8. Start Selection
9. End Selection

## Playing Multimedia Files

You select the type of multimedia file you want to use with the Media Player.

### Viewing multimedia files with media player

1. Choose **File**, **Open** from the menu bar.
2. In the **Open** dialog box, click the arrow to the right of the Files of type box to see the choices supported by your Media Player (see Figure 10.20).

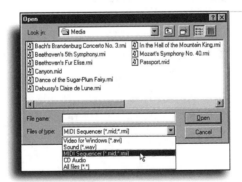

FIGURE 10.20

The multimedia file types supported by this Windows 98 installation are displayed.

3. Choose the multimedia file you want to play by double-clicking it.
4. Click the **Play** button to begin the fun.

## Insert Multimedia Files in Documents

One function the Media Player provides is the capability to grab a part of a file and insert it into a document. Normally, if you insert a multimedia object in a file you have to take the whole file. With the capability to take a specific portion of a video or audio file you can fine tune your document.

### Grabbing part of a multimedia file

1. Open the file and choose **Play** to start the playback.

2. At the point where you want your partial selection to begin, click the **Start Selection** button. Media Player inserts a beginning mark on the playback grid.

3. At the point where you want your partial selection to end, click the **Stop Selection** button. Media Player inserts an ending mark on the playback grid. The portion of the play-back grid representing your selection is highlighted (see Figure 10.21).

FIGURE 10.21

A couple of seconds of this music is exactly what I need for my document.

4. Choose **Edit, Copy Object** from the menu bar to place your selection on the Clipboard.

5. Open the document and place your insertion point where you want the icon for the selection to appear.

6. Choose **Edit, Paste** to place the selection in your document.

When the document is onscreen, double-click the object icon to play back the multimedia selection.

## Sound Recorder

The Windows 98 Sound Recorder is a tool you can use to record your own sound and then play it back or insert it into a document (see Figure 10.22). You need an input device (technical term for microphone) to do this, of course. Most of the time you'll be recording your own voice, either speaking or singing or yodeling if that's your best thing.

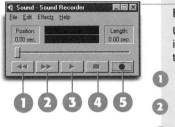

FIGURE 10.22

Use the sound recorder to immortalize your vocalized thoughts.

1  Seek starting point

2  Seek ending point

3  Playback

4  Stop

5  Record

**Recording a sound**

1. Clear your throat, gargle, and do your vocal warm up exercises.

2. Choose **File**, **New** from the menu bar.

3. Click the **Record** button

4. Speak up!

5. Click the **Stop** button.

6. Check it out with the **Playback** button.

7. Choose **File**, **Save** to make it all permanent.

You can also use the Media Player to play back your sound files.

## Volume Control

The Volume Control dialog box is always within easy reach, you don't have to open the Start menu to get there. Double-clicking the speaker icon on the taskbar opens the dialog box from which you can control the individual volume and balance levels (see Figure 10.23).

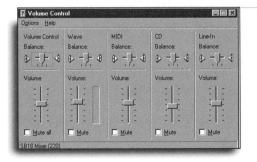

FIGURE 10.23

Balance or unbalance your speakers (depending on how they're positioned) and adjust the volume with the Volume Control dialog box.

If you just want to make a quick adjustment to the volume of whatever is coming out of your speakers, single-click the speaker icon on the taskbar. When the Volume Control dialog box appears (see Figure 10.24), move the slider up or down.

FIGURE 10.24

Make quick adjustments with a single click of your mouse.

Depending on your installation choices, you may have additional accessories available on your menu. Take the time to open them and experiment—you'll probably find at least one useful tool.

# Installing Software

The truth is, no matter how much you learn about Windows 98, the operating system itself isn't a whole lot of fun to play with. Nor can you use your computer very effectively if all you have on it is an operating system. To use your computer as a tool, and to get work done, you need software.

Today, most software comes on CD-ROM. In fact, it's difficult to find software that ships on floppy disks, although you can call the manufacturer and request floppy disks if you don't have a CD-ROM drive.

Almost all Windows programs follow the same procedures for installation. There's a setup program, and it requires you to answer questions and make decisions.

Before beginning the installation of any software, make sure all the software you were using is closed. No files or utilities should be open before starting software installation.

# Installing with CD-ROM AutoRun

Windows 98 has a feature called AutoRun, which can launch a program automatically when you insert a CD-ROM into your CD-ROM drive. The CD-ROM has to be programmed to take advantage of the AutoRun feature.

You'll know in a minute or two if your software CD-ROM uses AutoRun. Insert the CD-ROM and watch the Busy light on your CD-ROM drive. If it stays on more than a few seconds, stand by—something is probably going to happen automatically.

Software companies usually take one of three approaches to using AutoRun:

- The setup program launches automatically.
- A graphical window appears with icons for starting setup or browsing the CD-ROM.
- A dialog box appears, asking if you want to install the software. Answering Yes starts setup.

No matter how you get there, you'll have to get to the setup program in order to install the software.

There are some common themes to software installation, and understanding them makes the whole process a bit less intimidating:

- There's usually a license agreement you should read. You must agree to abide by the terms and you're asked to confirm that by clicking a dialog box button (usually Yes, but sometimes "I agree," and your software may present some other method of getting you to agree to the license).

- There may be multiple installation choices: Typical or Custom. You can always add and remove components later, so it's always safe to choose Typical. If there's a choice for Laptop and you're installing the software on a laptop computer, choose that option.

- The setup program usually tells you which folder it plans to use for the software. Unless you have some special reason to invent your own folder, it's a good idea to accept that choice.

- Many games offer you the opportunity to install some files on your hard drive and leave everything else on the CD-ROM. You should accept the invitation because games take up a great deal of disk space and your hard drive will lose the free space it needs to operate Windows efficiently.

- Some software programs tell you about their additions to your Start menu. Usually you're shown the name of a new program group. Accept that decision—there's absolutely no reason to change it.

- You may be told you have to shut down your computer and restart the operating system before you can use the software. Usually, there's a dialog box offered that lets you perform that task without going to the Start menu.

# Installing with Add/Remove Programs

If your software CD-ROM doesn't have AutoRun, you're in do-it-yourself land. Luckily, Windows 98 has a tool you can use for this manual labor.

The Add/Remove Programs application is a Microsoft wizard that gets you started with new software setup. Here's how to use it:

### Using Add/Remove Programs to install your software

1. Click the **Start** button and move your mouse pointer to Settings to display the Settings submenu.

2. Choose **Control Panel** from the submenu to open the Control Panel window.

3. Double-click the Add/Remove Programs icon to open its dialog box (see Figure 11.1).

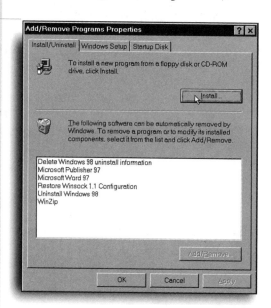

4. Choose **Install** to start the wizard.

5. The first wizard window tells you to put the CD-ROM into its drive (or put the first installation floppy disk into a floppy drive). Choose **Next** when your disk is in place.

6. The wizard searches your floppy drives and the CD-ROM drive, looking for a program to install. When it finds one, it displays it (see Figure 11.2). Choose **Finish** to confirm the wizard's findings and complete the wizard's work.

FIGURE 11.2

If the wizard is correct (which it usually is, which is why it's called a wizard), click Finish. Otherwise, choose Browse and find the right file.

**7.** The installation program for the software takes over and begins the setup of your new software. Just answer questions and provide information as requested.

## Helping the Add/Remove Programs Wizard

Unfortunately, the wizard isn't all that wise, and sometimes you need to give it some assistance. You see, the wizard thinks there should be a file named Setup.exe or Install.exe on the root of the disk. If there's not, the wizard displays a message telling you it couldn't find an installation program—sorry about that.

The wizard isn't the least bit inquisitive, there's no sense of exploration, and there's no wondering whether there might be a file named Setup.exe in a folder on the disk.

There are two ways to give the wizard a push:

- Read the instructions that came with the software and enter the correct name for the installation file. Some programs use filenames that reflect the name of the software, such as WildGameSetup.exe.

- Choose **Browse** and look in any existing folders for an installation file. Frequently, the folder names provide a hint about where to look: Look for folders named Setup or Install. Or, look for a folder named Win95 (there will probably be a folder named Win3 also, because the software has multiple versions for both versions of Windows).

Frankly, unless the software has an installation program that the wizard can find without your intervention, there's not much point in using the Add/Remove Programs application.

# Installing with the Run Command

If you have to browse the CD-ROM to find the installation program, you might as well use the Run command—it's faster and easier to get to (you don't have to open the Control Panel to find it). To install software with Run, follow these steps:

### Using the Run command to install your software

**1.** Click the **Start** button, and then click **Run** to open the Run dialog box (see Figure 11.3).

FIGURE 11.3

Enter a filename or enter a drive letter to get set to Browse.

**2.** Enter the filename for the installation program along with the drive letter (such as D:\Setup if your CD-ROM is drive D).

**3.** If the instructions tell you that the installation program is in a folder, enter the path to the file (such as D:\install\ Setup.exe).

**4.** If you don't know where on the CD-ROM to find the installation program, enter the drive letter for your CD-ROM followed by a colon (D:). Then choose **Browse**.

**5.** When the Browse dialog box opens, it displays all the folders on the CD-ROM disk, and all the program files (files with an extension of .exe). Move through the folders to find the installation program file.

6. When you find the right file, select it and choose **Open** from the Browse dialog box (or double-click it).

7. You're returned to the Run dialog box and that filename is in the Open box. Click **OK** to launch the installation program.

The installation program takes over, and you're off and running.

# Installing DOS Software

There is still a lot of DOS software around, and some of it may be exactly what you need to get your work accomplished. For example, DOS accounting software is still very popular because it runs faster than most Windows accounting programs. More important, many people feel it isn't necessary to have a lot of graphics and fancy screens to do plain, old-fashioned number crunching.

There are also some very useful DOS utilities, including DOS-based anti-virus programs that you have to use if a virus prevents you from starting your Windows 98 operating system. However, be selective about the DOS utilities you use. Anti-virus software is fine, but any utilities that manipulate files directly will mess up your long filenames, because DOS has no idea how to handle them.

While some DOS software comes with an installation program, the norm is that DOS programs do not have any program that installs the software package.

Read the instructions if there is a printed manual with your DOS software. If there isn't, look for a file named Readme.txt, Read.me, or Readme.1st on the software disk.

### Finding Readme files for installing DOS software

1. Open Explorer and double-click on the file.

2. If the file has an extension of .txt, Notepad opens. Read the file and, if necessary, print it.

**3.** If the file has an extension of .1st (or any extension besides .txt), double-clicking it brings up the Open With dialog box. Choose Notepad. Read the file and print it if you will need the information during installation.

## Using DOS Install Programs

If there is an installation program file for the DOS software, it is usually named Install (Windows installation program files are usually named Setup).

Most DOS installation programs require you to enter a DOS command that tells the software where to install the program. Here's a typical DOS installation routine, assuming the software comes on floppy disks. You'll notice that I use the term "directory" instead of folder. They mean the same thing, but folder is strictly a Windows term.

Don't use these steps until you have read the printed instructions or the readme file, because you may have to make some substitutions in the commands entered below. However, this should give you an overview of how DOS software gets installed.

### Typical installation routine for DOS software

**1.** Open an MS-DOS command prompt (choose MS-DOS Prompt from the Programs menu).

**2.** Enter **cd\** and press Enter to move up to the root directory of your hard drive.

**3.** If the instructions indicate that the installation program will create any directories that are needed automatically, move to step 6.

**4.** If the instructions indicate that the installation program must be told which directory to use (and the directory must exist), create the directory by typing **md name** (substitute the directory name for the word "name"). Make sure the directory name does not exceed eight characters. Then press Enter.

**5.** Move to the floppy drive by entering **A:** and pressing the Enter key.

**6.** At the A: prompt (A:\>), type **install a: c:** if the program
makes its own directory. Type **install a: c:\name** (using the
name you created) if you had to create a directory.

The installation program takes over, and if you're installing from
floppy disks, you'll have to insert additional disks when prompt-
ed. There is no need to restart your computer after the installation is complete.

However, you must type **exit** and press Enter in the MS-DOS
command window to close the window and end the DOS session.

The program will not appear on your Start menu. See Chapter
12 for information about starting programs that are not on the
Start menu.

## Installing DOS Software Manually

Many DOS software programs have no installation programs,
but they do provide instructions for installing the software properly. This usually involves creating a directory and copying all
the files into it. You can perform these tasks from Explorer.

### Manually installing your DOS software

**1.** Select Drive C in Explorer. If you have multiple hard drives
and want to install this DOS software on another drive,
select that drive in Explorer.

**2.** Right-click on a blank spot in the right pane, then choose
New, Folder from the shortcut menu that appears.

**3.** A new folder appears in the right pane; it's named New
Folder and the name is highlighted because it's in edit mode
(see Figure 11.4). Type a new name for this folder, and use a
maximum of eight characters for the name.

**4.** Place the software program floppy disk into Drive A.

**5.** Use the scroll bar in Explorer to move above your hard
drive's listing in the left pane and select the floppy drive.
This displays the contents of the floppy drive in the right
pane.

FIGURE 11.4

Create a new folder to hold
your DOS software.

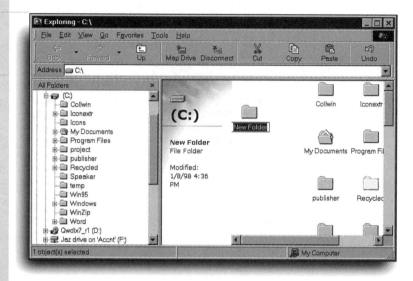

**6.** Press **Ctrl+A** to select all the files in the right pane. Then right-click any file and choose Copy from the shortcut menu.

**7.** Move to the new folder you created and right-click on it, then select **Paste**.

**8.** If there are additional floppy disks, repeat the process until all the files on all the floppy disks have been moved to the new folder.

Alternatively, you could perform the entire operation from an MS-DOS command prompt (I always do it this way; I think it's much faster).

### Installing DOS software from an MS-DOS command prompt

**1.** Open an MS-DOS command prompt.

**2.** Enter **cd\** and press Enter to move to the root directory of your hard drive.

**3.** Enter **md name** (substituting the name of the directory you want to create to hold your DOS software). Press Enter.

**4.** Enter **cd\name** (substituting the name of the new directory) and press Enter to move to the new directory.

5. Put the floppy disk with the DOS software in Drive A. Then enter **copy a:\*.\*** and press **Enter**. All the files are copied to the new directory because you issued the command from there.

6. If there are additional floppy disks, put the next disk in the floppy drive. Press **F3** (which repeats the last DOS command).

7. Repeat as necessary.

Your DOS software is installed. See Chapter 12 to learn how to run it.

# Installing Downloaded Software

Most of us download software from the Internet—it's a source of great utilities, interesting and useful shareware, and updates to our existing software.

## Installing Self-Extracting Software

Most downloaded software is in the filename form filename.exe. This is a self-extracting compressed file, which means a number of individual files have been scrunched together to save space (and downloading time).

Double-clicking on the file extracts all the individual files. You'll want to have some control over where those files reside, so it's always important to create a new folder to hold the files. In fact, I think it's a good idea to keep the self-extracting file in the same folder I create to hold the extracted files. Here's my approach, which is safe and easy:

### Installation of self-extracting software

1. In Explorer, select your hard drive. Then right-click on any blank spot in the right pane and choose **New**, **Folder** from the shortcut menu.

2. Name the new folder something that relates to the software you downloaded.

**Close the MS-DOS command window after extraction**

Sometimes a DOS command window opens and the individual filenames are displayed as they're extracted. If the extraction program doesn't close the DOS window, you'll have to do it.

3. Move to the folder that holds the files you download from the Internet and right-click on the file you downloaded.

4. Choose **Cut**, and then move to the new folder. Right-click on the new folder and choose **Paste**.

5. Double-click on the downloaded file to begin the extraction process.

## Installed Zipped Software

Some downloaded programs are compressed with a program named WinZip (or PKZip, which is the DOS zip program). This is a terrific utility that you can use to uncompress downloaded files. More important, you can use WinZip to compress files yourself, which is a great way to put a group of files into one file if you need to send them to someone over the Internet or on a floppy disk. In fact, you can use WinZip to put files together on floppy disks to back them up.

If you have downloaded a software program that is zipped, you'll have to go back to the Internet and download WinZip. You can find it at **http://www.winzip.com**. Double-click on the file (it's named Winzip95.exe) and it will self-extract and install itself into Windows 98.

After WinZip is installed, right-click the downloaded software named *filename*.zip. The shortcut menu now contains a new command: Extract To. Select the command and follow the instructions to use WinZip to extract the downloaded software.

## Setting Up Extracted Programs

Tip

If the self-extracting file is too large to fit on a floppy disk (many of them are), then you can either keep the original file in the extraction folder you created or put it back in your Internet download directory. If hard drive space is a problem, just delete it, and if you need it again, you can download it again.

After you self-extract or unzip downloaded software, one of the extracted files should be named Setup.exe. Double-click it to start the installation of the program, and follow the instructions.

If the program has a default folder for installation and it creates that folder, when the installation is over you can delete the folder in which you extracted the files. However, I always copy the original self-extracting file to a floppy disk so I have a copy of the software. I consider downloaded software to be the same as purchased software, and I certainly keep the original disks of any software I buy.

## Installing .inf Downloads

Some downloaded software, particularly operating system utilities, don't have a Setup.exe file. Instead, after extraction, there is a file (or multiple files) with a filename extension of .inf (which means the file has installation information).

Right-click the .inf file and choose Install (the shortcut menu adds the Install command when you right-click .inf files).

These files generally don't have complex setup programs for installation, but some may require that you restart your computer before using the utility.

# Uninstalling Software

These days, software that is written specifically for Windows 98 (or Windows 95 or Windows NT 4) frequently includes an Uninstall program so you can remove the software if you find you don't use it. The reason you need an uninstall program is that it's almost impossible to find all the files that were installed when you set up the software. Files are placed in a variety of folders, including Windows 98 system folders, and entries are made to the Registry. Without an uninstall program, you'd never get rid of the software.

To uninstall software, one of the following facts must be true:

- The submenu for the software program on your Programs menu must include a listing called Uninstall.
- The program must be listed on the Add/Remove Programs dialog box (in Control Panel).

If there is a submenu Uninstall program, just select it. You'll be asked to confirm the fact that you want to uninstall the software. Say Yes.

If there is no Uninstall program in the software's menu choices, double-click the Add/Remove Programs icon in the Control

Panel. Then select the software you want to remove, choose Add/Remove, and follow the instructions.

If the software isn't listed in the Add/Remove Programs list box, you'll have to remove it manually. This can be a daunting task because there are probably files for the software in folders above and beyond the software folder.

## Uninstalling Shared Files

During the Uninstall process, it's common to see a dialog box telling you that Windows 98 is about to uninstall some files that are shared by other programs. You're given an opportunity to skip those files, leaving them on your system. Here's how to decide:

**Reinstalling shared files**

If you do accidentally uninstall a shared file that another program needs, you'll probably get an error message the next time you use the software that needs those files. Just re-run the installation program for the software to replace the shared files. You won't lose or damage any data files.

- If the software you're uninstalling isn't a suite (such as Microsoft Office), the files are probably shared only among the various features of the software and it's okay to remove them. You can be sure it's okay if the shared files have the program's name or part of the name. For example, if you're uninstalling software named Widgets and the shared file-names all start with "Wid," it's safe to remove them.

- If the software you're uninstalling is part of a suite of programs, it's probably not a good idea to uninstall shared files unless you're uninstalling every program in the suite.

The big problem with installing software is underestimating the amount of hard drive space today's software uses. This is especially true of games, and if your computer is shared with your children, you probably have plenty of games or educational programs. When you install them, choose the configuration that lets you use the software from the CD-ROM (some files will be transferred to your hard drive, but millions of bytes will remain on the CD).

# Using Software

# Using Software

It's interesting to poll people who spend a lot of time in front of a computer about what they do. In the office, most people spend the majority of their time using one software program. Very few people in the accounting department spend time using graphics software, and if your job involves creating reports and letters, you probably don't spend much time using a spreadsheet program.

At home, however, it's different. Not just because individual family members have their own favorite programs, but because each person who uses the computer tends to move from program to program. Pay your bills with accounting software, write a couple of letters, and finally log on to the Internet for your e-mail and some Web browsing.

The point is that the real purpose of using a computer is to get something accomplished in a software application. Learning to open, use, and close software efficiently and safely makes your time in front of the computer more productive.

# Launching Software

The one thing that all software programs have in common is that they have to be opened and closed with some form of keystroke or mouse action. A common term for opening software is "launching," which is a pretty good description of the process. One minute it's not visible, the next minute it's on your screen waiting for you to go to work.

The variety of ways in which you can launch a software program depend on how the program was installed and whether it takes advantage of Windows 98 features (such as the Programs menu).

**SEE ALSO**

➤ *For information on installing software, see Chapter 11, "Installing Software."*

## Using the Programs Menu

Most of the time, the software you install will create a listing for itself on your Programs menu. Getting there is easy.

### Opening software from the menu

**1.** Click the Start button.

**2.** Move your mouse pointer to Programs to display the Programs menu.

**3.** Click on the listing for the software you want to use.

Some software doesn't just create a listing—it creates a folder in which there are a group of listings. You can tell folders from individual listings by the arrows that appear to the right of an item on your Programs menu (see Figure 12.1). When your mouse pointer is on the folder, the submenu appears, and you can click the program listing to launch the software.

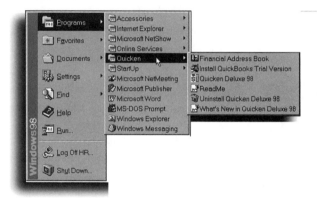

**FIGURE 12.1**

An arrow on a Programs listing indicates there's another menu with additional choices.

## Using Explorer

You can also launch software from Explorer (or from My Computer). All you have to do is find the program's executable file (that's the techie way of saying the file that controls the program) and double-click it. Here are some helpful guidelines:

- Most program files have an extension of .exe.

- Some DOS software starts with a batch file, which has an extension of .bat.

- You may have some older software installed on your system that has an extension of .com (although those programs are very rare these days).
- Usually you can locate and identify the folder that contains the program file. Folder names usually contain some form of the software name.

The only reason to go to all the trouble of using Explorer or My Computer to launch software is because the software is not listed on your Programs menu. This can occur when you install older Windows software, DOS software, or a downloaded utility.

## Using Shortcuts

You can save yourself some work by putting the program on your Start menu or on the desktop as a shortcut.

- To place the program on your Start menu, drag the program file to the Start button. The program listing will appear at the top of your Start menu (see Figure 12.2).

**FIGURE 12.2**

When you drag a program file to the Start button, the program listing leaps to the top of your Start menu instead of appearing on the Programs menu.

- To create a desktop shortcut, drag the program file to the desktop.

The listing on the Start menu is also a shortcut; it just isn't on the desktop.

# Configuring DOS Program Shortcuts

Shortcuts for DOS programs make sense because DOS installation procedures don't place listings on your Programs menu.

When a DOS program runs, it runs in a space created for it by Windows 98, and that space can be thought of as a virtual DOS computer. It's a little, self-contained world of DOS, almost as if you created a computer within a computer.

Frequently you have to tweak the way a DOS program's virtual computer is configured in order to get maximum performance out of the software. You can do this from the shortcut icon.

### Configuring DOS shortcuts

1. Right-click the shortcut icon and choose Properties from the shortcut menu.

2. Move to the Program tab (see Figure 12.3).

**FIGURE 12.3**

Get maximum performance by tweaking the environment for DOS software.

3. Enter a location for the working folder (the title of the text box says Working, but it means working folder). Usually it's best to make sure the working folder is the folder in which the software files reside.

**4.** The Run box is for specifying the window that's created when the software is first launched. You can choose among Normal, Maximized, or Minimized.

**5.** Select **Close on exit** to make sure the MS-DOS command prompt window closes when you exit the software (otherwise you'll have to do it yourself).

There are other tabs on the shortcut Properties dialog box, but most of the time you won't have to mess around with their settings. If you're having problems with the software, it's a good idea to get some expert help in changing the settings on the other tab.

# Saving Your Documents

Most software requires you to click the mouse or enter some keystrokes in order to save the document you created while you worked in the software.

## How Save Works

The way documents are saved is the same whether you're using Windows or DOS software. The keystrokes needed to make it happen differ, but the effect is identical.

When you create a new document and save it, you must name it. The document is saved to a disk (usually a hard disk, but you can save documents to removable disks if you enjoy working very slowly).

The next time you open the document in the same software, a copy of the document is loaded in the software window. The original document remains on the disk. After you make changes, you save the document again. The new document, as it exists in your software window, is saved to the disk and replaces the copy that was on the disk. (Some DOS software asks if you want to replace the current copy, and you should answer Yes.)

Each time you save, the document that's in your software window is saved to disk, replacing the last saved disk copy.

---

**Some software saves as you go, automatically**

Many accounting programs and other database software save your entries as you make them. It's automatic and it makes sense for the way databases work. The efficiency of databases is that data entry is fast and repetitive (sometimes called "crunching"). Stopping to save each time you enter data would be nerve wracking and nonproductive.

## Using Save As

After a document is saved, you can use Save As to save the document as something else:

- Save the document with a different name, which leaves the original disk file unchanged. Now you have the last version and the current version as separate files.

- Save the document in a different format. Usually you do this because you have to give the document file to somebody who doesn't have the software you have.

When you use Save As, the document that was on the disk when you opened a copy into your software window is not changed. You have two versions (with two separate names) of the document on your disk.

## Closing without Saving

Sometimes it's a good idea to close a file without saving it. Picture this: You've created a document and saved it. Later you open the document and work on it. You get fancy-schmancy and experiment with features that don't work the way you expected them to. You've ruined your document.

Close it. Or exit the software. Either way, you'll be asked if you want to save the document. Answer No. The messy document in your software window disappears and the original document on the disk is unsullied.

# Using Multiple Windows

You can work in more than one window at a time in Windows 98. The most common form for this feature is having multiple documents open in your favorite software program. Two spreadsheets, three letters, two graphics—that's all done with multiple document windows within a single software program.

You can also open more than one software program, and have multiple software windows. In fact, you can do both.

The technical term for working in multiple software programs simultaneously is *multitasking*, and it's one of the powerful features of the Windows operating systems.

Just open a software program, then open another one. Voilà, you're multitasking. You can keep going, opening more software as you need it, without closing the software you've already opened. I routinely have four or five programs open and there are plenty of people who feel they cannot be productive without eight or 10 programs open.

## Understanding Foreground and Background Windows

When there are multiple software windows open, one of them is the active program. The active program is the one that receives your keystrokes and mouse clicks. That program is said to be running in the foreground. The title bar for the foreground program is different than the title bar for the background programs.

All the other software windows are running in the background. There are rules about how foreground and background programs behave:

- Foreground programs receive the output of your keyboard or mouse.

- Background programs can continue to work and can do any task except receive keystrokes or mouse clicks.

- When a background program wants to pass an important message to you (an error message or a message that says that something has been accomplished), it puts itself in the foreground.

- When a background program needs keystrokes or mouse clicks to continue its work, it puts itself in the foreground.

For example, the first thing in the morning when I sit down in front of my computer, I start a series of events. Let's look at "a day in the life of a computer user" with me as the heroine of the story. I'll lay out the plot in the order in which it occurs:

1. I double-click the Dial-Up Networking connection to my Internet service provider.

2. The software accesses the modem and dials the phone. It's the only process running, so it's the foreground process.

3. I open Internet Explorer. IE becomes the foreground program because it received the last mouse click. My Dial-Up Networking connection is the background program. It continues to do its work, none of which requires input from me, so it stays in the background.

4. In the background, my Dial-Up Networking connection connects to the ISP host computer and runs the script that enters my username and password. It waits while the host computer accepts the name and password.

5. I launch Outlook Express to collect my email.

6. I open Microsoft Word (eventually I have to get some work done, so I might as well open the software), which becomes the foreground application. Internet Explorer, Outlook Express, and the Dial-Up Networking connection are all in the background.

7. When the Dial-Up Networking connection completes its work and a connection is established, the program sends me notification. The programmers designed notifications as foreground tasks, and, thus, the notification dialog box is automatically sent to the foreground (see Figure 12.4).

8. I click the Internet Browser title bar (or taskbar button, depending on which is handier) to bring it into the foreground and select the bookmark for the local newspaper. Outlook Express is downloading my mail in the background.

9. While I'm reading the paper, Outlook Express finishes downloading my mail. When all the mail is transferred, it notifies me that I have mail.

I can continue switching among all the open programs, selecting a foreground program as I need it. If a background program needs something from me or needs to tell me something, it will place itself in the foreground.

FIGURE 12.4

The Dial-Up Networking software automatically popped a dialog box into the foreground to send me an important message.

Incidentally, printing, downloading, and connecting to other computers can all take place in the background.

**SEE ALSO**

➤ *You can decide which colors to use to differentiate foreground and background software windows. See Chapter 8, "Personalizing Your Desktop," to learn about desktop schemes.*

# Using the Clipboard

The Clipboard is an area of memory that Windows 98 reserves to hold data for you. Once you've placed data on the Clipboard, you can drop it anywhere. This is how you move data between documents in a software program, and between programs when you're multitasking.

### Using the Clipboard

1.  Select the item you want to work with. It could be a word, a paragraph, or multiple paragraphs from a word processing document. It could be a series of cells from a spreadsheet

program. The software you're working in has rules and shortcuts for selecting information.

2. Choose **Edit**, **Cut** from the menu bar of the software program if you want to remove the item from the current software and place it in another software program. The item is on the Clipboard.

3. Choose **Edit**, **Copy** from the menu bar if you want to leave the item in the current software and place a copy of it in another software program. The item is on the Clipboard.

4. Move to the program that will receive the item (use the program's button on the taskbar or click the program's menu bar if it's visible). That program is now in the foreground and will respond to keystrokes or mouse clicks.

5. Move your mouse to the location in the document where you want to place the item. Choose **Edit**, **Paste** from the menu bar. The contents of the Clipboard are now in the target software's document.

The contents you placed on the Clipboard are still there. In fact, you could move to another software program (or open a new program) and paste the contents of the Clipboard again. And again and again.

The contents of the Clipboard stay there until:

- The next time you select an item and choose Cut or Copy.
- You shut down your computer.

# Exiting Software

Just as you have to use the Shut Down command to close down Windows 98 in an orderly fashion, you have to exit software as well. It's important to have an orderly shut down of software programs, and you never want to shut down your computer without shutting down all your open software programs first.

**Right-click instead of using the menu bar**

Most software, if it's written for Windows 98, will let you cut, copy, and paste by right-clicking and choosing those commands from the shortcut menu.

Windows software has several ways to implement the exit command:

- Choose **File**, **Exit** from the menu bar.
- Click the X in the upper-right corner.
- Right-click the software's button on the taskbar and choose **Close**.

If you have a document "live" in the software window and you've made changes since the last time you saved it (or you haven't saved it all yet), the software will ask you if you want to save the document. Answer Yes or No as the moment requires (and name the file if it hasn't yet been saved). The software then shuts down.

Opening and closing software while keeping multiple programs on your screen is a wonderfully productive feature. However, if you notice that your system is slowing down a bit, shut down a couple of programs. All this multitasking takes resources and memory, and the configuration of your computer may limit the amount of multitasking you can do.

# Printing

# Installing a Printer

No matter what software you're using as you work at your computer, eventually you'll want to print a document you've created. Otherwise, the only way anyone else will see your work is if you have them stand behind you and look at your monitor. Incidentally, in the computer world the jargon for a printed document is "hard copy" (the soft copy is the file on your computer).

You're the one who decides what to print and when to print it; your software takes care of sending your document to the printer; but it's really Windows 98 that does all the work. In fact, even though your software thinks it's sending your document to the printer, it's not. Windows 98 intercepts the document and takes over, handling all the printing processes.

The first thing you have to do is install a printer. In fact, you have to install a printer twice, once physically and once for Windows 98. The physical installation is easy, take the printer out of the box, plug it in, attach a cable between it and your computer, put paper and ink (or toner, or a ribbon) in it and you're done.

The Windows 98 installation is even easier. To get started, all you have to do is put your original Windows 98 CD-ROM in the CD-ROM drive (or have your Windows 98 floppy disks handy if you don't have a CD-ROM). Installing a printer in Windows 98 is accomplished in two steps:

1. You have to tell Windows 98 where your printer is (which means how it's connected to your computer).

2. You have to copy the drivers for your printer onto your hard drive so Windows 98 can use them when you want to print.

To make it all even easier, there's a Windows 98 wizard that walks you through the entire procedure. You merely answer questions and supply some information and the wizard takes care of everything.

# Understanding Drivers

All printers are designed to receive, interpret, and understand instructions. These printer instructions (also called printer codes) make everything happen as you send a document to your printer. There are instructions for printing fonts, setting margins, grabbing paper from the right tray (if there are multiple trays), and even ejecting the pages.

All those instructions are in files we call *printer drivers*. Printer drivers are written specifically for individual printers, the code that's sent to eject the page to one printer may mean something else if it's sent to a different printer (perhaps it makes all the text bold).

# Using the Printer Wizard to Install a Printer

When you're ready to install your printer in Windows 98, there's a wizard to guide you.

### Installing a printer

1. Click the **Start** button, and then choose **Settings**, **Printers** from the **Start** menu to open the **Printers** folder. (Alternatively, you can double-click **My Computer**, and then double-click the **Printers** folder.)

2. Double-click the **Add Printer** icon in the **Printers** folder. This launches the opening window of the Add Printer Wizard. This first graphic is an introduction; there's nothing you have to do except choose **Next** to get started.

3. The wizard needs to know where this printer is located (see Figure 13.1). A local printer is one that's attached to your computer. A network printer is attached to another computer on your network. For now, we'll assume you have a local printer (if you're installing a network printer, see "Installing a Network Printer," later in this chapter). Choose **Next**.

4. On the next wizard window, find the name of your printer manufacturer in the left pane and select it. The right pane lists all the printers from that manufacturer that are supported by Windows 98 (see Figure 13.2). Scroll through the list

### Understanding ports

Your computer has several ports built in and you can peek at the back of your computer to see them. Most computers have one parallel port (also called LPT1 and sometimes called printer port). You can recognize this port because it's a 36-pin female connection. Most computers also have two serial ports, which are used mainly to connect a mouse and an external modem. Serial ports (also called COM ports) come in two sizes: 9-pin and 25-pin. Frequently, there is one of each size. Serial ports have male connectors.

If you have a modern computer, when you're installing a printer you may see that the parallel port description includes the phrase "ECP Parallel Port." ECP stands for Extended Capabilities Port. This means your parallel port is capable of performing a higher level of communication between the printer and the computer. For example, the printer can send you messages such as "hey, the toner level is getting low." More important, these ports handle data better, so printing is much faster. To get the most out of an ECP port (especially the two-way conversations), you have to buy a printer cable that supports ECP. Even without special cable, though, you'll print faster with an ECP port. Incidentally, if you see references to EPP (Enhanced Parallel Port) support in your computer manual, it's a similar capacity. Microsoft supports only ECP with its operating system and drivers, but the port itself will probably support both standards.

to find your printer model. (If you can't find your model, stand by a second; we'll get to a solution for that a bit later in this chapter. Read the section "If Your Printer Model Isn't Listed.") Choose **Next** when you have made your selections.

**FIGURE 13.1**

Specify whether the printer you want to use is attached to your computer or to another computer on a network.

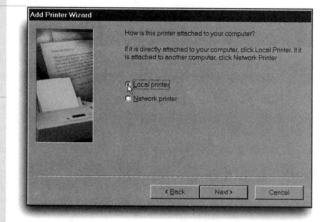

**FIGURE 13.2**

Be careful to choose the exact model to make sure the right drivers get installed.

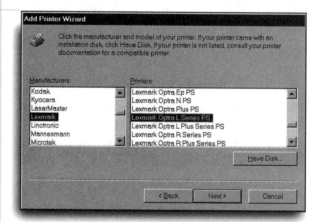

5. Select the port you used to attach your printer to your computer (see Figure 13.3). Most printers use LPT1, which is the computer name for a parallel port. Choose **Next** to move ahead.

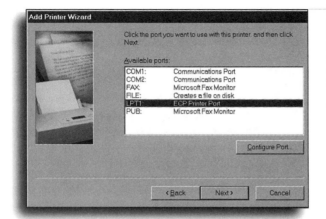

FIGURE 13.3
Pick your printer port. Usually it's LPT1, so that selection is highlighted automatically.

**6.** The next wizard window has two important items: naming your printer and deciding whether it is your default printer (see Figure 13.4). A name is suggested and usually it's perfectly suitable, but you may have some compelling reason to change it. If this is the first printer you are installing, the wizard has specified it as the default printer, assuming that this is the printer you'll want to use with all your windows software. (If it's not the first printer you're installing, the wizard specifies **No** but you can make this new printer the default by clicking **Yes**.)

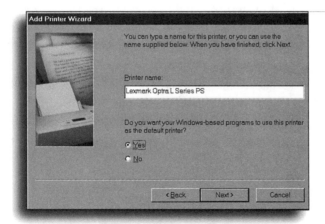

FIGURE 13.4
You could name your printer after your dog or your grandmother, but usually the printer's real name is an appropriate choice.

**7.** You're almost finished, and the wizard displays a window asking if you'd like to print a test page after the drivers have been installed. Always say **Yes**; it's the only way to know if this printer is going to work when you need it. Then choose Finish.

Sit back and relax a minute while the files are copied from your Windows 98 CD-ROM to your hard drive. If you used floppy disks to install Windows 98, you'll be told exactly which disk to insert into your floppy disk drive.

Then the test page is sent to the printer, and Windows 98 asks if it printed correctly.

If the test page did print correctly, read it to see that Windows 98 has offered congratulations for accomplishing the installation of your printer. There's also some technical information about the printer and the drivers it uses; it's boring and you don't really need the information for anything. Tell Windows 98 that the test page is fine by choosing **Yes** on the message box.

If the test page didn't print or it printed strange characters (the computer jargon for this is "garbage"), tell Windows 98 about it by clicking **No** on the message box.

## Using the Printer Troubleshooter

If the test page didn't print properly or at all, Windows 98 launches the printer troubleshooter. Troubleshooters are part of the Help file system and they work by asking questions and then offering suggestions based on your answers.

The troubleshooting process starts with some of the obvious potential problems (see Figure 13.5), and then escalates the complexity of its questions to dig deeper into the problem. The troubleshooter continues to ask questions and make suggestions until you answer Yes, indicating "that fixed it." Each time the troubleshooter makes a suggestion that doesn't work, it offers another one, and keeps making suggestions until it runs out of alternatives. At that point, it admits defeat and tells you to look for help from a technical support desk.

**FIGURE 13.5**

Windows 98 troubleshoots printing problems by asking questions and making suggestions.

## If Your Printer Model Isn't Listed

Sometimes you can't find your exact printer model in the list of available printers. That means Windows 98 does not have drivers for that printer. Don't panic; it's quite easy to resolve this problem. In fact, you have two choices for end-running this roadblock:

- You can pick a printer that uses the same codes and driver instructions as your printer. This is called *emulation*, and the documentation that came with your printer probably has a section on emulation. Or you can call the manufacturer and ask about emulation.

- You can provide your own drivers. Don't worry, you don't have to write a whole software program; you can get them from the manufacturer. Most manufacturers keep printer drivers on the Internet and you can download them. Before you go to any trouble, though, peek inside the box your printer was packed in and see if you find a floppy disk that is labeled Windows 98 drivers or something similar.

To use emulation, just select the emulated printer instead of your own printer during that part of the installation process. You'll know as soon as the test page prints whether or not it worked.

To use printer drivers you obtained from manufacturers, just use the Have Disk feature of printer installation.

### Using manufacturer disks to install a printer

1. When the list of manufacturers and models appears, choose Have Disk. The Install From Disk dialog box appears (see Figure 13.6).

**FIGURE 13.6**

You have to tell Windows 98 where you put the printer driver files.

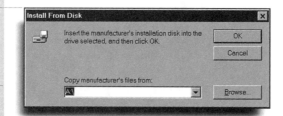

2. If the printer drivers are on a floppy disk in Drive A, click **OK**.

3. If you downloaded the drivers, enter the drive letter for your hard drive to replace the A:\ drive that's preselected. Your hard drive is probably C: (don't forget the colon after the drive letter). Then choose **Browse** to see a dialog box that lets you browse through the folders on your drive. Find the folder and file you need and select it.

4. The rest of the printer installation process is exactly the same as discussed earlier.

**Using downloaded drivers**

Many downloaded drivers are compressed into one file when you download them. Be sure to follow any instructions for decompressing the file before you use it.

## Installing a Network Printer

If you work on a network, there's a good chance there's no printer attached to your computer. Few companies can afford to give every user a printer, and it makes much more sense to have a large group of users share a few printers.

To print to a shared printer, you have to install it in Windows 98 just as if you were installing a printer that you connected to your computer.

## Installing a network printer

1. Open the Printers folder and double-click the **Add Printer** icon as described earlier in this chapter.

2. When the Add Printer Wizard asks how the printer is attached to your computer, choose **Network**, and then choose **Next**.

3. The next wizard window asks you to enter the path or queue name for the printer you want to install. You probably don't know that information offhand (there's no reason to know it; even I don't have the paths for printers on my system memorized and I'm the administrator). Just click the **Browse** button to tell Windows 98 to look for the available printers.

4. The Browse for Printer dialog box appears. Only the computers on your network that have printers attached to them appear in the dialog box (which I think is pretty clever and a great timesaver).

5. Expand the information about the computers by clicking the plus sign next to the computer icons (see Figure 13.7). All the printers attached to each computer are displayed. (If you already know which computer has the printer you're looking for, you have to expand only that computer.) Select the printer and click **OK** to return to the wizard window.

6. There's another question on that window to answer. When you use a shared computer, you have to tell Windows 98 whether or not you print from MS-DOS programs. Even if you don't have DOS software, if you ever use the command line to copy a file to a printer, you're printing in DOS. If you think you might need this capacity, select **Yes**. Windows 98 will ask you to configure the operating system to capture the printer port on your computer. As long as you don't have a printer attached to your computer, do it—it's okay, trust me. (If you do have a printer on your computer and are installing an additional printer, say **No** to the question about printing from MS-DOS.) Check out the section on capturing a port if you're the type who's curious about the technical stuff that operating systems do.

FIGURE 13.7
Select a printer

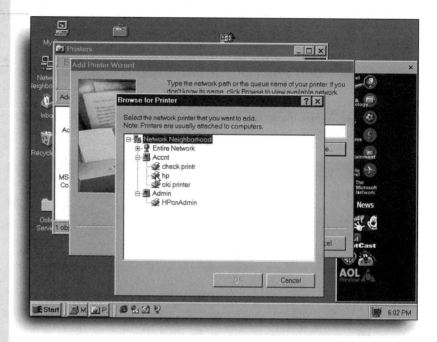

**7.** The rest of the installation proceeds exactly the same as installing a local printer. Well, except when you want to see if the test page printed correctly, you'll probably have to take a walk.

If there are multiple printers available on the network, you can install as many of them as you care to. Just repeat the installation process from scratch for each printer you want to install. Don't forget that only one printer can be designated the default printer. Each time you say "make this the default printer," the last default printer you chose loses that designation. In fact, you can change the default printer at will if you've installed multiple printers, and that's covered in the next section of this chapter where we talk about configuring printers.

## Understanding Paths for Computers

If the connected printer is on a Windows 98, Windows 95, or Windows NT machine, there's a path to it. However, instead of typing a path the way you do for a folder on your computer (`c:\foldername`), the path to a connected computer has a format called UNC (Universal Naming Convention). This format is used for shared resources on remote computers, and it follows the form `\\computername\resource_name`. For instance, if the printer you want to install is named HP_3rd_floor and it's attached to a computer named AccntgDept, the UNC is `\\accntgdept\hp_3rd_floor`. Because capitalization doesn't matter for a UNC, it's usually faster to ignore the Shift key when you're typing.

If the connected printer is on a NetWare print server, there's a queue name for it. You may not be able to find the right queue easily with Browse so ask your network administrator for the name of the printer queue. In this example, we're assuming the printer is connected to a Windows computer.

## Capturing a Port

MS-DOS is a pretty dumb operating system and it doesn't really "get" the whole idea of shared resources. It can't go out and find connected computers and printers by peeking through the network wires the way Windows 98 can.

Because there's no expectation that DOS will find connected resources, software written for DOS doesn't think about them, either. MS-DOS software asks you to tell it where your printer is and the only answer it accepts is a port. Because Windows 98 captures the port for you, you can lie to your DOS software by saying your printer is on LPT1. Windows 98 will grab (capture) any print job headed for the port and send it to the connected printer.

# Getting the Most Out of Your Printer

Different printers have different capabilities. Some printers can do wondrously clever things, such as print on both sides of the paper automatically, or grab different paper from different trays without your intervention. This means you can have letterhead in one tray and plain paper in the other tray, or you can have letter-size paper in one tray and legal-size paper in the other.

You just have to specify the paper when you're preparing to print from your software; the printer driver knows which paper is in which tray and sends the right codes to the printer. For those of us who started working with computers when printing meant dot-matrix printers, this stuff is really amazing.

You can view, change, and tweak the capabilities of your printer (we call this configuring a printer). The configuration options can be viewed in the printer's Properties dialog box, and all you have to do is select or deselect the options you want to use.

### Configuring a printer

1. Open the Printers folder from My Computer or the Settings menu item on the Start menu.

2. Right-click the printer icon to see the shortcut menu and choose **Properties** (it's the last choice on the menu).

3. The Printer Properties dialog box displays and you can begin the configuration of your printer.

Now, I'm stuck; I can't give you explicit instructions. Your printer and my printer probably don't display the same Properties dialog box. In fact, no two of the printers on my network display the same Properties dialog box.

The best I can do is present an overview of the type of options you might find and what they mean. Some of them are more important than others, and some of them are boringly technical.

To give you a general idea of some of the differences you might find, look at Figure 13.8. The Properties dialog box on the left is for a laser printer and there are six tabs needed to cover the variety of options available for this printer. On the other hand, the Properties dialog box on the right is for an inkjet printer, which has far fewer capabilities, and there are only two tabs available to play around with.

As you move through the tabs to consider your own printer's configuration, you'll find some of them far more interesting than others. We can discuss some of the performance options before we move on to the more mundane technical stuff.

**Printer drivers control the configuration**

The configuration information is controlled by the printer driver you installed, which knows everything there is to know about the printer and its capacities. The printer driver installs itself with a bunch of default options, which are assumptions that are made about how you want to use this printer, and you'll probably find the default configuration is just fine.

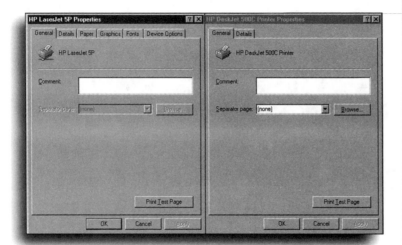

FIGURE 13.8
A laser printer has many more
options than an inkjet printer.

## Configuring Graphics Options

If most of your printing is text-based or even if you print some
graphics (the grid lines around a spreadsheet or a table), you
probably can get adequate, readable hard copy without printing
at 600 dpi. If your laser printer is capable of 600 dpi, change the
configuration option on the Graphics tab to make 300 dpi the
new default. Then, for those once-in-a-while print jobs that
require better print quality, click the Setup button (in some software the button says Options or Printer Options) and increase
the resolution.

Printing at lower resolution has two benefits:

- You'll save a lot of money on toner/ink cartridges.
- Printing is much faster.

## Configuring Paper Options

Windows 98 makes an assumption that your printing needs are
limited to standard letter-size paper. If you have a printer that's
used for legal work, and nobody ever puts letter size paper in the
tray, you have to reconfigure the printer. Move to the Paper tab
of the printer's Properties dialog box and select the paper that is
the default for this printer (see Figure 13.9).

**More dots mean better resolution**

Dpi means dots per inch, and
it's a measurement of the den-
sity of printing. The more dots
of toner/ink laid down in each
inch, the crisper the resolution.

FIGURE 13.9

Some printers have a remarkably robust capability for paper handling.

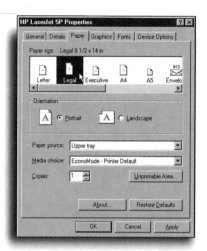

Many printers present an opportunity to design your own paper size. Perhaps there's some weird and strange paper size that is used for certain office documents. Or maybe your Aunt Lynn gave you personalized stationery for your birthday and explained she had it custom designed just for you. The fact that it's 5.7" high and 4.5" wide won't matter because you can match it and use it using the paper named Custom (if custom designing paper is available for your printer, it's the last choice when you scroll through the paper choices).

There's a neat thing about paper sizes and your ability to use them at will—Windows software works with you to make it easy. When you print from a Windows software application, the Print dialog box has a Properties button (see Figure 13.10). After you create a document that's designed for a particular paper size, choose File, Print, and then use the Properties button to change the paper configuration for this document. (Don't forget to change it back.) You can even specify the tray (or specify manual feed if the paper doesn't fit properly in any tray).

Oh yes, I guess I should remind you that you have to go to the printer and physically put this custom-designed paper in, but you've probably figured that out for yourself.

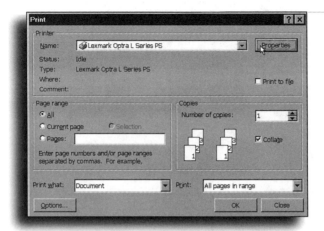

FIGURE 13.10
Click the Properties button to change the paper configuration for the printer when you're ready to print.

## Configuring Device Options

For most laser printers, the Device Options tab is for tweaking (see Figure 13.11). You can play with the options on this tab to try to enhance your printer's performance. Actually, one item isn't a tweaking item, you may have to correct the information the printer driver uses. That item is memory, and if your printer has more memory installed than the display indicates, change the value in Printer Memory field to match the amount of installed memory for this printer.

This memory usage configuration can be tricky, like trying to fix a wobbly three-legged table. But if you get it just right, you can make a real difference in the performance you get from your printer.

When you send any document to the printer, the printer driver goes into "fast mathematical calculation" mode. It looks at the document and does a calculation to see how much memory is required to print the document. Then it compares that figure to the amount of memory in the printer. If the needed memory is more than the memory of the printer, the document won't print. You'll see an error message (usually something like "document is too large for printer memory") and some lights on your printer might start blinking, or a light that isn't usually on will suddenly light up, or the printer LED panel (if there is one) will flash a number or a message.

**Device options may be different for your printer**

Some printers, especially high-end PostScript printers, present entirely different options for Device Options. The dialog box selected for this example represents commonly seen options.

FIGURE 13.11

You can change the way your printer uses memory to see if performance improves.

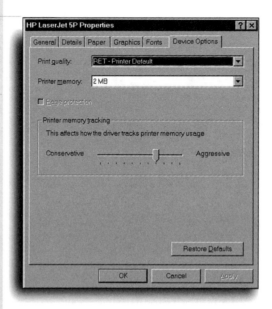

If your printer's Device Options tab displays a Printer memory tracking slider bar, you can configure the way the printer driver performs its calculations. In effect, that means you can control the way the printer uses memory.

If you tell the printer driver to be more aggressive about trying to print a document that is just on the edge of "maybe it needs more memory than the printer has," you'll find that sometimes the document will make it. When it doesn't, however, it's after a very long wait and that isn't terribly productive.

If you tell the printer driver to be more conservative about the way it does its calculations, you're telling the driver to err on the side of safety. You'll see more error messages that there isn't enough memory to print your document (although some of those documents might really have been able to get through the process). Then, you can make changes in the document or the printer configuration to print a modified version. For example, to overcome the problem of too much graphic for too little memory, you could try one of these tactics:

- Make the complicated graphic smaller.

- Make the complicated graphic less complicated by removing a border or removing one layer of decorative graphical elements.

- Lower the graphics resolution of the printer for this print job.

The memory tracking option isn't important if you do text-based work, but if you do a lot of graphics, you should move the slider along until you find you're getting as much out of the printer and its memory as you can. Be sure to write down what you do each time you make a change so you can approach this experiment with all the efficiency of a lab scientist.

## A Trick for Producing Good Graphics

I learned a trick years ago about getting complicated graphics out of a printer at low resolution, and still getting hard copy I could send out without being embarrassed. I would print the graphic at a low resolution just to get it out of the printer. The graphic didn't look terrific; it looked "soft and fuzzy" instead of "crisp." The reason for that is there are fewer dots in each inch and you're really seeing the spaces between the dots when you print at lower resolution. Then I'd copy the document on a good copier, setting the copier for reduction. Even a 20 percent reduction helps enormously. What reduction does is close up some of the spaces between the dots, making the document look crisper. For really important stuff, I'd take my printout to a copy shop and have them use a powerful copier or even a stat machine. Another trick I learned when doing this was to keep more expensive, coated paper around for these situations. Regular paper has some rag content and it actually absorbs some of the toner, which makes the problem worse. Coated paper doesn't absorb and therefore you start with a crisper image. In fact, whenever I printed anything that was going to be reproduced on a copy machine (even if it were all text), I used coated paper. Try this if you put out the company newsletter or any other document that will be copied or is going to a printing company that's using offset printing.

## The Care and Feeding of Printers

Printers need some TLC, although the technical jargon for this is usually "preventive maintenance."

Printers are dust collectors. It's not really dust—it's lint from the paper, but it piles up like those dust balls that grow under beds. A computer vacuum is a good investment because cleaning dust from printers (and computers) saves repair costs. Do not use your household vacuum to clean your printer; if you don't have a computer vacuum, buy canned air and blow the dust out.

Laser printers need to have the wires and paper guides cleaned, and you should do this every time you change cartridges (or toner if your laser is a toner-replacement printer). Approach this task gingerly and gently; a Q-tip is your best tool.

# Printing Your Document

Finally, your printer is installed, tweaked, tested, and ready. You have created a magnificent document and it's time to share it with the world. From the menu bar of your software window, you've chosen **File, Print**. Two procedures occur at this point and we'll discuss both of them in this section:

- You choose the options you need from the Print dialog box.
- The printing process begins.

## Using the Print Dialog Box

When the Print dialog box appears in your Windows software, you have a number of options for creating a hard copy of your document (see Figure 13.12). Use these guidelines to understand the important options on this dialog box:

- The default printer is assumed, but if you have multiple printers, you can select a different one. Usually, you change printers to match the options needed to print this particular document.

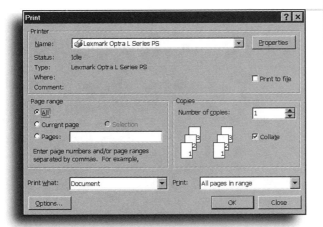

FIGURE 13.12
Use the Print dialog box to set options for printing the document, and to reset printer capabilities to match the document.

- You can opt to print the entire document or specific pages (enter a range of page numbers with a dash, as in 2-6, or enter individual page numbers with commas, as in 2,4,7). Choose **Current page** to print the page on which your cursor is. (If you've selected some portion of your document, you can print just the selected items.)

- If you want multiple copies of the document, specify the number. Select the **Collate** button to print the pages in order, and then print the next copy in the same order. Deselect the **Collate** button to print multiple copies of the first page, then multiple copies of the next page, and so on.

- The Print field in the lower-right part of the dialog box offers three options: **All pages in range**; **Odd pages**; **Even pages**. Use these options if you want to print on both sides of the paper but your printer does not offer duplex printing (this is the "do it yourself" method for double-sided printing).

- Choose **Properties** to open a Properties dialog box for the printer if you have to change printer options to print this document. For example, you may need to change the paper size or the tray.

Click that **Print** button and go back to work in your software. Your document is now officially a "print job."

**Limited options available from the print dialog box**

When you choose Properties from the Print dialog box, you do not see all the tabs in the printer's Properties dialog box. You see only the options for printing documents such as paper type or graphics resolution.

# Understanding Spooling

Windows 98 performs some work on the file, getting it ready for your printer. It renders graphics, makes sure the data format and the size of the data match what your printer can handle, makes sure the instruction codes match what your printer can understand, and generally manipulates the file in a number of complicated ways. As it does all of this, it saves its work to a file, which it places on your hard drive in the folder `\Windows\Spool\Printers`, (assuming your Windows 98 directory is named Windows).

The process of taking the print job and turning it into a file is called *spooling*, and the folder is called your *spooler*. All of this happens in the background; you don't see it and you don't have to wait for it to complete before you can go back to work in your software program.

When the file is saved to the spooler, the filename format is `filename.spl`, where *filename* is your document name and the .spl extension indicates it is a spool file.

In addition, Windows 98 keeps notes about the spool file such as the name of the user who sent the print job, the type of data in the file, and other details. It puts those notes into another file which is also saved in the spooler and named with the format `number.shd`, where *number* is the job number and the extension .shd means "shadow file."

Now there are two files: your print job and the shadow file created by Windows 98. Those files sit in the spooler, waiting to be sent to the printer. That lineup of files waiting for their turn at the printer is called a *queue*.

The files in the queue stay there until they have their turn at the printer and printing is finished (unless you remove them, which is covered in the next section of this chapter). If the power fails and your computer shuts down (and the printer does, too), those files are still in the queue and they'll print when everything is up and running again.

**The spool takes up disk space**

The spooler is one of the reasons you have to keep an eye on the amount of free space on your hard drive.

# Controlling Print Jobs

While these spooled files are being written to your hard drive and waiting to be printed, you can manipulate them. You can stop, start, cancel, or eliminate any print job that is in the queue. Why would you want to do this? Good question, and here are some good reasons:

- You've sent a large print job that will take a long time to print and you suddenly realize you have to make changes in the document. You can stop the job from printing.

- The printer is stuck or slowed down by a complicated print job that could wait until later, but the next print job is a document that must be printed and distributed immediately. You can cancel the unimportant job, or you can move the important job up ahead of the unimportant job in the queue.

- The first page of a large print job has come out of the printer and there's a problem. The fonts are wrong or there are garbage characters, or there is some other serious problem. There's no point in looking at page after page of a bad print job, so you should cancel the job.

## Viewing the Printer Dialog Box

You can see what's happening to your print jobs in the printer's dialog box. To open the dialog box, follow these steps:

1. Open My Computer, and then open the **Printers** folder (or click **Start** and choose **Settings**, **Printers** from the Start menu).

2. Double-click the icon for your printer to open the printer's dialog box.

The dialog box displays the current printer queue. Your options for manipulating the printer and the print jobs depend on what's in the queue and the current state of any particular print job. Let's track a print job by watching the display in the printer's dialog box.

**Quick access to an active printer**

While your printer is actually printing, there's a printer icon on the taskbar tray. You can double-click that icon to open the printer's dialog box.

To illustrate, I sent a 17-page document to a local printer, opening the printer's dialog box so I could watch the events. Figure 13.13 shows the spooling process.

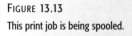
FIGURE 13.13
This print job is being spooled.

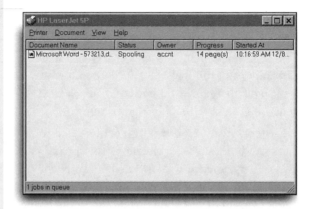

There isn't much I can do to manipulate the file at this point because things move much too fast. By the time the queue was displayed on the dialog box (meaning the amount of time it took to place the display on my screen, which must be nanoseconds, don't you think?), the spooling was already 14 pages in on its goal of spooling 17 pages. By the time I moved my mouse to the listing, spooling was finished. If the print job had been many pages of large graphics (complicating and therefore slowing down the rendering process), I probably could have manipulated the item. When I checked again, printing had started (see Figure 13.14).

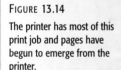
FIGURE 13.14
The printer has most of this print job and pages have begun to emerge from the printer.

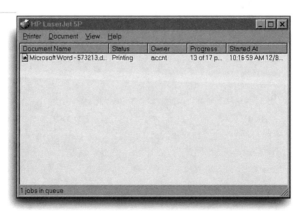

At this point, it's technically possible to stop this print job or pause it. However, the number of pages that have been sent to the printer make it apparent that it's too late to manipulate the job. By the time I get my mouse to the print job listing and right-click to see the shortcut menu that shows me my options (or click a menu item to see the options), the printer will have all the pages. Remember that because the printer itself has memory and a certain number of pages have been printed, there are pages in the printer's memory. If I stop the print job at the dialog box, the printer continues to print whatever is still in memory (which can be a great many pages if the pages are mostly text).

## Manipulating the Spooler Options

The way this print job was spooled and printed matches the configuration options in the Properties dialog box for this printer. You have some options for the manner in which spooling and printing takes place and now that you understand what happens when you print, those options will make more sense to you. Let's look at the spooling options, which are reached by following these steps:

1. Open the Printers folder and right-click the printer icon. Choose **Properties** from the shortcut menu.

2. Go to the **Details** tab (all printer Properties dialog boxes have a Details tab).

3. Choose **Spool Settings** to bring up the **Spool Settings** dialog box (see Figure 13.15).

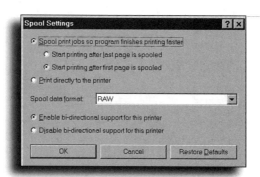

**FIGURE 13.15**
You can change the way spooling works, or eliminate it altogether.

**4.** You can change the spooler so it starts printing after the last page is spooled. This means that all the resources in the Windows 98 printing system are concentrated on spooling instead of continuing to spool additional pages while sending the first page to the printer. The upside of that is you get back to full speed in your software faster. The downside is that you're using more disk space.

**5.** You can bypass the spooler by selecting **Print directly to the printer.** You won't like this—when you send a document to the printer, your software slows down until the printer has finished processing all the pages (even fast printers are much slower than the disk-based spooler). This option is usually used to test printing when you're having a problem and you want to see if bypassing the spooler eliminates it.

## Manipulating the Print Jobs

Now that we all understand what's going on, and how fast everything moves through the spooler, it's time to examine realistically the kind of controls you have over printing.

You can control both the printer and the individual print jobs from the printer's dialog box. Let's open a busy printer's dialog box using the steps described earlier (open the Printers folder and double-click the printer icon). Figure 13.16 shows a six-job queue, and we can use the items in this dialog box to discuss all the things you can do (one of which I've already done).

FIGURE 13.16

The printer's dialog box displays information about every print job in the queue.

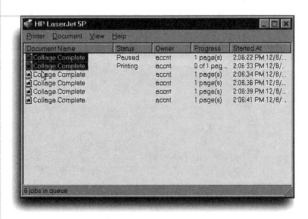

Here are the important things to know about viewing a print queue:

- The document name, along with the software that sent the print job, is displayed.

- The current status of the individual print job is shown if it is spooling, printing, or paused. Otherwise, the status column is blank, which means "sitting patiently waiting its turn."

- The user who sent the job is listed, as is the time the job arrived at the queue.

- By default, jobs are printed in the order in which they arrive in the queue.

- The size of the job is shown in the Progress column (depending on the type of data you're sending, the size can be reported in either pages or bytes).

- If there is a problem at the printer, an error message displays on the title bar of the dialog box, or in the Status column of the print job that is currently printing (or in both places). It's not uncommon to see an "out-of-paper" message here.

The first thing to notice about this particular queue (you probably already have) is that the job at the top of the queue is paused. The job next in line is printing.

## Pausing Printing

You can pause any print job, or you can pause the printer. The most common reason for pausing a print job is because a job behind it is more important and you want to let it "print through" (and I don't even play golf—I just know the term). The most common reason for pausing a printer is to change something physical, such as the paper, or the tray (if you have one tray slot and have to alternate between the legal-and letter-size trays).

- To pause a print job, right-click its listing and choose **Pause Printing**. Pausing an individual print job doesn't stop all printing; it stops only that job and all the print jobs behind it keep going.

**Use the menus**

If you aren't in the mood for right-clicking, the same options are available for manipulating individual print jobs in the Document menu on the menu bar of the dialog box.

**Manipulating network printers requires rights**

You can't automatically manipulate a network printer the way you can your local printer. If you don't have the necessary permissions to access the printer, you'll have to ask a network administrator to pause or cancel any jobs that require those actions.

- To pause the printer, choose **Printer**, **Pause Printing** from the menu bar. All the print jobs in the queue are paused.

- To resume printing, follow the same steps you used to pause printing. The pause menu item is a toggle; the first time you click it a check mark appears to indicate that pause is active and the second time you click it the check mark is removed and printing begins.

## Removing Print Jobs

As with pausing, you can remove individual print jobs from the queue or remove all the print jobs currently headed for the printer.

- To remove a print job, right-click on its listing and choose **Cancel Printing**.

- To remove all the print jobs, choose **Printer**, **Purge Print Jobs** from the menu bar.

## Changing the Order of Print Jobs

If you have several print jobs in the queue and you want one to print ahead of another (or after another), select the job and drag it to the appropriate point in the queue. You cannot change the order of the document that is printing and you cannot move a print job ahead of a document that is printing.

# Printing to a File

Printing to a file means taking that spool file (the one with all the rendering, instruction codes, and other technical stuff in it) and sending it to a file on your disk instead of sending it to a printer. The important part of that sentence is the fact that the codes are in this file and that means it can be printed only by that printer model.

The disk file that results from printing to a file is not the same kind of file that your software sends to the printer, and it's not the same kind of file that sits in the spooler. A printer disk file is a unique animal and there's only one way to turn it into hard copy—you have to copy it to the printer using a DOS command.

**Printing a file document is a two-step process**

1. From your software, print your document to a file instead of a printer.

2. Copy the file to the printer to get a hard copy.

## Saving the Document as a Print File

To print a document to a file instead of sending it to your printer, follow these steps:

1. In your software program, when you have finished creating the document, choose **File**, **Print** from the menu bar.

2. When the Print dialog box appears, select **Print to file** (see Figure 13.17). Then click **OK**.

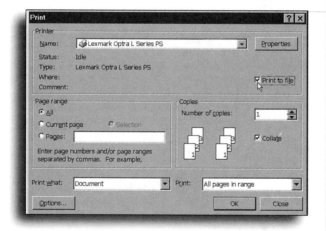

FIGURE 13.17

Select **Print to file** on the Print dialog box to change the target port/printer to a file.

3. The Print to File dialog box opens, which is like a Save As dialog box (see Figure 13.18). Choose a folder to save the file in and give the file a name. The automatic extension for a printer file is .prn.

FIGURE 13.18

Save a print file the same way you save any file.

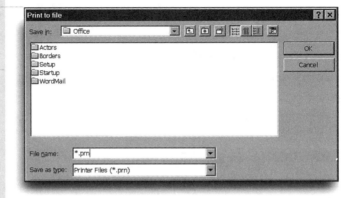

## Printing a Print File

When you are able to get to a computer that's connected to the printer, you can print the file. To do so, follow these steps:

1.  Open an MS-DOS command session by choosing Programs, MS-DOS Prompt from the Start menu.

2.  Enter **copy \path\filename.prn lpt1: /b**, where:

    - **\path** is the name of the directory into which you saved the file.

    - **filename** is the name you gave the file.

    - **lpt1:** is the printer port (if the printer is attached to lpt2, use **lpt2:**).

    - The **/b parameter** tells the Copy command that you are sending a binary file, not a next file.

You can also send this command from the Run dialog box on your Start menu. However, because Run expects the name of a software application, you have to warn it you're using a DOS command instead of the name of an executable file.

For the Run dialog box, the command is **command /c copy \path\filename.ext lpt1: /b**.

- The word **command** tells Run you are entering a command.

- **/c** tells the command processor to carry out the command and then stop.

---

**LPT1, prn—Six of one, half a dozen of the other**

The command **copy \path\ filename.ext prn /b** also works if your printer is attached to lpt1, because the operating system translates a target destination of "prn" as "lpt1."

## Uses for Print Files

Once you start to think about it, there are a lot of ways to use this feature. Here are a few to jump-start your own thinking about how your situation would be made easier by using print files.

- You create a document at home and want to print it at your office (the office has better printers). The software you use at home doesn't exist at the office, so you can't bring the document file to work and load it into the office software.

- You create a document you want to give a hard copy of to someone who doesn't have the software you used.

- You create a document at work that would look much better if it were printed on a powerful fancy PostScript printer, but there's no such printer you can connect to.

- You create a document that is going to be printed by a printing company that has a Linotronic or Varityper printer and you have no access to one.

Now, if you remember what I said earlier about printer files containing all those codes that are specific to the printer, you're asking the question, "But how do I do that if the printer that will ultimately print this document isn't the same printer I prepared it for?"

The answer is, "You can't." That is, you cannot send a print file that was prepared for your HPIII and send it to an Apple PostScript printer or a Linotronic. You have to prepare the print file for the same printer that will be used as the target of the copy command that prints your print file.

Okay, now you're saying, "But I don't have a Linotronic printer." The answer is, "You can if you want to." Install it. You can install any printer you want to because during the installation, Windows 98 cannot peer out from the monitor and say, "Hey, wait—I don't see a Linotronic printer there." Just lie. Tell Windows 98 you have a Linotronic (or any other printer on the list of available printers) connected to LPT1. It doesn't matter if you already have a printer connected to LPT1; it doesn't matter

**No printer at home or on the road?**

To learn about non-printing (deferred printing), which is an issue when you're not at your usual computer location, read Chapter 22. There's information about offline printing tricks you'll need if you travel with a computer.

if you never use LPT1 because the printer you use is a network printer. This is one lie you cannot get caught telling.

When you add additional printers, Windows 98 assumes they are not the default printers so you won't accidentally print to one of these "phantom printers" from your software.

When you want to use this printer to create a print file, select it from the list of printers in the Print dialog box and then choose **Print to file**. The resulting file can be sent to anyone with a real printer of that type.

# Tricks, Tips, and Troubleshooting

There are some tricks to using, installing, and configuring printers that will save you time and energy. This section is an assortment of things I've learned to do in my constant effort to avoid any more work or exertion than is absolutely necessary.

## Quick Printing

You're in front of your computer working on a spreadsheet, and somebody asks for a printed copy of a document you prepared in your word processor. You don't have to open the word processor; simply use the **Open** icon to open a dialog box to find the file, load it in the word processor window, choose **Print**, choose **OK** in the Print dialog box, close the word processor, and go back to work in the spreadsheet program. Whew! That's too much like work.

Find the file in Explorer and right-click its icon. Choose **Print**. Everything else that has to happen (see the long list enumerated in the previous paragraph) happens automatically and you just keep working in your spreadsheet program while it happens.

Every tips and tricks book or article I've seen about printing in Windows 98 includes a way to print quickly by dragging a file from Explorer to a desktop shortcut for the printer. I think right-clicking is faster, but to make sure I'm covering all bases, I'll include this tip. Here goes.

Or, for quick printing, find the file in Explorer and drag it to a printer icon on your desktop.

Of course, you need a printer icon on your desktop, so here's how to get one:

1. Open the Printers folder on an empty desktop.
2. Right-drag the icon for your default printer to the desktop.
3. Release the mouse button and choose **Create Shortcut(s) Here** from the menu that appears.

Now, when you want to print in a hurry, use these easy steps:

1. Minimize the software window you're working in to see the desktop.
2. Open Explorer and find the file you need to print.
3. Drag the file to the printer icon.
4. Restore the software window and go back to work.

This is even easier if you keep a shortcut to Explorer on the desktop, too (I couldn't live without it). To put a shortcut to Explorer on the desktop, follow these steps:

1. Open Explorer and go to the Windows 98 folder (which may or may not be named Windows).
2. Find the file named Explorer and right-drag it to the desktop.
3. Choose **Create Shortcut(s) Here** from the menu that appears when you release the mouse button.

If you right-click a file and there is no Print command on the shortcut menu, dragging that file to a desktop printer icon won't work either. The reason is that the file is not associated with a software program so Windows 98 doesn't know which program to load.

**SEE ALSO**

➤ *To learn about file associations, turn to Chapter 4.*

## Restoring Printing Defaults for Software

When you print with either method (right-clicking or dragging to a desktop printer icon), you'll find that for most Windows software, the printing options that were selected when you last closed that software remain in effect. If you shut down the software after printing to a file, quick printing will display a dialog box asking you to name the disk file you're printing. You have to be careful to restore the default print options before you exit the software.

On the other hand, the next time you open the software normally, the print options are restored to default; it's part of the opening process the software goes through. It would be easier if the return to defaults took place when you closed the software, but that's not the way most software is written.

## Clone Printers for Specific Options

If you find yourself printing a great many documents that require changing the options on a printer before you can send the print job, save yourself some work. Invent a new printer with those options already set.

For example, suppose your printer is set for 300dpi (even though it's capable of 600dpi) to save toner and because most of your printing is text based. However, once in a while, perhaps every 10 print jobs or so, you have to change the resolution to 600dpi because the graphics in your document have to look terrific (you're doing a presentation for the people who get to vote on your annual raise).

If you had a printer that was configured for 600dpi, you wouldn't have to go through all those steps in the Print dialog box (open the Properties for the printer and change the resolution).

Clone your printer and configure it for the settings you need by following these steps:

1. Install the printer using the same steps detailed earlier in this chapter.

**2.** At the point in the installation where you have to name the printer, pick a name that describes what you're doing (for example, HP5-600dpi).

**3.** After the installation is complete, right-click the printer's icon and change the settings to match your needs.

You can do this as often as you want, cloning your printer for printing to a file, using a different paper type, or for any other configuration options.

Then, when you need those options, you just choose that printer from the list of printers in the Print dialog box.

Remember that for many programs, the printer that's selected when you exit the software is the printer that's used for quick printing, so get in the habit of restoring the default printer before you exit the software. Just open the Print dialog box, select the default printer, close the dialog box, and exit the software.

## Create a Universal Print to File Technique

Earlier in this chapter, we talked about printing a document to a file and then sending it to the printer via the command line. Remember that this file is filled with all the special codes provided by the printer driver, so it can be sent only to the printer model for which it was created.

But, there's a way to create a print file that will work for everyone. It creates a print file that has no special codes, so that any printer can handle the contents of the file. The only drawback is that the contents must be plain text.

In fact, you can use this printer for direct printing—it's not limited to printing to a file.

This is all possible because Windows 98 includes a generic, text-only printer in the list of supported printers. You can use this printer to send a document to any printer, as long as the document is text and you don't care about fancy formatting of the text.

**To install this printer, follow these steps:**

1. Open the **Printers** folder and double-click Add Printer to begin the installation of a new printer.

2. Select **Local Printer** and choose **Next**.

3. Select **Generic** as the manufacturer in the next wizard window (see Figure 13.19).

FIGURE 13.19

The manufacturer known as generic makes only one model, but it works with every printer.

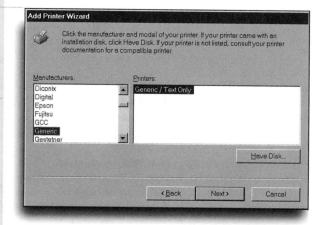

4. Use LPT1 as the port and name the printer (the suggested name "Generic/Text Only" is perfectly fine).

5. If you have a real printer attached to LPT1, it's okay to say **Yes** to the test page. If you normally use a network printer and will use this new printer only for printing to a file, turn down the offer to print a test page.

6. Choose **Finish**, and when the files have been transferred from your Windows 98 disk to your hard drive, the new printer is in your Printers folder.

Incidentally, you can use this printer to test your real printer if you experience problems while printing. If a document will print to this printer but not to your real printer, it indicates some problem with the printer driver for your real printer. Delete and reinstall the real printer to freshen the driver files. If a document won't even print to this printer, you probably have a hardware problem.

# Shadow Files Aren't Deleted

Earlier in this chapter, I explained the files Windows 98 creates when sending print jobs to the spooler. The shadow file for each print job remains in the spooler subdirectory if you have your spooler configured to start printing after the first page is spooled. The process of rebooting your computer and restarting the operating system deletes these files.

However, if you don't regularly shut down your computer and restart it, the files continue to pile up in your spooler (I rarely restart my computer, so I find lots of shadow files in the spooler; they have the extension .shd).

The files do no harm except to take up disk space, and if disk space is a problem, you should either reboot more often or delete the files manually.

# Using Manufacturer Software

Some manufacturers (most notably Hewlett-Packard) supply software disks when you purchase a printer. Some of the utilities on the software are quite useful, but some features just won't be used because Windows 95 handles those functions or there are functions you don't ever need.

If you feel you want to use the software, the trick is to perform the installation so that the software utilities are launched only when you need them. Otherwise, the software is always there, taking up memory and resources.

The truth is, the only really useful utility I've encountered is the HP realignment for DeskJet printheads, which is pretty clever.

Printing is one of the functions you'll use more often than any other. It's the "global application" for computing. Installing, configuring, and tweaking your printing capabilities is worth the effort, because afterward you can click the print icon on any toolbar and know you'll get what you need.

There's nothing difficult or super-technical about installing and using a printer in Windows 98, but you must test your printer and its configuration carefully. Printing is one of the most important, and commonly used, functions in computers.

*IV*

# Working with Hardware

# Installing Basic Devices

# An Architectural Overview of the PC

Computer hardware used to be difficult to install and configure properly because of the various possible conflicts that can occur between hardware devices. In this chapter, we'll take a look at some popular PC add-on hardware devices, and I'll explain how Windows 98 helps to ease the pain of hardware installation problems. Until recently, installation of new hardware in a PC wasn't very user-friendly, and conflicts between hardware devices used to be the norm. Luckily for us, that's all changed now. A basic PC consists of a few main components and various specialized add-on components. The various hardware components of a typical PC system are:

- A processor, such as an Intel Pentium chip
- Input and output devices, such as a keyboard and a monitor
- Memory in the form of RAM, ROM BIOS, and data cache (pronounced "cash")
- Expansion bus slots
- Hardware interface ports, such as communications ports and printer ports
- Long-term storage devices, such as floppy and hard disk drives
- A power supply

In addition, there are numerous add-on peripheral devices and adapter cards available.

# Hardware Conflict Hotspots

At the heart of the PC is the Basic Input/Output System (BIOS), which controls how resources are used. The problem with legacy (old) PC hardware devices is that they expect to use specific resources within the computer, and these resources are quite limited in number. Two or more devices may claim the same resource, and then you have a hardware conflict. There are four major hardware resources that are involved in conflicts:

- Input/Output (I/O) port addresses
- Interrupt Request (IRQ) numbers
- Bus memory addresses
- Direct Memory Access (DMA) channels

Let's look at each of these a little more closely to understand the kinds of conflicts that can occur in your PC hardware.

## I/O Port Addresses

Your computer uses I/O addresses to communicate with adapter boards installed in the system's expansion bus slots. Adapters utilize a range of addresses, and these addresses are typically written using a numbering system based on 16 rather than 10. Base-16, called *hexadecimal*, is easier for computer programmers and hardware engineers to work with than base-10, which is just plain old decimal. A few examples in hexadecimal, or hex for short, are numbers like 01F0 (496 in decimal) or FB3C (64,316 in decimal). If two or more adapters claim the same I/O address, a conflict occurs.

## Interrupt Request Numbers

A computer can efficiently process tasks you've given it, yet still interrupt what it's doing to do your bidding when you type at the keyboard or move the mouse. Any task that's interrupted is stored in an area of memory called the *stack*, and when the interruption is finished, the original task resumes.

PCs use a system of hardware interrupts to allow a smooth flow of data for all its component parts. For instance, when a hard disk controller needs to perform the physical disk actions needed to rename a file, an interrupt is used to accomplish the task. Interrupts have varying priorities within the system, ranging from zero (highest priority) to 15 (lowest priority). Interrupts are requested from the system using interrupt request numbers, or IRQs. An IRQ is assigned to each device in the system, and some IRQs can be shared among devices.

## Bus Memory Addresses

Some devices use portions of the system's random access memory (RAM) to store information that's critical to proper performance. Unfortunately, there's only a limited amount of memory available for the data bus. The problem, similar to I/O addressing, is that devices may use overlapping memory ranges, and this causes a hardware conflict.

## DMA Channels

Direct memory access channels allow an adapter to send data directly to system memory without generating an interrupt to the microprocessor. This makes DMA the ideal choice for high-speed devices that must transfer data quickly. DMA channels are scarce, and devices must contend for them.

# Understanding Plug and Play

A few years ago, hardware vendors came up with a great idea—a new way for hardware devices from various manufacturers to cooperate with one another within a computer system. The idea was to have each piece of hardware configure itself without conflicting with any other hardware in the system. This idea of user-friendly self-configuration grew into the hardware specification called *Plug and Play*.

There are three main Plug and Play components:

- A Plug and Play BIOS
- Plug and Play hardware devices and device drivers
- A Plug and Play operating system, such as Windows 98

If all system components are Plug and Play-compliant, there's usually no problem with hardware conflicts. However, if you've got a mixture of Plug and Play and non-Plug and Play devices in your PC, conflicts are likely.

## What Is Plug and Play?

With the computer's resources being used by so many different types of devices in the system, imagine the difficulty in finding available settings, without conflict, when installing a new adapter. Using trial and error to change various IRQs, DMA channels, I/O addresses, and bus memory addresses can quickly become a nightmare.

In the old days (just a few years ago), most devices used small jumper pins to set I/O addresses, IRQ numbers, and DMA channels to some specific range or number. For example, if a newly installed sound card conflicted with some pre-existing device, this would generally be resolved by trial and error, moving the jumper for a given resource and trying again (and again) until everything worked properly. That's where Plug and Play comes in.

There are many types of Plug and Play devices, but each must meet certain requirements:

- Each device must identify the services provided and the system resources needed.
- Each device must have a unique identity within the system.
- Each device must identify the software that drives it.
- Each device must be configurable by software.

Plug and Play-compliant devices each communicate with the BIOS to find out which resources are in use and which are

**Plug and Play conflicts**

The Plug and Play specification allows the BIOS to change resources automatically for Plug and Play devices as needed when the system boots. This occurs before Windows 98 is even loaded into memory, and if non-Plug and Play hardware causes a conflict that Plug and Play can't resolve, Windows 98 may not start at all!

**Resolving conflicts in Safe Mode**

Microsoft created Windows 98's Safe Mode to allow the system to load Windows 98 with a minimal set of drivers and allow manual configuration by way of software. Software-configurable Plug and Play devices can use virtual jumpers to change I/O and bus addresses, and DMA or IRQ numbers. This eliminates the need for hardware jumpers on most adapters.

available, and then each politely claims an unused resource as its own.

# The Universal Serial Bus (USB)

The Universal Serial Bus (USB) is a new type of bus architecture that provides a single bus for peripheral devices like game controllers, serial and parallel ports, and scanners. Because USB represents a new specification for hardware design, USB hardware is completely Plug and Play-compliant, without the problems inherent in older legacy hardware.

USB is a fast and inexpensive bus for communications and input devices, and a computer with USB capabilities allows you to attach any USB device to any USB connector at any time. Windows 98 is fully USB aware, and will therefore recognize any new USB device as soon as the device is plugged into a USB port. Windows 98 will then load any necessary software drivers and make the device available for immediate use.

# Types of Devices

There is an ever-growing market for PCs, and the add-on device market is booming. There are so many types of devices available that I can't cover them all, but I'll touch on the most popular ones.

Devices are grouped into two general categories: internal and external, and these are further broken into smaller, more detailed groups. The type of hardware interface a device uses to communicate with the PC determines which general group a device belongs to. Let's look at these groups to see what categories various basic devices fit into.

## Common Internal Devices

Internal devices are designed for semi-permanent installation. They are usually plugged into an expansion slot or are connected by a cable to an adapter card that is plugged into an expansion slot.

Basic internal devices fall into these categories:

- Data storage devices, including DVD drives, CD-ROM drives, floppy disk drives, hard disk drives, tape drives, and Zip drives.
- Add-on adapter cards, such as modems, network interface cards (NICs), sound cards, SCSI controllers, and video display adapters.

## Data Bus Expansion Slots

Computers have several internal architecture schemes that determine what particular flavor of device you should buy for your PC. There are four common bus architectures you should be aware of:

- Industry Standard Architecture (ISA) bus
- Extended ISA (EISA) bus
- Video Electronics Standards Association (VESA) bus, also called the VESA Local (VL) bus
- Peripheral Component Interconnect (PCI) bus

ISA has been around the longest and was extended with the EISA specification. Since EISA is an extension of ISA, an old ISA adapter card will work in an EISA bus—it's the same type of card slot on the bus. Because their architectures are quite different from ISA/EISA, the VL and PCI buses use a different type of card slot on the bus, smaller and more efficient.

The design of a PCI slot is completely different from that of ISA or EISA. In fact, a PCI adapter card must be plugged into a PCI expansion slot upside down from an ISA or EISA card. That is, when inserting a PCI card into an expansion slot, the card's electronic components are on the opposite side of the card from an ISA or EISA card's components.

Many systems these days have a mixed-bus architecture that supports both types of expansion slots, and these are typically referred to as either ISA slots or PCI slots. The VL bus and EISA bus have faded away over the last few years in favor of the PCI/ISA bus, so it's getting harder to find adapter cards for these buses.

# Common External Devices

Unlike internal devices, external devices are very flexible because you can easily transfer them from one computer to another. By simply unplugging an external device from one PC and plugging it into another, most of the work is done. If both machines have the proper software drivers to run the hardware, there is usually little or no additional configuration.

Basic external devices fall into these categories:

- Serial port devices
- Parallel port devices
- SCSI devices

## Serial Port Devices

Serial port devices connect to a serial communications (COM) port on the back of the PC. There are four standard COM ports: COM1, COM2, COM3, and COM4. COM1 is shared with COM3, and COM2 is shared with COM4, making COM port selection a possible point of conflict for systems using multiple serial devices.

Serial devices typically include communications devices such as modems, but also include devices as diverse as printers, scanners, and mice.

## Parallel Port Devices

Parallel port devices connect to a parallel (LPT) port on the back of the PC. There are four standard LPT ports: LPT1, LPT2, LPT3, and LPT4, but most PCs have only one physical LPT port. The others are usually virtual ports created by the operating system.

Parallel port devices include printers, DVD drives, CD-ROM drives, tape drives, ZIP drives, and external hard drives.

### Small Computer System Interface (SCSI) Devices

External SCSI (pronounced "scuzzy") devices connect to an available external SCSI port. Up to seven SCSI devices can attach to a SCSI controller, and each must have a unique SCSI ID number to prevent conflicts.

External SCSI devices include DVD drives, CD-ROM drives, tape drives, ZIP drives, and external hard drives.

# Using the Add New Hardware Wizard

Adding new hardware to your PC shouldn't be a tedious chore. That's why Windows 98 includes wizards to break complex tasks down into simple steps. After adding a new device to your computer, Windows 98 may or may not recognize it automatically. In a perfect world, Windows 98 would recognize every piece of hardware, install the drivers for it automatically if needed, and you'd be ready to go. Unfortunately, this isn't a perfect world.

For one reason or another, Windows 98 often doesn't recognize newly installed devices automatically. When this occurs, you can use the Add New Hardware Wizard to tell Windows 98 everything it needs to know about the new device. You access the Add New Hardware Wizard from the Control Panel, as shown in Figure 14.1.

**FIGURE 14.1**

Access the Add New Hardware Wizard from the Control Panel.

# Adding New Hardware

To tell Windows 98 about some new, as yet undetected hardware device, launch the **Add New Hardware** Wizard from Control Panel. The opening screen gives a description of the wizard. To begin installing your new hardware, click the **Next** button.

Windows 98 is going to search for new Plug and Play hardware automatically, as shown in Figure 14.2.

**FIGURE 14.2**

The Add New Hardware Wizard tells you that it is going to search for new Plug and Play hardware automatically.

## Automatic Plug and Play Hardware Detection

Windows 98 first attempts to find any new Plug and Play hardware that may have been installed. To start the process, you must select the **Next** button, as shown in Figure 14.3.

**FIGURE 14.3**

The Add New Hardware Wizard searches for Plug and Play hardware.

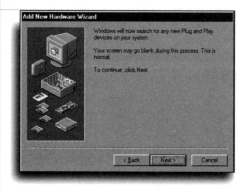

Because most add-on devices are now Plug and Play-enabled, this should detect the hardware and display it in a dialog box like the one shown in Figure 14.4.

FIGURE **14.4**

The Add New Hardware Wizard displays a list of Plug and Play devices found.

Even if there is only one item in the list, you must select it and click **Next**. Windows 98 will then attempt to load the driver. If the drivers aren't available on your hard disk, Windows prompts you for the location of the drivers. After the driver is loaded, you will often need to reboot your system.

If the hardware you are trying to set up is not displayed in the list, select the option, **No, the device is not in the list,** as displayed in Figure 14.4. Then you would choose the **Next** button. Windows then displays the screen shown in Figure 14.5.

FIGURE **14.5**

The Add New Hardware Wizard lets you choose whether windows should search for new hardware.

## Automatic Non-Plug and Play Hardware Detection

Letting Windows 98 attempt to detect the hardware is a good first choice. This process, as shown in Figure 14.6, can take a while, but if Windows finds the hardware successfully, it automatically knows which driver software to load and tries to do so. If the drivers aren't available on your hard disk, Windows prompts you for the location of the drivers.

**FIGURE 14.6**

The Add New Hardware Wizard searches for non-Plug and Play hardware, usually for quite a long time.

## Selecting Hardware on Your Own

If Windows 98 can't detect your new hardware, or if you are sure of the manufacturer and model, you can select the hardware on your own. To do this, start the Add New Hardware Wizard and tell Windows 98 not to search for the new hardware, as shown in Figure 14.7.

**FIGURE 14.7**

To select hardware on your own, you must tell Windows 98 not to search for the new hardware.

With this approach you simply choose the hardware from a category list, as shown in Figure 14.8, and then select the manufacturer and model of the device as in Figure 14.9.

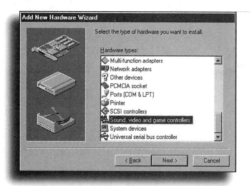

**FIGURE 14.8**
Choose a device category from the device list.

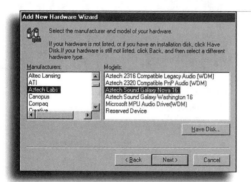

**FIGURE 14.9**
The Add New Hardware Wizard contains lists of many types of devices from hundreds of manufacturers.

After the driver installation is complete, Windows usually prompts you to restart your computer.

## Using Drivers from the Device Manufacturer

If the drivers for your new hardware aren't included with Windows 98, you can use drivers supplied by the manufacturer. Typically, drivers ship with the device, usually on floppy disk or CD-ROM. Many vendors also offer updated device driver files on their Web sites. To use a device driver from the manufacturer, simply click the **Have Disk** button in the Add New Hardware Wizard.

Some devices have custom features that require specialized drivers. Manufacturers usually ship a driver disk with a setup program for these devices. For example, the Microsoft IntelliMouse has a special wheel located between the mouse buttons. The IntelliMouse Setup program installs and configures everything automatically.

## What To Do When Problems Occur

Sometimes, when installing new hardware, things just don't go as planned. Maybe the new device simply won't work properly. More drastically, Windows 98 might lock up intermittently, might crash without warning, or might not even start at all.

If the device doesn't work like it should, or at all, the Device Manager is the answer. Using the Device Manager (explored later in this chapter), you can find and resolve conflicts quickly.

# Other Installation Wizards/Processes

In addition to the Add New Hardware Wizard, there are several other wizards and processes you can use to install drivers for new hardware. Each of these is similar in appearance and use. They are typically reached through the Control Panel, as you can see in Figure 14.10, where seven device configuration icons are highlighted.

These seven device configuration icons are:

- Mouse
- Game Controllers
- Keyboard
- Modems
- Multimedia
- Display
- Network

FIGURE 14.10
These seven selected Control Panel icons are used for device configuration.

## Mouse Installation

Buying and installing a new mouse is an easy task. For the most part, you just plug in the new mouse, start the computer, and you're ready. Some mice have special features like extra buttons or a mouse wheel.

### Installing a new mouse

1. Plug the mouse into your computer.
2. Start your computer.
3. To configure your mouse, launch the Mouse applet from the Control Panel.
4. Select the Buttons tab to set the mouse button configuration and double-click speed, as shown in Figure 14.11.
5. Choose the Motion tab, as shown in Figure 14.12, to set the mouse pointer speed and, optionally, to enable mouse trails. Mouse trails are useful mainly on notebook computers, allowing you to see the pointer movement better.
6. Click the **OK** button.

Many specialized models, such as the Microsoft IntelliMouse, come with a simple setup program on a disk that ships with the mouse, extending the Mouse applet in the Control Panel to allow configuration of the custom features of the mouse.

FIGURE 14.11

Choose the Buttons tab to set
the mouse button configuration and double-click speed for
your mouse.

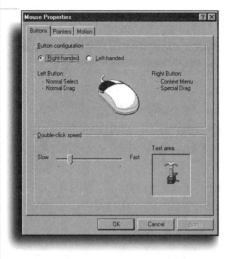

FIGURE 14.12

Choose the Motion tab to set
the mouse pointer speed and,
optionally, to enable mouse
trails.

## Game Controller Installation

Installing a game controller such as a joystick is just as easy as
installing a mouse.

### Installing a game controller

1. Plug the game controller into your computer.

2. Launch the Game Controllers applet from the Control
   Panel.

**3.** Choose the **Add** button, as shown in Figure 14.13.

FIGURE 14.13

Choose the Add button to add a new game controller to your system.

**4.** Select the proper manufacturer and model from the device list, as shown in Figure 14.14.

FIGURE 14.14

Select the proper game controller from the Windows 98 device list.

**5.** Click the **OK** button.

## Keyboard Installation

Installing a new keyboard is just as easy as installing a mouse or a joystick, but before you begin, make sure the computer is powered off.

### Installing a keyboard

1. Plug the keyboard into your computer.

2. Start your computer.

3. Launch the Keyboard applet from the Control Panel.

4. Choose the Speed tab to set the character repeat rate and cursor blink rate, as shown in Figure 14.15.

5. Choose the Language tab to add new language capabilities to your keyboard. Click the **Add** button and select the new language from the language list, if desired (see Figure 14.16).

6. Choose the **OK** button.

FIGURE 14.15

Choose the Speed tab to set the character repeat rate and cursor blink rate.

FIGURE 14.16

Choose the Language tab to add new language capabilities to your keyboard.

## Modem Installation

The Modems applet in the Control Panel is your gateway to the Install New Modem Wizard, discussed in detail in Chapter 16. To call up the wizard, choose the **Add** button found in the Modems applet, as shown in Figure 14.17.

**FIGURE 14.17**

Add a new modem using the Modems Properties dialog box, accessed via the Modems applet in the Control Panel.

**SEE ALSO**

➤ *To install a modem, see page 389*

➤ *To configure a modem, see page 392*

➤ *To configure dial-up networking, see page 407*

# Installing Display Devices

New display devices, including video adapter boards and monitors, are easy to install and configure in Windows 98. The Display applet in the Control Panel is the place to start. I'll show you how to drill down into the display properties to install and configure drivers for video adapters and monitors. Let's start with installing drivers for a newly installed video adapter board.

## Installing a New Video Display Board

If Windows 98 doesn't recognize your newly installed video display adapter, you can specify the proper device drivers using the Display applet.

### Configuring video adapter drivers

1. Start the Display applet from the Control Panel, or right-click the desktop and select Properties from the context menu that appears.

2. When the Display Properties dialog box appears, choose the **Settings** tab as shown in Figure 14.18, revealing the Advanced Properties button.

3. Choose the **Advanced** Properties button to bring up the Advanced Display Properties dialog box.

**FIGURE 14.18**

On the Settings tab, you'll find the Advanced Properties button.

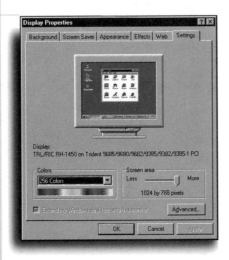

4. The Adapter tab shows information about the current video adapter, as shown in Figure 14.19. Choose the **Change** button to bring up the Select Device dialog box.

5. At this point, you simply select the proper manufacturer and adapter model from the hardware list (see Figure 14.20), or install a manufacturer-supplied driver by choosing the **Have Disk** button as you saw earlier.

Be sure to choose carefully. If you pick the wrong driver, your display may not work properly. If this occurs, start Windows 98 in Safe Mode and use this same process to install the correct driver.

FIGURE 14.19
From the Adapter tab, you can easily change video drivers by clicking the **Change** button.

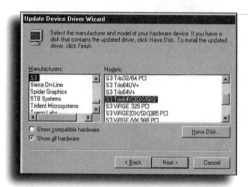

FIGURE 14.20
Select the proper manufacturer and adapter model from the hardware list.

## Installing a New Monitor

If Windows 98 doesn't recognize a newly attached video monitor, you can specify the proper type using the Display applet. The steps are almost identical to those for installing a new video display adapter.

### Setting the monitor type

1. Start the Display applet from the Control Panel, or right-click the desktop and select Properties from the context menu that appears.

**2.** When the Display Properties dialog box appears, choose the Settings tab as shown in Figure 14.18 above, revealing the Advanced Properties button.

**3.** Choose the **Advanced** Properties button to bring up the Advanced Display Properties dialog box.

**4.** The Monitor tab shows information about the current video monitor, as shown in Figure 14.21. Click the **Change** button to bring up the Select Device dialog box.

**FIGURE 14.21**

From the Monitor tab, you can easily change video monitors by clicking the Change button.

**5.** At this point, you simply select the proper manufacturer and model from the hardware list, as shown in Figure 14.22, or install a manufacturer-supplied driver by choosing the **Have Disk** button as you saw earlier.

**FIGURE 14.22**

Select the proper manufacturer and model from the hardware list.

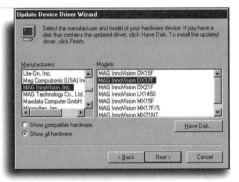

If you're not sure of the manufacturer or model, you can pick one of the standard monitor types from the hardware list, as shown in Figure 14.23.

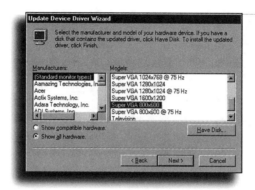

FIGURE 14.23

If you're not sure of the manufacturer or model, you can pick one of the standard monitor types from the hardware list.

# Installing Basic Network Devices

Networks are becoming commonplace both in the workplace and at home. For a few hundred dollars, you can even have a high-tech computer network in your own home. All you need is a network interface card (NIC), also called a network adapter, a hub to connect NICs to each other, and the data cables to connect the NICs to the hub.

In Chapter 20, I discuss what kind of fun you can have with networking, but for now let's just get the hardware set up—specifically, a NIC. You will typically use steps similar to the following to set up other kinds of adapter cards.

## Installing a Network Interface Card

Almost all new network adapters are fully Plug and Play-compliant. Windows 98 can install drivers for most of these automatically, but sometimes you have to do it yourself, especially with the older, legacy cards.

### Installing a network adapter

1. Begin by launching the Network icon from the Control Panel, revealing the Network dialog box shown in Figure 14.24.

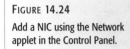

FIGURE 14.24

Add a NIC using the Network applet in the Control Panel.

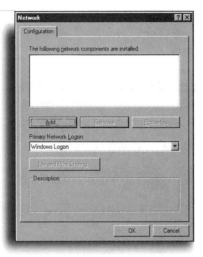

2. Select the **Add** button to bring up the Select Network Component Type dialog box and highlight the adapter in the list (see Figure 14.25).

FIGURE 14.25

Select the adapter from the network components list.

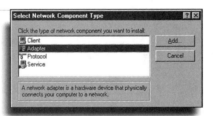

3. Select the **Add** button to bring up the Select Network Adapters dialog box.

4. Select your adapter from the Windows 98 hardware list, or choose the **Have Disk** button to use a driver supplied by the manufacturer. Figure 14.26 shows an adapter manufacturer and model selected in the Select Network Adapters dialog box.

5. Choose the **OK** button to add the adapter to your network configuration.

The end result of these steps can be seen in Figure 14.24, where networking components are installed and ready.

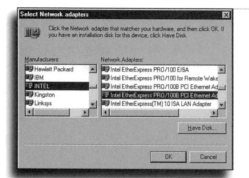

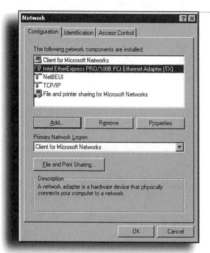

A minimal network would consist of two PCs linked by data cables. All that's needed now to create a minimal network is connectivity to another computer, allowing file and printer sharing between the two machines.

## Connecting to a Hub

Data cables plug into the NIC on one end and a standalone device called a hub on the other. Hubs are available with various numbers of these cable connections, or ports. An inexpensive 8-port hub can be found at most computer stores alongside the network adapter cards.

# Understanding the Device Manager

The Device Manager is the keeper of your computer's hardware configuration. It's a powerful, user-friendly tool that lets you perform some important types of hardware configuration and troubleshooting. The Device Manager reads and writes information about devices to the system Registry database, so be careful when making changes.

## Viewing Properties for Troubleshooting

When using the Add New Hardware Wizard or a Control Panel applet to install drivers for new hardware in a PC that uses legacy hardware adapters, there will often be hardware conflicts. Figure 14.28 depicts a dialog box that Windows 98 displayed when I installed a new sound card in my computer.

**FIGURE 14.28**

This dialog box shows a Windows 98 warning of a hardware conflict between Plug and Play and legacy adapter cards in a PC.

To view the devices installed on your system and check their properties, including drivers and resources, launch the System applet in the Control Panel (see Figure 14.29). When the System applet appears, select the Device Manager tab to get a good look at your system's component devices.

Notice in Figure 14.30 that the offending device contains a small exclamation icon in the device list. This signifies a problem of some sort.

## Resolving Hardware Conflicts

Most hardware conflicts aren't hard to resolve; it just takes a little trial and error. A peek at the offending device in the Device Manager usually reveals the conflict quickly. Let's take a look at how to fix these annoying glitches.

FIGURE 14.29

The System applet is the gateway to the Device Manager.

### Resolving a hardware conflict

**1.** Launch the System applet in the Control Panel and choose the Device Manager tab.

**2.** Click the offending device in the device list, which should have a warning icon to its left (see Figure 14.30).

FIGURE 14.30

The Device Manager reveals hardware problems quickly, displaying a warning icon to the left of conflicting devices in the list.

**3.** Choose the **Properties** button to bring up the Properties dialog for the device.

**4.** The Device Status box on the General tab warns of any device conflicts that may be present.

**5.** Choose the Resources tab to see exactly what resources the device is using and what resources are conflicting. This is where Windows 98 really shines. By clicking each resource in the list, you can see exactly where the conflicts occur (see Figure 14.31).

**FIGURE 14.31**

The Resources tab shows exactly which resources a device is using and which resources are conflicting.

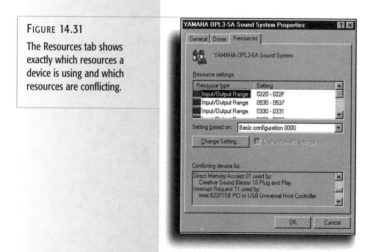

**6.** Eliminate the conflict from each affected resource by choosing the **Change Setting** button, which brings up the resource editing dialog box shown in Figure 14.32.

**FIGURE 14.32**

Eliminate conflicts from affected resources by editing resource usage values.

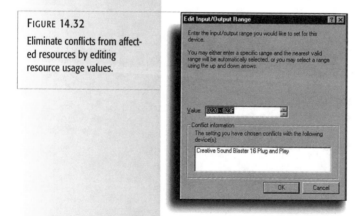

**7.** Click the up/down control arrows next to the resource value, keeping an eye on the message in the Conflict Information box. Change all offending resource values until there are no conflicts (see Figure 14.33).

FIGURE 14.33
When a free resource value is located, the conflict disappears.

By choosing the **Properties** button, as shown in Figure 14.30, the problem is immediately obvious—the device is trying to use resources that are already in use by other devices. In this instance, there are multiple conflicting resources including DMA channels, I/O addresses, and IRQ numbers.

To resolve these conflicts, you must try changing each conflicting resource value individually until a free resource is located.

# Hardware Profiles

A Hardware Profile is a device list that tells Windows 98 about all the devices in your computer, along with their configuration settings. This allows you to select multiple hardware configurations for your computer, which you may need if you have device conflicts that you can't resolve due to legacy hardware. You can copy a Hardware Profile to allow special hardware configurations. Figure 14.34 shows the Control Panel's System applet with the Hardware Profiles tab selected.

**FIGURE 14.34**

The Hardware Profiles tab, selected in the System applet, allows you to create custom Hardware Profiles.

## Copying a Hardware Profile

To create a new Hardware Profile, choose the **Copy** button from the Hardware Profiles tab. When the dialog box shown in Figure 14.35 appears, type the name of the new profile.

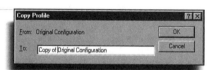

**FIGURE 14.35**

This dialog box allows you to name your new Hardware Profile.

The new profile is then available in the Hardware Profiles list, as shown in Figure 14.36. When you reboot your PC, you'll see a new text-based menu appear before Windows loads into memory. This menu lets you choose which hardware profile to load. By choosing the new profile, you can now enable and disable certain devices, or change their settings, without fear of crashing your system. The original profile still contains the correct device information. That is, by choosing a certain Hardware Profile when your system boots, you can specify which device to activate depending on your needs.

FIGURE 14.36

The new Hardware Profile is now available in the Hardware Profiles list.

## Disabling Devices in a Hardware Profile

When a legacy device just won't cooperate with the Plug and Play devices in your computer, you can disable it in the current Hardware Profile. To disable a device in a Hardware Profile, perform the following steps.

### Disabling a device in a Hardware Profile

**1.** Launch the System applet in the Control Panel.

**2.** Choose the Device Manager tab, and select the device to disable in the current profile.

**3.** Choose the **Properties** button.

**4.** From the General tab of the Properties dialog box for the device, in the Device Usage area, click the check box next to Disable in this hardware profile.

# Installing Multimedia Devices

Install a CD-ROM

Install, configure, and troubleshoot your sound card

Configure multimedia

# Introducing Multimedia

*Multimedia* is an all-encompassing term that's used to describe the audio and video capabilities of a computer. The problem is those capabilities differ depending on the hardware that's installed in your computer.

The permutations and combinations of available hardware are too immense to guarantee that this chapter will cover your situation exactly. Therefore, this chapter is an overview of what you can do with multimedia hardware and software. Once you understand what does what, and how it does it, you'll be able to get the most out of your multimedia capabilities.

The one fact that's certain is that if your computer has a CD-ROM and a sound card, you can avail yourself of some level of multimedia.

# Installing a CD-ROM

Installing means both attaching the hardware to your computer, and telling Windows 98 you have a CD-ROM and making sure Windows 98 can find it.

## Installing the Hardware

The physical installation of a CD-ROM is a matter of attaching a cable from a drive controller to the CD-ROM. That sounds much simpler to do than it actually is. There are a lot of traps to fall into.

The drive controller to which you attach your CD-ROM can be a SCSI controller, an IDE controller, or a proprietary controller from the manufacturer of the CD-ROM. If you're not comfortable setting up SCSI adapters or cabling devices, get a hardware guru to install the CD-ROM.

## Telling Windows 98 About the CD-ROM

After you add the CD-ROM to your computer, Windows 98 will probably recognize it when you start your computer. Once the device is recognized, the correct drivers are installed and you can begin using your CD-ROM.

## Manually Installing the CD-ROM

If Windows 98 doesn't automatically recognize and install your CD-ROM, you'll have to install it manually.

### Installing drivers manually

1. Click the **Start** button and choose **Settings**, **Control Panel** from the Start menu.

2. Double-click the **Add New Hardware** icon in the Control Panel.

3. When the first wizard page appears (which is an introduction to the wizard and a reminder to close any open programs), click **Next**.

4. On the next wizard page, you're told that Windows will search for any new Plug and Play devices. Click **Next** to let the search begin.

5. After a bit of time, the wizard displays a list of the hardware it found. If it found the correct device, click **Next** and follow the instructions to perform the installation.

6. If the wizard didn't find any new Plug and Play devices, the next step is to try to find new devices that are not Plug and Play–compatible (see Figure 15.1). Select **Yes** and then click **Next** to let the wizard make the search. (The next wizard window tells you what the process is for performing this search.)

7. If the device is found, it's installed. If not, you're notified that the search failed. Choose **Next** in the notification window to install your controller manually.

FIGURE 15.1

Windows 98 likes to find devices on its own.

8. Choose the type of device your CD-ROM is connected to and choose **Next**. Here's what you have to know about selecting the device:

   - Choose **SCSI controller** if your CD-ROM is connected to a SCSI adapter.
   - Choose **Hard disk controller** if your CD-ROM is connected to an IDE or EIDE controller.
   - Choose **CD-ROM controller** if your CD-ROM is connected to a proprietary controller that came with the CD-ROM.
   - If your CD-ROM is connected to your sound card, check the documentation that came with the sound card to see the controller type.

9. On the next wizard page, choose the manufacturer and model of the controller that matches yours and choose **Next**. If your manufacturer and model is not listed, and you have tried the generic drivers without success, you'll have to obtain drivers from the manufacturer.

10. If you have Windows 98 drivers on floppy disk or you have downloaded them, choose **Have Disk** and follow the instructions to install the drivers.

## Using MS-DOS Drivers for Your CD-ROM

If Windows 98 absolutely cannot find your CD-ROM device, it's probably not a supported device. However, you can load the drivers in Config.sys and Autoexec.bat during your computer's startup (this means you're loading real-mode, 16-bit devices) and then you'll be able to access the drive.

Consult the documentation for your CD-ROM device to install the drivers and add the appropriate lines to those boot files. Be sure the line in Autoexec.bat points to the Mscdex.exe file in the \Windows\Command folder.

Also, load Smartdrive from \Windows\Command to improve the performance of the CD-ROM.

## Configuring the CD-ROM

After the installation, you can configure and tweak the CD-ROM to ensure it operates at its best performance level.

### Configuring your CD-ROM drive

1. Right-click the My Computer icon, and then choose **Properties** from the shortcut menu.

2. When the System Properties dialog box opens, move to the Device Manager tab.

3. Select the CD-ROM and choose **Properties**, and then go to the Settings tab of the Properties dialog box (see Figure 15.2).

FIGURE 15.2

Set options for the CD-ROM in its Properties dialog box.

**Use the Shift key to stop AutoRun**

If AutoRun bothers you more often than is convenient, you don't have to change the Auto insert notification option to stop it. Just hold down the Shift key when you insert a CD-ROM in the drive.

**4.** Some people change the Auto insert notification option, which is a feature that notifies Windows 98 whenever you insert a disk. As a result, you can see the disk name next to the CD-ROM icon in My Computer. It also enables AutoRun, which launches CD-ROMs with AutoRun files. If you deselect this option, you'll have to open CD-ROMs manually by double-clicking the CD-ROM icon in My Computer.

**5.** If you have some particular reason to change the drive letter assigned to the CD-ROM, you can enter a new Start and End drive letter (use the same letter for both options to force the new drive letter for the CD-ROM).

**6.** Click **OK** when you finish making any changes (or choose Cancel if you haven't made any changes) to close the Properties dialog box. Then click **OK** to close the System Properties dialog box. If you made changes to the CD-ROM options, you're notified that you must reboot to have them take effect.

**Use the Letter Range option for jukeboxes**

Windows 98 supports CD-ROM changers (jukeboxes), and if you're using one, you have to reserve a range of drive letters to cover the maximum number of disks your device can use. Each disk needs its own drive letter.

## Tweaking Advanced CD-ROM Settings

If your CD-ROM audio or video seems to jump or skip, the default settings for the CD-ROM cache may not match what your CD-ROM drive needs.

You can experiment with the settings to see if you can improve performance. This tweaking is performed in the System Properties dialog box.

### Improving CD-ROM performance

**1.** Right-click My Computer and choose **Properties**.

**2.** When the System Properties dialog box appears, move to the Performance tab.

**3.** Choose **File System**, and then move to the CD-ROM tab (see Figure 15.3).

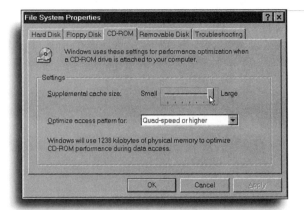

FIGURE 15.3
Experiment with performance levels to get more out of your CD-ROM.

4. Try moving the Supplemental Cache Size slider a bit to the right. This earmarks more RAM for caching data from the CD-ROM drive. If the slider is already far to the right, try moving it to the left to assign less RAM to the caching operation.

5. The access pattern should match the rated speed of your CD-ROM (check the documentation or look at the drive bay, because many CD-ROM drives have the speed printed right on the bay).

**Why changing the cache can help**

*Caching* is a technique of keeping data in a special area of memory, and it's very effective when the data is reused frequently. The software program looks at the cached data first and then looks at the drive. However, many multimedia software programs don't reuse data very much (if at all), and making the cache smaller actually helps their performance.

# Installing a Sound Card

A sound card is a device that translates the digital data in sound files to analog data that speakers can understand (speakers are not digital animals). Most sound cards are automatically found and recognized by Windows 98 when you next start the computer after inserting the card. However, if that doesn't occur, you can install the card manually.

### Installing the card manually

1. Click the **Start** button, and then choose **Settings**, **Control Panel** from the Start menu.

2. Double-click the **Add New Hardware** icon in the Control Panel.

**3.** When the first wizard page appears (it's informational), choose **Next**. The wizard searches for Plug and Play devices. It probably won't find one (or it would have found the new sound card when it searched during startup).

**4.** When the wizard fails to find a new Plug and Play device, choose **Next** and then tell the wizard not to search for the new hardware. Choose **Next** to start the manual installation.

**5.** In the Hardware types list, choose **Sound, video and game controllers** and choose **Next**.

**6.** Select a manufacturer and model from the next wizard page (see Figure 15.4).

FIGURE 15.4

Tell the wizard the make and model of your sound card.

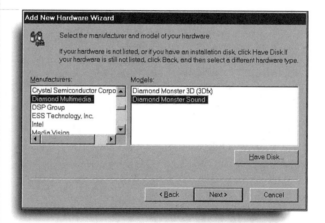

**7.** The wizard copies the driver files to your hard drive. Continue to follow instructions and, finally, click **Finish**.

## Check for Settings Conflicts

A common reason for Windows 98's failure to recognize a sound card is a conflict with an existing device. If the settings on the sound card conflict with any other device that's already installed in your computer, you'll have to change the sound card settings. Each device in your computer must have unique IRQ and I/O settings, and it's not uncommon for sound cards to encounter conflicts. You must change the IRQ and I/O settings directly on the sound card (usually by moving jumpers right on the card). Check the documentation that came with the sound card to see how to make these changes. Then install the sound card and make sure the settings in Windows 98 match the physical settings.

In fact, it's a very good idea to know all the IRQ and I/O settings that are already in use in your system.

### Tracking IRQ and I/O settings

1. Right-click My Computer and choose **Properties** from the shortcut menu.

2. When the System Properties dialog box opens, move to the Device Manager tab (see Figure 15.5).

**FIGURE 15.5**
Settings for all the devices in your system are found in the Device Manager.

3. Choose **Print**, and then select **System summary** as the Report type.

4. Click **OK** to start printing and close the Print dialog box. Then click **OK** again to close the System Properties dialog box.

The printed report enumerates each IRQ and I/O address used by the devices in your computer.

## Recording Sound

After your sound card is installed, if you have a microphone you can record your voice. There's no setup for a microphone; just attach it and your sound card will use it.

If you don't have a microphone, you can record from your boombox by connecting the Line Out plug to the Line In plug on your sound card.

# Configuring Multimedia

The multimedia software and drivers in your Windows 98 system depend on the hardware in your computer and the installation choices you made.

The Multimedia icon in the Control Panel offers some very basic configuration choices; they're shallow because essentially the hardware does what it does, and the software you use does what it does.

The real excitement for those who love the action of robust multimedia comes from third-party software companies. The assortment of multimedia products is growing daily and the Internet is a great source of information and multimedia files.

The fact is, you'll have more success in enhancing the performance of your multimedia shows by paying attention to hardware. Aim for these minimum requirements:

- A powerful video controller with plenty of memory and the capability to display HighColor or TrueColor.
- A 16-bit audio card with MIDI capabilities.
- A CD-ROM with quad speed or better.

Those items are more important than an overabundance of RAM or the megahertz speed of your processor. (Well, don't take that to extremes; you should have at least 48MB of RAM if you're serious about multimedia and I doubt if you'd be happy with a 90MHz processor—in fact, a Pentium 166MMX is recommended for some of the popular voice-recognition software.)

# Setting Multimedia Options

There are a few options you can change to match your equipment and needs in the Multimedia Properties dialog box.

### Accessing multimedia configuration settings

1. Click the **Start** button, and then choose **Settings**, **Control Panel** from the Start menu.

2. Double-click the **Multimedia** icon to open the Multimedia Properties dialog box.

### Setting Audio Options

When the Multimedia Properties dialog box opens, the Audio tab is in the foreground (see Figure 15.6). Here you have the ability to select the preferred device for both playback and recording. If you have multiple sound cards in your machine, the Audio tab lets you select the device that you want to use as the default. While there are software packages available that will make use of multiple sound cards, most Windows programs—including the operating system itself—only want to know about one device at a time.

FIGURE 15.6

Setting your preferred audio device.

Each of the preferred Playback and Recording devices has an Advanced Properties button. When you choose it, the Advanced Audio properties dialog box for the Playback device opens.

Use the Speaker tab to configure the speakers attached to the sound device. Use the drop-down listbox shown in Figure 15.7 to choose the configuration that comes closest to matching yours.

**FIGURE 15.7**

Whether you stole the family stereo speakers for your computer or opted for bargain-basement speakers, you should find a configuration that works with your system.

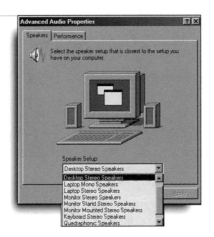

Move to the Performance tab to configure the technical settings for the sound card (see Figure 15.8).

You should probably leave the settings as they are unless you're very comfortable with the hardware technical specifications for computer audio. Changing them can drastically affect how well your computer responds during playback of sounds. Choose **OK** to return to the Audio tab of the Multimedia Properties dialog box.

On the Audio tab of the Multimedia Properties dialog box, there are buttons to the left of the Preferred Device—one for Playback controls and the other for Recording controls. Use these buttons to see and adjust the respective volume controls.

FIGURE 15.8
The technical information might be useful if you're conferring with a support person, but there's rarely any reason to change settings.

At the bottom of the Multimedia Properties Audio tab are two check boxes:

- Select **Use only preferred devices** to limit the use of the device you've declared to be the preferred device. Software that can use multiple devices won't see anything except the preferred device.

- Deselect **Show volume control on the taskbar** (it's selected by default) if you don't want the volume control icon on your taskbar tray.

## Setting Video Options

Move to the Video tab to set options for playing video files (see Figure 15.9).

You can specify a size for the window that opens when you play a video file, or you can select Full screen. (By default, the window that opens matches the size of the video clip.)

Click the arrow to the right of the Window box to choose a different size. The other choices are: Double original size; $\frac{1}{16}$ of screen size; $\frac{1}{4}$ of screen size; $\frac{1}{2}$ of screen size; or Maximized. As you select an option, check the preview monitor on the dialog box to see the effect.

The best performance usually comes with original size, especially if you don't have all sorts of hardware bells and whistles in your computer.

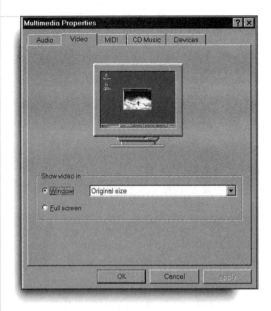

## Configuring MIDI

Move to the MIDI tab of the Multimedia Properties dialog box if you want to install a MIDI instrument and configure it.

The *Musical Instrument Digital Interface (MIDI)* is a system for recording and playing music. Instead of saving a copy of the sound in a file, MIDI saves the musical notes, along with information about the duration of each note. Playback is a matter of sending the information to the musical instrument being used, which is frequently attached to a serial port. This could be a synthesizer or any other musical instrument with a computer interface.

The music industry is using MIDI more and more for soundtracks, and if you get your hands on a MIDI instrument for your computer, you'll be delighted at the music you can compose and play.

### Installing a MIDI instrument

1. Select **Add New Instrument**.
2. When the MIDI Wizard launches, supply the information as needed.

**3.** As each new instrument is added to the list, you can configure its channel by selecting **Custom Configuration** and then choosing **Configure**.

## Setting Up CD Music

If you like playing your favorite music discs in your computer's CD-ROM, you can configure the CD-ROM properties for that purpose (see Figure 15.10).

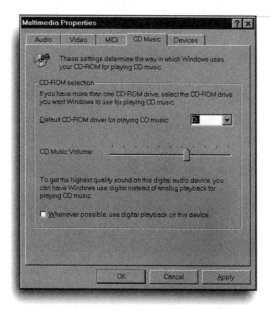

**FIGURE 15.10**
Putting a music disc into a CD-ROM is certainly more fun than putting a software disk in.

Follow these guidelines to complete the configuration:

- If you have multiple CD-ROM drives, earmark one for music.
- Adjust the volume by moving the slider bar. Of course, if you work in an office, headphones are a must.
- If you have a digital device (such as a USB connection) for your speakers, you can select digital playback for your music discs. However, this disables headphones.

**USB and IEEE 1394 connections**

USB (Universal Serial Bus) is a new class of hardware that's probably best described as a serial port on steroids. If you have a USB port, you can plug any USB device into it. All USB devices have a plug that matches the USB port connection. Most USB devices provide powerful digital functions.

IEEE 1394 is another powerful type of port that you can install on your computer. It works similarly to USB (in fact, the end result is impossible to tell apart).

The devices are not interchangeable and intercompatible. You cannot plug an IEEE 1394 device into a USB port.

Windows 98 supports both of these new hardware classes. At the moment, these ports are used for multimedia devices (for example, broadcast TVs) and they bring a great deal of power to multimedia.

## Using Your PC Speaker Instead of a Sound Card

No sound card? No problem! Microsoft has a clever utility that lets you hear some sound files through your PC speaker. You won't play Bach, but you can have the fun of playing .wav files for sound effects and short bursts of music.

The program is called Speak and it's available on the Microsoft Internet site (go to **ftp://ftp.microsoft.com/SoftLib/ MSLFILES**). If you use FTP, go to **ftp.microsoft.com** and move to the Softlib/MSLFILES folder. Then download Speak.exe and install it.

### Installing PC-Speaker

1. Open Explorer.

2. Create a new folder on your hard drive (name it something that will remind you that it contains the Speak program).

3. Move Speak.exe into the new folder.

4. Double-click on the Speak.exe file.

5. An MS-DOS command window opens to extract the compressed files in Speak.exe. You're asked if you want to extract the files; enter **Y** to indicate Yes.

6. Close the MS-DOS command window and close Explorer.

7. Open the Control Panel (choose **Settings**, **Control Panel** from the Start menu).

8. Double-click the **Add New Hardware** icon and choose **Next** when the introductory wizard window appears.

9. In the next wizard window, choose **No** to tell the wizard not to search for your new hardware. Then choose **Next**.

10. When the list of hardware types is displayed, choose **Sound, video and game controllers**. Then choose **Next**.

11. The list of manufacturers and models appears. Click the **Have Disk** button.

12. In the Install From Disk dialog box (see Figure 15.11), enter **c:\speaker** (substitute the name you gave the folder for "speaker"). If you can't remember the name, enter **c:\** and then choose **Browse** to find the folder. Then click **OK**.

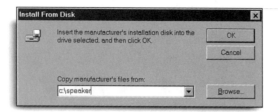

FIGURE 15.11

Tell the wizard where you put your new speaker software.

**13.** The wizard finds the driver and shows you a new device named Sound Driver for PC-Speaker in the Select Device dialog box. Because this is the only device in the list, click **OK**. Then choose **Finish** from the last wizard window.

After the driver is copied, the PC-Speaker Setup dialog box appears (see Figure 15.12). Until you have tried the speaker, you probably don't know whether you want to change any settings, so leave the defaults alone.

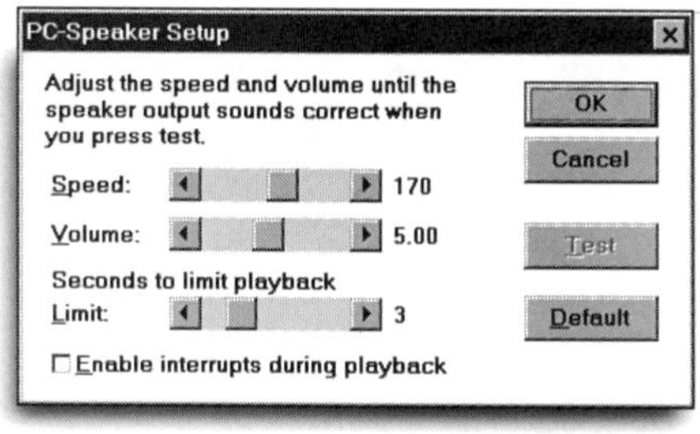

FIGURE 15.12

You can set the speaker settings now, or wait until you've used the device for a while.

A dialog box appears offering to restart your computer in order to have this new device work. Accept the invitation.

After you restart your computer, you can use Sound Recorder to play .wav files through your speaker. No other multimedia audio program works with PC-Speaker, only Sound Recorder.

You can configure PC-Speaker, changing the settings to tweak the performance.

### Tweaking PC-Speaker

**1.** Choose **Settings**, **Control Panel** from the Start menu.

**2.** Double-click the **Multimedia** icon to open the Multimedia Properties dialog box.

**3.** Move to the Devices tab. The Audio Devices listing now has a plus sign (+), indicating a device is installed. Click the plus sign to see the device listing (see Figure 15.13).

FIGURE 15.13

The PC-Speaker is now listed as a valid multimedia audio device.

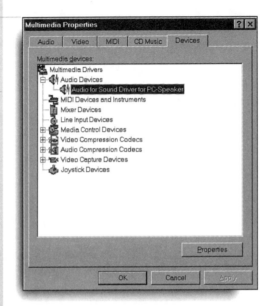

**4.** Select the PC-Speaker device and choose **Properties**, **Settings** to see the same Settings dialog box you saw during installation.

**5.** Make any changes you want and click **OK**.

Once you have the ability to hear .wav files, you can go into the Sounds icon in Control Panel and assign amusing musical sounds to events such as opening software, shutting down Windows, seeing informational dialog boxes, and so on.

If you have a computer that was preconfigured as a multimedia machine (which means state-of-the-art hardware), you'll have a wonderful time with multimedia software.

# Taking Advantage of MMX Processors

If you have an MMX processor, you can take advantage of the new games and multimedia software on today's market. MMX is the jargon for the Intel Pentium Multimedia Extensions that have been added to the latest and greatest Pentium processor. Software companies can write software that uses this chip's capabilities to provide incredibly rapid audio and video playback. MMX is built into today's Pentium II chips.

# Communicating with Windows 98

# Modems

# Choosing a Modem

A *modem* is a device that takes computer data (which is digital) and translates it into a form that a telephone line can handle (the telephone line is analog). This process is called *modulating*. At the other end, there's a modem attached to a computer and it takes the analog data from the phone line and translates it into digital data that the receiving computer can handle. That process is called *demodulating*. The modulate-demodulate function of the device produced the word *modem*.

If you have a choice, the considerations that go into buying a modem can be very confusing. The reason I say "if you have a choice" is that most of the computers that are sold today have modems preinstalled. That hasn't always been the case and it's a direct response to the popularity of the Internet.

## Modem Features

Modems have a wide variety of features and you'll want to buy one that gives you what you need without spending additional money for functions you'll never use. Here are some general guidelines about modem functions:

- *Data modems* are basic modulating-demodulating devices that transmit data over a telephone line between your computer and another computer. That other computer may be an Internet connection, America Online, CompuServe, or a Dial-Up Networking connection to your office. If you're not just going to dial out, but want to let other computers dial into your computer, make sure the modem is auto-answer capable.

- *Fax modems* have all the capabilities of data modems in addition to enabling you to use the modem to connect to a fax machine. Installing a fax modem means you can send a fax directly from your computer; you don't have to print the document and walk it to a free-standing fax machine. In fact, most Windows 98 software has the capability to fax the document you're working on without launching a separate faxing software application. To receive faxes, the modem must be auto-answer capable, although I've never seen a fax modem that wasn't.

- *Cellular modems* are usually sold in the form of PCMCIA cards that you install in a laptop computer, and all of them that I've seen are data/fax–enabled. They connect to a cellular phone, which means you can use them when you don't have access to a phone jack. Some of the marketing hype for these modems includes the fact that you can send or receive a fax from your car. That may sound productive and efficient, but as a driver it makes me nervous to think that some of the cars streaming along with me on the highway are being driven by some techy who thinks it's neat to drive and fax at the same time.

- *Voice modems* have the additional capability of handling voice mail. (To use this feature, you have to install the appropriate answering machine software.) Every voice modem I've seen is also a data/fax modem. Voice modems don't always have the terminology "voice modem" in their model names, but usually you'll see some phrase such as "with voice mail capabilities" or "personal voice mail software included."

Confused enough? Wait, there's another decision to make: speed.

## Modem Speed

The speed of a modem determines the amount of time it takes to transmit data. This becomes important if you pay by the minute for your access to a host system, and the extra dollars invested in a faster modem are amortized very quickly. Even if you don't pay for the time you use online, there is that old adage "time is money," and most of the time that's a point of view that can be defended with financial data (especially if you're using your modem in the office).

Modem speed is rated by the number of bits the modem can transmit in a second, and the speed rating is expressed as XXXXbps, where the XXXX is the modem's speed. For example, you can buy a modem that operates at 28.8Kbps (the K means thousand) or 33.6Kbps.

The lowest speed you should consider is 28.8Kbps. The current state of the art is 56Kbps, but there's a problem at the moment with that speed—it is just in the process of being standardized. That means that you cannot guarantee that a certain brand of modem that operates at 56Kbps will talk to a different brand operating at the same speed (at the time of this writing, the standards had just been agreed upon by several modem manufacturers, so by the time you read this all manufacturers may be building 56K modems that all talk to each other). All other speeds are standardized and you can rest assured that you'll be able to connect with any other modem.

When two modems of varying speeds connect, the connection proceeds at the speed of the slower modem. When two modems of the same speed and the same brand/model connect, the connection often proceeds at a higher speed than the rated speed.

There's often a substantial difference in price as modems get faster, but this is one device that you should consider spending money on. You'll hear a lot of so-called experts (your friends who have been using computers and modems for a long time and have firm opinions) that there's no point in buying a 33.6 modem because most of the connections you reach are probably operating at 28.8. Bullfeathers! A month from now those 28.8 connections will be at 33.6, and six months from now they'll be at 56.

Now that I've recited all these explanations of speed, there's something to add. Lots of times it doesn't matter; your modem doesn't work at its rated speed anyway. That's because modems and communications software are designed to keep an eye on the data being transmitted. Without going into all the long, techie, boring engineering stuff, the bottom line is that if the receiving modem thinks the data is bad, it will ask that it be re-sent, and if there seems to be a real problem in transmitting clean data, the modems will slow down in an effort to get a good transmission.

# Telephone Lines and Modems

Most of the problems with data corruption during transmission are caused by your telephone lines. Some of these problems can be eliminated by you; others will require the cooperation of the telephone company.

Data is transmitted via squawky noises (I'm sure there's a technical term for that but if you listen to it while data is being sent over a modem, you'll hear squawky noises). The pitch and sound of each noise is meaningful and is translated on the other end into characters. If you permit an extraneous noise to join the flow of data, the receiving computer cannot interpret it. The following are the most common extraneous noises that either corrupt or interrupt data transmissions:

- The sound of an extension telephone being picked up. This is made worse if the person who picks up the telephone talks ("Hello, is somebody on this line?").
- The sound (beep) made by call waiting when somebody tries to call you while you're using your modem. Fortunately, you can disable call waiting when you dial out (and we'll go over that in this chapter).
- Static on the telephone lines. This can be caused by a number of problems (squirrels chewing on your lines, telephone lines that are old and the insulation is wearing out, or just general problems with lines that the telephone company is experiencing). These problems have to be resolved by the telephone company.

I have one more thing to add to your confusion; there's one more choice to make: external or internal?

# External Versus Internal Modems

An external modem attaches to one of the serial ports on your computer (desktop computers usually have two serial ports; laptops usually have only one).

An internal modem is inserted in a bus (slot) in your motherboard (or a PCMCIA card in a laptop). Internal modems are also serial port devices, and when you install an internal modem, you also give yourself another serial port, which becomes the next available COM port. If you have two serial ports (called COM1 and COM2), the internal modem becomes COM3.

There's no right or wrong decision here, and there's really no strong advantage of one over the other. I like external modems because I have more control over them. If something strange happens, I can turn the modem off and on (the only way to turn off an internal modem is to shut down the computer). I also like the fact that I can see those little lights blinking on and off, assuring me that data is still being transmitted when things are moving so slowly that I'm afraid something has gone wrong.

Internal modems are almost always less expensive and they let you keep your serial port(s) for other devices, such as a mouse or a serial port printer or any other serial device. The real downside to an internal modem is that you have to open your computer to install it.

## ISDN Devices

One device growing in popularity is the Integrated Services Digital Network (ISDN) device. People refer to ISDN devices as if they were modems, but they're not. They can claim membership in the modem family only because they, too, transmit data between computers.

ISDN devices don't use normal telephone lines—they use ISDN lines. More and more telephone companies are making ISDN lines available, but you have to check with your local telephone company to see if the service can be connected to your computer (if not, wait a few months and try again).

ISDN lines are digital so the ISDN device doesn't have to modulate or demodulate the data. But the real advantage is that they're much faster than telephone lines—this is a phone line on steroids.

There are two types of ISDN lines available from most telephone companies: Basic Rate Interface Services (BRI) and Primary Rate Interface Services (PRI).

BRI is a copper-wire service that is capable of transmitting at speeds of 64Kbps or 128Kbps. The choice of speeds is a result of the fact that BRI service is a two-channel service, each of which transmits at the rate of 64Kbps. When you set up your ISDN device, you can opt to use both channels for your transmissions (giving you 128Kbps) or use each channel separately, giving you slower connections but the ability to use each of them simultaneously. You can dial out to two separate locations, or dial out to one while receiving transmissions from another computer on the other channel. (Actually, there's a third channel in BRI service, and it's used to send signals to the receiving ISDN device but doesn't transmit data.)

PRI service uses fiber-optic cable and transmits at speeds that reach 1.5 million bps.

ISDN devices cannot talk to modems; the other end of your transmission must also be an ISDN device.

Even though ISDN lines are much more expensive than plain old telephone service (POTS), if you're being charged for usage, the blazing speed of your data exchange amortizes the cost.

## TV Cable Modem

A new and exciting technical breakthrough is the ability to go online through your cable television company. This is a whole new definition of speed!

The service is so sparse at the moment that it's difficult to talk about what you can expect in the way of services and cost, but I can give you some general descriptions of how the service works.

The modem you use for cable access is specifically designed for cable. Most of the time, your cable company supplies the modem (most cable companies rent the modem to you and the rental cost is part of the monthly charge for the service).

Cable access is not dial-out modem access. You are part of a network. In fact, a network interface card (NIC) must be installed in your computer so you can join your cable company's network. The NIC has a 10Base-T connection to the cable modem. The cable modem has a co-ax connection to your cable TV co-ax line (which has a splitter to divide your television service from your modem service). The cable company installs all of this for you.

Because the cable company can't run cable from your location to its server, you join the network through a modem. This is called dial-in networking, except you're not dialing in if you define dialing as something involving a telephone line. When your computer is on, you're on the network. You cannot have a connection "timeout"; you are never unconnected. You get to your email, the Internet, FTP, and all the other online services through the cable company's network.

If you already have a NIC installed in your computer, you can add a second one for your cable networking. The protocol that's bound to the card is TCP/IP and the Identification tab on the Network applet in Control Panel points you to the cable company's network. It also gives your computer a static IP address, and if you know your way around TCP/IP communications, that provides some very interesting possibilities for accessing your computer from any remote site that also has cable access on this gigantic network. This can also be a serious security problem because technically you're just another network node and as this technology grows, so will the number of hackers. Think about using a stand-alone computer for this service. In fact, the most efficient way to approach this is to run this service as a stand-alone service with two NICs in the computer. Only connect the "real" network NIC to cable when you want to transfer files you've downloaded to another computer on your network. Then pull that plug!

The speed of a TV cable connection is astounding. As an example, let's say you have to download a 2MB file. Here are the numbers:

- A 28.8 modem will download the file in slightly over nine minutes.
- An ISDN connection will have this file downloaded in just a tad over two minutes.
- A TV cable connection puts this file on your local drive in 10 seconds.

Even as this service grows in popularity, which reduces the speed to some extent (this is network traffic so it slows down as more and more nodes join the network and crowd the available band-width), this service will continue to outpace any other current connection type.

Because this connection is ongoing, you don't pay for time; you pay a monthly flat fee. At the moment, that fee is around $40/month (including the modem rental).

You cannot run a web site or fax from TV cable connections—yet.

# Installing a Modem

After you complete the physical installation of your modem, you have to perform a Windows 98 installation. Fortunately, Windows 98 has an easy-to-use modem wizard that walks you through the process.

If your modem is already connected to your computer when you first install Windows 98, the Plug and Play feature of Windows 98 will probably kick in. Windows 98 will figure out whether there's a modem attached to your computer and automatically start the Install New Modem Wizard. In fact, even if you add a modem later, the next time you start the operating system, the same thing will happen.

If your modem isn't Plug and Play–enabled, you can start the installation manually. We'll cover those steps here and even if Plug and Play launched the installation of the modem, the basic approach is the same and the wizard windows are the same.

## Using the Add New Modem Wizard

To install a modem in Windows 98, be sure your modem is con-nected and turned on. Put your Windows 98 CD-ROM in the CD-ROM drive (or, if your version of Windows 98 came on floppy disks, have those disks handy).

### Adding a new modem

1. Click the **Start** button and choose **Settings**, **Control Panel** from the Start menu.

2. Double-click the **Modems** icon.

3. The Install New Modem Wizard opens (see Figure 16.1). By default, the wizard is prepared to find your modem and detect its properties automatically. The best approach is to let this happen (you can manually select your modem during the installation process if the wizard makes a mistake). Choose **Next** to get the installation process started.

**FIGURE 16.1**

Installation starts with the wizard offering to do all the work.

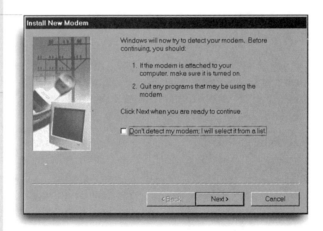

4. The wizard searches your serial ports, sending out signals that are designed to find a modem. When it finds one, it queries the modem to learn more about it (see Figure 16.2).

5. The wizard displays the name or model of the modem it has found. If it's correct, choose **Next**. If the displayed information is wrong, choose **Change** and select your modem manually, click **OK**, and then choose **Next** (see Figure 16.3).

6. The next wizard window announces that installation is complete. Click **Finish**. The necessary files have been copied to your hard drive.

Skipping automatic detection

If you choose to skip the automatic detection process when your first begin the installation, the manufacturer/model list in Figure 16.3 is presented. You'll also have to tell the wizard which serial port your modem is using.

**FIGURE 16.2**

When the modem is located, Windows 98 interrogates it to learn more about it.

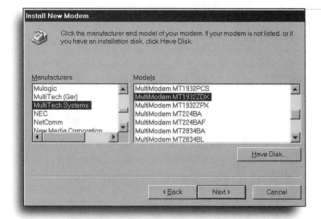

**FIGURE 16.3**

Select the manufacturer and the model from the list of supported modems.

## If Your Modem Isn't Listed

If the auto detection chooses the wrong modem or doesn't find your modem, you must use the list of manufacturers and models to select your modem manually. If your modem isn't there, you have three choices for remedying the situation:

- Select **Standard Modem** from the Manufacturers list and then choose a speed from the Models list (there aren't any models listed, just speeds).

- Select a modem that your modem emulates (check the documentation that came with the modem to see what the emulations are).

- Use drivers provided by your manufacturer.

If you opt to use manufacturer drivers, you must make sure the drivers you received from the manufacturer are for Windows 98. These drivers either arrive on floppy disks with your modem or you can call the manufacturer for them. In fact, you can probably get them from the manufacturer's Internet site, but because you don't have a modem, that could pose a problem. So, ask a friend to get the drivers for you and give them to you on a floppy disk.

### Installing your own drivers

1. In the first wizard window, select **Don't detect my modem** and choose **Next**.

2. When the list of manufacturers and models is displayed, choose **Have Disk**.

3. The Install From Disk dialog box appears (see Figure 16.4). Tell the wizard where to find the driver files and follow the instructions to complete the installation (which is the same as the process described earlier).

FIGURE 16.4

Confirm the fact that the floppy disk containing the files for your modem are in Drive A by clicking **OK**, or browse your hard drive to find them if you transferred them there.

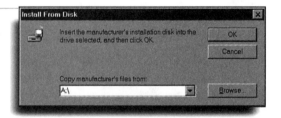

## Configuring Your Modem

When your modem installation is complete, the Modem Properties dialog box appears and you can begin configuring the modem (see Figure 16.5).

If you want to wait until another time, you can get to this Properties dialog box by double-clicking the Modem icon in the Control Panel. (Double-clicking that icon produces a Properties dialog box when a modem is installed, and launches the Add Modem Wizard when no modem is installed.)

The properties for the modem are set by the driver you installed (the Windows 98 installation process is really nothing more than installing a driver for the modem onto your hard drive). The driver knows all the codes to send the modem to make it do its job.

## General Modem Properties

When the Properties dialog box appears, the General tab is in the foreground. These settings, and the settings on the Diagnostics tab, are system settings. Each modem in your system also has its own Properties dialog box and settings, and we'll cover those first.

The modem is highlighted and you can choose Properties to view or change the settings for this particular modem (see Figure 16.6).

- The Port to which the modem is connected shouldn't be changed unless you physically move the modem. If you do, use the down arrow next to the Port box to choose the new port from the list of available ports.

- The Speaker volume is adjustable (if your modem has a speaker) and I find it best to set it for enough volume to

**14.4 isn't a valid speed**

If you're using a 14,400bps modem, do not set the speed for 14,400. That's an artificial setting used by modem manufacturers that isn't supported by any operating system. You may find you have trouble connecting with other modems. By the way, it's time to get a faster modem.

hear a dial tone and the squawky noises that indicate the modem has made contact with another modem (I just like the reassurance). If you use your modem for voice mail, and the software doesn't use your sound card, you'll probably find that regardless of the volume, it will be hard to understand messages.

- The maximum speed is an "okay, go for it" number. You can set it far higher than the rated speed of your modem without doing harm, and some people insist that it increases speed.

**FIGURE 16.6**

You can configure the basic settings for your modem.

## Modem Connection Properties

Move to the Connection tab to see the configuration options that are set by default for your modem (see Figure 16.7).

The specifications in the Connection preferences sections are the default settings for most computer-to-computer communication processes. If you dial into a host computer (perhaps a mainframe), that computer may need different settings, which are detailed in the instructions you receive for dialing in. However, the software you use to make that connection probably has an options dialog box, and you should make the changes there (those settings will override these default settings while the connection is live).

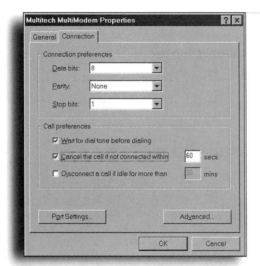

FIGURE 16.7
You may want to change the
settings that determine when
you automatically disconnect.

Years ago, communications software was not as robust as today's
software and you had to dial a number through the telephone
instrument before you could tell the modem to connect. Your
Windows 98 software doesn't have that requirement, so don't
touch the setting that tells the modem to wait for a dial tone
before dialing.

You can use the other call preferences to determine how you
want to force an automatic disconnect.

- It's a good idea to cancel a call if there's no connection within a certain amount of time (unless you really love to listen
  to the sound of a phone ringing).

- Configuring the modem to Disconnect after an idle period
  (idle means no data exchange and no keyboard or mouse
  activity) is designed to force your modem to hang up
  because you've probably forgotten you're online. This is
  useful if you pay for online time or if you use the household
  phone line. (This is another feature that is probably an
  option you can select in your communications software, so
  there's no need to make an absolute configuration change
  here.)

The Port Settings and Advanced options should be left in their default state unless you're given specific changes by the host system you're dialing into.

If you make changes in any of the modem's Properties, choose **OK** to save them. Otherwise, choose **Cancel** to return to the General Properties dialog box.

## Setting Dialing Properties

Choose Dialing Properties on the General tab to tell Windows 98 how you want to dial out when you use your modem. The dialing Properties dialog box appears and you can select the options you need (see Figure 16.8).

**FIGURE 16.8**
Specify any special dialing needs you have to effect a clean connection.

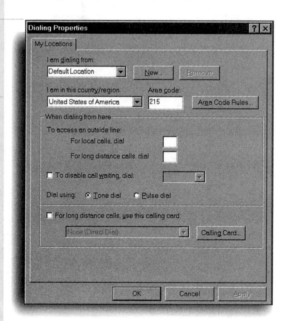

The nifty feature here is that you can have as many sets of dialing properties as you need. This is usually important only for laptops, because it would be unusual for you to carry a desktop computer around to various locations.

For example, my laptop has quite a few sets of dialing properties. I have one that assumes I'm in a hotel room and want to use my credit card (it dials 8,0, then the number I want to call; then my credit card number is punched in automatically). I have another one that assumes I'm in a corporate environment (it dials 9, then the number I want to call). And, I have one for each of the places I visit regularly, mostly relatives and friends (the dialing properties are set up for credit card use). The actual number I want to call is established by the software I'm using and the local access number I need in that city.

### Configuring dialing options

1. Name the location if you think you may add additional locations (otherwise, Default Location will probably serve just as well as "Home" or "Office"). If you have an existing location and want to add a new one, choose **New**, which produces a dialog box asking you to give the new location a name.

2. Enter your area code so the system knows when you're dialing out-of-town. When you do dial out to a different area code, Windows 98 will dial a "1" automatically.

3. If you need to dial a number in order to access an outside line (usually necessary for a business phone system), enter that number (it's usually a 9).

4. If you need to dial a number in order to access a long distance line in a business system, enter that number in the box named "for long distance." Do not use this box to indicate a "1" for normal long distance calls; this is only for those business phone systems that require a special character for permission to dial long distance.

5. If you use a calling card and want every call charged to it, select that option. The Calling Card dialog box appears and you can select the method you want to use for charging your calls (see Figure 16.9), or you can invent your own (see the section "Adding a Credit Card Carrier" later in this chapter). Then enter your calling card number and click **OK**.

FIGURE 16.9

You can use a wide variety of calling card services if you want to charge your call to your account.

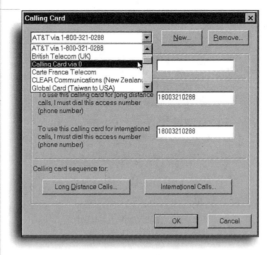

**How to determine tone service**

You cannot assume that because you have a touch-tone phone that you also have tone service on your telephone line. Here's how to tell: Press and hold any number on your telephone. If the tone continues as long as you're holding down the key, you have tone service. If the tone stops even though you're continuing to press the key, you have pulse service.

**6.** If you have call waiting, select that option and then enter the dialing sequence needed to disable it. The common choices are available; just click the arrow to the right of the text box to see them and select the one that works for your telephone company. When your modem connection is closed, call waiting returns automatically.

**7.** Specify whether your telephone service is tone (push button) or pulse (rotary).

**8.** Click **OK** when you finish setting your dialing options.

## Adding a Credit Card Carrier

If your long distance carrier or the service you use when charging your calls to a card isn't listed, you can create your own credit card carrier listing.

### Adding a credit card carrier

**1.** When the Calling Card dialog box appears, choose **New** and enter a name for this credit card service and then click **OK**. A message appears telling you that you must now enter the rules for using this card. Click **OK**.

2. The Calling Card dialog box now displays this new calling card name. Enter the information so you can make calls with it.

3. To configure long distance calling rules, choose **Long Distance Calls** to bring up the Calling Card Sequence dialog box (see Figure 16.10).

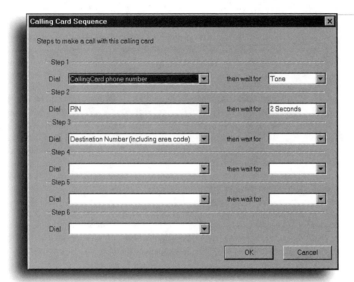

FIGURE 16.10
You have to specify the number and special characters needed to charge your calls.

4. Each text box has a drop-down list available with the common choices for the field. If you don't know what to enter, contact your calling card company.

5. When you are finished, click **OK**. Then click **OK** on the Calling Card dialog box to return to the Dialing Properties dialog box. Click **OK** again to return to your Modems Properties dialog box (where you click **OK** again to close it).

Figure 16.11 shows a typical set of dialing sequences. This Calling Card requires a 0 before the number being dialed. Remember that the actual number that's being dialed is contained in the communications software; these are only the instructions.

FIGURE 16.11

This set of instructions dials "0," then the number being called.

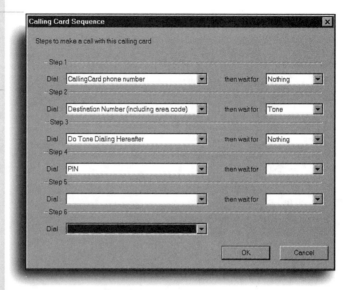

## Modem Diagnostics

Move to the Diagnostics tab of the Modems Properties dialog box to see a list of devices installed on your serial ports (see Figure 16.12).

FIGURE 16.12

The serial ports are displayed along with any devices attached to them.

You can test the modem and view the commands that control it by choosing More Info. Be sure your modem is on. It takes a few seconds for the system to find the modem and interrogate it, and then it displays the commands it sent and the modem's response (see Figure 16.13). If you're having problems with your modem and call a support technician at the manufacturer, this information will probably be useful.

**FIGURE 16.13**

The command codes sent to the modem, and the response to those codes, are displayed when you test the modem.

# Understanding Unimodem

Microsoft has taken the common modem codes and instructions and included them in a driver named Unimodem (named because it is a universal modem driver). This driver, which is part of Windows 98, is capable of controlling most of the modems in use today.

As of this writing, the latest version of this driver is Unimodem V, which has support for a number of communications features, including:

- Data communications
- Fax communications
- Voice communications

- Recording to and from the handset
- Recording to and from the telephone
- Speakerphones
- Caller ID
- Distinctive ringing
- Call forwarding

You can download UnimodemV by going to **http://support. microsoft.com/download/support/mslfiles/unimodv.exe**. The file is compressed and when you double-click on it in Explorer, it expands into a directory of your choice. The Readme.txt file gives full instructions on upgrading your modem to use Unimodem V.

If you install Unimodem, it's important to make sure you have the latest version.

### Ascertaining the version of Unimodem

1. In the subfolder \Windows\System (assuming Windows is the name of the directory that holds your Windows 98 software), find the file named Unimodem.vxd.

2. Right-click on the file and choose **Properties** from the shortcut menu.

3. Move to the Version tab. The Description line has the file description followed by (Version X.X).

## Using Phone Dialer

Because you have the modem, and your modem probably has a second jack for a telephone instrument, you might as well let the modem dial your regular phone calls for you. This is a great way to have access to speed dialing.

Be sure the modem is connected to the wall jack using the wall jack plug. Then plug your telephone into the modem's telephone plug. When you aren't using your modem, your telephone works normally.

To add a speed dial feature to your telephone, use the Microsoft Phone Dialer.

**Adding a speed dial number**

**1.** Click the **Start** button, and then choose **Programs**, **Accessories** from the Start menu.

**2.** In the Accessories menu, choose **Phone Dialer**. The Phone Dialer opens (see Figure 16.14).

**FIGURE 16.14**
The Phone Dialer is ready to accept your speed dial list.

**3.** To add a new speed dial number, click a blank speed dial button. This displays the Program Speed Dial dialog box, where you fill in the name and telephone number for this entry (see Figure 16.15).

**FIGURE 16.15**
Enter a name or nickname, along with that person's phone number.

**4.** Choose **Save** to save the entry, or choose **Save and Dial** to save the entry and dial the number.

**5.** To dial an entry, open the Phone Dialer and click the appropriate speed dial button. Don't pick up the telephone.

**6.** When the connection is made, the Phone Dialer tells you to pick up your telephone receiver and click the Talk button (see Figure 16.16).

FIGURE 16.16

Pick up the phone, click **Talk** and talk.

**7.** To change or delete an entry choose **Edit**, **Speed Dial** from the menu bar.

**8.** When the Edit Speed Dial dialog box opens, select the button you want to change. Then change either the name or number, or delete them to empty the button.

The Phone Dialer is just one of many communications programs available to you once you've installed a modem.

# Going Online

# Setting Up Online Services

Online services are connections to online computers. Those computers may be connected to the Internet, or may be proprietary systems with their own features. However, these days almost all the popular proprietary systems also provide gateways to the Internet, so I guess it's fair to say that online services means Internet services, except that these services offer special features not available to the standard run-of-the-mill Internet service provider.

Windows 98, just like Windows 95 and Windows NT 4, provides Dial-Up Networking services so you can establish a connection to an Internet service provider.

However, if you want to use a proprietary service such as AOL or CompuServe, you previously had to get the software from the service and install it. Not anymore. Windows 98 builds in quick and easy installation for some of the popular proprietary online services.

To begin, open the Online Services folder on your desktop to see the online service providers you can access (see Figure 17.1).

FIGURE 17.1

Set up online services from the desktop.

The icons in the folder are shortcuts to software that must be installed from the Windows 98 CD-ROM.

If the Online Services folder isn't on your desktop, it means it wasn't part of the installation of the operating system. You can install it now using the procedure for adding operating system features after you've installed the operating system. You'll need your Windows 98 CD-ROM.

### Adding online services

1. Open the Control Panel window.
2. Double-click the Add/Remove Programs icon.
3. Move to the Windows Setup tab.
4. Scroll through the list to find Online Services, and click the check box of the service you want to install to put a check mark in it (see Figure 17.2).

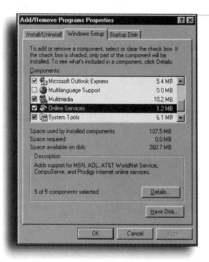

**FIGURE 17.2**
You can install additional operating system components at any time with the Windows Setup dialog box.

5. Click **OK**.

Each of these services includes a setup program that's very easy to understand. Just double-click on the proprietary online service you want to use and you'll be taken through the installation of that service in a setup wizard.

## Configuring Dial-Up Networking

For standard run-of-the-mill Internet service providers, there usually isn't any sort of easy setup wizard. For these, you need to use dial-up networking.

Setting up dial-up networking assumes that you have a modem hooked up to a phone line so you can dial out, and that the server you are calling is set up to accept incoming calls. If both of those conditions are true, you can set up dial-up networking.

To set up dial-up networking, open My Computer and then open the Dial-Up Networking folder. (If the Dial-Up Networking folder isn't there, you didn't install the communications features for Windows 98. Go to the Control Panel, select Add/Remove Programs, and install Communications from your Windows 98 CD-ROM.)

When you open the Dial-Up Networking folder for the first time, the only option (icon) available is Make New Connection.

### Creating a new connection

1. Double-click on the Make New Connection icon to launch the Make New Connection Wizard (see Figure 17.3).

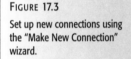

FIGURE 17.3

Set up new connections using the "Make New Connection" wizard.

2. Type in a name for this connection. Use a descriptive name such as the name of the computer you are dialing into.

3. The wizard enters the device (usually a modem) that you'll use for communications. If you have an additional device, you can change the default. Choose **Next** to move on.

4. Enter the **area code**, **phone number**, and the **country code** for the location of the server you are calling. Then choose **Next**.

5. The wizard tells you you're done (see Figure 17.4). Wasn't that easy? Choose **Finish**.

**FIGURE 17.4**
Congratulations, you're ready to connect!

An icon for your new connection resides in the Dial-Up Networking folder in My Computer. Double-click it to use it.

While you're connected, an icon displays on the taskbar. Right-click the taskbar icon and choose Disconnect when you want to hang up.

# Refining the Connection

You can tweak and refine the settings for a dial-up networking connection. The properties for dialing and the properties for the host computer can be configured for accuracy and efficiency.

## Working with Dialing Properties

To edit an existing dial-up networking connection, right-click on its icon in the Dial-Up Networking folder and choose **Properties** from the shortcut menu.

The General tab of the connection Properties dialog box contains the dialing information, in addition to the modem that's used for this connection.

If the telephone number changes, this is the place to modify that information. You can also tweak or change the settings for your modem by clicking on the Configure button to bring up the Modem Properties dialog box (see Figure 17.5).

FIGURE 17.5

You can fine-tune your modem settings in the Modem Properties dialog box.

You can modify the volume on the modem if it is supported by your modem, and you can set the maximum speed at which your modem can connect using this connection and port. I always set the speed for the highest available speed regardless of the rated speed for my modem.

Use the Connection tab of the modem Properties dialog box to set the data bits, parity, and stop bits for your modem. Then specify your preferences for calling out. You can also change error control and flow control settings and log file settings by using the Advanced button, and buffer control settings using the Port settings button. Refer to your modem documentation and the system administrator for the server you are connecting to if you think that any of these settings may need to be changed.

Use the Options tab to set the controls you need for the terminal window and special dialing properties (such as waiting for a credit card tone if you use a credit card number).

There's also an option to display the modem status, which means a progress bar will display on your screen while the connection is being made.

## Connecting to Different Server Types

Dial-Up Networking supports several different server types. The type of server you select for a connection determines how your computer can talk to the server on the other end of your connection. The "languages" spoken by the computers are called communications protocols, so the type of connection determines which protocols can be used.

Server types are defined on the Server Types page in the Connection Properties dialog box (see Figure 17.6).

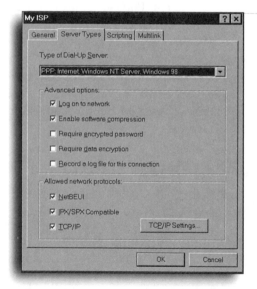

Specify the advanced options and select the network protocols that are expected for this connection.

The advanced options and the available protocols vary depending on the type of dial-up server and the protocols available on your computer. Some of the common specifications are shown in Table 17.1.

TABLE 17.1  **Communication protocols and options for different server types**

| Server Type | Advanced Options | Allowable Network Protocols |
| --- | --- | --- |
| NRN: Netware Connect | Log on to network | IPX/SPX–compatible |
| PPP: Windows 95, Windows 98, Windows NT 3.5+, Internet | Log on to network, enable software compression, require encrypted password | NetBEUI, IPX/SPX–compatible, TCP/IP |
| SLIP: Unix Connection | Log on to network | TCP/IP |
| Windows for Workgroups and Windows 3.1 | Log on to network | NetBEUI |

As you can see in Table 17.1, dial-up networking with a PPP connection (Point-to-Point Protocol) offers the most options. This is the type of connection you can use with Windows 95, Windows NT 3.5 or later, Windows 98, or the Internet. The connection allows logging on to the server, compressing data, and encrypting passwords for secure connections. You can usually use NetBEUI or IPX/SPX protocols, as well as TCP/IP, the protocol used for Internet and World Wide Web communications.

## Setting Up Logon Scripts

Sometimes you're asked to enter information during the logon process. For example, you might have to enter your username and your password, and perhaps you have to respond to prompts from the host system.

It's really boring to enter the same information every time you log on to the server, so simplify the process with a script. Then, let the script do all of the repetitive boring stuff when you log on.

To accomplish this, you must create a script file, and then assign the script file to a specific dial-up connection.

## Creating a Script File

The basic component of a script is a *command*, which is a simple instruction to the computer. An *expression* results in a value that can be used in a command. An example of a simple command with an expression is

```
transmit "John Doe^M"
```

where the command tells the computer to send the literal string `"John Doe"` followed by a `"^M"` character to insert a carriage return.

The scripting language is a fairly simple programming language that you should be able to learn on your own, especially if you have any knowledge of programming languages. There is a complete language reference file named `script.doc` that you can find in your Windows directory. The file can be opened and printed using Notepad or WordPad.

Save the file in your `Windows\Accessories` directory with an extension of .scp; for example, mylogon.scp. If you use WordPad, you have to be sure to save the file in ASCII/Text format.

There are several examples of scripts already in the Accessories directory:

- `CIS.scp` demonstrates logging on to CompuServe and changing your port.
- `PPPMenu.scp` demonstrates using a PPP connection for logging on to a system that uses a menu system.
- `SLIP.scp` demonstrates how to log on to a host using a SLIP connection.
- `SLIPMenu.scp` demonstrates how to use a SLIP connection to log on to a host that uses a menu system.

If you can find a script that is close to what you want, make a copy of the script file, save it under a unique name, and modify it to suit your needs.

## Assigning the Script File to a Dial-Up Networking Connection

After you create the script file, you can assign it to a dial-up networking connection so it runs automatically each time the connection is used.

To assign a script file to a connection, right-click the Connection icon and choose **Properties** from the shortcut menu. Move to the Scripting tab (see Figure 17.7).

**FIGURE 17.7**

The Scripting tab of the Dial-Up Networking Connection.

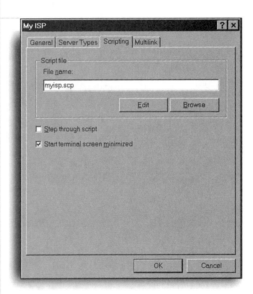

Enter the path and name of your script file, or choose **Browse** to locate it. Browse the directories to locate the script file you want to associate with the connection.

You can also check **Step** through script to execute the script a line at a time, which can be helpful for troubleshooting. Deselect the **Start terminal screen minimized** option if you want to see a display of the script as it is being executed.

# Dial-Up Networking and the Internet

Before you can use the Internet, you have to have a place to get online. You have a choice of letting Microsoft set you up with a connection to Microsoft Network (MSN), or you can set up your own connection through a local Internet service provider or through your business.

You don't connect your computer directly to the Internet. Instead, you connect to a *server* that is connected to the Internet. In turn, that server has an industrial-grade connection to the Internet and a bank of dial-in telephone lines that let multiple users connect at one time. That is true with any Internet connection, including the commercial Internet services.

When you set up your own Internet account, the Internet server that you dial in to belongs to an Internet service provider (an ISP). When you call an ISP to set up an account, you will be given an account with a username and a password, and a phone number that you can dial to make a connection. In addition, you will probably be given vital information about the ISP, such as the following:

- The host name and domain name of the ISP. The domain name is the part of your Internet email address. For example, in the address jdoe@grandcanyon.com, "grandcanyon" is the domain name, and the server at "grandcanyon" is where you are connecting to the Internet.

- The IP (Internet Protocol) address of the Domain Name Server (the DNS). The IP address is a registered numeric address that identifies a particular computer on the Internet. It will be in a format such as "111.22.3.45" with a series of one-, two-, or three-digit numbers separated by periods.

This information is important when you set up dial-up networking to an ISP or to any other host computer (such as an Internet server at your office).

## Refining Your Dial-Up Connection to the Internet

How does all this relate to the dial-up networking connection we defined earlier? The connection has to be refined with the specific information about your ISP. You can do the setup using the Internet Connection Wizard from the Windows Desktop, or you can modify your setup using the Internet Properties dialog box.

### Refining your Internet connection

1. Open the Control Panel and click on the Internet icon, and then move to the Connection tab (see Figure 17.8).

**FIGURE 17.8**

Enter detailed information about your Internet connection in the Internet Properties dialog box.

2. Create a new dial-up network connection, if you want to, by choosing **Connect**. The Connection Wizard opens to create a new dial-up networking connection. For an existing dial-up connection, select **Connect to the Internet Using a Modem**, and then choose **Settings** to display the Dial-up Settings dialog box (see Figure 17.9).

3. Select the connection you want to work with, and modify the basic settings so your computer makes connections the way you want it to. You can modify these settings at any

time. For example, you may find that your **Disconnect if idle for** setting is too short, so you can either set a longer disconnect interval or deselect it altogether. Click **OK** to save your changes when you are done (or choose **Cancel** to exit the dialog box without saving any changes).

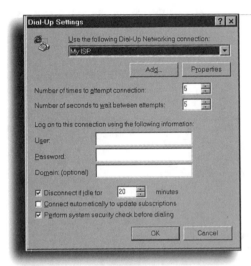

## Setting Up a Proxy Server

If you are connecting through an office Internet account, the chances are good that you're connecting through what is called a *proxy server*. The server acts as a proxy for you, so you do not connect directly to the Internet.

The proxy server is a buffer between you and the Internet. It does all the connecting for you. When you request a URL, the server retrieves the requested web page from the Internet and then relays the downloaded page to your computer. The relay takes place so quickly that you will not even be aware of it. The proxy server helps keep your corporate data safe from intruders. The proxy server provides what is called a *firewall* between you and the Internet.

You are probably wondering why you need a dial-up connection, because the proxy server is on the local area network in your office and you're already connected by cable. The reason? You can dial into the proxy server from home.

If you are using a proxy server to connect to the Internet, there is some additional tweaking you can do to refine your connection.

**Refining the connection to a proxy server**

1. From the Connection tab of the Internet Properties dialog box, select **Access the Internet using a proxy server,** and then choose **Advanced** to display the Proxy Settings dialog box (see Figure 17.10).

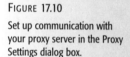

FIGURE 17.10

Set up communication with your proxy server in the Proxy Settings dialog box.

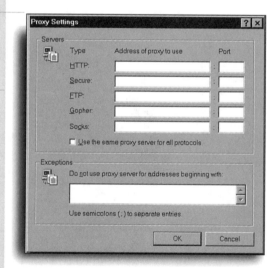

2. In the **HTTP proxy** field, enter the Web address of the proxy server. This can be a server name, such as **www.myserver.com,** or enter the numeric (IP) address of the server. You will have to get this information from your network administrator. HTTP stands for Hypertext Transport Protocol. It is the protocol used to transmit web pages.

3. Set the **port** to **80,** unless you are instructed to set it to something else. This is the default port number used on the Internet by most servers. The port is a numeric address used internally by the computer to communicate with the outside world.

**4.** If you are using the same proxy server for different types of Internet protocols, select **Use the same proxy server for all protocols**. All of the other protocol types will be grayed out, and will automatically use the same proxy you specified for your HTTP proxy. The other proxies are used in special situations on the Internet, such as when you connect to a secure server, when you send or retrieve files from an FTP server (using File Transfer Protocol), or when you search the Internet through a Gopher server. If you need to use any of these other protocols, the proxy server has to be set up to use them, and you need an address to access the proxy server.

**5.** If you want to specify different servers for the different protocols, you will have to specify addresses for each individual proxy type.

**6.** Because you know that web sites inside your organization's firewall are safe, you can access them directly without going through the proxy server. You don't have to access them locally—you can go through your proxy server to the Internet, and then come back in through your web server to retrieve web pages—but it is more direct to retrieve pages directly from the web server. To do this, enter local addresses in the **Exceptions** field at the bottom of the dialog box. For example, enter **www.myserver.com** to go to all web sites that begin with that address, e.g. **www.myserver.com/ homepage**.

# Dial-Up Networking and Other Servers

The Internet is probably the most popular reason to connect to a server using a dial-up connection, but you can connect to other servers, and you can use communication protocols other than TCP/IP. In fact, corporate networks are likely to use another protocol just to ensure that the network cannot be invaded by someone using an Internet connection.

If you are using a PPP dial-up connection (Point-to-Point Protocol), you can select or deselect any of the available protocols. If you are using a server type that does not support PPP, you are restricted to the protocol offered by that server type.

When you attempt to connect to the server, you may be required to provide login information on a terminal screen when you first connect. If this happens, you must have the modem properties set to bring up the terminal window after dialing. To accomplish this, open the Connection Properties dialog box and choose **Configure** on the General tab to open the modem Properties dialog box. Move to the Options tab and select **Bring up terminal window after dialing**.

# Configuring Internet Explorer 4

Offline surfing the Active Desktop

Channels

Secure Web surfing

# Offline Browsing

When you browse the World Wide Web, the Web pages you encounter are downloaded to your computer as HTML (Hypertext Markup Language) files. They're normally stored in a Temporary Internet folder within your Windows subdirectory. You can configure IE4 to determine how many files are held in the folder until they're automatically discarded. While the files are held in the folder, you can display them by choosing their origin (the page on which you originally found them). IE4 checks this folder to see if the page exists before moving to a Web site to fetch it, which speeds everything up when you use the Back and Forward buttons.

If you launch IE4 when there is no connection, you're given the option of browsing offline. When you offline enter a URL address to visit a Web page, that Web page is displayed if the HTML file is still in your Temporary Internet folder. If it's not, you see a message telling you that the page is not available in offline mode. You will be given a choice of connecting to the Internet or canceling out of the dialog box.

What can you see when you browse offline? In addition to HTML files in your Temporary Internet folder, you can see any Active Channel subscriptions that have been downloaded (see "Using Active Channels to Automate Your Browsing"). With the Active Desktop, you can also use the browser's *address bar* to open any file on your computer by entering the full pathname and address.

# Active Desktop

The Active Desktop can transform the Windows desktop into a Web page, so you can open your word processor or spreadsheet with a single click, and just as easily you can travel to your favorite Web site. The Active Desktop keeps track of where everything is so you don't have to worry about the details.

You have the option of using some of the Active Desktop features such as single-click icons, or sticking with the familiar double-click navigation. Regardless of your configuration

options, you can get to IE4 and all of its features from the
taskbar, because IE4 creates its own icon set.

# A Tour of the Active Desktop

When you have the Active Desktop enabled, your desktop is
your computer's home page. You can still display shortcuts and
folders on your desktop, but added to those common elements
are windows into a customizable Web world.

What are your interests? Do you like to keep up with sports
scores? You can have a sports ticker on your desktop showing
up-to-the-minute scores. The weather? You can display a weather map. Travel? You can show a map. The stock market? You can
display a stock ticker on your home page. Combined with an
Active Channel navigation bar, you can go to favorite sites on
the Internet as easily as you can go to programs on your personal computer. That is the appeal behind the Active Desktop.

You can quickly activate the Active Desktop or put it to rest so
you can work locally with your desktop applications.

## Starting the Active Desktop

When you have Windows 98 installed on your computer, display
the Active Desktop floating menu by right-clicking on your
Windows desktop. The menu is shown in Figure 18.1.

**FIGURE 18.1**

A right-click displays the Active
Desktop floating menu.

Select **View as Web Page** to turn the Active Desktop on or off.
When you view the desktop as a Web page, the Active Desktop
elements are visible. When you view the desktop without the
Active Desktop, it will look just like the traditional Windows
desktop.

## Customizing the Active Desktop

There are a lot of ways you can customize your Active Desktop, including copying a Web page as wallpaper or designing your own home page. Here are some of the ways:

- Define how links to applications, files, and folders from icons on your desktop should be treated—as Web links (single-click) or as Windows shortcuts (double-click).
- Define how folders should be displayed.
- Add Active Desktop content.

## Working with Links

Standard links to applications, files, and folders from icons on your desktop can be defined as underlined hypertext links, or as standard Windows shortcuts. You can make shortcuts to applications, files, and folders.

### Configuring links

1. Right-click on the Windows Desktop and select **Properties**.
2. Click on the Web tab to display the Web Properties page.
3. Click on the **Folder Options** button at the bottom of the page. A prompt will be displayed asking if you want to close the Display Properties box and open the Folder Options dialog box. Answer **Yes** to display the dialog box shown in Figure 18.2.
4. On the **General** tab, select **Web Style** to make all items open with a single click. If you want to refine the settings, you can select **Custom** so you have more control over how links and Web content are handled on the Active Desktop. **Web Style** will make all icons on your desktop into hyperlinks.
5. On the **View** tab, configure the manner in which you want icons and links to display.
6. On the **File Types** tab, define which applications are used to display files based on their three-character file extension.

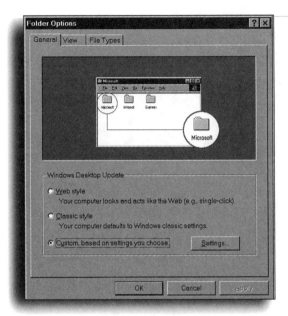

FIGURE 18.2
Define Web properties for a
folder in the Folder Options
dialog box.

## Displaying Folders

You can customize the display of an individual folder, or you can make a single folder look the way you want it to, and then make all of the other folders look the same when they are viewed as Web pages.

### Customizing a folder

1. Open the folder you want to customize.

2. Choose **Customize this Folder** from the **View** menu to start the Customize This Folder Wizard (see Figure 18.3).

3. Select **Create or edit an HTML document** if you are proficient at HTML and want to create a customized HTML page to display the folder. You can also create Web pages using FrontPage Express, or save an HTML page as a background picture.

4. Select **Choose a background picture** if you want to use a picture as a background for the folder.

5. Select an image to use as a background.

**Lost your menu bar?**

If you cannot see the menu bar in IE4, you are probably looking at the browser in a full-screen window. To see the toolbars and the menu bar, click on the Fullscreen icon. You will then see the familiar toolbars.

FIGURE 18.3

Use the Customize this Folder Wizard to create a fancy design for the folders on your desktop.

**6.** Click on **Next** and then **Finish** to complete the background customization.

You can further customize the appearance of the folder by selecting **Folder Options** from the **View** menu and selecting options on the View tab. Play with these settings until the files in your folder are displayed they way you want them.

## Add Active Desktop Content

*Active content* is the hallmark of the Active Desktop. It means that Web pages are updated automatically (you can watch the data change).

The content of the Active Desktop is downloaded to your computer's memory, and is updated on a schedule that you determine. This minimizes the amount of traffic on the Internet, and at the same time maximizes the amount of information that you can see. You can quickly view what is important to you without having to browse through the Web to locate the information. If you are a quick reader, you can keep up with your world on-the-fly as you navigate around your desktop.

You can select from several Active Desktop elements provided in a gallery on the Microsoft Web site, or search the Web for other sites that are defined as Active Desktop sites.

### Adding content to the Active Desktop

**1.** Right-click on the desktop and choose **Customize my Desktop** from the Active Desktop menu item. This opens the Display Properties dialog box with the Web tab in the foreground (see Figure 18.4).

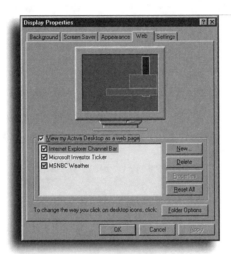

FIGURE 18.4
Use the Web tab to customize your active desktop.

**2.** Choose **New** to add an element to your desktop. The New Active Desktop Item dialog box appears, inviting you to visit the Microsoft Web site to see the available active desktop items. Choose **Yes** to connect to the gallery and pick the elements you want to use on your desktop.

Now let's take a quick tour of the Microsoft Gallery, where you get your Active Desktop content.

## Walking the Halls of the Microsoft Gallery

When you go to the Microsoft Gallery to select items for your Active Desktop, you see a wide variety of items (see Figure 18.5).

The Gallery holds a number of links that can be placed on your Active Desktop. The links are categorized into topics such as News, Sports, and Entertainment.

**FIGURE 18.5**

The Microsoft Gallery is a
source for Active Desktop
items.

Meander through the gallery—there's information about the
links (click a link to see the information). As you find the links
you want to add to your desktop, choose Add to Active Desktop
(see Figure 18.6). You can add the link, or subscribe to the
service.

Now, before you panic, understand that subscribing doesn't
mean that you have to pay for the content. It just means that the
content will be downloaded to your computer automatically, if
you so choose.

To find out what subscribing means, you can click on the
Customize Subscription button to see the Subscription Wizard
(see Figure 18.7). This wizard gives you the option of updating
manually or on a variety of schedules, including the channel
publisher's recommended schedule; on a daily schedule; a weekly
schedule; or even a monthly schedule. If you don't like those
options, you can create a new schedule or edit an existing
schedule.

If you choose the **Dial as needed if connected through a
modem** check box, your scheduled connection will take place
automatically when the time comes (assuming your computer is
running).

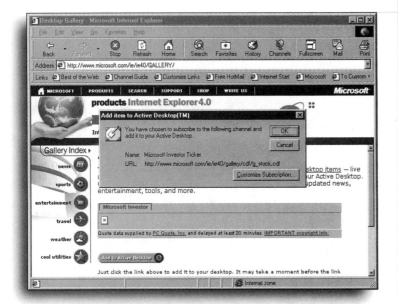

FIGURE 18.6

Read about the link, and then add it to your desktop.

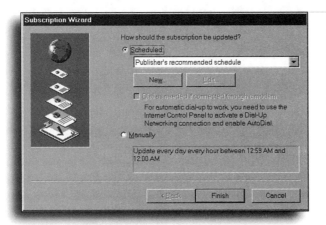

FIGURE 18.7

Use the Subscription Wizard to schedule updates to your Active Desktop items.

On the second page of the wizard (displayed by clicking on the easily overlooked Next button at the bottom of the page), you have the option of entering a username and password if the site you have chosen requires you to register each time you visit.

Creating a new schedule involves filling out a single page form that gives you flexibility about how often the channel gets updated. Choose **New** to display the Custom Schedule dialog box, which enables you to specify the time of day to call the channel's home Web site (see Figure 18.8). This means you can schedule an update in the middle of the night when there is less traffic on the Web, and when you are not using your computer for work.

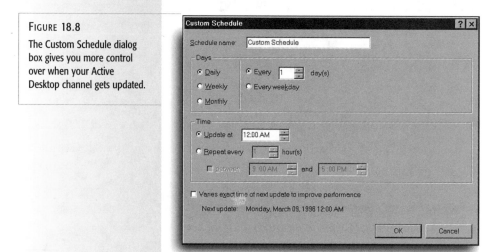

The end result of all the updating is that you end up with a new element on your Active Desktop.

## Other Subscription Options

You can be as creative as you want on your desktop. You are not limited to the Active Desktop content provided by Microsoft in its gallery. Do you want to add a Dilbert link? Maybe you want to add a link to your hometown newspaper's home page? Or maybe you want to keep an eye on your competitor's Web page.

Does all that sound too much like work? Then you can create your own home page using a tool such as the Microsoft FrontPage Express, and include a picture of your spouse, your children, your pets, or links to your own favorite Web sites.

To accomplish this, right-click on the desktop and choose **Customize my Desktop** from the Active Desktop menu item to bring up the Display Properties box. On the Web tab, select **View my Active Desktop as a Web Page**. Then choose **New** to display the New Active Desktop Item dialog box shown in Figure 18.9.

**FIGURE 18.9**

Do you want to go to the Microsoft Gallery?

Choose **No** to display the New Active Desktop Item dialog box (see Figure 18.10).

**FIGURE 18.10**

Enter the URL of the item you want on your desktop.

Enter the URL of the Web page you want on your desktop, or select a graphic or another Web page from your local system using the Browse button. Choose **OK** to put the object on your Active Desktop.

**Use a Web page as wallpaper**

Try copying your favorite Web page as wallpaper, or as an HTML page. It will give you a good place to start when you begin designing your desktop.

# Using Active Channels to Automate Your Browsing

*Active Channels* provide a way to subscribe to information in a similar fashion to the Active Desktop. You can locate your favorite information sources quickly.

Channels can be accessed quickly and easily from the Windows desktop by clicking on the Channel shortcut icon (the satellite dish) on the taskbar.

Even better, a bar of channel shortcuts, called the Channel Guide, can sit right on your desktop (Figure 18.11).

FIGURE 18.11.

The Active Channel Guide sits on the Windows desktop.

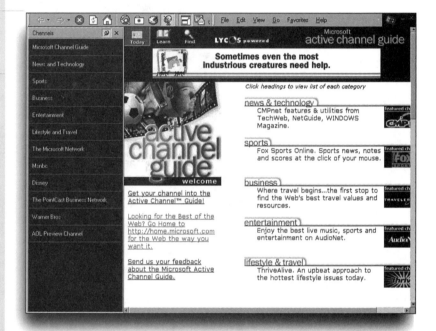

To access a channel to which you have subscribed, all you have to do is click on its icon on the Channel Guide. The link will launch IE4 and display the selected channel in a full screen.

Click the Active Channels icon on the taskbar (it looks like a satellite dish) to launch IE4 and travel to the Microsoft Active Channel Guide page (see Figure 18.12).

This Active Channel Guide page serves several purposes:

- It provides a number of featured links of the day in major categories such as news, sports, and business. Other links are accessible from the Channel Guide, which slides onto the left side of the screen when you move the cursor against the left border of the page.

- It provides a chance to learn about Active Channels. There is a good overview of Active Channels, plus links that bring up specific instructions on how to add a new channel to the Channel Guide, how to subscribe to a channel, and how to display a channel in the browser.

- It provides a search facility you can use to look for other Web sites that have been designed to work as Active Channels.

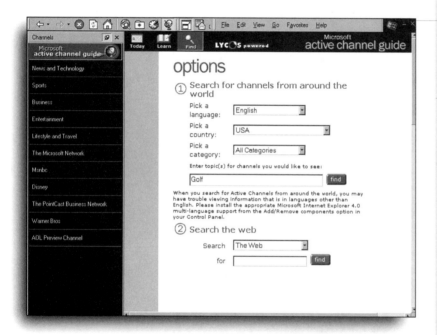

## Using the Channel Guide

The Channel Guide sits on your Windows desktop and provides a link to a preset group of Active Channels. If you click on a channel link, you are automatically connected to the Internet so you can view the content in the channel. (Downloading Web pages from the site may be fine if you are working in an environment where you have a constant high-speed connection to the Internet, but in most instances, it is no different from ordinary Web surfing.) After you set up the Channel Guide, you'll notice a difference in the way everything works.

To set up the Channel Guide, click on the Channel icon or the Channel Guide link. This displays the Microsoft Active Channel Guide window. Slide the cursor to the left edge of the screen to see the Channel Guide. Click on the Push pin icon to make the Channel guide stick in the open position, or click on it again to let it automatically slide back off the screen whenever the cursor is not pointing at it.

Point to the Channel Guide. As the cursor slides over different categories, a category icon displays. Click once on a category and it will expand to reveal a list of available Active Channels. The categories include:

- News and Technology
- Sports
- Business
- Entertainment
- Lifestyle and Travel

The other items listed on the default Channel Guide are links that lead directly to Web sites.

If you want to add an Active Channel to the Channel Guide, click on the Channel link to see a preview of the channel. You're given an opportunity to subscribe to the channel so you can see the full content.

If you don't see the channel you want, you can search for other sites that are set up to serve Active Channels to your computer.

### Searching for an unlisted channel

1. Choose **Find** at the top of the screen.
2. Enter a word to describe the topic you want to search for. For example, I entered the word "golf" (see Figure 18.13). To search channels worldwide, click **Options**, and enter the topic.

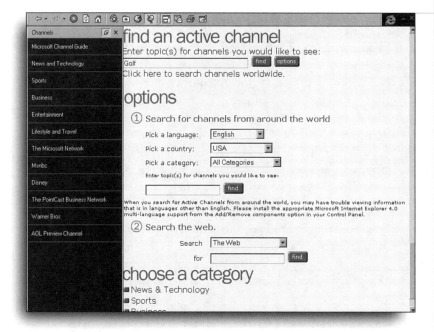

**FIGURE 18.13**

Search for an Active Channel using a simple keyword, or refine your search using a variety of options.

3. Choose **Find**.

4. After a few seconds, you will see a list of links to Web pages on the selected topic that support Active Channels. For golf, it found 21 listings.

5. Click on the link to the listing you want to add, and then subscribe to that channel. Subscribing to a channel is the same as subscribing to an Active Desktop element. You can accept the publisher's recommended schedule, or you can establish your own schedule. If a channel has reasonably static information on it, for example, you can download the channel once a day, and then view the channel while working offline.

6. After you have subscribed to a channel, you can view it by clicking on the channel's icon in the Channel Guide. The Channel Guide lists all channels available on your computer, whether you subscribe to them or not.

**Refining your search**

You can refine your search using a variety of options. For example, you can search for sites in a particular language and country, or search only pages that are categorized under particular topics.

## Making Your Own Web Site into an Active Channel

The advantage of having your Web site defined as an Active Channel is that you can control what content is received by subscribers to your site. If you are familiar with the terminology, this is called push technology. The subscriber connects to your site at the time defined in the subscription, and then everything that you have defined gets pushed across the Internet to the client computer so it can be viewed while connected or offline. If you are a business user, it is a great way to help your clients tap into the resources you provide for them.

To become an Active Channel provider, there are specific steps you need to take. You need to modify your site, you need to submit an application to be included in the Channel Guide, and you have to be a member of the Microsoft Site Builder Network. This is an advanced feature for Web developers.

A link on the Microsoft Channel Guide page takes you to information that describes in detail how you can convert a Web site into an Active Channel. It is mentioned here for the sake of those who may be interested in developing an Active Channel site, but the information is not really needed if you are just an end user.

# Working with Security in IE4

The World Wide Web, incredible as it may seem, is no more than a few years old. In that short time, the Web has already had to overcome a reputation for lawlessness and undisciplined growth. When people made jokes about practicing safe computing, they weren't kidding. There is a lot of content available on the Web, and it isn't all necessarily fit for everyone.

Web security has two distinct areas: Making your computer more secure when you download Web pages from the Internet, and making sure that information is secure when you send private information over the Web.

# Security Zones and Safe Surfing

When you open a Web page, what happens in the background is that essentially you give permission to another computer to send information to your computer. That information comes to your computer in the form of a page that is coded with HTML tags. Those tags tell your Web browser, Microsoft IE4, how to interpret and display the page.

Embedded in the HTML code that you download from the Web may be a variety of scripts and active programs such as *applets* or *agents* that can be run on your computer.

In an ideal world, these downloaded programs make surfing the Web more exciting and relevant. At their most obvious, these downloaded programs can do things like adding sound and motion to a Web page. More important, though, is the fact that these programs can run on your computer, and can potentially do anything that you can make a program do. They can copy information from a file and process that information to make your world easier for you. They can verify information about you and help you work in a secure environment. But on the dark side, these programs could potentially copy files and send them to someone else without your even knowing it. They could steal your password. They could reformat your hard drive. In short, downloaded programs could contain just about any type of computer virus invented by hackers.

The problem is, how do you know if a program is friendly or fiendish? You have to depend on two things: the intelligence of your computer to screen out downloaded programs from certain sites; and your ability to determine which sites you want to trust, and how much you want to trust them. Determining which sites to trust is the key to *security zones*.

IE4 divides the Web into four different Security Zones with different levels of security:

- The *Local Intranet Zone* is where you keep your local intranet Web pages that do not require a proxy server. Pages in this zone are defined by the intranet administrator using an Internet Explorer Administrator's Kit. These sites are assigned medium security, by default, but you may want to set the security level to low.

- The *Trusted Sites Zone* is where you keep sites that you trust. These are sites that you know are reputable, so you can freely download files and programs without worrying too much about downloading harmful or malicious programs. This zone has low security.

- The *Restricted Sites Zone* is where you put sites that you do not trust. This zone has high security, which means that nothing aside from straight HTML-coded content gets downloaded without your explicit permission.

- The *Internet Zone* is the default zone for anything that is not specifically in one of the other zones. The Internet Zone has medium security.

Files on your local computer are not assigned to any security zone. In order to take full advantage of the security zones, you have to set up security levels for the zones, and you then have to assign Web sites to the zones.

## Defining Security Levels for Zones

You can change the default security settings for a Security Zone.

### Configure security settings

1. Select **Internet Options** from the IE4 **View** menu.

2. Move to the Security tab (see Figure 18.14).

3. Select the security zone you want to modify.

4. Select a security level for the zone. You can set security to High for zones you don't trust, Medium, or Low (zones that you trust completely). You can also choose **Custom**, then choose **Settings** to define specific security behavior for different types of Web content, including ActiveX and Java security. If you change your mind, click the Reset button to return the custom settings to High, Medium, or Low.

5. When you are done, click **OK** to close the Internet Settings dialog box.

**FIGURE 18.14**
Modify the security settings for security zones in the Internet Options dialog box.

## Assigning a Web Site to Another Security Zone

When you first begin using IE4, everything is in the Internet Zone, which has a medium security setting by default. That means, for example, that your computer will not run unsigned ActiveX controls, and will prompt you before IE4 runs any ActiveX controls that are not marked as being safe. If you do a lot of browsing on certain sites, you might decide that you want to move those sites to another Internet Zone.

There are two types of site you can move to your Trusted Sites Zone: sites served by a secure server (an https: server); or sites from which you are absolutely sure you're willing to accept all content.

The Restricted Sites Zone holds any sites that you do not trust, and therefore want to enforce high security when you visit those sites. For example, if you suspect that you downloaded a virus from a site, you may want to add it to this zone to ensure that you are informed before anything from the site gets downloaded to your computer.

### Adding trusted sites

  **1.** From the IE4 browser, choose **Internet Options** from the **View** menu and move to the **Security** tab.

**Moving sites is a limited activity**

You can only move sites to your Trusted Sites Zone or your Restricted Sites Zone. All sites not in one of those zones is by default in the Internet Zone. The Local Sites Zone is only used if you are on a LAN, and only the system administrator can place sites into the zone.

**2.** Select the zone to which you want to add sites in the zone selection field.

**3.** Choose **Add Sites** (the Add Sites button is only available if you are in the Trusted Sites Zone or the Restricted Sites Zone). This opens the dialog box shown in Figure 18.15.

FIGURE 18.15

Adding sites to the Trusted Sites Zone.

**4.** If you want to put only secure servers in your Trusted Sites Zone, check the box at the bottom of the dialog box to indicate that you want to require verification for all sites in this zone. If this is checked, you can only access servers that use an https: secure Internet protocol. The check box does not show up on the Restricted Sites page.

**5.** Enter the **URL address** for the site that you want to add. If you opted to require verification for secure sites, only http: sites can be added.

**6.** When the site URL is entered, choose **Add** to add the site to the list of trusted or restricted sites.

**7.** If you want to remove a site from the zone, highlight the site's URL and choose **Remove**.

**8.** When the zone is set up the way you want it, click **OK** to save your changes.

When you next open any of the sites listed in your Trusted Sites Zone, the sites will automatically have low security enforced, or whatever security level you have selected for sites in the Trusted Sites Zone.

When you next attempt to download any of the restricted sites, you will be able to view the site, but high security will be enforced automatically, because the site is in your Restricted Sites Zone.

## Using Certificates

When you travel to another country, in most circumstances you have to present a passport at the border. The passport identifies you to the representative of the country you are visiting.

But why does the other country trust you? Think about it for a minute. I can scan your picture and put it into a document that says "Passport" in big letters across the top. I'll even put your name and your birthdate on it, and if you want, I'll sign it. But will it get you through an international border? I doubt it. The other country will not accept this bogus document, because they do not know me, and therefore they do not trust me. They will accept passports that are issued only by authorities they trust.

With computers, the same paradigm is true. When you visit a secure site (a Web site that runs https: protocol, which means that it uses SSL [Secure Socket Layers]), that secure computer wants to know who you are, and will demand that you prove your identity. Likewise, you want to know that you are talking to the correct computer, and not to someone who has intercepted your communication and is masquerading as the secure computer. So you and the other computer show each other certificates issued by somebody you both trust.

IE4 has a complete list of Certificate Authorities that issue secure certificates. You can decide which authorities you want to trust. When you connect to a secure site, there is a background conversation (unseen by you) that takes place between your computer and the secure site before you can connect. Your computer demands that the secure site show a certificate that can be trusted. When the certificate is shown (electronically, of course), your computer can compare this certificate with the certificate issued to that secure site by a recognized Certificate Authority. If the two certificates match, then your computer knows that the site is authentic.

Likewise, the secure site demands that you prove your identity. Your identity can come from one of two sources: a Personal Profile document that is encrypted on your computer, or a Personal Certificate issued by one of the recognized Certificate Authorities.

Now don't throw up your hands in despair. You don't have to remember all this. In fact, you hardly need to do anything—the computer does it all for you. If you need a certificate in order to access a site, you will be told how to acquire one. Once you have one, the exchanging of certificates takes place in the background without your knowing anything about it, except maybe remembering a username and password when you log onto the secure site. The following couple of paragraphs will tell you all you need to know about your certificates.

## Deciding Which Certificate Authorities to Trust

You can view the list of all Certificate Authorities and place a check mark next to any authority you want to trust. In other words, if you don't trust passports issued by Lower Elbonia, you don't have to accept them.

### Looking at certificate authorities

1. Choose **Internet Options** from the View menu.

2. In the Internet Options dialog box, move to the Content tab (see Figure 18.16).

FIGURE 18.16

Work with security settings from the Content page of the Internet Options dialog box.

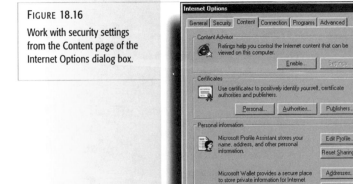

**3.** Choose **Authorities** to display the Certificate Authorities
dialog box (see Figure 18.17).

FIGURE 18.17

Place a check mark next to the
Certificate Authorities you want
to trust.

**4.** Select the **Issuer Type**. You can select authorities to trust
for Network Server authentication, Network Client authentication, secure email, and software publishing.

**5.** For the Issuer Type, scroll the list of authorities and place a
check mark next to any authority you want to trust. To
select or deselect an authority, click on the check box.

**6.** If you want, you can view the certificate issued by this
authority. Click on the authority to highlight it, and then
choose **View Certificate**. An example of a certificate is
shown in Figure 18.18. Notice that you can click on different field names to display the subject, the issuer of the certificate, the effective date and expiration date of the
certificate, and the "fingerprint," which is a digital key used
to decrypt communications that use this certificate.

**7.** To delete a certificate, highlight the certificate and choose
**Delete**, and then confirm the deletion. Without the certificate, you may not be able to access some sites. An example
of the Delete dialog box is shown in Figure 18.19.

FIGURE **18.18**
You can view details for any certificate stored on your computer.

FIGURE **18.19**
Before you delete a certificate, you have a chance to verify that you really want to do this.

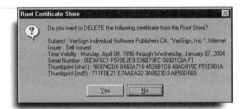

## Working with Personal Certificates

When you work with sites that require a certificate, you're instructed about the methods for obtaining a certificate. When you receive a certificate in a file, you can import it and maintain a list of personal certificates.

### Importing a personal certificate

1. Choose **Internet Options** from the **View** menu.

2. In the Internet Options dialog box, move to the Content tab.

3. Choose **Personal** in the Certificates part of the Contents page to display the Client Authentication dialog box. This dialog box consists of a list of personal certificates and three buttons: Import; Export; and View Certificate.

4. Choose **Import** to locate and import a file that contains a certificate.

5. Highlight an existing certificate and choose **Export** to export a certificate to a file so it can be transferred to another computer.

**6.** Highlight an existing certificate and choose **View Certificate** to view details regarding the certificate.

The certificates in your Personal Certificates list enable your computer to identify itself positively to secure servers. Using the fingerprint of your certificate, information can be encrypted and sent securely to the secure server on the other end. The secure server will then use its copy of the same certificate to decrypt the information you send. That is the essence of how secure commerce happens on the Web.

## Storing Personal Information in a Personal Profile

The Personal Profile is used to record personal information about you. When you connect to a Web site that requires personal information, you won't have to type it in as long as you give the site permission to access your Personal Profile.

Whenever a site wants to access your Personal Profile, you will be told. You can determine the site's URL, what information is being requested (you can block release of information that you want to keep private), how the information will be used, and whether the requesting site uses SSL, that is, is site-secure. If it is secure, you will have the option to check the certificate before granting access to your profile.

### Configuring your personal profile

**1.** Choose **Internet** **O**ptions from the **V**iew smenu.

**2.** Move to the Contents tab.

**3.** Choose **Edit Profile** to display the Personal Properties dialog box. The first tab is shown in Figure 18.20. Notice that default information is already filled in when you open the dialog box.

**4.** If you want to fill in your email address, type it in the Add New field, and then choose **Add**. The email address will be placed in a list of email addresses at the bottom of the page. If you have multiple email addresses, you can specify which address should be used as a default address.

**5.** Enter optional information on any of the other tabs in the Personal Properties dialog box. This includes Home,

**About the Other button**

The Other button in the Certificates section displays a list of publishers to whom you subscribe. These are the providers of Active Desktop and Active Channel content that you subscribe to.

Business, Other (miscellaneous information), NetMeeting (described in Chapter 19) and DigitalIDs (Personal certificates used for encrypting email from specific email addresses).

**6.** When you are finished, click **OK** to save your profile.

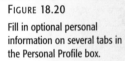

FIGURE 18.20

Fill in optional personal information on several tabs in the Personal Profile box.

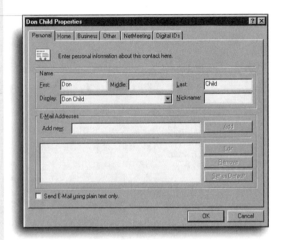

If you've been sharing information with various sites and decide to stop sharing with any of those sites, you can force all sites to request anew the right to access your Personal Profile. To reset the permissions to ground zero, choose Reset Sharing on the Content tab of the Internet Properties dialog box.

## Using the Microsoft Wallet to Store Financial Information for Net Commerce

The Microsoft Wallet is similar to the Personal Profile, but it is more secure. It contains information you can safely use in Internet commerce without worrying about the possibility of theft. When you want to buy something over the Web using IE4, the information is readily available in your "wallet," but the information can be released only with your explicit permission.

The Wallet holds two types of information: Address information and Payment information.

## Entering Address Information into the Wallet

Address information can be entered for any addresses to which you want online orders sent. When you create an address, you have a choice of entering the information from scratch or looking up the information in the Windows Address Book.

### Entering address information

1. Choose **Internet Options** from the View menu.

2. Move to the Contents tab.

3. Choose **Addresses** in the Personal Information section at the bottom of the page. This displays the Address Options dialog box with a list of addresses currently in your Wallet. The addresses are identified with a descriptive phrase, such as "My office." You can edit or delete any address by highlighting an address and choosing **Edit** or **Delete**.

4. Choose **Add** to add a new address. The Add a New Address dialog box appears, shown in Figure 18.21.

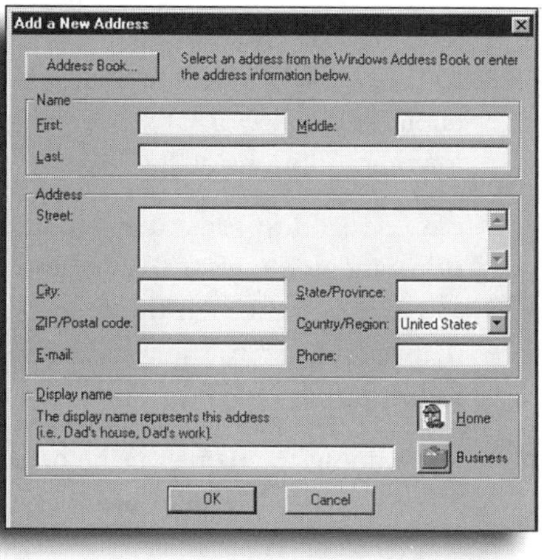

FIGURE 18.21
Use this page to add new addresses to the Microsoft Wallet.

5. Enter address information, including a display name that will be used to distinguish this address from others in the list of addresses.

6. Alternatively, choose **Address Book** to display a list of names from the Windows Address Book.

7. When you are done, click **OK** to add the address.

## Adding Payment Information to the Wallet

Payment information consists of credit card information that can be used to order items online. Entering payment information brings up a wizard that will ensure that information gets entered accurately. Choose **Payments** on the Content tab of the Internet Options dialog box to see the Payment Options dialog box (see Figure 18.22).

Choose **Methods** to select the payment methods you may want to use. A list of possible methods displays; select or deselect your choices. Choose **OK** to save your choices and return to the Payment Options dialog box.

Choose **Add** to add a new credit card. Then select the method of payment you want to add, and the appropriate wizard starts to guide you through the process of entering credit card information. The steps the wizard takes you through include the following:

- Adding the name on the credit card, the number, and expiration date. The number is checked by the system to ensure it is valid.

- Adding or selecting the billing address for the credit card. The name can be selected from the list of addresses you have already entered, or you can add a new address from within the Payment Wizard.

- Adding a password that is required before anyone can use the credit card information. You will be asked to re-enter the password to verify how it was added.

When you are done, the Wizard will save the payment information and redisplay the Payment Options dialog box, which will now show the new credit card information.

With the Wallet and the Personal Profile set up, you are ready for just about any eventuality when it comes to online browsing and online shopping.

# Using Internet Explorer 4 Features

Browsing in Fullscreen mode

Screening Web content

Sending and receiving email in Outlook Express

Working with newsgroups in Outlook Express

Online meetings

Launching applications from IE4

## Using the Explorer Bar

The Explorer Bar will be familiar to those who read the previous chapter's discussion of the Active Channel Guide. The Explorer Bar sits on the left side of the screen, and it will slide off the screen when you are not using it. It can be made to "stick" on the screen, though, by clicking on a Pushpin icon at the top of the Explorer Bar. The Explorer Bar is like a temporary "frame" that appears beside your Web page until you close it by clicking on the X in the top corner of the bar.

# Browsing in Fullscreen Mode

IE4 has some terminology that could be confusing, because the definition of full screen is not the same as maximized. When you use IE4 in maximized mode, it looks very much the same as it looks in a window.

However, the IE4 toolbar has a button named Fullscreen, which toggles the display between the normal window (toolbar icons across the top of the window, and the URL address box below the toolbar) and a display in which more of the window is used for content. When you work in Fullscreen mode, the toolbar icons are minimized and the URL address box disappears (see Figure 19.1).

**FIGURE 19.1**

Use IE4 in Fullscreen mode to fill your window with content.

When you work in Fullscreen mode, you can view the Explorer Bar by clicking the Channels icon. However, to access the URL Address box or the menu bar, you must click the Fullscreen icon to toggle the display back.

The Fullscreen display is a great feature because it makes the screen much less cluttered. You'll use History and Favorites more than you did with earlier Web browsers, because you don't have to toggle back to a normal display in order to access the Address Bar.

## Playing Favorites

Favorites are Web pages that you want to revisit. To make it easier to revisit them, save them to a Favorites folder. Click the Favorites icon on the toolbar to display the Favorites Bar (see Figure 19.2).

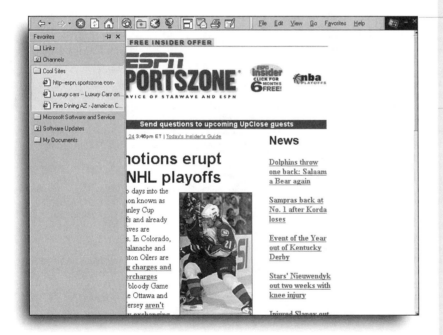

There are several Favorites subfolders built into IE4 by default, for example

- Channels (Active Channels)
- Links (same as on the Links toolbar)
- Subscriptions
- My Documents

It's easy to add a new site to your Favorites folder. When you arrive at a site, choose **Add to Favorites** from the F̲avorites menu to see the Add Favorite dialog box shown in Figure 19.3.

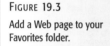

**FIGURE 19.3**

Add a Web page to your Favorites folder.

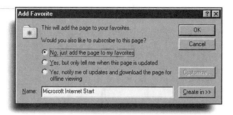

From the drop-down Favorites menu (visible only when you toggle away from the Fullscreen), you can manage your favorites by creating new folders and grouping your favorites in those folders with the Organize Favorites dialog box (see Figure 19.4). You can drag and drop, or use the buttons to move, delete, or rename your favorites.

**FIGURE 19.4**

Organize your favorites using the familiar Windows dialog box.

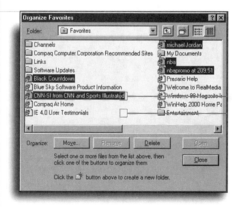

## Exploring the Search and History Bars

The Search Bar and the History Bar are also displayed in the Explorer Bar along the left side of Web pages. Take the name literally. Select your favorite search engine and try searching for Web pages on one of your hobbies. Take a look at the History Bar and see which Web pages you visited yesterday, or last week.

As you explore all of the Explorer Bar elements—Channels, Favorites, Search, and History—you'll find they are greatly improved over similar functions in earlier versions of Microsoft Internet Explorer.

# Moderating Your Children's Surfing with the Content Advisor

Within IE4, you can control the Web content that is presented to your computer. You can use this to protect your children, yourself, or anyone else who might be using your computer. The Internet is still pretty much of a wild frontier, and if you look hard enough, you can find just about anything. The settings on your Content Advisor let you narrow the scope of the content you access. You can be as strict as you want to be, with settings on a sliding scale for several types of content.

### Controlling the content accessible from your computer

1. Select **Internet** **Options** from the **View** menu.

2. Move to the **Content** tab, where the top section is the Content Advisor.

3. Choose **Enable** to begin the process of setting up the Content Advisor.

4. The Create Supervisor dialog box appears so you can enter a password, and then enter it again to confirm it. This password must be used whenever you want to control content. Click **OK** to continue.

5. The Content Advisor dialog box displays (see Figure 19.5). Select a Rating Category (for example, language, nudity, sex, violence) to display a slider bar on the Ratings page. The ratings are provided by RSACi, a rating organization (choose **More Info** to learn about RSACi).

6. Move to the **General** tab to select additional options:

   * Permit users to see sites that have not been rated.

   * Set the Content Advisor to permit a password that allows users to see restricted content.

   * Change the Supervisor password.

**Understanding the levels**

For each rating category, you can move a slider to set the rating level for anything from zero to five. Zero means that only very mild content is allowed, and a five allows virtually any content to be viewed within the selected category.

FIGURE 19.5

Select a rating category and
slide the bar to the appropriate level.

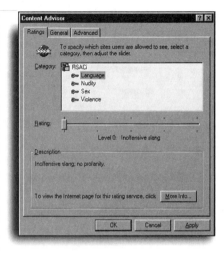

**7.** Move to the **Advanced** tab to select other rating systems to use with the Content Advisor. The system you select must be in a ratings file (with a .RAT file extension) on your local drive. If you want to use a rating system other than the default RSACi system, you have to enter the name of the rating bureau.

**8.** Click **OK** to save your settings. A message box informs you that the ratings are now being enforced. You can turn them off at any time by choosing **Disable** on the Content tab of the Internet Options dialog box (you need the password, of course).

After the Content Advisor is enabled, moving to a page that is unrated or that exceeds the ratings you specified produces the Content Advisor message box shown in Figure 19.6.

FIGURE 19.6

Access to restricted sites is
blocked unless you know the
password.

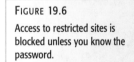

# Using Outlook Express for Internet Email

You can use Outlook Express to send and receive email and participate in Internet newsgroups when using IE4. Outlook Express is an integral part of the IE4 browser. You can start Outlook Express from within IE4 either by selecting **File**, **New**, **Message** from the drop-down menu, or by clicking the Mail icon and then selecting **New Message**. However, you can also open Outlook Express directly by clicking its icon in the Quick Launch tray of the Taskbar, and then clicking on the Compose Message icon.

You should have already set up your system so that it works with email (see Chapter 18 "Configuring Internet Explorer 4"). If you have not, the Inbox Setup Wizard will appear when you attempt to send your very first email message. With suggestive dialog boxes, it will walk you through the process of collecting your account and connection information. It will also create an address book and a personal folder to complete and store your profile. When you finish the steps in the Inbox Setup Wizard, you will be ready to send email.

## Sending Mail

The following procedure shows you how to send a mail message from within Outlook Express using your default profile.

### Sending a mail message

1. Click on the Compose Message icon to open a new message form (see Figure 19.7).

2. Enter the email addresses of the recipient (and anyone to whom you want to send a CC), or select names from your Personal Address Book. To look up a name, click on the To or CC button to display the address book (see Figure 19.8).

   In the address book, simply highlight a name on the left, and then click on a button (To or Cc) to move the name into the appropriate field. Click **OK** to return to the message form.

FIGURE 19.7

The New Message screen is used to create email messages.

FIGURE 19.8

The Personal Address Book can be used to choose recipients in your email message.

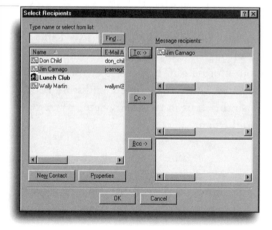

3. Enter a Subject line for your message. This is what the other person will see before she opens the message, so try to make it informative.

4. Enter the body of your message in the large field at the bottom of the New Message window. You can use simple word processing and text-formatting tools to enhance your message, because this is a *rich text* field.

5. When you are done with the message, click on the Send icon (it looks like an envelope). The message is placed in your Outbox until you connect to the mail server, at which point it's sent.

## Attaching Files in Email Messages

When you send an email message, you are not restricted to text, pictures, and links. You can also attach files of any sort, such as program files, zipped files, sound files, movie files, and so forth.

Attaching files is simple. When you are composing a message, there is an Insert File icon that looks like a paperclip.

To attach a file, click on the Insert File icon to display an Insert File dialog box, locate the file you want to attach, and click on the Attach button. The file will be attached at the bottom of your message, and will be sent as part of the message.

If you want to attach a link, make sure that Format, Rich Text (HTML) is selected from the drop-down menu in the message window. Click in the message where you want the attachment to appear, then highlight hyperlink text and select **Insert**, **Hyperlink** from the drop-down menu. Enter the URL of the Web site to which you want the text linked.

To attach a picture, select **Format**, **Rich Text** (HTML), position the cursor where you want the picture inserted, and select **Insert**, **Picture**. In the dialog box that is displayed, select the picture you want to insert. If the other person cannot view your pictures, select **Tools**, **Send Pictures with Image** and then resend the message.

When you receive a message with an attachment, you can double-click on the attachment to see it in its native application. For example, if you receive an attachment created with Microsoft Word, the attachment will be opened in Word. You can also save the attachment by selecting **File**, **Save Attachments** from the drop-down window.

## A Signature Look for Your Mail Form

Okay, so you have a distinct personality and you want to make your messages stand out, but the templates just aren't enough. What else can you do? You can create your own form with a unique background, a unique font, your own tag line or a *Signature* (or *Sig*) file, or you can attach a *vCard* business card.

### Creating a customized mail form

**1.** Select **Tools, Stationery** from the drop-down menu in Outlook Express. The Stationery dialog box will be displayed (see Figure 19.9).

**FIGURE 19.9**

Create a customized mail form in the Stationery dialog box.

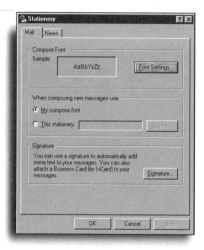

**2.** If you want to use a unique font for your stationery, select the font in the Compose Font field. Click on the **Font Settings** button to select a font.

**3.** Enable the Compose Font by selecting **My compose font** in the When composing new messages use section.

**4.** Alternatively, you can select existing stationery to use for you messages. When you click on **This stationery** and press the **Select** button, you will see a list of stationery (see Figure 19.10).

**FIGURE 19.10**

Select or modify Microsoft stationery for your custom mail template.

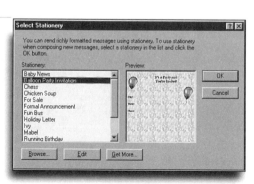

Select the stationery you want, and then you can modify it by clicking the **Edit** button. This will launch Microsoft FrontPage Express so you can modify the stationery to your liking, or create your own stationery starting with the selected template. After you complete your stationery selection, be sure to click **OK**. The Stationery dialog box will then list your selection in the This stationery field.

**5.** Click on the **Signature** button to add signature text or a business card to your messages. You will see the Signature dialog box (see Figure 19.11).

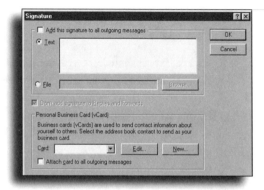

FIGURE 19.11
Add a signature line to your messages using the Signature dialog box.

In this dialog box, you can type in a text message or locate the name of a *sig* file, a file that has your signature line(s) in it. If you want your message to be attached automatically to all outgoing messages, click to add a checkmark next to **Add this signature to all outgoing messages**. You will then have the option of turning this off for messages that are either replies or forwards.

The Personal Business Card portion of this dialog box (called a vCard, for *virtual* business card), lets you select a Contact profile from your personal address book. This will automatically add the name, address, telephone number, and email address from the address book to the bottom of every message. This information will be in a format that can be electronically captured by the person receiving your message. They will then have the option of putting the information directly into their address book.

**6.** When you are done, click **OK** to save your changes and close the dialog box. If you click **Apply**, this is the equivalent of saving your changes without closing the dialog box; the changes will become effective even if you cancel to get out of the dialog box.

After you set up your personal stationery, it will be used every time you create a new message by clicking the Compose button. If you want to create a message using another type of stationery, select **Compose**, **New Message Using** from the drop-down menu, and select another stationery (or no stationery) for this one-time message.

## Receiving Mail

Outlook Express is where you send and receive mail, work with addresses, and participate in newsgroups. You can start Outlook Express by clicking on the Read Mail or Read News icons in IE4, or by clicking on the Outlook Express icon on the taskbar. You will then see the Outlook Express Home Page (see Figure 19.12).

FIGURE 19.12

The Outlook Express home page lets you read and send messages and work with newsgroups and addresses.

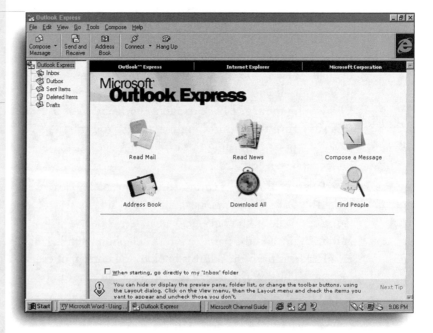

To read your messages, do one of the following:

- Click on the Read Mail icon.
- Click on the Inbox link.

You will then see a screen that is divided into three parts: the navigation links on the left; a list of messages on the top; and a preview of the highlighted message on the bottom, as shown in Figure 19.13.

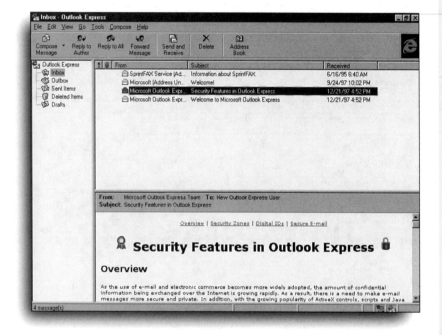

**FIGURE 19.13**
You can preview messages in the Inbox.

Before you open a message, notice the links at the top of the screen. You can compose a message, but you can also reply to the author of the message that you have highlighted. If there are others addressed in the message, you can reply to all of them, or you can forward the message to someone who is not addressed. You can also connect to your Internet Mail server to send and receive mail, you can delete mail, or you can work with your address book. But we are here to read mail.

Double-click on the message that you want to read in a full screen. If necessary, click on the Expand icon in the upper-right corner to expand the message so it can be viewed in the full screen. It will look similar to the message displayed in Figure 19.14, which is being displayed as rich text so it can include graphics, links, formatted text, and so forth.

FIGURE 19.14

Read rich-text messages in a full screen.

**Signing and encrypting messages**

The Sealing Wax icon in Figure 19.14 means that a message has been digitally signed by the author. The Lock icon means that the document has been *encrypted* so it can only be read by someone with access to your encryption key, for example, the person to whom you addressed the message. You can sign or encrypt messages by clicking on the appropriate icon at the top of the message form before it is sent.

You can use all of the standard mail icons and menu commands from the full window. You also have the option of sending your message to the printer, or copying it to a file (mail is saved in a file with a *.eml* file extension) and then deleting the original from your Inbox.

You may want to check out the drop-down menus in the full screen display as well. One menu item in particular is useful. Under the drop-down Tools menu, you will find the Inbox Assistant. When you click on it, you will see a list of rules that are applied to incoming mail that meets certain criteria. If you don't have any rules set up, or want to set up new rules, you can click on the Add button in the Inbox Assistant to display the Properties dialog box (see Figure 19.15).

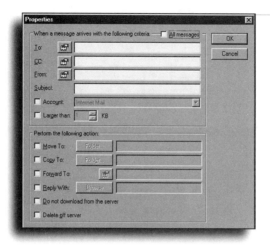

FIGURE 19.15

Set up rules that determine how your mail is handled when it arrives in your Inbox.

Using the Properties dialog box, you can do things like have all of your mail from certain individuals copied into a folder and deleted from the server. Or, you can have all of your mail forwarded to another email account while you are on vacation, and have a stock reply forwarded to the sender telling him when you will be back.

When you are done reading your mail in a full window, close the window and return to your Inbox.

Notice on the navigation links by your Inbox that you can also go to other folders besides your Inbox. The other folders include the following:

- *Outbox*  This holds all of your outgoing mail until you connect to the mail server—for example, by clicking on the Send and Receive Mail icon.

- *Sent Items*  This holds messages that you sent to your outbox after electing to save the messages.

- *Deleted Items*  These are items that you have deleted from your Inbox. They will stay in the Deleted Items view so you can retrieve them, if necessary. To delete a message permanently, highlight the message in the Deleted Items view and press the Delete key.

- *Drafts*  This folder holds messages that you have written and saved, but have not yet sent. You can reopen the message at a later time, edit it, and then send it. That will change it from Draft status to Sent status, and put it into another folder automatically.

## Adding People to the Address Book

To get full use of your email, you will want to add the email addresses of people with whom you communicate. To add someone to your address book, click on the Address Book icon in Outlook Express, and then click on New Contact in the Address Book window. You can also add new contacts while addressing a message.

The Address Book Profile for a person consists of several pages of information, most of it optional (see Figure 19.16).

FIGURE 19.16

The Profile dialog box consists of several pages of information about a contact.

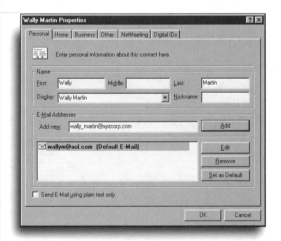

The most important information is obviously the person's name and email address. To add an email address, enter the address in the Add new: field, and then click on Add. Other information includes:

- Home is used for home address and phone number, and Web home page.

- Business is used for the same information for the person's business.

- Other is for miscellaneous information about the person. Also, if she is added to a *group*, then group membership will be noted on the Other page.

- NetMeeting is used to set up an email address and server for Net conferencing.

- Digital IDs keeps track of any digital IDs you have for encryption and secure communications.

The other interesting thing you can do with the Address Book is to create a mailing group. Rather than entering several names into a memo, you just have to enter the group name, and the message will be sent to each person in the group.

### Creating a mailing group

1. Click on **New Group** in the Address Book. The Group Properties dialog box will be displayed (see Figure 19.17).

FIGURE 19.17

Add people to a group in the Group Properties dialog box.

2. Give the group a name. To send a message to the members of the group, you can address the name you enter here.

3. Click on **Select Members** to display a list of people in the Address Book. For each contact you want to add to the group, highlight the name in the list and click on **Select** to add them to the group.

4. Click on **New Contact** to add a person to the address book and to the group at the same time.

5. Enter miscellaneous notes about the purpose of the group in the **Notes** field.

6. When you are done, click on **OK** to save the group.

# Using Outlook Express with Newsgroups

A *newsgroup* is a single place where people with a common interest can post messages and read messages from others in the group. There are hundreds of newsgroups on just about any topic you can imagine.

The newsgroup is hosted on a news server. As long as your ISP has a link to the newsgroup, you can subscribe to it. There is no charge to subscribe to a newsgroup. When you have a subscription, the newsgroup gets downloaded to Outlook Express so you can read and participate in the newsgroup. If you do not have a subscription, you can still read the newsgroup directly from the news server, as long as your ISP provides a connection to that server.

## Connecting to a News Server

To use Outlook Express for newsgroups, select **Go**, **News** from the drop-down menu. If you have not previously defined a news server, you will see an Internet Connection Wizard. In this wizard, you enter the following information, with just a single piece of information on most screens:

- *Display Name*  The name that is displayed when you post to a newsgroup.

- *Email Address*  Your email address, so people can send messages directly to you, or post responses to the newsgroup.

- *NNTP Server*  The name of the news server from which your ISP gets its newsgroups. NNTP is the name of the Internet protocol used by news servers. It is comparable to HTTP, which is used for retrieving Web pages.

- *Account Name*  A friendly name for the account, so that when you want to work with the news server, you can call it "Quark," or whatever you want.
- *Connection Type*  The type of connection used with this news server. You can have a dial-up connection, a network (LAN) connection, or a manual connection where you can decide how to connect when it's time to download the newsgroup. If you select a dial-up connection, you can select an existing connection or set up a new connection.

## Selecting and Subscribing to Newsgroups

When you first set up your news server, you will be asked, at the end of the setup process, whether you want to subscribe to any newsgroups. You can subscribe at that time, or you can subscribe later.

### Subscribing to a newsgroup

1. Click on the link (the friendly name of your news server) in the Outlook Express folder list to go to your news server folder.

2. If you have not yet subscribed to any newsgroups, you will see a prompt box asking if you want to see a list of available newsgroups. Click on **Yes** to display a list. If you have already subscribed to at least one newsgroup, you can display the list by clicking on the **News Groups** icon that is displayed at the top of the page when you are on a news server page.

3. You will be connected to the news server and will see a list box with a list of newsgroups on the server. Locate a newsgroup to which you want to subscribe, and click on the **Subscribe** button.

4. Click on **OK** when you are done setting up newsgroup subscriptions.

You will notice that you can manage all your subscriptions in the list box, which has separate pages for all newsgroups, subscribed newsgroups, and new newsgroups.

## Reading and Posting to Newsgroups

To read a newsgroup, click on it in the news server folder. If you want to read it offline, you can click on the group and select **File**, **Properties** from the drop-down menu. Go to the Download page and select options for downloading.

Newsgroups can become very active. On the drop-down menu, there are several commands that can be used to manage the newsgroup. For example, you can display only messages that you have not yet read, or you can set up filters for the newsgroup.

To post to a newsgroup, highlight the newsgroup and click on the Compose button. When composing messages, you have the option of submitting to a single newsgroup, or to multiple newsgroups. You can read a message and compose a response to it. You also have the option of cancelling a message after it has been composed by opening the message and clicking on Cancel.

There are a lot of options available for working with newsgroups—too many to cover here. Every newsgroup is a world of its own. Sign up for a newsgroup that matches your interests, and then explore the newsgroup. Compose messages and respond to those messages that interest you. Explore the options for reading and posting, and you will soon feel comfortable. It is a form of collaborative email.

# Getting Together for a NetMeeting

The Internet is becoming more of a two-way medium. A lot of the IE4 browsing activity, from Java applets to subscribing to Active Channels to the Active Desktop, involves more interactivity than what used to be available on the Web. NetMeetings and other Internet Call applications push that interactive envelope one step further.

NetMeetings are a way to live on the cutting edge of computing. You've seen the cartoons of someone on the telephone looking at a video screen of the person on the other end in hair curlers or unshaven. You've probably also heard the stories of how people use the Internet to talk for "free" to someone on the far side of the world. Both of these are examples of what NetMeetings do. You can connect with someone else who is also on his computer, and you can talk to each other via voice, via video, via a computer chat, via a "whiteboard" where each of you can see what the other is drawing on his computer.

NetMeeting is the Internet Call software component of IE4 that makes these futuristic scenarios possible today.

NetMeeting is similar, in a way, to newsgroups, in that you have to set up a unique connection that is used for the purpose of sharing. In this case, the sharing can be done either over the Internet or over a local area network. The difference is that you do not use the email software, Outlook Express. Instead, you and the person with whom you meet must use NetMeeting.

To start up NetMeeting, select **Go**, **Internet Call** from the IE4 drop-down menu.

NetMeeting will start up as a separate application, displaying the interface shown below (see Figure 19.18).

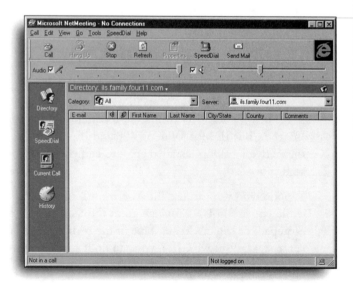

**FIGURE 19.18**

Use NetMeeting to place an Internet call and work directly with another user over the Internet or over a network.

When setting up NetMeeting for the first time, a wizard will walk you through setting up speakers, a microphone, and a camera, if you have one. You will be provided with a list of directory servers, or you can use your own server over a local area network. And you will be able to set up a default call type, for example, business, personal, or adult.

Notice some of the options that are available in Figure 19.18. First, you have to place a call to the person you are meeting with. You can either call them directly, or find them in one of several NetMeeting directories. After you place a call the first time, you can "speed dial" to reconnect with the same person. If their computer answers the call and the person you want is on the other end, you are in business.

During the current call, you can use video, share files with one or more people connected to the same meeting, chat, or use a whiteboard. And, of course, you can talk to the other person via a microphone and hear her through your computer's audio.

To modify your settings, you can select Tools, Options from the drop-down menu inside NetMeeting.

Want to have a meeting?  Tomorrow at 9:00 a.m. I'll be there—will you?

# Using Other Applications with IE4

IE4 is primarily a Web browser. That means that its purpose is to render HTML documents into Web pages, whether those pages be on your local computer, on an intranet, or on the Internet. But IE4 for Windows 98 and IE4 for Windows 95 with the Active Desktop installed are also launching pads for other applications.

Suppose you want to use the Microsoft Notepad application while you are in IE4. You can go to the Start button and locate Notepad, or select Go and type in the command to launch Notepad.exe. But with IE4, you can do it with one less step.

You can use the Address Bar (where you type in a URL to go to a Web page) to start applications. For example, to start Notepad, type **Notepad** on in the Address Bar and press the Enter key. Notepad will start up right away.

If you want to start an application that is not a standard component of Windows 95 or Windows 98, type in the full path to the application to launch it. For example, you could type "C:\Apps\ Lotus\Notes.exe" to launch Lotus Notes from within a Lotus directory.

Default helper applications are launched from the drop-down Go menu within IE4. You have seen how to use Outlook Express for Mail and News, and NetMeeting for Internet Call applications. You can change the default program used for any of these functions by selecting **View**, **Internet Options** and going to the **Programs** tab to specify another program to be used for mail, for news, or for Internet calls.

PART

*VI*

# Using Windows 98 on a Network

# Networking with Windows 98

# Logging On to a Network

If you're using Windows 98 in an office, the odds are pretty good that you're connected to a network. Being on a network gives you some advantages that stand-alone computer users don't have:

- There is software you can use on other network machines (usually servers) so you don't have to keep buying larger hard drives to add the software you need.
- You can share resources such as printers, CD-ROM drives, and modems.
- You can share files with other users without having to transfer them to floppy disks and walk them to the other person (the jargon for that is "sneaker net"). And, you can share very large files that wouldn't fit on a floppy.
- You can exchange email messages with other people in your company in a matter of seconds.

**Null passwords are passwords**

If your network logon is set up so that you don't have to enter a password, that's called a null password and it's a form of a password (it's sort of like having the Enter key as a password). It works like a password because if somebody enters any characters in an effort to guess your password, he or she is denied entry to the network.

One of the built-in functions for networking is the need to identify every user who wants access to the network resources. Another built-in function is security. To fulfill both of these requirements, you must go through a process of logging on to the network. You must enter your username (which may or may not be your real name) and you must also enter a password.

Most companies use either Windows NT networking or Novell NetWare networking, or both. There are some other network operating systems (NOS), but the vast majority of corporate systems run NT or NetWare NOS.

After your computer and operating system finish their startup routines, you're asked to log on to the network. The information that makes the logon work is contained in two places: your local computer and the network server.

- Your local computer establishes the network your computer joins, and launches the correct logon sequence.
- The server has your username and your password. They must match the information you present to the server, or the logon fails.

It's not a good idea to mess around with your network configuration unless you're comfortable with networking protocols and services (or your network administrator has asked you to make changes). However, you can view the information on your local computer.

**Checking your network settings**

1. Open the Control Panel and double-click on the **Network** icon.

2. In the Configuration tab, the network components that are installed in your computer are displayed, along with information about your primary logon (see Figure 20.1).

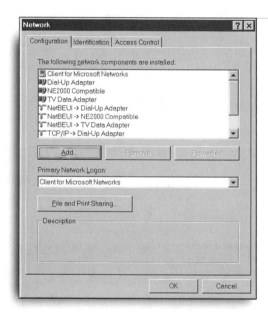

**FIGURE 20.1**

The installed networking components are listed in the Configuration tab.

3. If you need to change the Primary Network Logon, click the arrow to the right of that option to see the choices (see Figure 20.2):

   • Client for Microsoft Networks logs you on to a Microsoft NT network.

   • Client for NetWare Networks logs you in to a NetWare server.

**More jargon to get used to**

Windows NT uses the term "logon" for joining the network, and Novell NetWare uses the term "login." As picayune as that one letter difference may seem, I'm so conditioned to using the correct terminology that you'll find that all references to specific networks use the appropriate term. I just didn't want you to think I was inconsistent or mixing the two words willy-nilly.

* Windows logon is for working only on your local machine. No server validates your username and password.

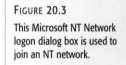

**FIGURE 20.2**

Your options may differ from the logon choices for this computer.

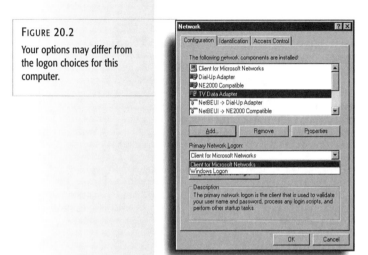

## Logging On to a Windows NT Network

The common NT Network logon requires that you log on to a domain server with a username and password that has been registered in the domain (see Figure 20.3).

**FIGURE 20.3**

This Microsoft NT Network logon dialog box is used to join an NT network.

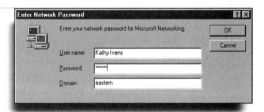

If your network has multiple domains, you may be asked to change the domain you log on to.

### Changing the logon domain

1. Click the **Network** icon in Control Panel.

2. In the Configuration tab, select **Client for Microsoft Networks**, and then choose **Properties**.

3. When the Properties dialog box opens, change the domain name to the appropriate one (see Figure 20.4).

4. Click **OK**. Then click **OK** again to close the Network dialog box.

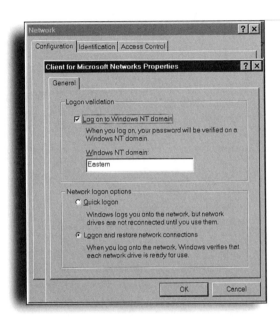

The processes that occur after you log on to an NT network are determined by the system administrator and the way the network is configured. There may be a script that runs to set up your network environment. This environment could include the folders and files you're permitted to access and it may even log you in to a NetWare network via the NT server (instead of forcing you to log in to the NetWare network with a dialog box). If you have different passwords for each network in a multiple network environment, you will be asked to enter a password for the second logon.

## Logging In to NetWare

Novell NetWare is by far the most popular network operating system used in the business world. Windows 98 provides support for accessing NetWare networks.

There are a couple of configuration options to choose from for joining a NetWare network:

- Microsoft Client for Netware
- Novell NetWare Workstation Shells (there is one for NetWare 3.x and one for NetWare 4.x)
- Gateway Services for NetWare

For the first two options, the login procedure for NetWare isn't as definitive as it is for a Windows NT network, which always displays the same logon dialog box. You may see a dialog box, you may see a menu system that asks you to enter a name and password, or you may be at a command prompt that says "Enter your Login Name." Just follow the directions.

The last option (gateway) doesn't have to be set up on your computer. It's used by the Windows NT server you log on to. That server is a client for the NetWare server and provides a gateway to that NetWare server for all its own clients.

After you've joined a NetWare network you can use the services and features of NetWare. Usually there's a login script that sets drive mappings, permissions, and other environmental settings.

If you're used to Windows, there are a few things to get used to in NetWare:

- NetWare uses the concept of *Volumes*, which are physical parts of a drive that are established as discrete partitions. The first volume of a NetWare system that has multiple volumes is usually named SYS, the second is usually named VOL1, then VOL2, and so on. This naming scheme isn't required, but it's commonly used.
- Most of the functions for manipulating and handling NetWare volumes and files are performed at the command line. Your permission level determines which NetWare functions you can use.

Even though the Windows 98 client for NetWare provides many functions via graphical dialog boxes, the command line functions are usually more robust. For example, if you enter **whoami** at the command line of a NetWare server you see your username, the name of the server you logged into, your connection number (NetWare tracks logged users in the order in which they join the server), the version of NetWare being run, and your login time. You can add parameters to the command to get even more information. The Windows 98 version of WHOAMI tells you only your username and connection number.

# Understanding Peer-to-Peer Networking

When you join a network and you are connected to a server, that's client/server networking. Your local computer is the client, although you'll also hear the term *workstation* used for a client computer. There are probably lots of other workstations that connect to the server, and you all have the same working environment: You can use the folders and files on your local computer or on the server. Figure 20.5 is a representation of a standard client/server network.

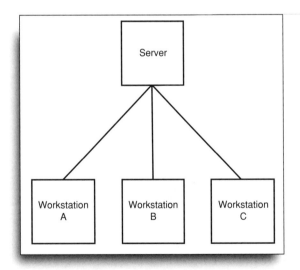

FIGURE 20.5

Each workstation can access files on the server as well as the local computer.

Peer-to-peer networking is a scheme in which every computer on the network can access every other computer on the network, as illustrated in Figure 20.6.

**FIGURE 20.6**

Each workstation can access files on every computer on the network.

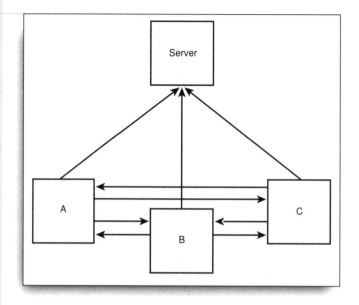

## Joining a Peer-to-Peer Network

Windows 98 workstations can exist in a pure peer-to-peer network environment or in a mixed environment. In many corporate networks, Windows 98 workstations log on to a server, establishing a client/server relationship. Then, these workstations can also use the peer-to-peer environment to communicate with all the other computers.

There are three ways to join a network and enjoy peer-to-peer network features:

- Log in to a NetWare server (establishing a client/server relationship) and also have a peer-to-peer relationship with all the Windows 98, Windows 98, Windows NT, and Windows For Workgroups computers on the network.

- Log on to a Windows NT server by joining a domain, and also have a peer-to-peer relationship with all the Windows 98, Windows 98, Windows NT, and Windows For Workgroups computers.

- Log on to a Windows network by joining a workgroup and network strictly in a peer-to-peer fashion.

**Domain versus workgroup**

A *domain* is an administrative unit of a Windows NT network. User logon names and passwords are validated by a domain controller and permissions for accessing resources on the server(s) are administered by a user with administrative rights.

A *workgroup* is a group of connected computers that share common resources (such as printers, CD-ROM drives, folders, and files). There is no central validation of logon names and passwords.

The ideal combination, in my view, is a network that is both client/server and peer-to-peer. Users log in to a server, so there is the security of validation of users and there is also some ability to control user environments. Once users are logged in, they're free to access any other resource on any other computer.

## Managing Peer-to-Peer Access

In a peer-to-peer environment, every computer is a server, because when a computer's resources are accessed, it becomes, by definition, a server. You have some control over the way your computer is used when it is acting as a server.

For one thing, no user can access any resource on your computer unless you establish settings that make that resource shareable.

The other control you have is a Windows 98 tool called Net Watcher, which lets you see and control the people who are using resources on your computer.

### Controlling shared resources

1. Open the **Start** menu and move to the **Accessories** menu.
2. In the **System Tools** submenu, choose **Net Watcher**.
3. When the Net Watcher window opens, you can see whether or not any other user is accessing your computer (see Figure 20.7).
4. The default view is By Connection, and you can select a user to see which resources that person is using.
5. Use the **View** menu to change the way you view your computer's server activity—the other choices are By Shared Folders or By Open Files.

You can use the toolbar icons to manipulate the activity. It's not considered cricket to disconnect a user without warning, however. And, above all, close the file the user is accessing before disconnecting the user to avoid file corruption.

One of the tools in Net Watcher is the capability to use Net Watcher on another computer, and that feature is called *remote administration*. Remote administration has to be configured for a computer before you can administer that computer remotely (and you must enable remote administration before anyone can administer your computer).

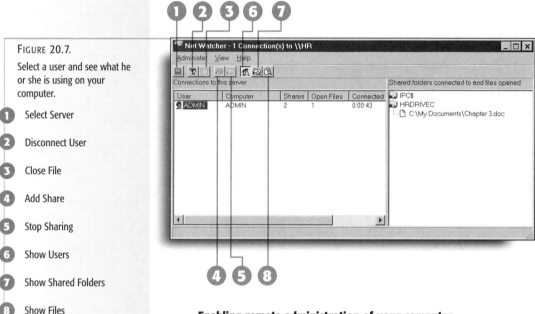

FIGURE 20.7.

Select a user and see what he or she is using on your computer.

**1** Select Server

**2** Disconnect User

**3** Close File

**4** Add Share

**5** Stop Sharing

**6** Show Users

**7** Show Shared Folders

**8** Show Files

### Enabling remote administration of your computer

1. Open the **Passwords** icon in Control Panel and move to the Remote Administration tab.

2. Select **Enable remote administration of this server**.

3. Optionally, enter a password that users must enter before they can administer your computer. Then reveal that password only to those users who should have this permission.

SEE ALSO

➤ *Learn about setting up shared resources in Chapter 21, "Sharing Files and Printers."*

# Using Network Neighborhood

The easiest way to move around a network is to open Network Neighborhood (see Figure 20.8).

There is also a display of Network Neighborhood in Explorer, and you can see all the connected computers on your network by clicking the plus sign to the left of the Network Neighborhood object (see Figure 20.9).

FIGURE 20.8

The computers on the network are represented by icons in Network Neighborhood.

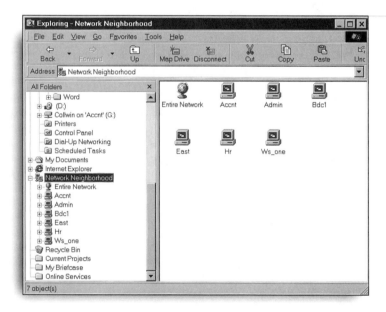

FIGURE 20.9

If you prefer a two-pane hierarchical view, browse your network in Explorer.

Regardless of the tool you use to access the other computers on your network, you can open each computer to see its shared resources. Some computers share only folders, others may have devices attached that are shared (such as printers, modems, or CD-ROM drives). Figure 20.10 shows two computers that have been expanded in Explorer. Each has a number of shared resources.

FIGURE 20.10

The left pane shows the shared folders for a computer, the right pane shows all the resources.

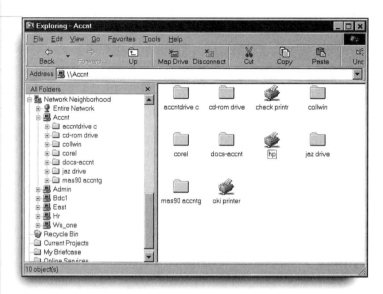

Notice that you don't see anything in the left pane except drives and folders that are shared. You must select the computer in Explorer to see any shared printers in the right pane.

On the other hand, if you open a computer in the Network Neighborhood folder, the folder that opens shows you all the resources (see Figure 20.11).

FIGURE 20.11

Network Neighborhood shows you all the shared resources for each computer on the network.

You can open any folder to access the files in the folder and manipulate (copy, move, delete, and so on) them across the network.

However, just because you see a shared resource doesn't mean you'll be able to access it. Users can set permissions (as well as passwords) for access, and you may not be given the password or you may not be included in the list of the favored few. If this occurs, a no-nonsense message makes it clear (see Figure 20.12).

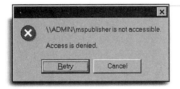

**FIGURE 20.12**
A short message tells you when you're not permitted to access a resource.

Here are several other important facts to bear in mind:

- If any of the computers on your network are running Windows NT and have installed NTFS as the file system (an advanced file system available for Windows NT), those users can manipulate permissions at the file level. Windows 98 machines can only set sharing and permissions down to the folder level. Therefore, you might get into a computer's folders but be unable to access certain files.

- When you access a hard drive of another computer, you'll see the Recycle Bin. It is NOT the Recycle Bin for that computer, it is your own Recycle Bin. If you open it you see all the files you've deleted on your own local drive.

- The shortcut menu that appears when you right-click on a shared resource on another computer has only a few commands. For any resource except a printer, you can map the resource to a drive letter. For a printer, you have an option to install it as a network printer so you can use it.

Take some time to open Network Neighborhood and explore the shared drives, folders, and devices on the other computers on your network. You may find some resources you didn't even know were there.

# Mapping Drives

*Mapping* is the process of assigning a letter to a shared folder or drive. The most common reason to map a drive is because typing a letter followed by a colon (which is the way you designate a drive letter) is far easier than entering the full name of the resource.

Remote resources are accessed by using the Universal Naming Convention (UNC), which is \\computername\shared_resource_name. For example, in Figure 20.13, the folder named docs-accnt on the computer named Accnt has a UNC of \\Accnt\docs-accnt.

## Mapping a Drive from Network Neighborhood

Open Network Neighborhood and then open the computer that has the resource you want to map (you could also open Explorer and expand the Network Neighborhood object).

### Mapping a resource

1. Right-click the resource and choose **Map Network Drive** from the shortcut menu.

**2.** The Map Network Drive dialog box appears and presents the next available drive letter in the Drive box and displays the UNC as the path (see Figure 20.14).

FIGURE 20.14

Windows 98 does all the work for you when you want to map a drive.

**3.** You do not have to use the drive letter that's presented. If you want to change it to a different letter, click the arrow to see the available drive letters (see Figure 20.15).

FIGURE 20.15

Choose any drive letter that isn't already being used to map a resource.

**4.** Select **Reconnect at logon** if you plan to use this resource most of the time. Your Windows 98 startup will include the process of mapping this resource to this drive letter.

**5.** Choose **OK** to map the resource to a network drive.

After you map a network drive, it appears in your system as just another drive, as if it were attached to your computer. The resource, using its drive letter, is listed in My Computer and Explorer (see Figure 20.16).

## Mapping from the Command Line

You can also map a drive from the command line. The command that's used for this is **net use**, and the syntax is **net use drive_letter: UNC**. For example, to map drive F: to a folder named PowerToys on a computer named Admin, the following

**Reconnecting at logon may not work**

If you choose to reconnect to the mapped drive at logon, the computer on which the drive resides must be up and running before your Windows 98 system starts. Nothing awful occurs if the resource isn't available because the remote computer isn't booted yet, you just get an error message stating that your computer was unable to connect to the mapped drive. You'll have to map it manually after the remote computer is running.

command is entered at an MS-DOS command prompt: **net use f: \\admin\Powertoys**. The system returns the message The command was completed successfully.

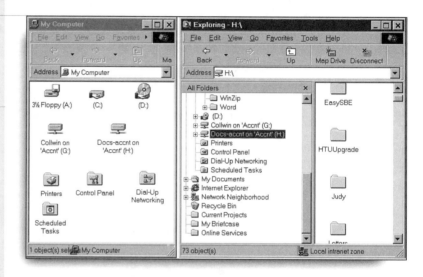

FIGURE 20.16

Mapped drives become part of your own system—you don't have to open Network Neighborhood to get to them.

If the drive letter is already in use by another resource, you're asked if you wish to continue. Answer Yes to map the new resource to the drive letter, which means you'll lose the mapping for the existing mapped resource. Answer No and enter the command again, picking a different drive letter for the resource. Of course, you can avoid this by glancing at My Computer or Explorer to see which drive letters are already in use.

This feature is useful for writing batch files. For instance, if you know you want to use several mapped drives, you can write a batch file and execute it instead of mapping a bunch of drives by clicking your way through Network Neighborhood.

I use batch files to map drives so I don't have to worry about which computers boot before other computers in order to make the Reconnect At Logon feature work. My mapping batch file looks like this:

```
net use f: \\east\projecttemplates
net use g: \\accnt\collwin
Net use h: \\admin\admindrivec
exit
```

The exit command closes the MS-DOS command window.

I put a shortcut to the batch file on my desktop so when I'm ready to use resources that are on other computers, I can double-click the shortcut.

# Working with Network Profiles

When you make changes to your desktop configuration, the next time you start Windows 98 your changes are there. If you share your computer with another person and you configure your computer to save profile information, you log on to your computer with a name so that Windows 98 knows which desktop configuration to load.

The same procedure is available on a network, and your network can be configured so that user profiles are stored on the server instead of on your computer. This means the information about the configuration of your desktop and the software you've installed on your computer is kept on a Windows NT server. When you log on to the server, it sends your configuration information to your computer.

This feature enables two special kinds of user profiles: Roaming Profiles and Mandatory Profiles.

## Using Roaming Profiles

A *roaming profile* (sometimes called a roving profile) is kept on the server you log on to. The server can be either a NetWare server or a Windows NT server.

When you make changes to your desktop configuration, the changes are saved at the server when you log off and shut down the computer. Because a copy of your configuration is saved on the server, no matter what computer you use to log on to that server, you'll see your own desktop.

As soon as you've completed the log on process, the server checks to see if you have your desktop configuration saved in a profile on the server. If you do, the server sends it to you. You could be using the computer in the next office, down the hall, or on a different floor.

There are a few things to be aware of to take advantage of roaming profiles:

- Roaming profiles are established and maintained on the server by the network administrator. In a Windows NT server, your profile information is stored in `\\Logon_Server\Your_Home_Directory`. In NetWare, the information is stored in your Mail directory. The administrator also makes registry changes in your computer.

- You must use the Microsoft Client service for joining the network. If you use Novell services to log in to a NetWare server, a roaming profile is not available.

- The computer you work on must log on to the same server as your regular computer does.

- You can make changes to the desktop configuration while you're at a borrowed computer and they'll be there when you return to your own computer (or use any other computer).

- Shortcuts on your desktop that don't have targets won't work. That means if you have a shortcut to a document on your regular computer, or a shortcut to a software program that isn't installed on the computer you're using, double-clicking the shortcut does nothing except produce an error message.

If your own computer is shared with another user, or if your job description means you work in a variety of departments during the day, this feature can be a terrific asset.

## Working with Mandatory Profiles

A *mandatory profile* is a profile that's etched in cement. Usually, it's the system administrator that does the etching.

Like roaming profiles, mandatory profiles are stored on the server you access to log on to the network. Unlike roaming profiles, however, you have no opportunity to make changes. Well, that's not true, you can make changes to your heart's content. However, the next time you log on, the changes aren't there.

If you're configured for mandatory profiles, don't waste your time making changes to the desktop.

**SEE ALSO**

➤ *To learn more about profiles on Windows 98 computers, see Chapter 9, "Tricks and Tips for Using Windows 98 at Home."*

# Troubleshooting Networking

There are all sorts of annoying, pesky network problems that crop up from time to time. Some of them are quite common, so it's probably a good idea to give you the solutions.

## You Can't Log On to the Network

Unfortunately, the error messages you see when logon fails are usually lacking in details. Telling you that you couldn't be logged on isn't terribly elucidating. Luckily, a Windows 98 computer can still be used for local work if the network logon fails. Try these solutions:

- Check the cable that's coming out of the back of your computer. Make sure it's there, and if it's a coax connection make sure it's firmly fixed. Don't yank (or it won't be firmly fixed any more), just jiggle.
- Call or yell for the system administrator to see if the server is down. If it is, there's nothing you can do and you'll have to work locally.
- Check the status of your Network Interface Card (NIC).

### Checking up on a NIC

1. Right-click My Computer and choose **Properties**.
2. When the System Properties dialog box opens, move to the Device Manager tab.
3. Click the plus sign next to the Network adapters listing, and then select your NIC (see Figure 20.17).

**4.** If there is an exclamation point next to the NIC listing, or if the listing isn't there, it's not functioning. You probably have to replace it.

**5.** If all looks normal, choose **Properties** to open the Properties dialog box for your NIC. Then move to the Resources tab. If there is a configuration problem you'll see an error message. You will have to re-configure it.

Most of the time, a configuration error appears after you've installed a new NIC or installed another device that uses the same IRQ or I/O Address as your NIC. These are technical specifications that guarantee that devices have unique specifications. To see the specifications for all the devices in your system so you can determine whether any two of them are bumping into each other, return to the Device Manager tab and choose **Print**. A complete listing of the specifications for every device in your computer is printed for you. You may need to call on an expert to help resolve these problems.

## You're Locked Out for a Bad Password

If your network is configured so that you're required to change your password at regular intervals, you're likely to forget your password just after one of those changes has occurred. If the network is set up for lockout, after three wild (and wrong) guesses, you're not allowed to try anymore.

You can't solve this yourself. You'll have to admit to the network administrator that you've forgotten your password. The administrator can issue you a new password and unlock your workstation so you can log on. Then, if you wish, you can change your password instead of using the one the administrator gave you (use the Password icon in Control Panel and just follow the easy instructions). The next step is to find a safe, secure place to write down your password. Pasting it to the monitor is not considered a good security tactic.

## You Are Denied Access to a Network Printer

If you cannot access a printer that's connected to another computer, it's probably not due to anything you did.

The first thing to check is whether or not someone has changed permissions on the printer (in most companies, printer permissions are available to everyone and it's unusual to have a printer with complicated permissions).

What's more likely is that the printer is connected to a Windows NT workstation instead of a Windows 98 computer or a server. Windows NT workstation only permits 10 users to access resources simultaneously. If this is the case (it's the most common cause of this problem), just wait. Or if your print job is important, convince some other user to wait.

The advantages of network computing are enormous. And, unless you're a system administrator, participating on a network is usually something that's problem-free.

# Sharing Files and Printers

# Setting Up File and Printer Sharing

One of the big advantages of having Windows 98 computers connected by cable is the capability to create peer-to-peer services. That means your peers—the other Windows 98 computers—can interact with each other. In fact, computers running other versions of Windows, such as Windows 95, Windows NT, or Windows for Workgroups, can join you. And you can all share each other's files, which makes it easier to exchange information when you're working on a common project.

## Enabling Shared Resources on Your Computer

Before you can let any other users share anything, you have to set up the sharing services. Until your computer knows that you're planning to share folders, the steps to set up shared files aren't available.

### Turning on sharing

1. Choose **Settings** and then choose **Control Panel** from the Start menu.

2. In the Control Panel, double-click the Network icon, which opens with the Configuration tab in the foreground.

3. Choose **File and Print Sharing** to open the File and Print Sharing dialog box (see Figure 21.1).

4. Select the appropriate check box to share files, printers, or both. Then click **OK** to return to the dialog box.

## Concerns About Sharing Printers

There are situations in which printers shouldn't be shared, and if a printer that's attached to your computer operates with special features you should not share it. Some of these seem obvious, but I've seen situations where shared printing was selected because users didn't think carefully about ramifications and just assumed that printer sharing is always safe.

If you work in the accounting department, don't share a printer that holds checks. It's not that everybody else in the company is going to write themselves an extra paycheck. Instead, one day you'll watch a 10 page report print out over the next 30 check numbers.

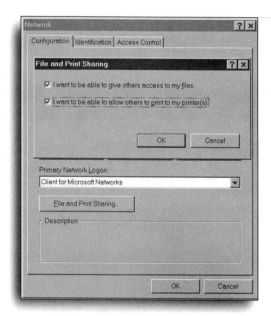

FIGURE 21.1
You can share your files, your printer, or both.

If your printer is used for special types of printing, either don't share it or set up careful security. This includes color printers or very high resolution printers that are earmarked for special projects. These printers tend to be expensive to operate and shouldn't be available for normal company printing.

## Securing Shared Resources

Now that you've established the fact that you want to share either or both of these resources, you must worry about security.

There are two ways to protect your shared files and printers:

- You can attach a password to the shared resource and give that password to those users you decide should have access to the resource.

■ You can specify a list of users who automatically have access to the resource.

You establish the security method in the Network dialog box.

### Configuring a security method

**1.** Move to the Access Control tab in the Network dialog box (see Figure 21.2).

FIGURE 21.2

Choose a security method for sharing your files and printers.

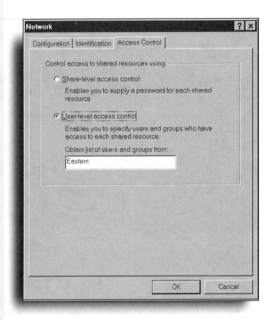

**2.** Select **Share-level access control** if you want to assign a password to each folder or printer you're sharing.

**3.** Select **User-level access control** to give specific users rights to the resources you're sharing. Then specify where the list of users comes from.

Usually there's only one list of users and groups for your network or domain. The only time you have a choice is if you log on to a network that has multiple domains and you have a choice of lists.

**4.** Click **OK** to save your new settings.

After you make your selections in the Network dialog box, you see a message telling you that these settings won't take effect until you restart the operating system. Choose **Yes** to restart your system.

When Windows 98 starts again, you're all set and you can begin earmarking the resources you want to share.

# Creating a Shared Folder

Before you mark a folder as shared, there are some considerations to bear in mind:

- When you share a folder, any subfolders it contains are automatically shared. This includes subfolders below subfolders. All the children of a shared parent folder are shared. You can, however, create a discrete share for a child folder and give it a separate password or user list for security.

- You can share a drive, which behaves as a shared folder so that all the folders and subfolders on the drive are shared. You can still individually share those folders if you want separate passwords or user lists for them.

- You cannot share files, only folders. Although you may see specific files being shared on your network, those files are on computers running file systems that permit file-level security. File sharing is not available for Windows 98.

## Setting Up a Shared Folder

You're all set, the configuration is complete. Now you have to set up the folders you want to share.

### Sharing a folder

1. Open Explorer or My Computer and move to the folder you want to share.

2. Right-click and choose **Sharing** from the shortcut menu.

3. When the Sharing tab of the Properties dialog box appears, choose **Shared As** and enter a share name for the folder. By

**Descriptive share names are better**

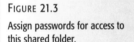

When you share a folder, its name is "advertised" across the network and the name may not be particularly enlightening to other users. In addition, that same name may exist on other computers (think about sharing the folder named "My Documents" if everyone uses Microsoft Office). Changing the share name doesn't change the folder name, the share name is for advertising purposes only. Therefore a share name like `AccntgDocs` clearly says that the documents on the computer named Accntg are available in this folder. Or, keep the share name the same as the folder name and use the description field to elucidate.

default, the share name is the folder name and you can keep that name or change it. Share names can contain up to 12 characters.

4. Enter an optional description of the shared folder in the **Comment** text box. The description appears in Network Neighborhood.

As soon as you've marked a folder (or drive) as shared, its icon changes in Explorer and My Computer. A hand appears under the folder's icon to indicate this is a shared resource.

## Configuring Share Access Security

The next thing you have to do is establish security for the shared folder. The process differs depending on whether you're using share access security or user access security.

If you've opted to secure the share with passwords, your sharing dialog box looks like the one shown in Figure 21.3.

**FIGURE 21.3**

Assign passwords for access to this shared folder.

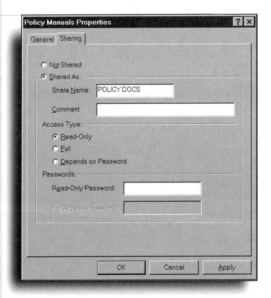

First, set the type of access you'll permit for this shared folder (by default it's assumed you'll give Read-Only permissions):

- **Read-Only** means that other users can open and view the files in the folder, but they can't change them. Anyone who knows the password can perform these actions.

- **Full** means that other users can do everything you can do to the files in the folder. Anyone who knows the password can perform those actions.

- **Depends on Password** means exactly what it says, because you'll have one password that gives Read-Only rights and another that gives Full rights. Then you share that password with users depending on the rights you want them to have.

Enter the password (or passwords) that users must know to access the folder. In case anyone's peeking over your shoulder, you'll see asterisks as you type instead of the actual characters you enter, so type carefully. Click **OK**.

After you enter the password(s) you're asked to re-enter your characters to confirm the password (see Figure 21.4). Click **OK**.

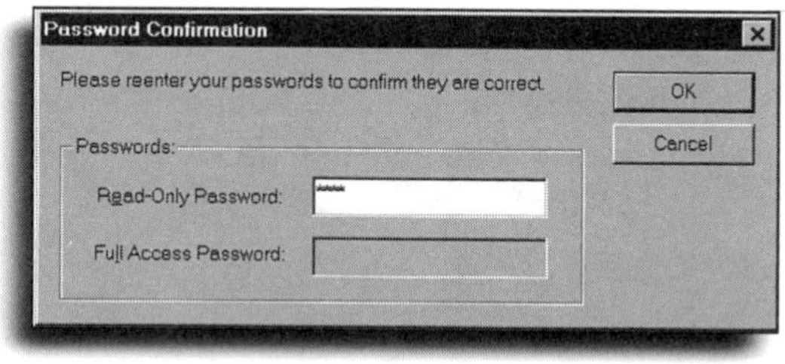

**FIGURE 21.4**
If you make a mistake you'll be told to try again.

Now you have to distribute the password to the favored few: those users you'll permit into this folder. You can use email, carrier pigeon, courier delivery, a telephone call, or just randomly stop people in the hallways. Anyone you tell the password to has access to your folder.

If the password becomes common knowledge and too many people are accessing the folder, or you change your mind about the user group you want to share the folder with, return to the dialog box, delete the password, and enter a new one. Then give that password to the users you select.

When a user opens Explorer or Network neighborhood and selects this folder, a password dialog box appears (see Figure 21.5).

**FIGURE 21.5**

Saving the password means this user only has to enter the password the first time she accesses the folder.

You don't have to enter a password. If you leave the password text box blank, everyone on the network can access this folder. Sometimes the folder should be available to everyone, and in that case save yourself and everyone else the work and skip the password.

## Configuring User Access Security

If you opted for securing your folders by naming the users who could access them, the Sharing tab of the Properties dialog box you see looks like the one shown in Figure 21.6.

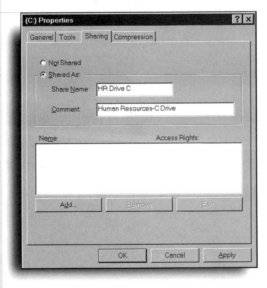

**FIGURE 21.6**

Add users and give them specific rights in this folder.

You have quite a few choices for giving rights to this folder:

- Let everyone in and limit their rights so they can't change any files.

- Choose specific groups (if you're on a domain and there are groups established) and give each group the same rights.

- Choose specific groups and tailor the rights on a group by group basis.

- Choose individual users and give everyone the same rights.

- Choose individual users and customize the rights on a per user basis.

It probably sounds more complicated than it is, so let's walk through a few examples. It's a two step process: select the group or individual user; then assign rights to that group or individual user.

### Assigning rights to SHARED resources

1. To select a group or user, choose **Add** to open the Add Users dialog box (see Figure 21.7).

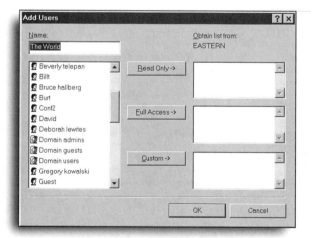

2. Select a group or user, or select multiple entries by holding down the Ctrl key as you click on each entry.

**Using the user list**

The user list is in alphabetical order, so groups and individuals are not displayed in separate parts of the list. In addition, there may be two types of groups available—the groups created automatically as part of the network operating system (for instance, on a Windows NT domain, those names start with the word "domain") and groups that have been created by the administrator. Your network administrator may not have created groups in addition to those groups automatically created by the network operating system.

**FIGURE 21.7**
The way to tell a group from a user is the icon—groups display two people, users display one.

**3.** Choose the appropriate rights to move that entry into the list box for that rights level. For example, choose all the entries you want to restrict to Read-Only access and choose **Read Only**.

**4.** Continue to put entries into each rights level (see Figure 21.8). Click **OK** when you finish.

**FIGURE 21.8**

It's easy to give some people limited rights, and other people more rights.

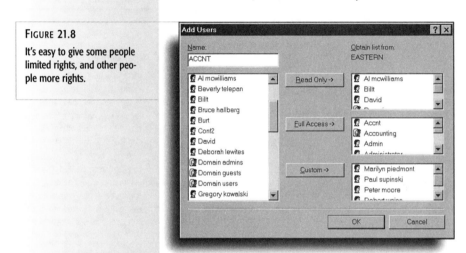

**5.** If you've assigned Custom Rights to anyone, you'll have to define what you mean by that. The Change Access Rights dialog box opens (see Figure 21.9) so you can assign exactly the rights you want these users to have.

**FIGURE 21.9**

Assign specific rights for the Custom Rights users.

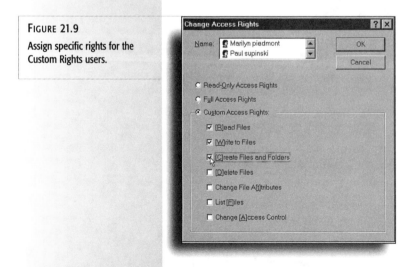

**6.** Select the rights you want these users to have, and then click **OK** to return to the Sharing tab of the dialog box.

The folder's dialog box now displays all the groups and users who can access this folder, along with the rights they have when they do so.

## Changing User Rights

If you want to change the rights for any group or user, return to the Sharing tab of the folder's dialog box and select that entry.

Choose **Remove** to prevent any access of this folder by this entry.

Choose **Edit** to change the rights for this entry. The Change Access Rights dialog box opens and you can change this entry's permissions (see Figure 21.10). If you choose **Custom**, you'll have to fill out the appropriate individual rights.

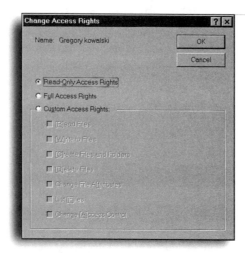

**FIGURE 21.10**
The existing rights level for the user is displayed when you use the Change Access Rights dialog box.

## Troubleshooting User Rights

Sometimes users cannot access the shared folder, and they complain to you about it. You check your access settings and you're sure you gave the user sufficient rights to get his work done.

What's happened is that the user is a victim of the "User Rights Pecking Order." There is a pecking order when you assign rights (the basic philosophy is to err on the side of caution):

- If you assign rights to an individual user and also assign rights to a group that user belongs to, the user rights take precedence over the group rights.

- If you assign different rights to different groups and a user is a member of both groups, that user is given the rights of the group that has less rights.

The real problem with opting for user rights instead of share rights is that every time a new user is added to your system or changes groups or changes jobs, you have to go back into your system and make adjustments. And, if you don't remember to delete those users who have departed your list can get extremely long and hard to work with.

## Sharing Subfolders

If you share a folder that has subfolders, by default all the sub-folders inherit the users and rights of the parent folder. You can change that scheme by assigning specific rights to any or all sub-folders. The most common use of this feature is to share your hard drive and then put tighter security on specific folders. For example, you might want to limit access to payroll or accounting information, and you'd probably want to deny access to the folder that holds your personal correspondence.

When you open the Sharing tab of a subfolder (or a folder, if the drive is shared), the N<u>o</u>t Shared radio button is selected. However, you're told that the folder is already shared and the inherited rights are displayed (see Figure 21.11).

You can accept the configuration or create a new configuration for this folder by using the same steps described previously.

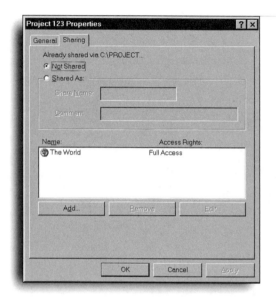

# Sharing Your Printer

Most companies don't buy a printer for every employee who uses a computer. Instead, they scatter printers around the building, each of them designed to be shared by a number of users. Sometimes those printers are attached to print servers, which are computers that exist specifically for providing printers. Some companies attach printers to user workstations and let other users access those printers. And, many companies do both.

## Configuring the Shared Printer

If you have a printer attached to your computer, you probably have to share it with other users on the network. This requires some simple configuration procedures.

### Sharing a local printer

1. Open My Computer, and then open the Printers folder.

2. Right-click the printer you want to share and choose **Sharing** from the shortcut menu.

3. The Sharing dialog box reflects the option you selected for security. Figure 21.12 is a printer that is shared with user access rights. A printer that is shared with share access rights would have a text box for a password.

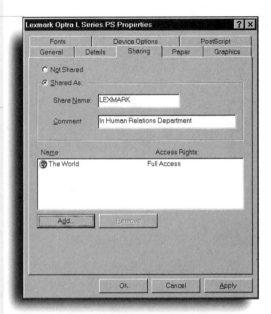

4. Create the security you need (if you need any) by using the same procedures described for sharing folders.

5. Click **OK** when you have finished setting up sharing for the printer.

Be sure you create a printer name and comment that's descriptive. Otherwise you'll have users sending print jobs from their software, then wandering the halls looking for the hard copy.

## Using Separator Pages

If a number of users share a printer, it's a good idea to configure the printer for *separator pages*. These are special pages that are printed before each print job. By the way, in a Novell NetWare system, these pages are called *banners*.

Separator pages can be a real necessity for a shared printer. Picture the scene after eight or nine different users send documents to the printer that's connected to your computer. You can watch the paper spewing from the printer as the outbound tray accumulates a large pile of paper. Is there anyone standing there to take the printouts? No, of course not, users rarely rush to the printer after they've sent a print job. They wait a while, then eventually they amble down the hall to the printer. The first user to arrive starts digging around, looking for his document. He has to read the first couple of words of each page to find it. In the process he may toss papers onto a table, put them back in the out-tray upside down or out of order, or create all sorts of havoc. It seems to get worse when additional users show up at the printer to claim their print jobs. They pass papers to each other "this isn't mine, is it yours?", and generally mess up everything.

Separator pages let a user rifle through the pile of printed pages to find a separator page with his name on it. Every page after the separator page, and until the next separator page, belongs to that user. No reading, no mess, no hassle.

All you have to do is tell Windows 98 to include a separator page, you don't have to create it or configure it or anything—it's really easy.

### Enabling separator pages

1. Open My Computer, and then open the Printers folder.
2. Right-click the printer you want to configure for separator pages and choose **Properties** from the shortcut menu.
3. When the Properties dialog box opens (see Figure 21.13), click the arrow to the right of the **Separator page** text box and choose **Full** or **Simple**:
   - Full separator pages have graphics. Use this choice for printers that print graphics quickly.
   - Simple separator pages are text, using the printer's built in default font. Use this choice for dot matrix printers or printers that print graphics slowly.
4. Click **OK** to close the dialog box.

Warning

The printer you configure for separator pages must be connected to your computer. If you choose a network printer, the system will let you go through all the steps. No error messages will be seen. But, no separator pages will ever print.

FIGURE 21.13

Choose one of the separator
page types for this printer.

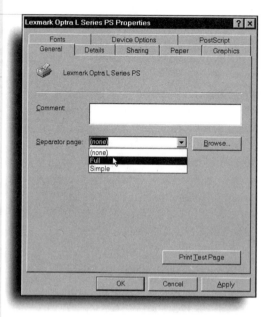

Sharing folders, files, and printers is part of networking. At least,
if you have to share, you now know how to protect the privacy
of the information that should remain private.

# Mobile Computing

# What's Mobile Computing?

Mobile computing is nothing more than using a computer when you're traveling. That includes traveling from the office to your home, if you take your work home with you. Mobile computing is growing at an incredible rate. Today's drummers (that's an old fashioned word for traveling salespeople) are expected to carry their offices in a laptop computer. Operating systems are adding features to help make all of this easier and more efficient, and Windows 98 has plenty of built-in support for all the nifty stuff laptops can do. Even if you've had your laptop for a long time and it doesn't have the state-of-the-art features, you'll find plenty of support for mobile computing in Windows 98. However, laptops frequently end up being used as desktops. After investing time and energy into putting all the right software and files on their portable computer, some people find it's smoother to work with that computer all the time.

# Using Hardware Profiles

*Hardware profiles* are startup options that load the correct device support for the way the computer is going to operate for a particular session. Typically this will mean that the system will be operating in multiple environments; connected to the office network, linked by phone, or just all by itself. Microsoft has built hardware profiles to allow the user to set up the machine to run best in these different scenarios.

One device that makes this much easier is a *docking station*. With laptops you usually use a docking station at work, so we will start with the 'docked/undocked' scenario.

## Understanding Docking

A docking station is a hardware device that has everything a computer needs except the computer. There's usually a mouse, a keyboard, a monitor, and a network interface card. The device has a cable and the connector for that cable matches a connector at the back of the computer.

When the portable computer is connected to this device, it's "docked." Removing the computer from the device (to travel with it) is "undocking."

There are two methods for docking and undocking: hot docking and not-hot docking (sorry, but there's no technical term I know of for that function). Hot docking means you can connect and disconnect from the docking station without even turning off the computer. Without hot docking, you must shut down the computer and turn off the power before connecting or disconnecting.

The choice is up to the computer, not you. Many of today's laptops come with hot docking support built in (that support requires both hardware and software features). Windows 98 understands and supports hot docking and will recognize the devices on the docking station as soon as they're hooked up. When the computer is undocked, Windows 98 recognizes that, too.

If you don't have a computer capable of hot docking, you have to create a way to boot your portable with the appropriate hardware configuration, otherwise Windows 98 won't find the devices in the docking station. In addition, of course, you need a set of configuration options for those times you're on the road and undocked.

The ability to create hardware configurations is what hardware profiles are all about. When you start your computer, you pick the profile that matches your current status and away you go.

## Creating Hardware Profiles

Hardware profiles aren't created just to load configurations for docked or undocked states, you can use them to tell Windows not to look for (or load) other hardware devices. For example, you may want to run the computer with or without a network interface device. Or, perhaps your portable computer lets you choose between a floppy disk drive or a CD-ROM drive in a particular slot. The hardware you want to use has to be supported with drivers, so having a hardware configuration for each permutation and combination of devices makes sense.

Creating a hardware profile is merely a matter of copying an existing profile and then enabling or disabling devices for the profile. (Your existing hardware configuration, created when Windows 98 was installed, is called the Original Configuration. It appears that way on the menus and in the Control Panel options unless you have changed it or upgraded from a system that had renamed it.)

### Creating a hardware profile

1. Choose **Settings**, **Control Panel** from the Start menu.
2. Double-click the System icon in the Control Panel and move to the Hardware Profiles tab (see Figure 22.1).

**FIGURE 22.1**

All computers have an existing hardware configuration.

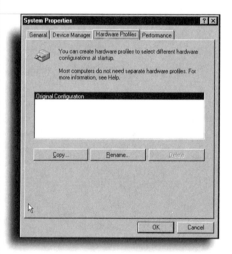

**Automatic configuration of docking profiles**

On some of the newer laptop computers, Windows 98 can figure out all on its own that you have a laptop with a docking station. When you install Windows 98 while the machine is in the docking station, the installation will figure it out and automatically create a docked and an undocked configuration on its own.

3. Choose **Copy** and when the Copy Profile dialog box appears, name the profile and choose **OK**. For example, use the name Docked if you're configuring your computer for docking.
4. Choose **OK** and make sure the new profile is selected (highlighted) in the Hardware Profiles tab.
5. Move to the Device Manager tab of the dialog box and click the plus sign next to the device type you want to add or remove from this hardware profile (clicking the plus sign expands the device type so you can see the actual device). Then select the device and choose **Properties**.

**6.** When the Properties dialog box for the selected device opens, look at the Device usage section at the bottom of the General tab. Enable or disable the hardware for the currently selected profile (see Figure 22.2).

**FIGURE 22.2**

The laptop display isn't needed when the computer is docked, because the docking station has a full size monitor attached.

**7.** Continue to select devices from the Device Manager tab and disable or enable them. Choose **OK** when you have finished setting the configuration for this hardware profile.

When you disable a device and choose OK, the next time you return to the Device Manager and check the properties for the device, an Enable Device button appears. Click it to enable the device and automatically remove the checkmark from the Disable option.

Think carefully about the configuration of your computer when you create your hardware profiles. If you have a CD-ROM in the docking station, create the hardware profile while you're docked so Windows 98 can find it. Always create the hardware profile while you're connected to the greatest number of devices that are affected by the profile.

The number of devices you have to manipulate for your hardware profiles depends on the equipment in your computer and the equipment that's only found on a docking station. For example, many laptop computers only have access to a CD-ROM drive when they're docked. My own laptop has a CD-ROM

**Disabling the video driver**

Note that on many laptops there is no option to disable the video driver. This functionality is controlled via a systems BIOS function—typically through a couple of keystrokes.

**Profiling your network card options**

You might want to select a network card to profile. Most laptops have slots that can hold a PC card for networking, but some docking stations come with NICs (network cards) built in. Disabling the PC card is usually pretty important in those cases because the network configurations could be different and interfere with each other.

drive that shares its drive bay with a floppy disk drive. I don't have to configure a hardware profile to have Windows 98 recognize whether I'm booting up with the CD-ROM drive or the floppy disk drive, because my laptop has a built-in Plug and Play feature for that. Other laptops that are capable of having multiple devices in a bay may need a hardware profile to load the correct drivers for the currently installed device.

Hardware configurations are not just for docking stations. Consider a laptop that sometimes you connect to the office network with your 3COM PC Card and sometimes you dial in on your PC CARD modem from home. If you have only one configuration the system will have to try both potential avenues for access to the office. This can slow things down. Some software is not as savvy as Windows 98 and will not operate correctly if it thinks there is supposed to be a network card present. So, we create two configurations, one called 'Office' with the 3COM network PC Card and modem enabled, and one called 'Remote' with only the modem enabled. Hardware profiles can really assist in making the system performance the best it can be.

### Choosing a Hardware Profile

After you've created an additional hardware profile, your system startup will include a message that asks you to choose a profile. The names of your profiles will be listed so you can choose the appropriate one.

If you have a newer laptop that is optimized for Windows 98, there's a good chance you won't see the message or have to choose. Windows 98 will determine the correct hardware profile automatically and load it without any intervention from you.

## Managing Power

Mobile users frequently need to rely on battery power (playing Solitaire on the airplane makes the trip less boring). Because modern laptops have full color displays, large hard drives, CD-ROM drives, and other power-consuming devices, battery life can be as short as the puberty period of a house fly.

# Understanding Power Management Capabilities

Windows 98 incorporates features that support some of the new power management capabilities available in modern laptop and desktop computers.

There are two levels of power management supported in Windows 98:

- *APM (Advanced Power Management)*. This feature is available on both laptop and desktop computers. In fact, if you're about to purchase a laptop you can probably take it for granted that APM is available. It means you can manage the way power is consumed by the components of your system. For example, if you have APM capabilities, you can power down the monitor and/or hard disk after a period of inactivity.

- *ACPI (Advanced Configuration and Power Interface)*. This feature is usually available on laptops, and is new enough that you can't take it for granted that the laptop you're considering has it. You must check the documentation to make sure that ACPI capability is built in to the computer. With ACPI, the power management tools are more refined and highly focused.

# Configuring Power Management

You can help conserve power to make your battery last longer by taking advantage of the power management features built in to Windows 98. Power management works on any device in your computer that is able to take advantage of this feature. After a period of inactivity, those devices are put to sleep, which means they shut down but they'll wake up as soon as you press a key or move the mouse. For most laptop computers, the hard drive and the screen are enabled for power management.

To configure power management, double-click the Power Management icon in the Control Panel.

## Configuring Power Schemes

When the Power Management Properties dialog box opens, the Power Schemes tab is in the foreground (see Figure 22.3). You can choose or create a power scheme and configure its settings.

FIGURE 22.3

Choose a power scheme for a laptop or desktop computer and specify the power management settings you want to use. Your machine's display may be different depending on the level of support your system has for this functionality.

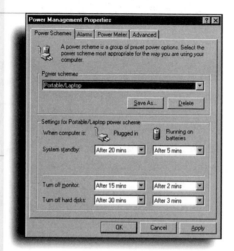

When you choose a power scheme (usually you have a choice between Portable/Laptop and Home/Office Desk), the default settings for that scheme are displayed.

- Change the settings and choose **OK** to make your choices the new settings for the scheme.
- Change the settings and choose **Save As** to create a new scheme based on your settings (you'll be asked to supply a name for the scheme).

## Configuring Alarms

If you don't see an Alarms tab on the Power Management Properties dialog box, it's because Windows 98 has determined that your computer doesn't support this feature.

If you do have an Alarms tab, you can specify the conditions for an alarm as well as the action that takes place (see Figure 22.4).

You can set up an alarm and a resulting action for low battery status or critical battery status, or both.

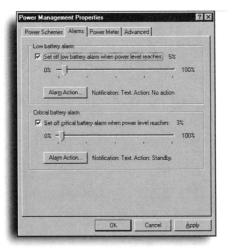

FIGURE 22.4
You can design a low battery alarm system for your laptop.

Depending upon the features available in your laptop, the choices displayed for actions differ. Choose the appropriate Alarm Action button to see what your computer offers (you should at least be able to set a sound alarm).

## Viewing the Power Meter

You can get information about the state of your battery from the Power Meter tab of the Power Management Properties dialog box (see Figure 22.5).

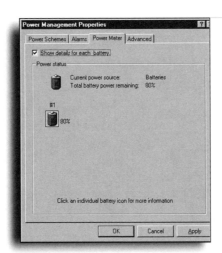

FIGURE 22.5
The percentage of battery life remaining displays on the Power Meter tab.

If you have ACPI features, double-click the battery icon to learn everything there is to know about that battery (the manufacturer, the model, all sorts of things that you probably don't really care about).

## Setting Advanced Specifications

The Advanced tab isn't really very advanced, at least not in the technical sense (see Figure 22.6). However, it does have a couple of useful settings.

**FIGURE 22.6**

Use the Advanced tab to set behavior options.

Choose **Show power meter on taskbar** to put a power icon on the taskbar tray. You can use that icon in the following ways:

- The icon always indicates the current power source (battery or AC).
- Single-click the icon to see a pop-up menu of the available power schemes, with the current scheme indicated by a bullet. You can switch to any other scheme from this menu.
- Double-click it to open the Power Management Properties dialog box.
- Right-click it to see a pop-up menu, each item of which displays a different tab of the Power Management Properties dialog box (see Figure 22.7).

Adjust Power Properties
**Open Power Meter**

**FIGURE 22.7**

Depending upon your computer and your configuration, your choices may differ.

Some laptops don't provide the choice to use power management intelligently. That is, if power management is on, it's on regardless of whether you're attached to an electrical plug or running on the battery. I find it annoying to have the screen go dark if I haven't used the keyboard or mouse for a while. I find it absolutely maddening to have to wait for the hard drive to wake up when I'm ready to work. I therefore frequently turn off the power management feature even if I'm operating on battery power. I prefer the shorter battery life to the annoyance. I reverse my thinking if I know I'll be working on battery power for an extended period.

## Using My Briefcase

If you're on the road a lot or do a great deal of office work at home, you can go crazy trying to keep track of documents you work on in both places. Which file is the latest version? Which files were changed and which were not? The Windows 98 Briefcase takes care of the tracking, so all you have to worry about is doing the work.

The way the Briefcase works is ingenuously simple:

- Copy files from your desktop computer to the Briefcase of your portable computer.

- While you're away from the office, open the Briefcase and work on the files. You must, of course, have the associated software on your laptop.

- When you return to the office, update your desktop files with the contents of your Briefcase.

**Power management isn't just for laptops**

There are power management features used by desktop computers as more and more "green" monitors and power-managed hard drives are being purchased. If you have a Power icon in Control Panel on your desktop, you'll see power management options to suit the devices in your computer.

Be aware that some older desktops with system BIOS settings for power management may not work well with Windows 98 unless you turn off the features in the BIOS or upgrade the BIOS. Refer to your computer documentation for procedures or call the vendor.

## Putting Files into the Briefcase

The first step is to move the files you're working on to the Briefcase. There are two ways to accomplish this:

- Between connected computers
- Between unconnected computers

Connected means a network connection, a direct cable connection, or a dial-up connection. If the computers are connected you can see folders for both computers.

Incidentally, Briefcase updates are accomplished by matching dates and times to find the latest version of the files. Make sure your laptop and desktop computers agree on the date and time.

## Packing the Briefcase with Connected Computers

If your desktop computer and your laptop are connected, you can drag the files you need from the desktop to the laptop. I find it easier to do the work from the portable computer, where the Briefcase that's my target is right on the desktop.

### Putting files into the Briefcase

1. On the laptop, open Explorer (you could also use Network Neighborhood). Position the Briefcase and the Explorer window so you can see both of them.

2. Move to the connected computer and the folder in which the documents you've been working on are located.

3. Select all the documents you want to put into the Briefcase on the laptop.

4. Drag the files to the Briefcase.

That's all there is to it. Incidentally, dragging files to the Briefcase doesn't move them (as dragging files between folders would), it copies them.

# Packing the Briefcase with Unconnected Computers

If you're not connected to your desktop computer, you have to pack your briefcase into a floppy disk. While this limits you to 1.44MB, that's generally plenty of space even if you're packing up multiple documents. This process starts at the desktop computer (where the files are).

### Putting a floppy disk into your Briefcase

1. Open Explorer (make sure you can see the Briefcase on the desktop) and select the files you want to pack into the Briefcase.

2. Drag the files to the My Briefcase icon.

3. Put a blank floppy disk into Drive A (put a label on it so you know this floppy disk is for the Briefcase).

4. Open My Computer.

5. Drag the My Briefcase icon to the Drive A icon in My Computer.

If the My Briefcase icon disappears from your desktop, don't panic, it's on the floppy disk. If you view the contents of the floppy disk in Explorer, you'll see the My Briefcase icon.

Pack the floppy disk into the carrying case for your portable.

# Working on the Road

Okay, pack up your laptop, say good-bye to everyone at the office, and hit the road. When it's time to work on your files, you have two choices for opening them: directly from the Briefcase, or from the software program.

You can open the Briefcase and double-click on the file you want to work with. The associated software program will launch automatically and the file will be in the software window, ready for your input.

You can also open the file from the software window. You might not have noticed it, but when you use the Open dialog box in Windows software, you can click the arrow next to the Look in box to move above your default documents folder, and above the hard drive, to get to the Desktop (see Figure 22.8).

FIGURE 22.8

Choose My Briefcase as the folder to open.

## Printing on the Road with no Printer

If you don't have a portable printer to carry with your portable computer, you really can't print any documents you work on while you're traveling.

However, you can just plunge right ahead and print the document by using the Print command in your software. An error message will appear to tell you that the printer isn't available.

Choose **OK** and the document is sent to the spooler, waiting for a chance to print it.

When you return to the office and reconnect your printer (or connect to the network if you use a network printer), a message appears automatically to remind you that you have print jobs waiting.

## Some Tricks for Printing on the Road

I've traveled and prepared documents that had to be distributed, but I rarely carry a portable printer. I've learned some tricks to get hard copies of documents.

If I'm staying in a hotel, I use my software and modem to fax the document to the hotel's fax machine, faxing right from the software. Most hotels also have copy machines so I can get as many copies of the fax as I need.

I've also faxed the document to a company fax if I'm traveling because I'm working at that company.

# Updating the Files When You Return

When you get back to your desktop computer, you can update the files. The files you changed will be replaced in their original location. Any files you didn't get around to working on aren't touched. You don't have to keep track of which files you changed, the Briefcase does it for you.

Reconnect the laptop to the desktop (or put the floppy disk with the Briefcase in Drive A). Then update the files.

### Updating files

1. Open My Briefcase (on the laptop if you're connected, from Drive A if you're not).

2. Choose **Briefcase**, **Update All** from the menu bar. The Briefcase checks its files against the date and day of the original files.

3. The Update My Briefcase window opens and displays the results of the comparison, indicating the files that need to be updated because they changed.

4. To update the files, choose **Update**.

It would be unusual not to update a changed file, but you're not locked into it. You can right-click on a file and choose Skip from the shortcut menu if you want to skip its update. The shortcut menu also offers a choice to update the file in the opposite direction, meaning the older file would replace the file you worked on (you'd be back where you started). One case when you might want to do this may be when you are working with a file that others might be able to get to. If someone else changes the document on a server, for example, you will not want to update the document as Windows 98 will not merge the changes, it will only replace the whole file.

# Troubleshooting My Briefcase

Sometimes you take a document on the road and while you're away somebody works on the document back in the office. The Briefcase will update the file in whatever direction is indicated

**Synchronizing doesn't merge changes**

Of course, if the file is on a server and your boss has changed the file with comments, replacing it might not be what you want to do. Note that synchronizing the file copies over, it doesn't merge changes.

**Some briefcases take over and automate the update**

If you use a docking station, you may find that as soon as you're docked the Briefcase automatically opens and presents the Update dialog box. If you have a laptop that has this type of sensory perception, it makes everything easier.

by the date and time the files were last modified. But one of you is going to lose the changes you made.

- You could print one of the files and enter the changes into the other file.

- If one set of changes isn't too extensive, select each change and copy it to the Clipboard. Then paste it into the other document.

- If the software that created the files can compare and merge two documents, unlink the files from each other and rename one of them. Then use that feature.

There is a way to break the relationship between a Briefcase file and its counterpart.

**De-synchronizing files**

**1.** Open the Briefcase and select the file you want to unlink.

**2.** Choose **Briefcase**, **Split From Original** from the file menu.

This breaks the link between the two files, and you cannot update them until you remove the file from the Briefcase and start all over with the file from the original source. When a Briefcase file is split from the original, it's called an orphan.

If I create an orphan, I've found it a good procedure to drag the file from the Briefcase to the desktop. I then rename it, and drag the newly named file to my documents folder. That way it's no longer in the Briefcase (and I can put the original back there when I have to) but it's also not floating around in orphan file heaven. It's available so I can look at it, grab data from it, or otherwise manipulate it. It turns out that most of the time I delete it, but I like the safety net I've created.

There's no reason to be less productive on the road than you are in the office if you establish the procedures you need. And, don't forget to phone in to the network so you can keep up with your email. Information about dial-up networking can be found in Chapter 17, "Going Online."

# Appendixes

# Advanced Disk Management

*A*

There are two choices for managing your drive(s) under Windows 98 that you can consider applying to your system: installing the FAT32 file system; and compressing your drive.

## Fat32 File System

Windows 98 offers the opportunity to use a file system called FAT32.

FAT (File Allocation Table) file systems have been around for a long time, starting with MS-DOS. FAT16 has been around since 16-bit computers and operating systems became the norm. Now comes FAT32, a more robust, more powerful version than its antecedents.

There are several advantages to be gained from this file system, and some disadvantages.

The most important improvements that you gain with FAT32 are the following:

- You can use a hard drive larger than 2GB without partitioning it.
- The cluster size is generally smaller and therefore disk storage is accomplished more efficiently.

- The root directory is positioned differently than it is with other file systems and can be relocated if there are physical problems with the drive.

- There are backup copies made of the FAT, which can make crashes easier to resolve.

On the downside, think about these facts:

- You cannot dual boot for multiple operating systems. In fact, even if the other operating system is on a different drive, you probably won't be able to use it after you install FAT32.

- If your computer has hibernating features in its power management set, you won't be able to use it.

- You cannot compress a drive.

- Older versions of MS-DOS and Windows can't read FAT32. This includes large media disk cartridges formatted in FAT32 or a hard drive that you move between machines.

For many people, the advantages far outweigh the disadvantages. For example, while you might think the last preceding downside fact would be particularly troublesome, the last version of Windows 95 (commonly referred to as OSR2 or Windows 95B) also supports FAT32, so many systems are already in place that make use of the extra features.

## Large Hard Drives

FAT32 file systems enable you to have a single partition for a drive larger than 2GB. Without FAT32, you must partition drives larger than 2GB into smaller logical drives, each no larger than 2GB in size. Incidentally, FAT32 requires a minimum drive size of 512MB.

## How the FAT Works

The FAT works under the concept of using clusters of data. These clusters each represent a single chunk of data, and they must all be the same size on a single disk drive. If a file's data is larger than a single cluster, then the first part of the data is stored in a cluster, and then the rest is stored in subsequent, but not necessarily sequential, clusters.

Here's where the File Allocation Table comes in: It's really just a table that lists all the clusters on the disk and whether or not they're being used. In a directory entry on the disk, a filename is associated with a beginning cluster number. The operating system then goes to the FAT to look up that cluster. If it's the last entry, it will have a particular value in it signifying it as such. If it's not the last cluster in the file, it will contain the number of the next one in the chain of data. The operating system keeps following this chain until it reaches the last cluster. An empty cluster is signified by a 0 entry.

The problem with the old FAT16 system was that each entry in the FAT was only 16 bits in size. Also, the FAT itself could only be a certain size in and of itself. This meant that the larger the disk, the larger the cluster size would have to be in order to be able to cover the entire disk. When you had a disk that was 2GB in size, the cluster size had to be 32KB.

The problem with such a large cluster size is this: You can't put multiple files into a single cluster. This means that a small file of 25 bytes would take up an entire 32KB of disk space, and a file of 33KB would take up 64KB as that extra kilobyte of the file was forced to take up an entire extra cluster. Smaller disks where a single cluster was only 4KB wasn't such a large waste of space, but the larger disks were just intolerable.

FAT32 solves the problem by allowing far more clusters on a single disk, which means that even extremely large disks will still have a cluster size of only 4KB.

Table A.1 shows a comparison between cluster sizes for a variety of partition sizes.

**Lost clusters**

Sometimes ScanDisk will refer to lost clusters. This occurs when the FAT lists certain clusters as being used, but nothing actually points to them, either via a directory entry or another FAT entry. This is essentially lost data on the disk because Windows 98 doesn't know how to get to the data through any normal channel. By converting the lost cluster to a file, ScanDisk is simply creating a directory entry that points to the first FAT entry of the chain of lost clusters.

TABLE A.1    **Cluster size comparisons**

| Partition Size | Cluster Size-FAT16 | Cluster Size-FAT32 |
|---|---|---|
| 512MB | 8KB | 4KB |
| 1GB | 16KB | 4KB |
| 2GB | 32KB | 4KB |

## Root Directory

In a FAT32 system, the root directory is not restricted to a specific location on the disk (as it is for FAT16 file systems). It is a contiguous section of disk that can be located anywhere. As a result, there is no limit on the number of entries you can have on the root directory. FAT16 file systems have a maximum of 512 entries (files and subdirectories) on the root directory.

## Converting to FAT32

**There's no going back**

If you convert your file system to FAT32, you cannot convert back to FAT16. You will have to repartition and reformat the drive, and then reinstall the operating system and restore your backed-up files.

Windows 98 includes a conversion program so you can convert your current file system to FAT32. Before you begin, back up your hard drive.

To start the conversion to FAT32, open the Programs menu and move to Accessories. In the System Tools menu, choose Drive Converter (FAT32).

The Driver Converter Wizard opens and performs the following tasks:

- Copies the conversion program to your root directory.
- Restarts your computer in MS-DOS mode.
- Runs ScanDisk on the drive.
- Converts the file system to FAT32.
- Restarts your computer, booting Windows 98.
- Runs the defragment utility (which takes a very long time).

# Compressing Your Drive

Windows 98 comes with DriveSpace 3, which you can use to compress your drive in order to gain more disk space from a small drive. Be warned that there are frequently problems with drive compression and you shouldn't consider this unless it's absolutely necessary (and even then, drives are not very expensive today; consider purchasing a larger drive).

DriveSpace 3 works on floppy disks and hard disks up to 2GB. It will not compress a disk that is running the FAT32 file system.

## How DriveSpace 3 Works

A compressed drive is not really a drive, it's a file. DriveSpace essentially takes all the data from the disk and creates a very large file into which all this data gets stored in a special format. Then, DriveSpace 3 tells the operating system that there's a host drive available. When Windows 98 goes to access the drive, it really goes through DriveSpace 3, which in turn does its magic of getting the requested data out of the file.

One large problem with DriveSpace 3 is that it requires Windows 98 to actually be running in order to access the compressed data. If you have any reason to boot your computer to MS-DOS mode (say, if you're running some game or other type of software that doesn't like Windows, or if you're using the Emergency Boot Disk to try and restore some settings), then you won't be able to access the compressed data. It will just look like an enormous file on the physical drive that was originally compressed.

## Running DriveSpace 3

To start DriveSpace 3, click the **Start** Menu, go to **Programs**, **Accessories**, **System Tools**, and click **DriveSpace**. When the DriveSpace window opens, choose the disk you want to compress and select **Drive**, **Compress**.

You will be presented with a dialog box displaying two pie charts, one showing the current free-space status of the drive and another showing you what it will be like after compression. This can be a good gauge of whether or not you'll really get enough savings to make the whole process worthwhile.

If you click the **Options** button, a dialog box will give you the option of selecting the drive letter to be associated with the compressed data, how much free space should exist on the compressed drive, and whether or not to use the old DoubleSpace format. If you think you will have to use this disk with an older version of Windows, then you should make sure the **DoubleSpace** box is checked. The compression won't be as good, but you'll be able to use it with older operating systems.

When you're ready to actually compress the drive, just click the **Start** button on the first dialog box. This will start the process moving along, and when it's done, you'll have a nifty little compressed area on your drive.

# Glossary

To help you keep up with the terminology and jargon that you run into as you use your computer, here's a glossary of terms.

**10BASE-2**   Coaxial network cable (it looks like a thin version of your television cable). It connects to the computer with a BNC connector.

**10BASE-T**   Network cable that looks like telephone wire and is used in Ethernet networks. The connection (plug), which also looks like a telephone plug (only a little larger), is called an RJ-45 connector.

**Active Desktop**   A new feature included in Windows 98 (and in Windows 95 in combination with Internet Explorer 4), the Active Desktop enables the display on your desktop of web pages and other objects that have live connections to the Internet or an intranet. The desktop becomes "active" in that such objects automatically update themselves to reflect new or changed content at the remote source. Unlike the still available Classic Desktop, the Active Desktop offers a uniform interface for accessing local, network, and Internet resources.

**Active window**   The window accepting input (sometimes called the window that has the focus).

**ASCII (American Standard Code for Information Interchange)**   A standard for characters that enables different makes and models of computers to communicate with one another. Generally, ASCII text contains only the characters found on the keyboard, with no pictures or formatting codes. Each ASCII character is assigned a number, and all computers use the same number-character conversion set.

**Associate**   To link a filename extension to a program. For example, the .doc filename extension is associated with Microsoft Word. When file extensions are associated with software, double-clicking on the file listing in Explorer opens the associated software.

**Backward compatibility**   The capability to use documents and functions from earlier versions of a software product.

**baud**   The speed of a modem (see **bps**).

**BBS (Bulletin Board Service)** A service you can contact by using a modem and a communications program such as HyperTerminal.

**Binding** The process that establishes communication between a network adapter driver and the driver for a network protocol.

**BIOS (Basic Input/Output System)** The part of your computer that controls the startup procedures, such as RAM tests, disk drive setup, and configuration (see **POST**).

**BIOS enumerator** In a Plug-and-Play system, the function that can identify all the hardware connected to the motherboard.

**Bookmark** To mark a page on the World Wide Web for quick access in the future. In Microsoft Internet Explorer, the term "favorite" is usually used instead of the term "bookmark."

**bootlog.txt** A file that you can create automatically during startup to track all the steps your computer took to load Windows 98. Errors and successes are noted in the file.

**bps (bits per second)** A measure of modem speed (see **baud**).

**Browse** To view drives, folders, and files by using My Computer, Windows Explorer, or a dialog box Browse button.

**Byte** The amount of space required to store one character.

**Cache** Pronounced *cash*. An area of RAM where frequently accessed data is stored to speed up access to it.

**CDFS (Compact Disc File System)** The system Windows 98 uses to manage files stored on a CD-ROM.

**CD-ROM (Compact Disc Read-Only Memory)** CD-style disks used in CD-ROM drives on a PC.

**Channels** Web resources you can subscribe to in order to keep up-to-date on information.

**Client** A computer on a network that uses the resources of another computer on the network (called the "server").

**Clipboard** An area in memory where data is stored temporarily so it can be pasted in a document.

**CMOS (Complementary Metal Oxide Semiconductor)** Memory kept by a small battery inside the PC that is used to manage the computer's settings (unrelated to the operating system).

**Codec** A system to compress and decompress digital video and audio files to minimize the amount of disk space they take up.

**Context menu** The menu that appears when you right-click an object. Also called a *shortcut menu*.

**Context-sensitive help** Onscreen help that relates to whatever you're trying to do at the moment. In Windows 98, you usually click the question mark (?) button to get context-sensitive help.

**Control Panel**   The folder in Windows 98 where you choose your settings and preferences and add new hardware and software.

**DDE (Dynamic Data Exchange)**   A process in which two separate programs can exchange data. It has been replaced by OLE in more recent versions of Windows.

**Default**   The selection that will be used unless you specify something else. For example, when you print a document, it is sent to the default printer unless you specifically choose a different one.

**Default icons**   The icons that appear on your Desktop automatically after installation of Windows 98.

**Desktop icon**   An icon that appears on the desktop, such as My Computer or the Recycle Bin.

**Device**   A general term for any piece of hardware you put into a computer or attach to a computer with a cable.

**Device driver**   A program that connects hardware to the operating system to make the hardware work.

**Dialog box**   A window with options you can use to select configuration or performance choices.

**Dial-up networking**   A Windows 98 service that lets a computer dial in to another computer and access its resources.

**Dimmed**   An option or command that's grayed out because it's not available at the moment. For example, Copy and Cut commands are dimmed when no data is selected, and Paste is dimmed when the Clipboard is empty.

**Directory**   An area on a disk that has a name and contains objects (either other directories or files). In Windows 98, the word *directory* has been replaced by the word *folder*.

**DMA channel (Direct Memory Access channel)**   A channel for transferring data between a device and memory without involving the processor.

**Dock**   To connect a portable PC to a docking station.

**Docking station**   A unit that connects a portable computer to desktop accessories such as a monitor.

**Document**   A file you create while using a software program.

**Domain name**   The location portion of an email address. For example, in **kathy@authors.com**, authors.com is the Internet domain name.

**DOS (also MS-DOS)**   The original disk operating system for the IBM PC.

**Download**   The process of copying a file from another computer on to your computer. This is the opposite of upload.

**Drag**   To hold down the mouse button while moving the mouse in order to move an object to a new location. At the target location, releasing the mouse button "drops" the object. The actions are frequently called "drag-and-drop."

**Driver**  A program that connects hardware to the operating system to make the hardware work. (Also called a "device driver.")

**Drop-down list**  A list of choices you can access in a text box by clicking the arrow to the right of the text box. Sometimes called a combo box.

**Email**  Electronic mail sent over a network or the Internet.

**Email address**  The address that identifies you on a network or the Internet.

**Explorer**  A browsing tool in Windows 98 that displays drives, folders, and files.

**File**  The basic unit of storage on a disk. For example, when you create and save a document, it's stored as a file.

**File sharing**  Allowing multiple PCs on a network to share the same set of files from one PC.

**Folder**  An area on a disk that has a name and contains objects (either other folders or files). Folders are also called directories.

**Free space**  The amount of space on a disk that is currently not being used to store files.

**Graphics**  Pictures.

**Graphics accelerator**  A hardware device that helps draw graphics on your screen faster.

**Hack**  Usually used to refer to the action of getting past security devices when accessing another computer. For many computer veterans, it means merely "working with computer code." For example, administrators who do troubleshooting frequently say they have to "hack the Registry."

**High Color**  A color scheme that shows close to photograph-quality color on a computer. Also called 16-bit color.

**Hot swapping**  A feature of some PC cards that enables you to insert or remove the card without turning off the PC.

**HTML (Hypertext Markup Language)**  A set of programming codes (called tags) that are used to add attributes such as bold or italic to text or to insert images and links to web documents and email messages.

**Hyperlink**  A spot on a web page or some link-enabled document that takes you to a new page when you click it.

**Icon**  A picture that represents an object.

**IEEE 1394**  A hardware standard for advanced digital ports and devices (see **USB**).

**Internet service provider (ISP)**  A service you dial into that connects your computer to the Internet.

**ISA (Industry Standard Architecture)**  A standard for a 16-bit motherboard bus (slot) that goes back to older computers.

**ISDN (Integrated Services Digital Network)**  A communications hardware device that works much faster than a modem.

**KB (Kilobyte)** 1,024 bytes.

**Kernel** The part of an operating system that interacts directly with the processor.

**LAN (local area network)** A network in which computers are connected by cable.

**Legacy** Older (pre-Windows 98) hardware devices and software.

**Local printer** A printer that's physically connected to your computer.

**Map** To assign a drive letter to a shared device on a local area network.

**MIDI (Musical Instrument Digital Interface)** A standard for composing and playing music on a computer.

**MIME (Multipurpose Internet Mail Extensions)** A protocol that permits email messages and attachments to contain more than plain text.

**MMX (Multimedia Extensions)** A feature in newer Pentium processors that helps multimedia applications run faster.

**Modem** A hardware device that connects your computer to a telephone line.

**My Briefcase** A desktop folder that lets you take documents out of the office and synchronize the changes you make with the original documents on your office computer.

**Network adapter card** A hardware device that you use to connect to other computers in a local area network. Also called Network Interface Card (NIC).

**Network printer** A printer physically connected to another computer on a LAN.

**Newsgroup** An electronic bulletin board on the Internet where people post messages (usually called articles).

**NIC (Network Interface Card)** (See **Network adapter card**)

**OLE (Object Linking and Embedding)** A feature in Windows that lets you take an object from one program and link it to a document prepared in another program. When the original object changes, its link in the second document changes as well.

**Password** A string of characters that must be entered in order to access protected data.

**Path** The location of a file described along with its drive, folder, and subfolder. For example, c:\My Documents\ Letters\Letter to Clinton.

**PC Card** An adapter card that fits into the PCMCIA slot of a portable computer.

**PCI (Peripheral Component Interconnect)** A standard for a motherboard bus (slot) that provides faster communication between the CPU and the 32-bit device installed in the PCI slot.

**PCMCIA (Personal Computer Memory Card International Association)** A standard that defines how PC cards work.

**Plug and Play**   A term for devices that can be installed and then recognized immediately by Windows 98.

**Plug-and-Play BIOS**   A Basic Input/Output System capable of recognizing and configuring Plug-and-Play devices during computer startup.

**Port**   A connector on the back of your computer into which you plug a cable that connects to some external device.

**POST (Power On Self Test)**   The process a computer goes through during startup to check hardware and load the basic drivers that control the hardware.

**Properties**   The characteristics of an object in your computer system. You can view an object's properties by right-clicking the object and choosing Properties from the shortcut menu.

**Recycle Bin**   A desktop folder that holds files you've deleted until you're sure you want to delete them permanently.

**Refresh**   To update the screen display so it shows current data.

**Registry**   The database where Windows 98 stores the settings for your system.

**Return to Application Interval**   The amount of time that elapses while printing is being processed before all the resources in your computer are returned to you.

**Root directory**   The highest level folder on a disk, designated by \. For example, c:\ represents the root directory of the C: drive.

**Select**   To choose the object(s) on which you plan to perform an action.

**Server**   A computer on a network that validates logons and/or holds files or printers that users share.

**Shortcut**   An icon that enables you to open a folder, document, or program without going through the Start menu.

**SIMM (Single Inline Memory Module)**   Circuit boards with RAM chips that have been soldered on.

**Startup menu**   A menu that can be displayed when Windows 98 starts, giving you choices about the way you want the operating system to load.

**Status bar**   The bar at the bottom of a window that provides information about the contents or the status of a selected object.

**Subfolder**   A folder within a folder.

**SVGA (Super Virtual Graphics Array)**   A video controller and monitor that permits higher resolution.

**Syntax**   The format for entering a command.

**Taskbar**   The area at the bottom of your screen that holds icons and buttons for access to system features.

**Title bar**   The area on the top of the window that displays the window's name and holds the Minimize, Maximize, and Close buttons.

**Toolbar**   A set of buttons and icons that provide one-click access to frequently used menu commands.

**ToolTip**  A small label that appears above or below a button or icon when you hold the mouse pointer on that button for a few seconds.

**Tray**  An indented section on the right side of the Windows 98 taskbar that holds icons representing system functions.

**True Color**  A scheme that shows photograph-quality color on your computer. Also called "24-bit color."

**UNC (Uniform Naming Convention)**  A method of identifying a resource by its path, which includes a computer name followed by the resource name. The computer name is preceded by two backslashes; for example, `\\Server\CommonApplications`.

**Unimodem**  A universal device driver for modems.

**Upload**  To copy something from your computer to another computer. This is the opposite of download.

**URL (Uniform Resource Locator)**  The address of a page on the World Wide Web (for example, **http://www. websitename**)

**USB device (Universal Serial Bus device)**  A hardware device that is designed for a USB port. This combination provides general digital data capabilities for audio and video.

**Usenet**  A service on the Internet for communicating through newsgroups. Each newsgroup specializes in a subject and users post messages/articles instead of communicating directly through email messages.

**VDM (Virtual DOS Machine)**  The environment created by Windows 98 to run DOS and Windows 3.*x* programs.

**VGA (Virtual Graphics Array)**  The type of display card and monitor that gives you rich color and graphics.

**Virtual memory**  Disk space that is used to hold data when you run out of RAM (the data is kept in a file called a "swap file").

# Index

incoming mail rules,
464-465
*Outbox folder, 465*
*reading messages, 462-464*
*sending Contact profiles
(personal business
cards), 461*
*Sent Items folder, 465*
*signatures, 461*
*viewing attachments, 459*
home page, 462
newsgroups, 468-470
*news server setup, 468-469*
*posting messages, 470*
*reading messages, 470*
*subscribing, 469*

## P

**Paint program, 247**

**paper options, printing,
301-303**

**parallel port devices, 334**

**partitions, FAT32 file
systems, 534**

**passwords**
changing, 219-220
forgotten passwords,
220-221
networks
*null passwords, 478*
*remote administration, 486*
*setup, 502-506*
*troubleshooting, 497*
protecting documents,
224-225
screen savers, 209-210
usernames
*deleting forgotten
passwords, 220-221*
*setting/changing, 219-220*

**pasting data, Clipboard,
286-287**

**paths**
computers, 298-299
files/folders, 74-75

**patterns, desktop, 199**
editing, 201-202
selecting, 200-201
versus wallpaper, 201

**pausing**
Disk Defragmenter, 144
printing, 313-314
scheduled tasks, 153

**PC-Speaker program,
374-376**
downloading, 374
installing/configuring,
374-375

**PCI (Peripheral Component
Interconnect) bus, 333-334**

**PC card icon, taskbar
tray, 34**

**peer-to-peer networking,
483-486**
access management,
485-486
joining networks, 484-485

**performance**
CD-ROM drives, 364-365
monitoring, System
Monitor, 145-147
*interpreting results, 146*
*selecting items for
monitoring, 145-147*
*toolbar, 145*
sound cards, 370-371

**Peripheral Component
Interconnect (PCI) bus,
333-334**

**permissions**
peer-to-peer networks,
485-486
Read Only, 225-226
shared resources, 501-503
*changing access rights, 509*
*folders, 506-509*
*troubleshooting, 509-510*

**Phone Dialer utility,
402-404.** *See also* modems

**pixels, screen resolution.** *See
screen resolution*

**playing**
CDs. *See* CD Player
accessory
games. *See* games
multimedia files
*Media Player, 258-259*
*PC-Speaker program,
374-376*
*video files, setting options,
371-372*

**Plug and Play, 330-332**
automatic hardware
detection, 336-337
configuring devices during
installation, 6
modem installation,
389-391
resolving conflicts, 331

**pointers, 170-174.**
*See also* mouse
animated, 173
changing, 168-170
diamond-shaped arrows,
36-37
installing, 171-172
moving, 14
*MouseKeys, 187-188*
schemes, 168-171
*3D, 169*
*saving, 170-171*
*selecting, 170*
speed, 172-173
ToolTips, *See* ToolTips
trails, 173-174

**ports**
IEEE 1394, 373
parallel port devices, 334
printers
*capturing, 299*
*ECP (Extended
Capabilities Port), 291*
*selecting, 292-293*
serial port devices, 334
USB (Universal Serial Bus),
332, 373

**POST (Power On Self
Test), 7**

**posting newsgroup messages
(Outlook Express), 470**

**power**
mobile computing power
management, 520-525
*ACPI (Advanced
Configuration and Power
Interface), 521*
*alarms, 522-523*
*APM (Advanced Power
Management), 521*
*battery meter icon, 34, 44*
*power schemes, 522*
*showing power meter on
taskbar tray, 524-525*
*viewing power meter,
523-524*